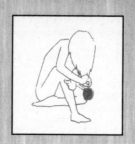

I RECENTLY MOVED AND
COULDN'T LOCATE ANY OF MY
ART SUPPLIES. THOUGH FOR
SOME REASON I HAD ORIGAMI
PAPER, SO THAT'S WHERE I
GOT THE RED FOR THE APPLE
IN THIS PICTURE.
- TSUGUMI OHBA

Tsugumi Ohba
Born in Tokyo.
Hobby: Collecting teacups.
Day and night, develops manga plots
while holding knees on a chair.

Takeshi Obata was born in 1969 in Niigata, Japan, and
is the artist of the wildly popular SHONEN JUMP title
Hikaru no Go, which won the 2003 Tezuka Shinsei
"New Hope" award and the Shogakukan Manga award.
Obata is also the artist of **Arabian Majin Bokentan
Lamp Lamp, Ayatsuri Sakon,** and **Cyborg Jichan G.**

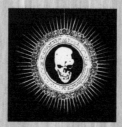

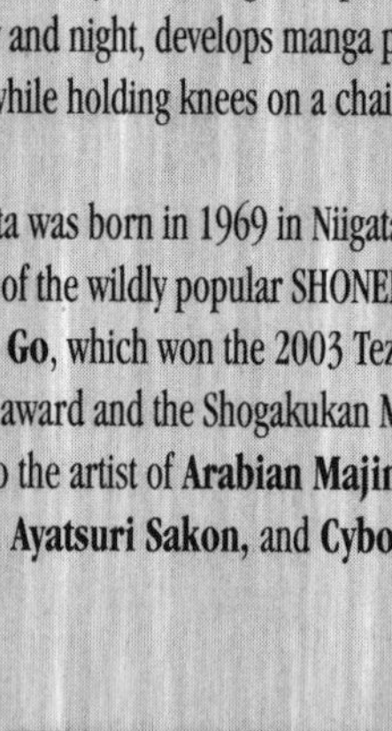

DEATH NOTE VOL 7
The SHONEN JUMP ADVANCED Manga Edition

STORY BY TSUGUMI OHBA
ART BY TAKESHI OBATA

Translation & Adaptation/Alexis Kirsch
Touch-up Art & Lettering/Gia Cam Luc
Design/Sean Lee
Editor/Pancha Diaz

Editor in Chief, Books/Alvin Lu
Editor in Chief, Magazines/Marc Weidenbaum
VP of Publishing Licensing/Rika Inouye
VP of Sales/Gonzalo Ferreyra
Sr. VP of Marketing/Liza Coppola
Publisher/Hyoe Narita

Printed in the U.S.A.

Published by VIZ Media, LLC
P.O. Box 77010
San Francisco, CA 94107

SHONEN JUMP ADVANCED Manga Edition
10 9 8 7 6 5 4
First printing, September 2006
Fourth printing, November 2007

THE WORLD'S MOST
CUTTING-EDGE MANGA

www.viz.com

SHONEN
JUMP
ADVANCED
www.shonenjump.com

SHONEN JUMP ADVANCED MANGA

DEATHNOTE
デスノート

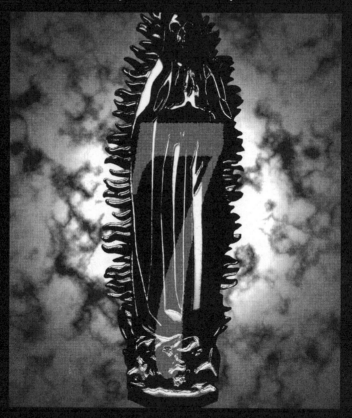

Vol. 7
Zero

Story by Tsugumi Ohba
Art by Takeshi Obata

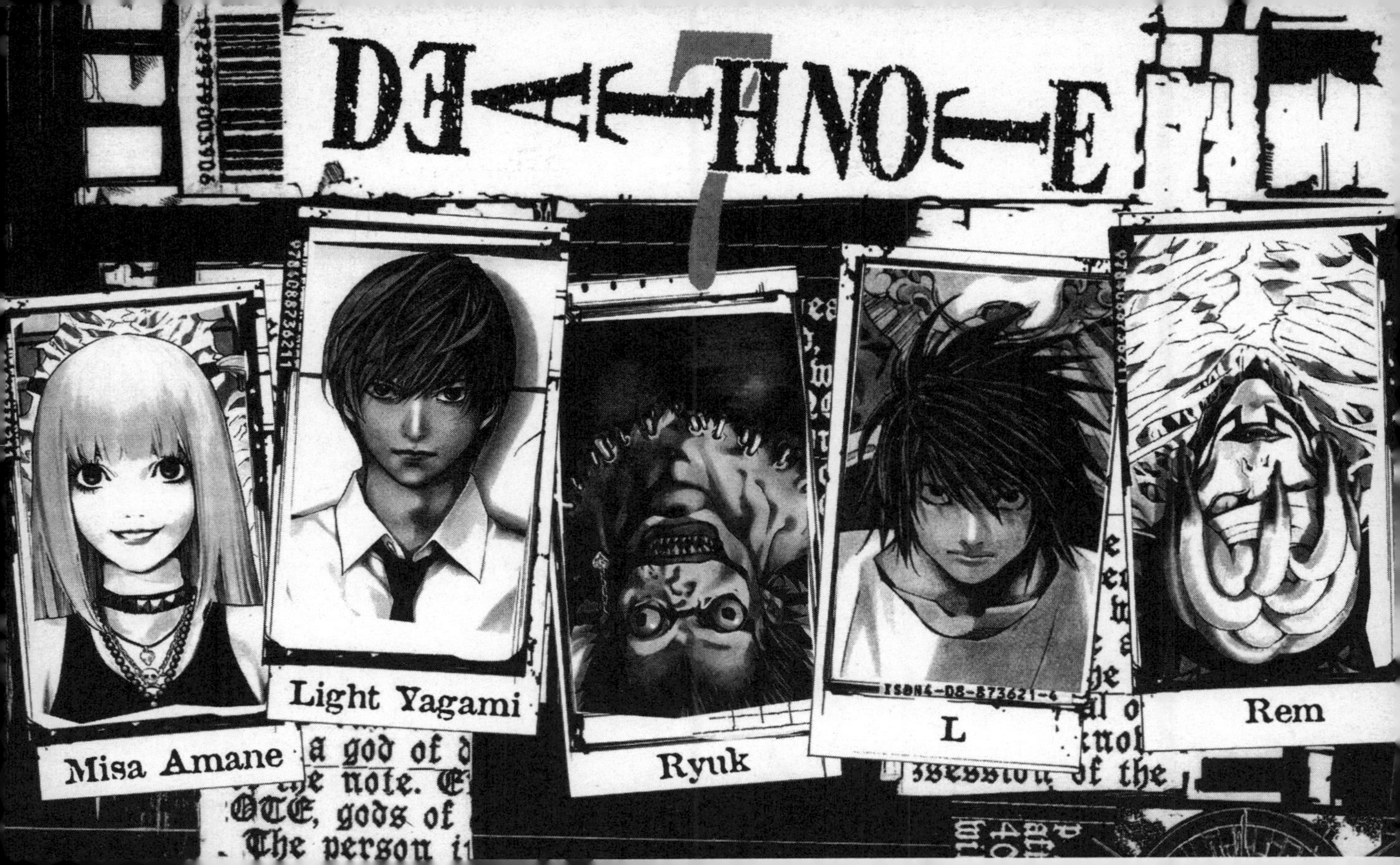
DEATH NOTE
Misa Amane
Light Yagami
Ryuk
L
Rem
ISBN4-08-873621-4
a god of d
the note. E
OTE, gods of
The person i
of the

Hatori
Ooi
Namikawa
Shimura
Takahashi
Higuchi
Kida
Mido
Soichiro Yagami
Watari
Mogi
Aiber
Aizawa
Matsuda
Wedy

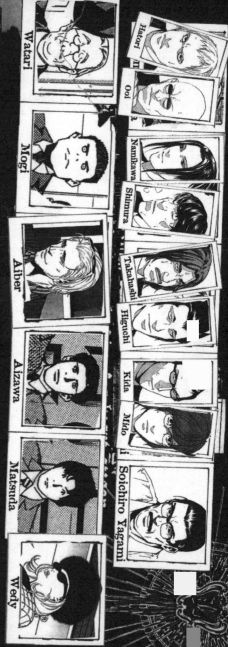

"THE HUMAN WHOSE NAME IS WRITTEN IN THIS NOTE SHALL DIE"... LIGHT YAGAMI, A STRAIGHT-A HIGH SCHOOL HONORS STUDENT, PICKS UP THE "DEATH NOTE" DROPPED BY THE SHINIGAMI RYUK INTO THE HUMAN WORLD. HALF DISBELIEVING, LIGHT USES THE NOTEBOOK, ONLY TO SEE THE PEOPLE WHOSE NAMES HE HAS WRITTEN DROP DEAD! INITIALLY HORRIFIED BY THE NOTEBOOK'S POWERS, LIGHT EVENTUALLY DECIDES TO USE THE DEATH NOTE TO PURGE THE WORLD OF VIOLENT CRIMINALS AND CREATE AN IDEAL SOCIETY. MEANWHILE, AS CRIMINALS WORLDWIDE START DYING MYSTERIOUSLY, THE ENIGMATIC L, A SECRETIVE GENIUS WHO SPECIALIZES IN SOLVING UNSOLVED CASES, ENTERS THE PICTURE. HE USES A TV BROADCAST TO ANNOUNCE HE WILL CATCH WHOEVER IS RESPONSIBLE, SETTING OFF AN ALMIGHTY BATTLE OF THE WITS BETWEEN LIGHT AND HIMSELF...

LIGHT BEGINS PASSING JUDGMENT ON ALL WHO STAND IN HIS WAY. HOWEVER, WITH HIS POWER OF DEDUCTION, L SETS HIS EYES ON LIGHT AS A POSSIBLE SUSPECT. WITH THE APPEARANCE OF MISA, THE "SECOND KIRA," LIGHT AND L JOIN FORCES IN AN INVESTIGATION THAT ENDS WITH MISA CAPTURED BY THE TASK FORCE. PUSHED TO THE BRINK BECAUSE OF HIS CONNECTION WITH THE CAPTURED MISA, LIGHT CHOOSES TO PUT HIMSELF IN POLICE CUSTODY! AND LIGHT FINALLY ANNOUNCES TO RYUK THAT HE IS FORFEITING HIS OWNERSHIP OF THE DEATH NOTE. WHAT IS LIGHT'S PLAN...? WITH THE APPEARANCE OF A NEW KIRA, LIGHT IS RELEASED AND, HANDCUFFED TO L, PURSUES THIS NEW KIRA. DETERMINING THAT THIS KIRA IS AN EMPLOYEE AT A LARGE CORPORATION CALLED THE YOTSUBA GROUP, THE TEAM WHITTLES DOWN THE SUSPECTS TO EIGHT. IN ORDER TO UNCOVER THE YOTSUBA KIRA, MISA IS SENT IN TO INVESTIGATE. THERE SHE IS REUNITED WITH THE SHINIGAMI REM, AND LEARNS THAT HIGUCHI IS THE NEWEST KIRA. MISA THEN ACTS ON HER OWN TO SECURE EVIDENCE FOR LIGHT AND L. WITH NO DOUBT LEFT, THE TASK FORCE MOVES IN TO APPREHEND HIGUCHI! AND NOW WITH, HIGUCHI COMPLETELY SURROUNDED...

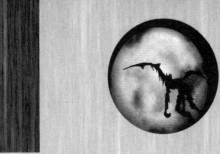

DEATH NOTE
Vol. 7

CONTENTS

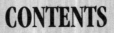

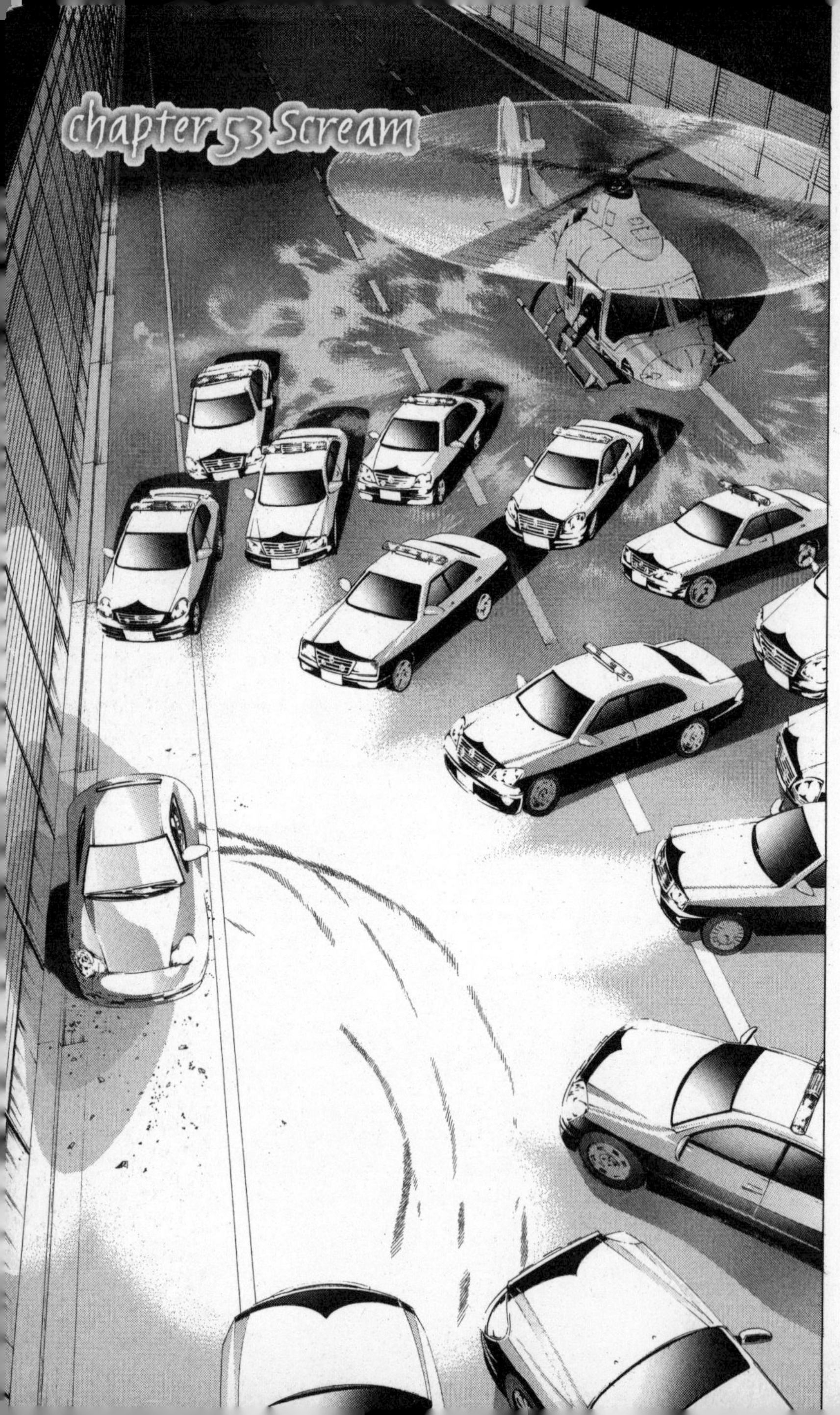
chapter 53 Scream

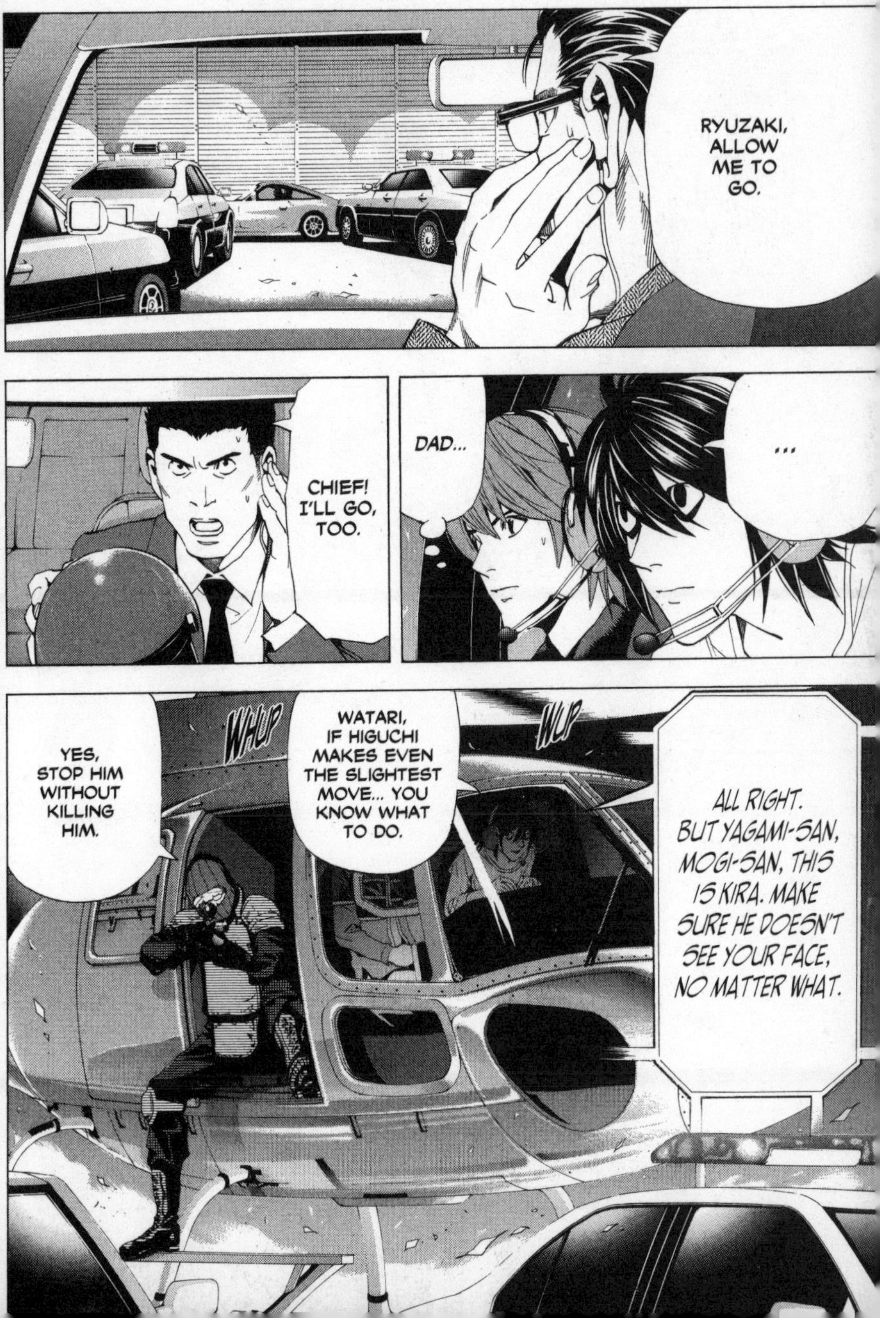
RYUZAKI, ALLOW ME TO GO.
...
DAD...
CHIEF! I'LL GO, TOO.
ALL RIGHT. BUT YAGAMI-SAN, MOGI-SAN, THIS IS KIRA. MAKE SURE HE DOESN'T SEE YOUR FACE, NO MATTER WHAT.
WUP
WHUP
WATARI, IF HIGUCHI MAKES EVEN THE SLIGHTEST MOVE... YOU KNOW WHAT TO DO.
YES, STOP HIM WITHOUT KILLING HIM.

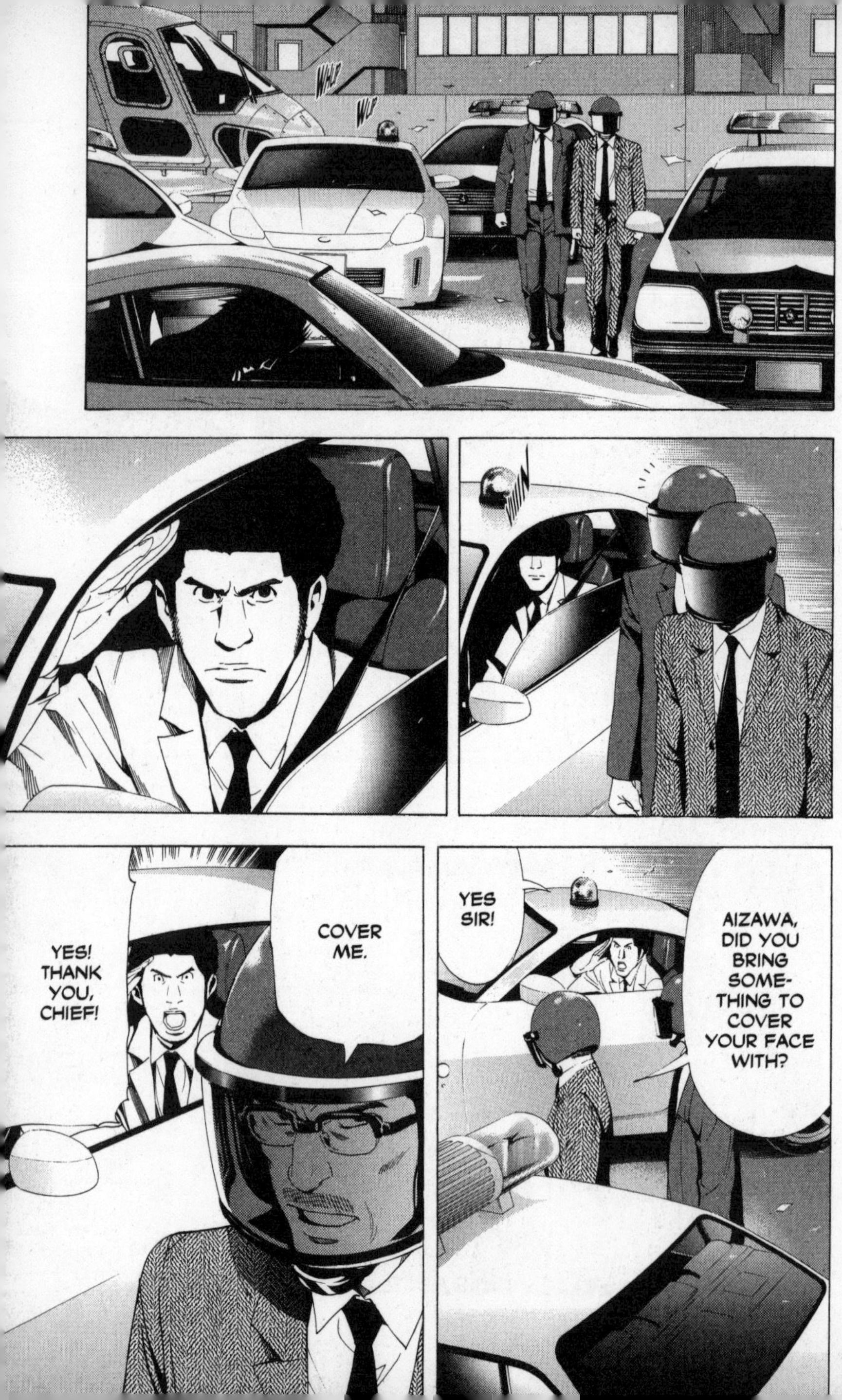
AIZAWA, DID YOU BRING SOME-THING TO COVER YOUR FACE WITH?
YES SIR!
COVER ME.
YES! THANK YOU, CHIEF!

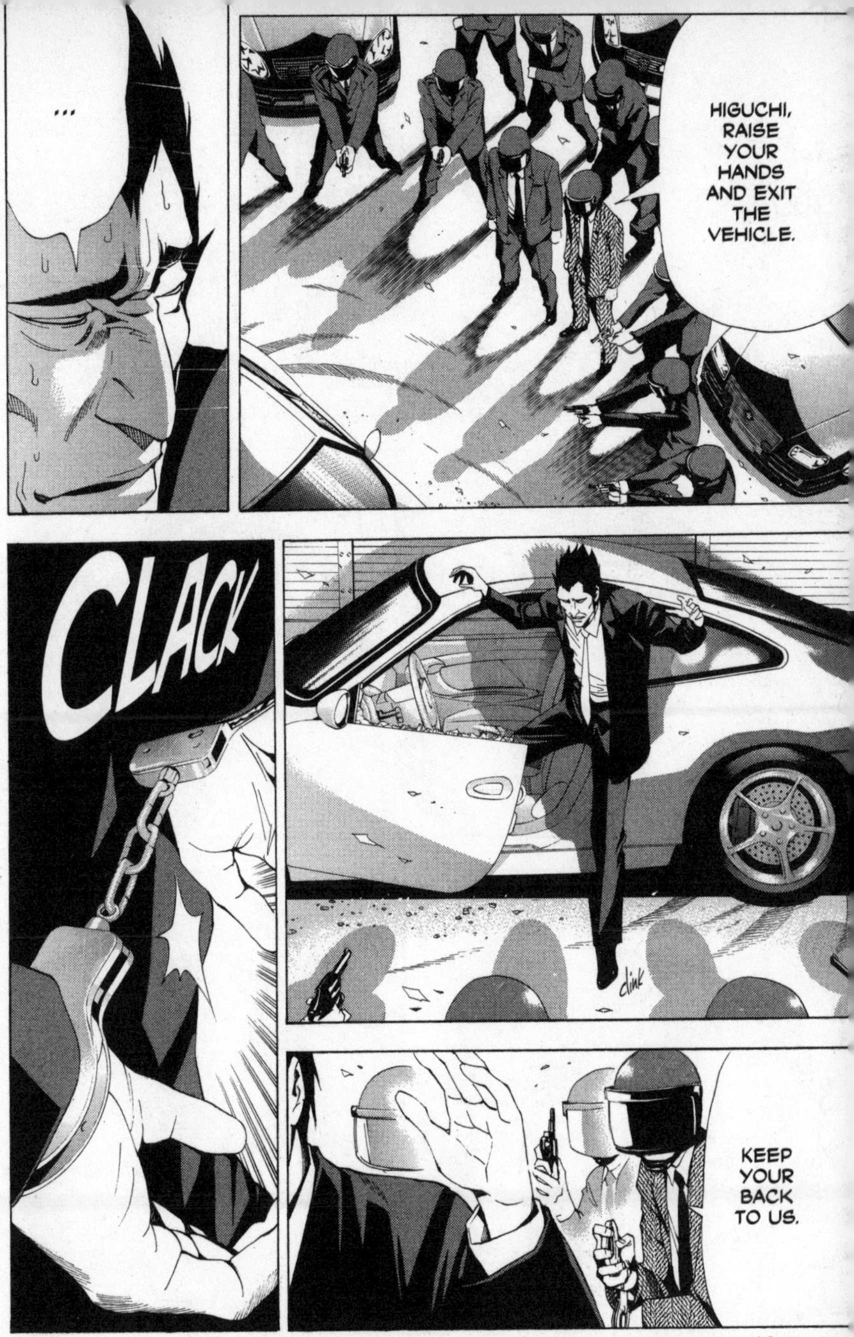
HIGUCHI, RAISE YOUR HANDS AND EXIT THE VEHICLE.
...
clink
KEEP YOUR BACK TO US.
CLACK

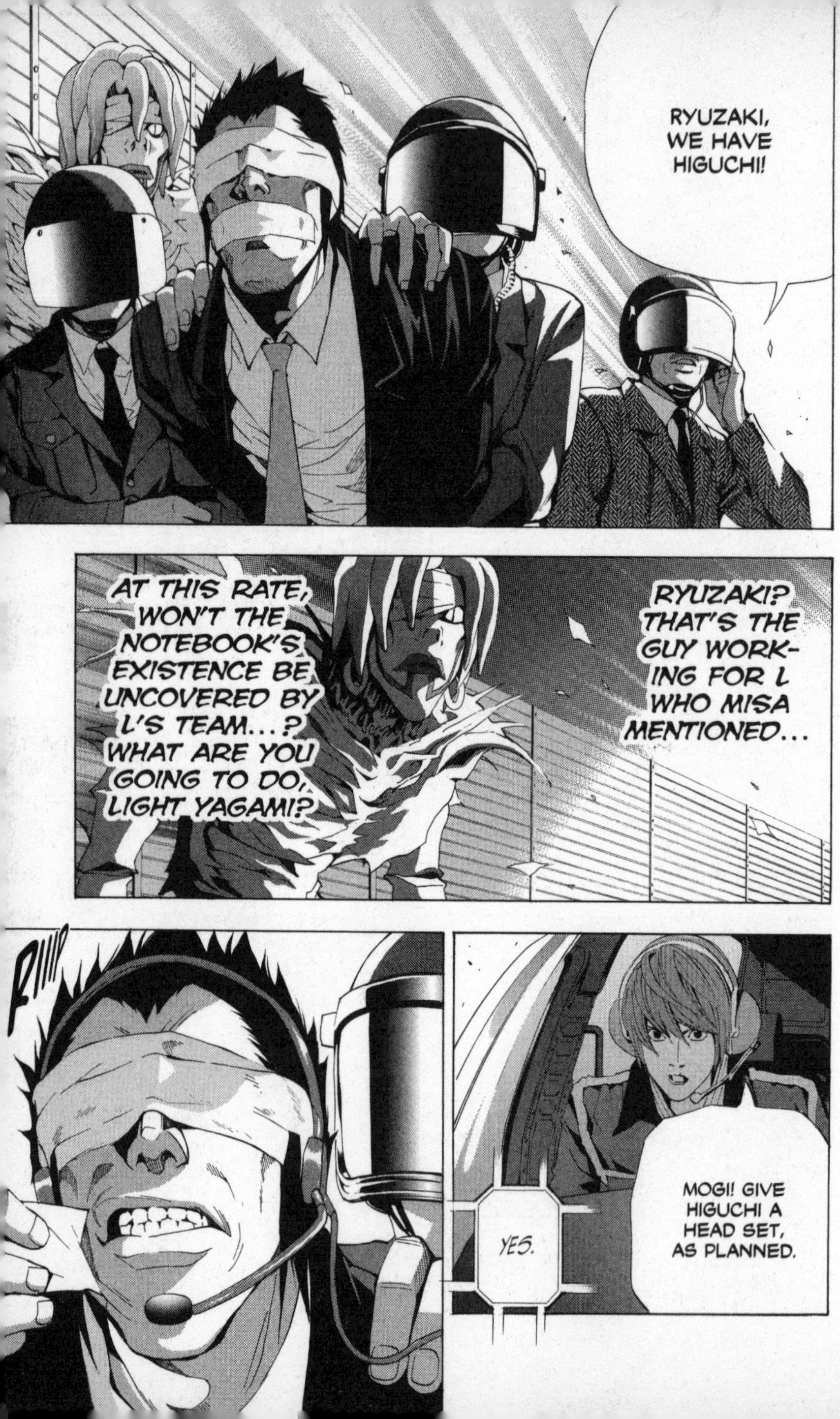
RYUZAKI, WE HAVE HIGUCHI!
RYUZAKI? THAT'S THE GUY WORKING FOR L WHO MISA MENTIONED...
AT THIS RATE, WON'T THE NOTEBOOK'S EXISTENCE BE UNCOVERED BY L'S TEAM...? WHAT ARE YOU GOING TO DO, LIGHT YAGAMI?
MOGI! GIVE HIGUCHI A HEAD SET, AS PLANNED.
YES.
RIIIP

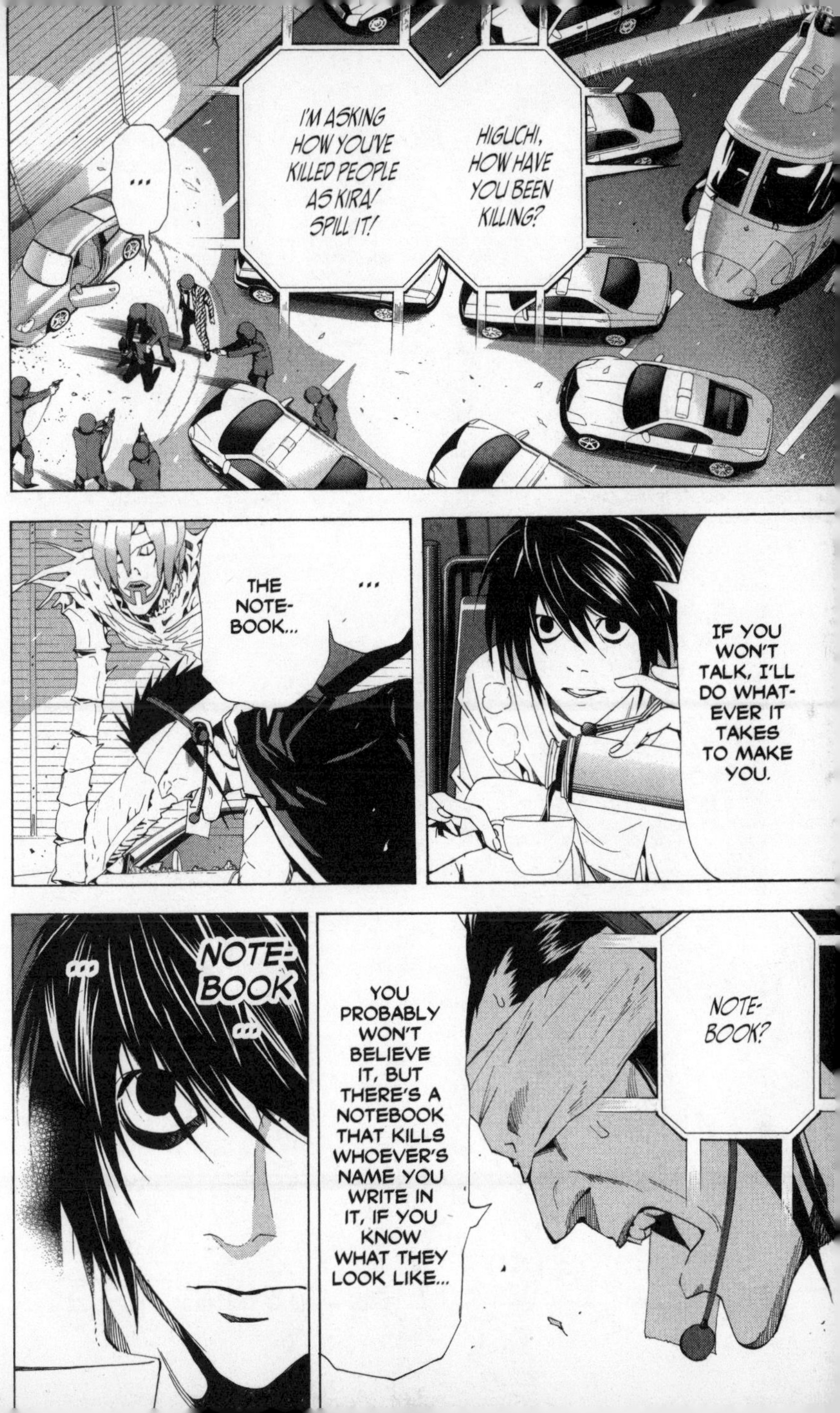
HIGUCHI, HOW HAVE YOU BEEN KILLING?
I'M ASKING HOW YOU'VE KILLED PEOPLE AS KIRA! SPILL IT!
...
IF YOU WON'T TALK, I'LL DO WHATEVER IT TAKES TO MAKE YOU.
...
THE NOTE-BOOK...
NOTE-BOOK?
YOU PROBABLY WON'T BELIEVE IT, BUT THERE'S A NOTEBOOK THAT KILLS WHOEVER'S NAME YOU WRITE IN IT, IF YOU KNOW WHAT THEY LOOK LIKE...
...
NOTE-BOOK
...

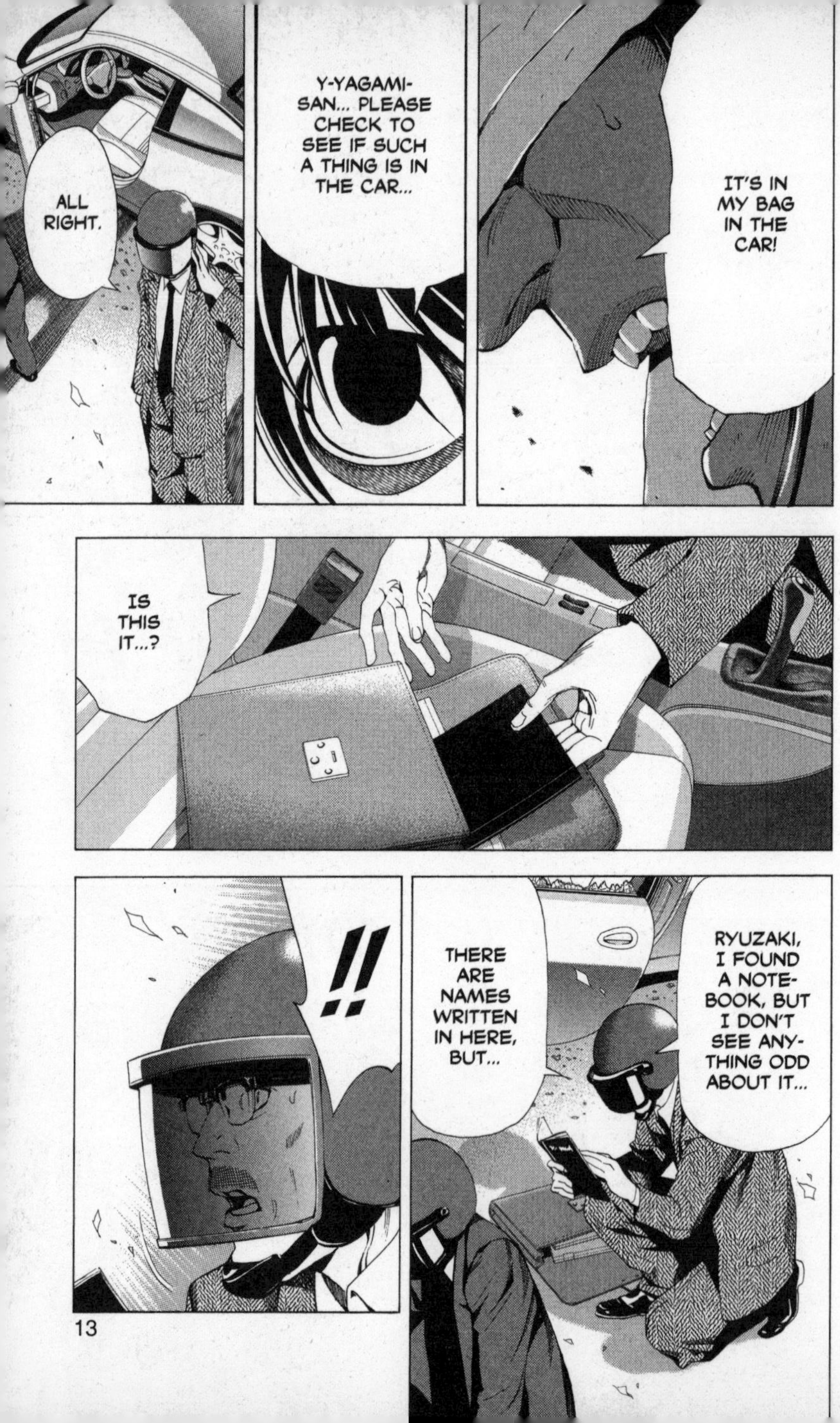
IT'S IN MY BAG IN THE CAR!
Y-YAGAMI-SAN... PLEASE CHECK TO SEE IF SUCH A THING IS IN THE CAR...
ALL RIGHT.
IS THIS IT...?
RYUZAKI, I FOUND A NOTE-BOOK, BUT I DON'T SEE ANY-THING ODD ABOUT IT...
THERE ARE NAMES WRITTEN IN HERE, BUT...
!!

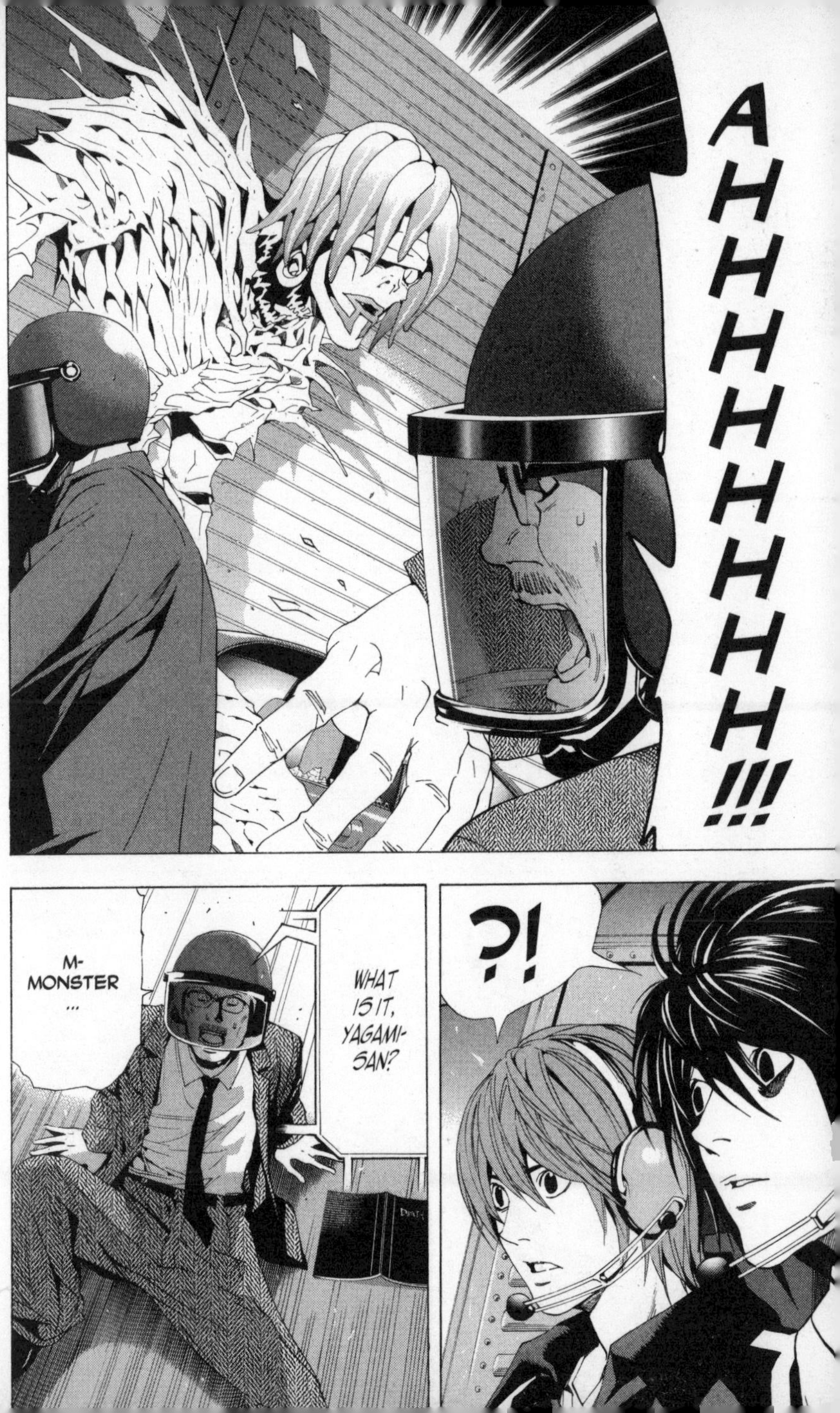
AHHHHHHHH!!!
?!
WHAT IS IT, YAGAMI-SAN?
M-MONSTER ...

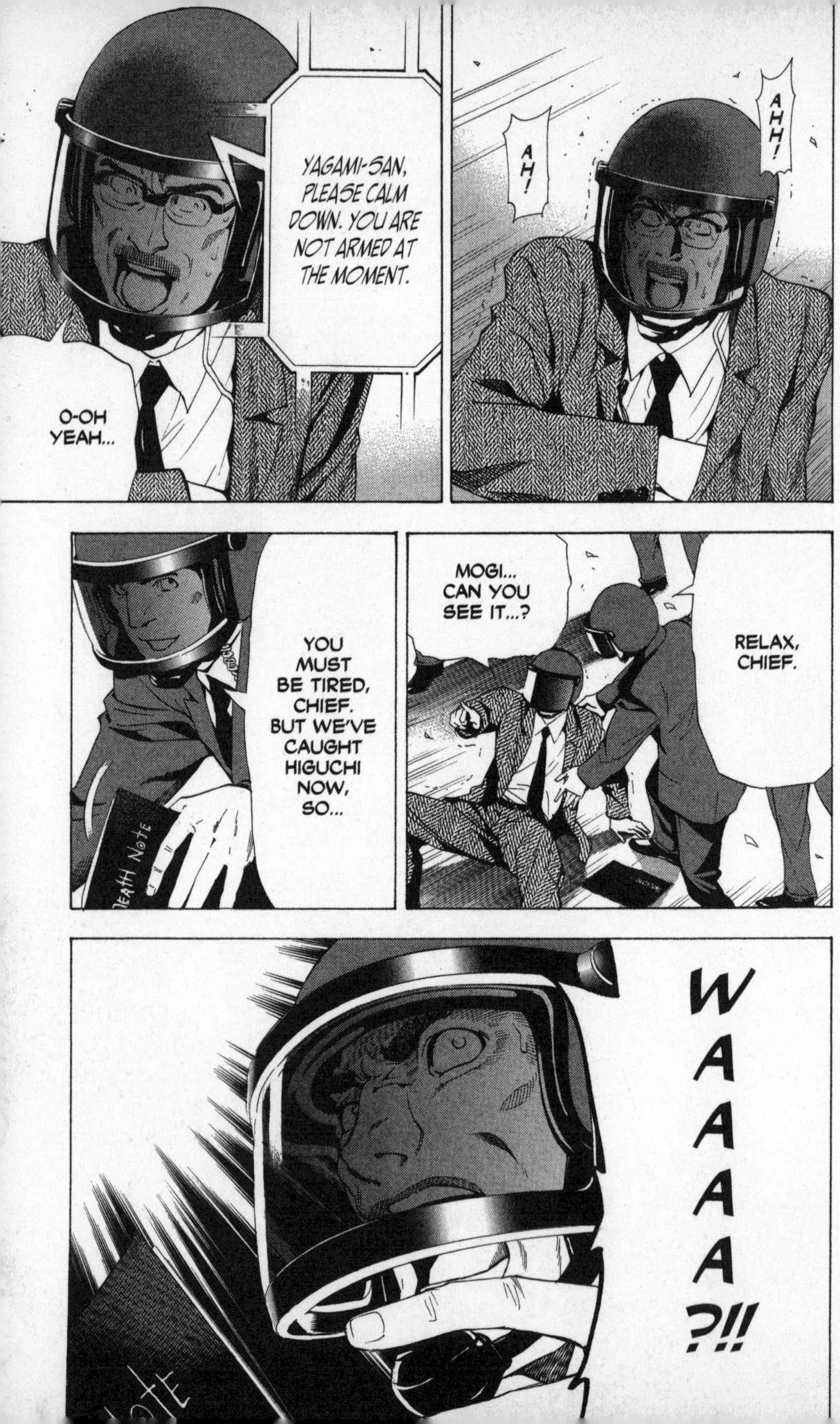
AHH!
AH!
YAGAMI-SAN, PLEASE CALM DOWN. YOU ARE NOT ARMED AT THE MOMENT.
O-OH YEAH...
RELAX, CHIEF.
MOGI... CAN YOU SEE IT...?
YOU MUST BE TIRED, CHIEF. BUT WE'VE CAUGHT HIGUCHI NOW, SO...
WAAAAA?!!

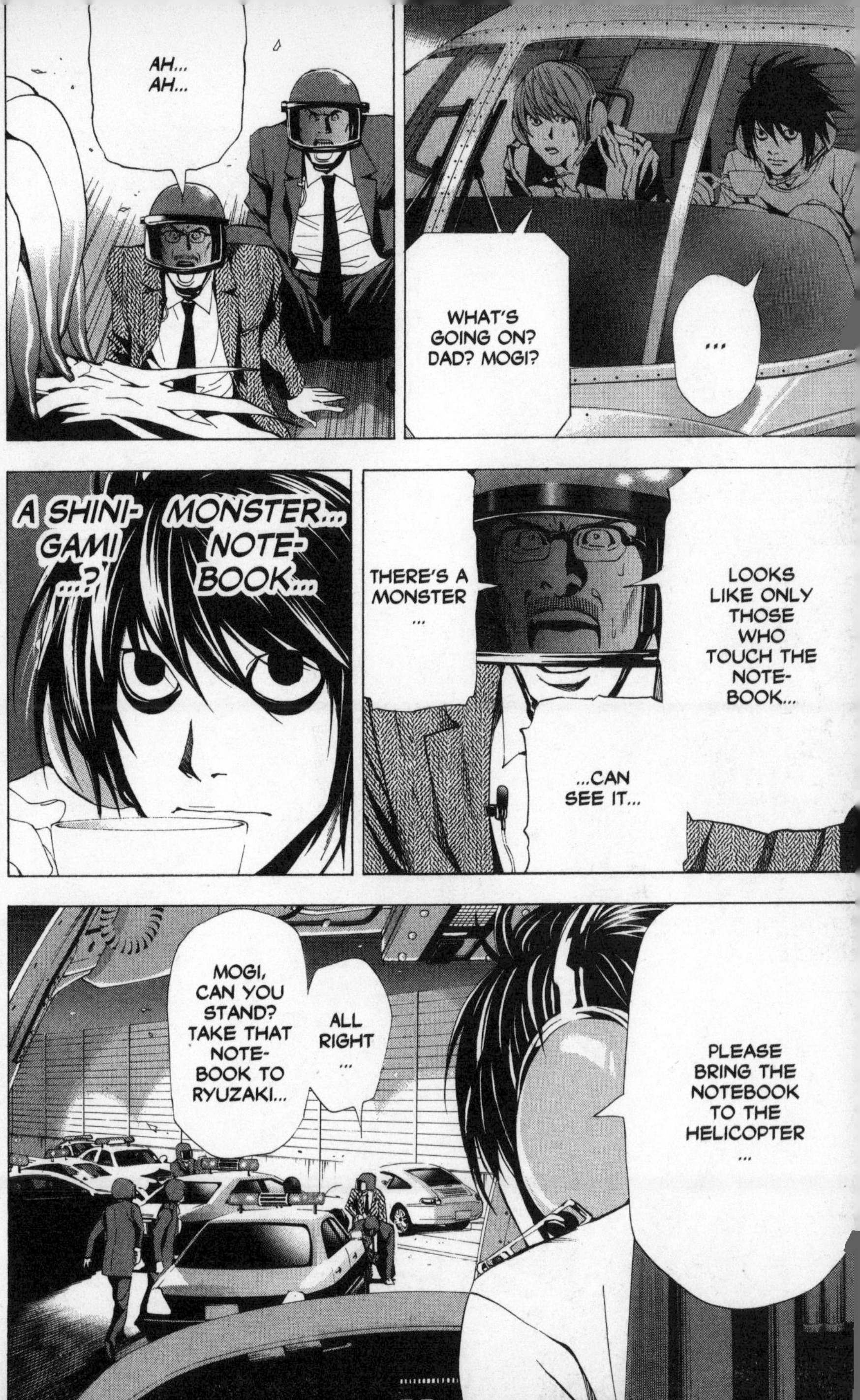
WHAT'S GOING ON? DAD? MOGI?
...
AH... AH...
THERE'S A MONSTER...
LOOKS LIKE ONLY THOSE WHO TOUCH THE NOTEBOOK...
...CAN SEE IT...
MONSTER... NOTEBOOK...
A SHINIGAMI...?
PLEASE BRING THE NOTEBOOK TO THE HELICOPTER...
MOGI, CAN YOU STAND? TAKE THAT NOTEBOOK TO RYUZAKI...
ALL RIGHT...

READ THIS WAY

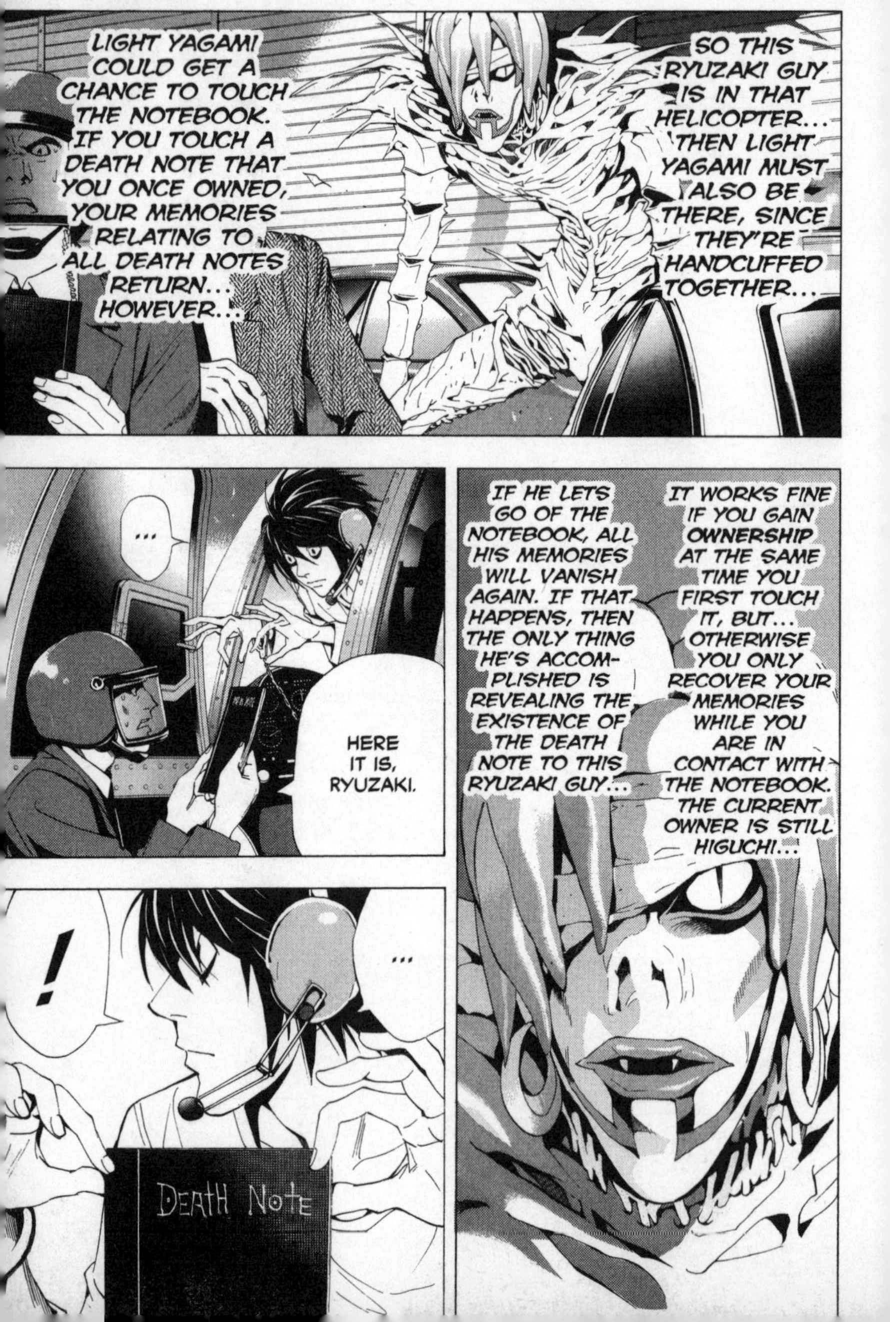
SO THIS RYUZAKI GUY IS IN THAT HELICOPTER... THEN LIGHT YAGAMI MUST ALSO BE THERE, SINCE THEY'RE HANDCUFFED TOGETHER...
LIGHT YAGAMI COULD GET A CHANCE TO TOUCH THE NOTEBOOK. IF YOU TOUCH A DEATH NOTE THAT YOU ONCE OWNED, YOUR MEMORIES RELATING TO ALL DEATH NOTES RETURN... HOWEVER...
IT WORKS FINE IF YOU GAIN OWNERSHIP AT THE SAME TIME YOU FIRST TOUCH IT, BUT... OTHERWISE YOU ONLY RECOVER YOUR MEMORIES WHILE YOU ARE IN CONTACT WITH THE NOTEBOOK. THE CURRENT OWNER IS STILL HIGUCHI...
IF HE LETS GO OF THE NOTEBOOK, ALL HIS MEMORIES WILL VANISH AGAIN. IF THAT HAPPENS, THEN THE ONLY THING HE'S ACCOM-PLISHED IS REVEALING THE EXISTENCE OF THE DEATH NOTE TO THIS RYUZAKI GUY...
HERE IT IS, RYUZAKI.
...
...
!
DEATH NOTE

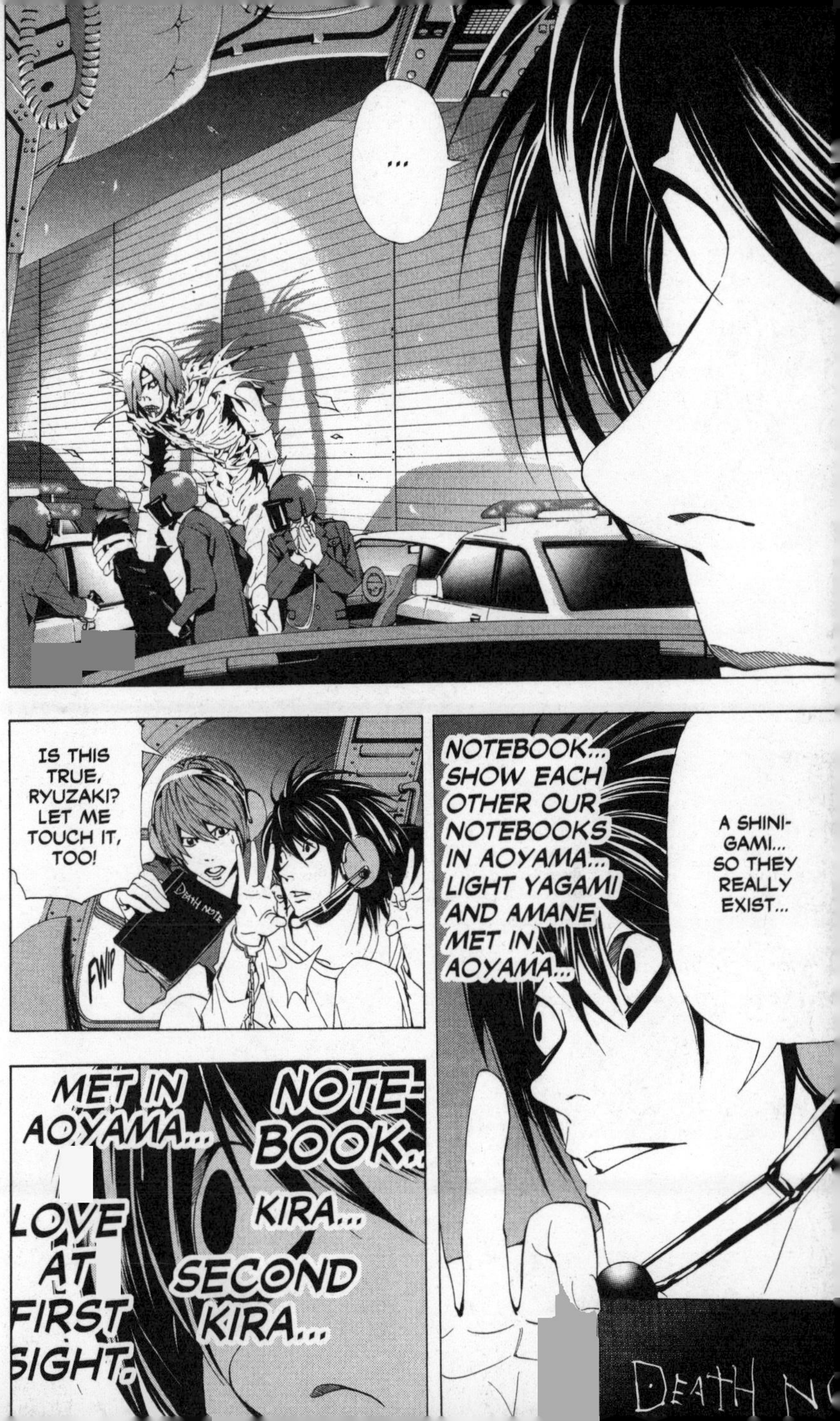
...
A SHINI-
GAMI...
SO THEY
REALLY
EXIST...
NOTEBOOK...
SHOW EACH
OTHER OUR
NOTEBOOKS
IN AOYAMA...
LIGHT YAGAMI
AND AMANE
MET IN
AOYAMA...
DEATH N
IS THIS
TRUE,
RYUZAKI!?
LET ME
TOUCH IT,
TOO!
DEATH NOTE
FWIP
NOTE-
BOOK..
MET IN
AOYAMA...
KIRA...
LOVE
AT
FIRST
SIGHT.
SECOND
KIRA...

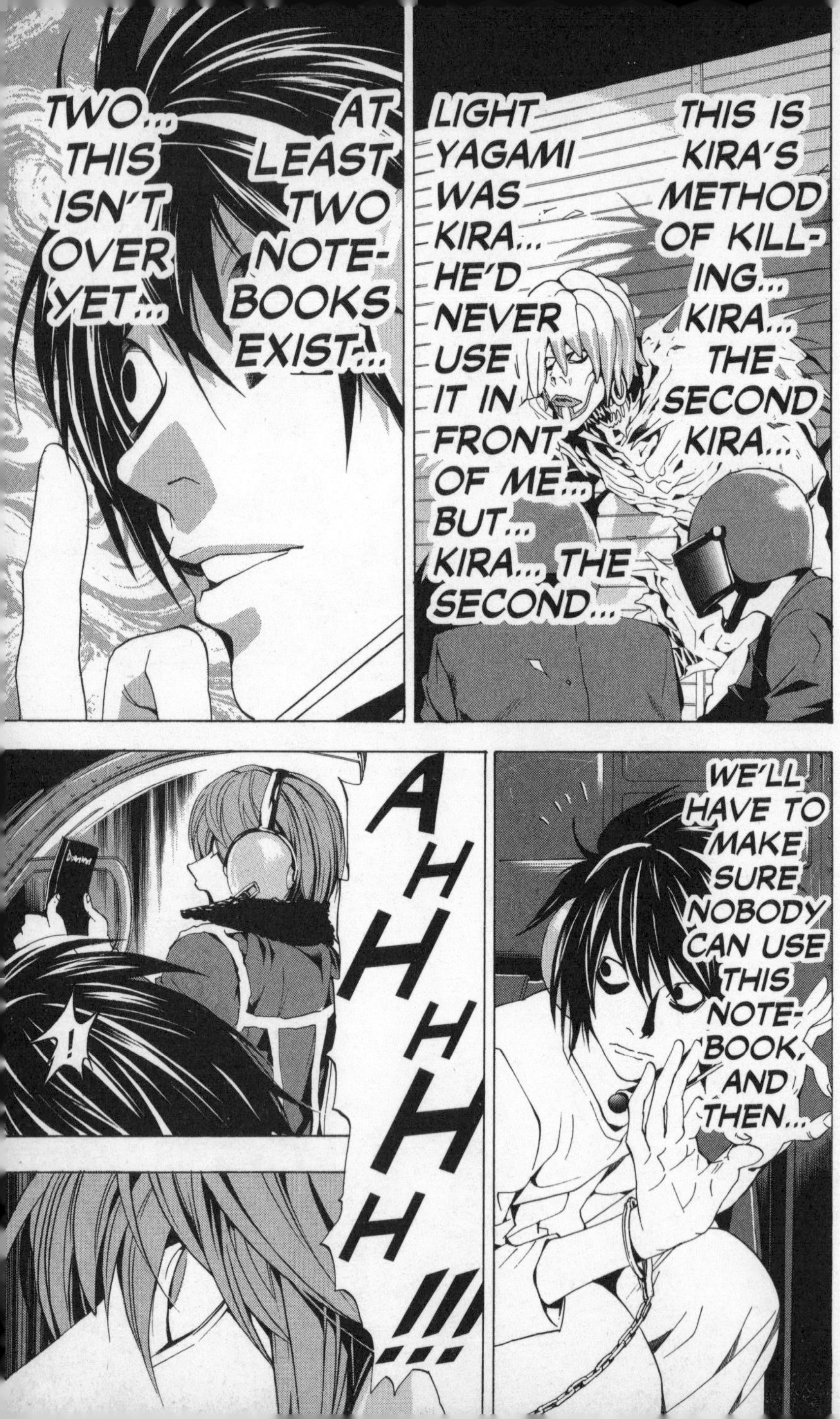
THIS IS KIRA'S METHOD OF KILL-ING... KIRA... THE SECOND KIRA...
LIGHT YAGAMI WAS KIRA... HE'D NEVER USE IT IN FRONT OF ME... BUT... KIRA... THE SECOND...
AT LEAST TWO NOTE-BOOKS EXIST...
TWO... THIS ISN'T OVER YET...
WE'LL HAVE TO MAKE SURE NOBODY CAN USE THIS NOTE-BOOK, AND THEN...
!
AHHHHH!!!

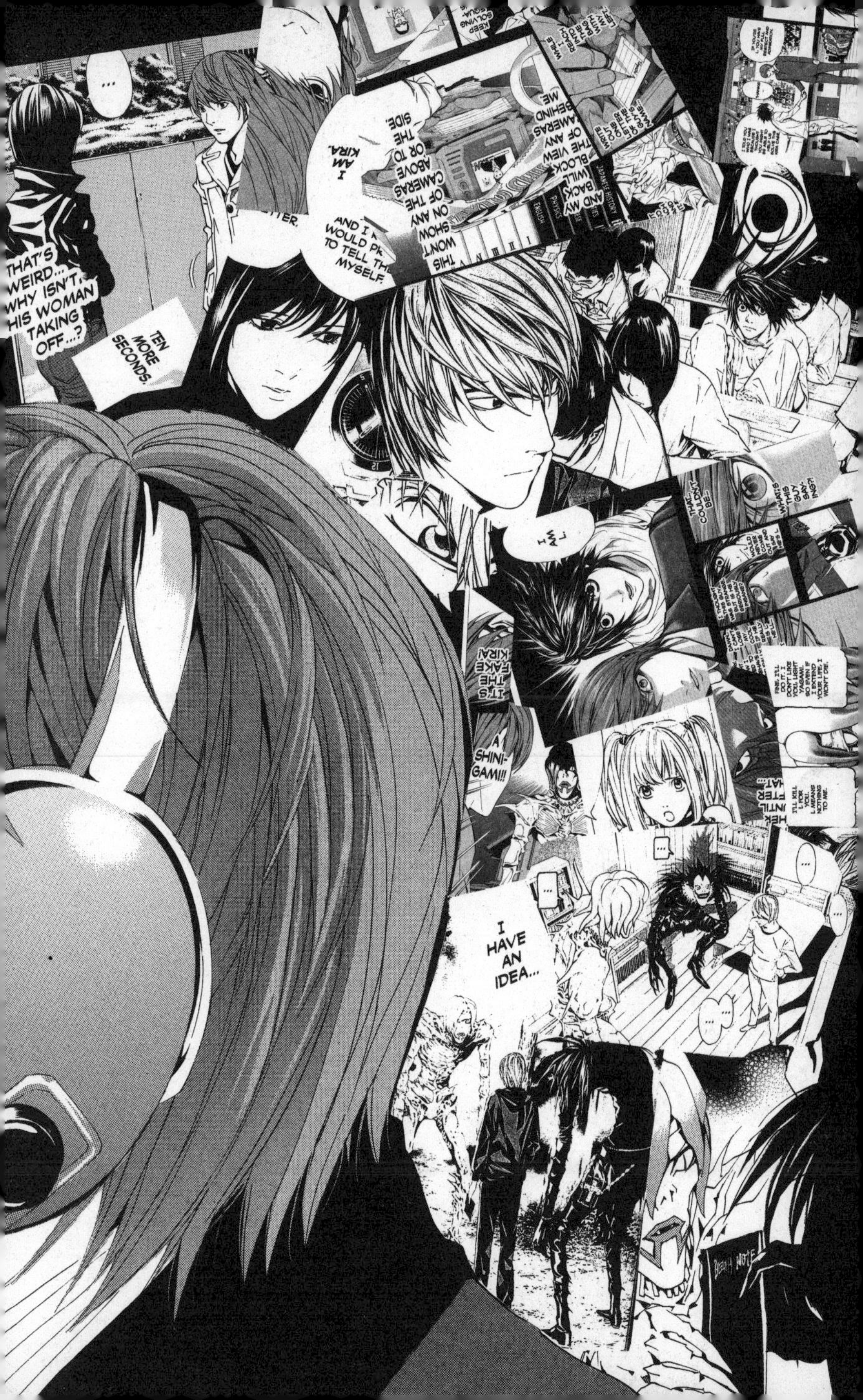

WHAT'S THIS GUY SAYING?
THAT COULDN'T BE...
THIS WON'T SHOW ON ANY OF THE CAMERAS ABOVE OR TO THE SIDE.
AND MY BACK WILL BLOCK THE VIEW OF ANY CAMERAS BEHIND ME.
I AM KIRA.
THAT'S WEIRD... WHY ISN'T THIS WOMAN TAKING OFF...?
TEN MORE SECONDS.
I AM L.
IT'S THE FAKE KIRA!
A SHINIGAMI!!
I HAVE AN IDEA...

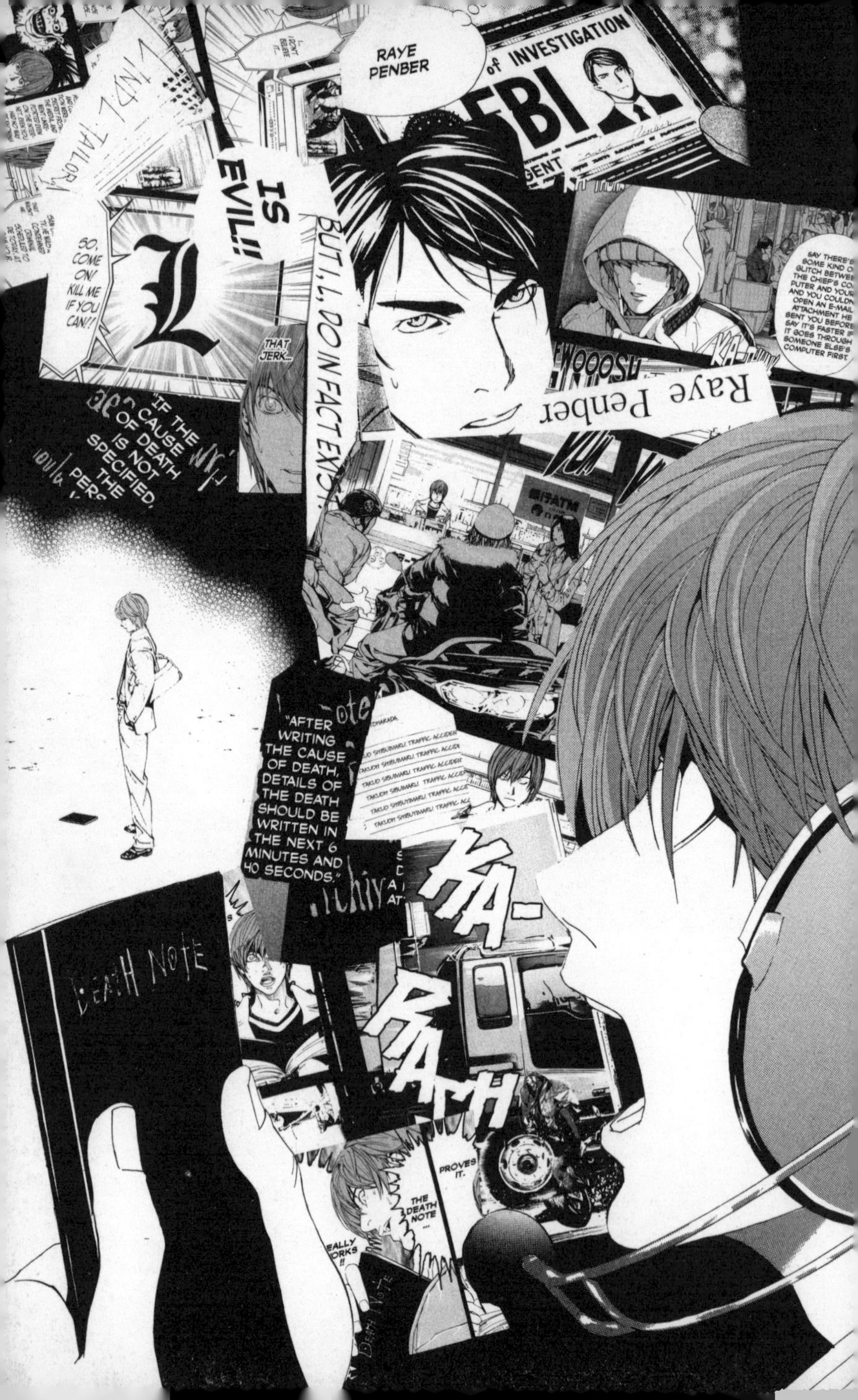
of INVESTIGATION
FBI
RAYE PENBER
IS EVIL!!
SO, COME ON! KILL ME IF YOU CAN!!
THAT JERK...
BUT I, L, DO IN FACT EXI
WOOOSH
Raye Penber
"IF THE CAUSE OF DEATH IS NOT SPECIFIED, THE
"AFTER WRITING THE CAUSE OF DEATH, DETAILS OF THE DEATH SHOULD BE WRITTEN IN THE NEXT 6 MINUTES AND 40 SECONDS."
KA-
PROVES IT.
THE DEATH NOTE ...
DEATH NOTE

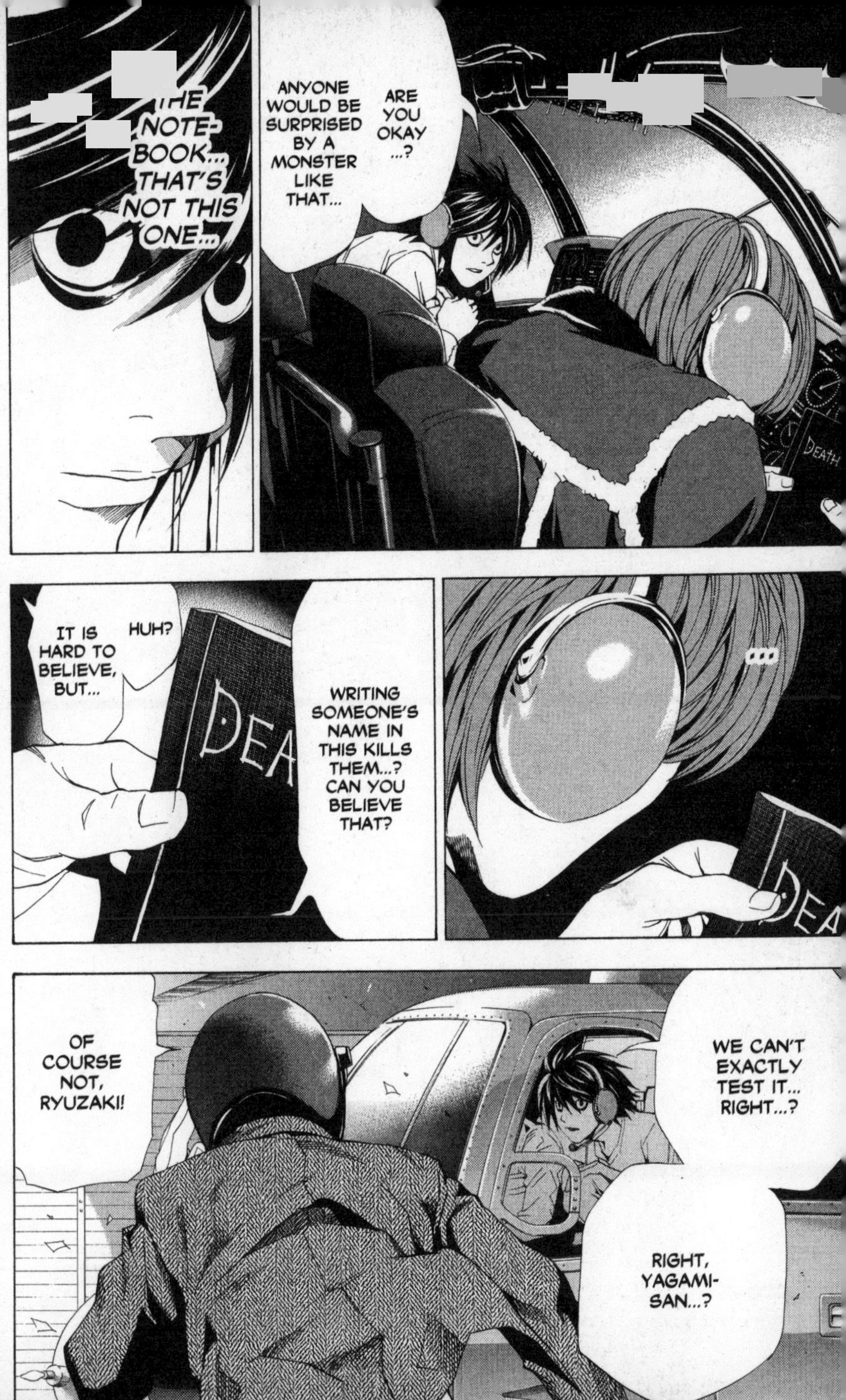
ARE YOU OKAY ...?
ANYONE WOULD BE SURPRISED BY A MONSTER LIKE THAT...
DEATH
THE NOTE-BOOK... THAT'S NOT THIS ONE...
...
WRITING SOMEONE'S NAME IN THIS KILLS THEM...? CAN YOU BELIEVE THAT?
HUH?
IT IS HARD TO BELIEVE, BUT...
WE CAN'T EXACTLY TEST IT... RIGHT...?
RIGHT, YAGAMI-SAN...?
OF COURSE NOT, RYUZAKI!

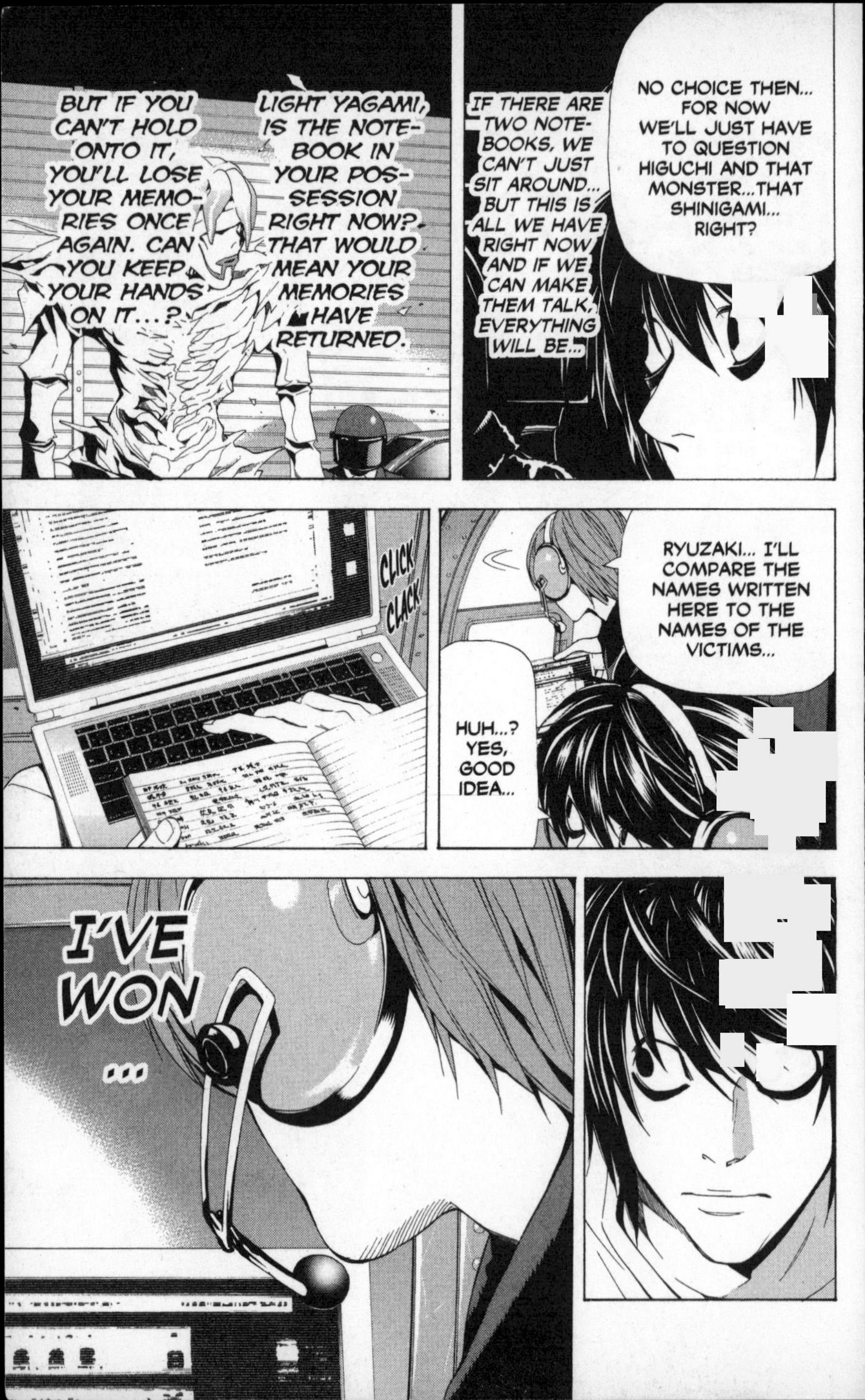
NO CHOICE THEN... FOR NOW WE'LL JUST HAVE TO QUESTION HIGUCHI AND THAT MONSTER...THAT SHINIGAMI... RIGHT?
IF THERE ARE TWO NOTEBOOKS, WE CAN'T JUST SIT AROUND... BUT THIS IS ALL WE HAVE RIGHT NOW AND IF WE CAN MAKE THEM TALK, EVERYTHING WILL BE...
LIGHT YAGAMI, IS THE NOTEBOOK IN YOUR POSSESSION RIGHT NOW? THAT WOULD MEAN YOUR MEMORIES HAVE RETURNED.
BUT IF YOU CAN'T HOLD ONTO IT, YOU'LL LOSE YOUR MEMORIES ONCE AGAIN. CAN YOU KEEP YOUR HANDS ON IT...?
RYUZAKI... I'LL COMPARE THE NAMES WRITTEN HERE TO THE NAMES OF THE VICTIMS...
HUH...? YES, GOOD IDEA...
CLICK
CLACK
I'VE WON ...

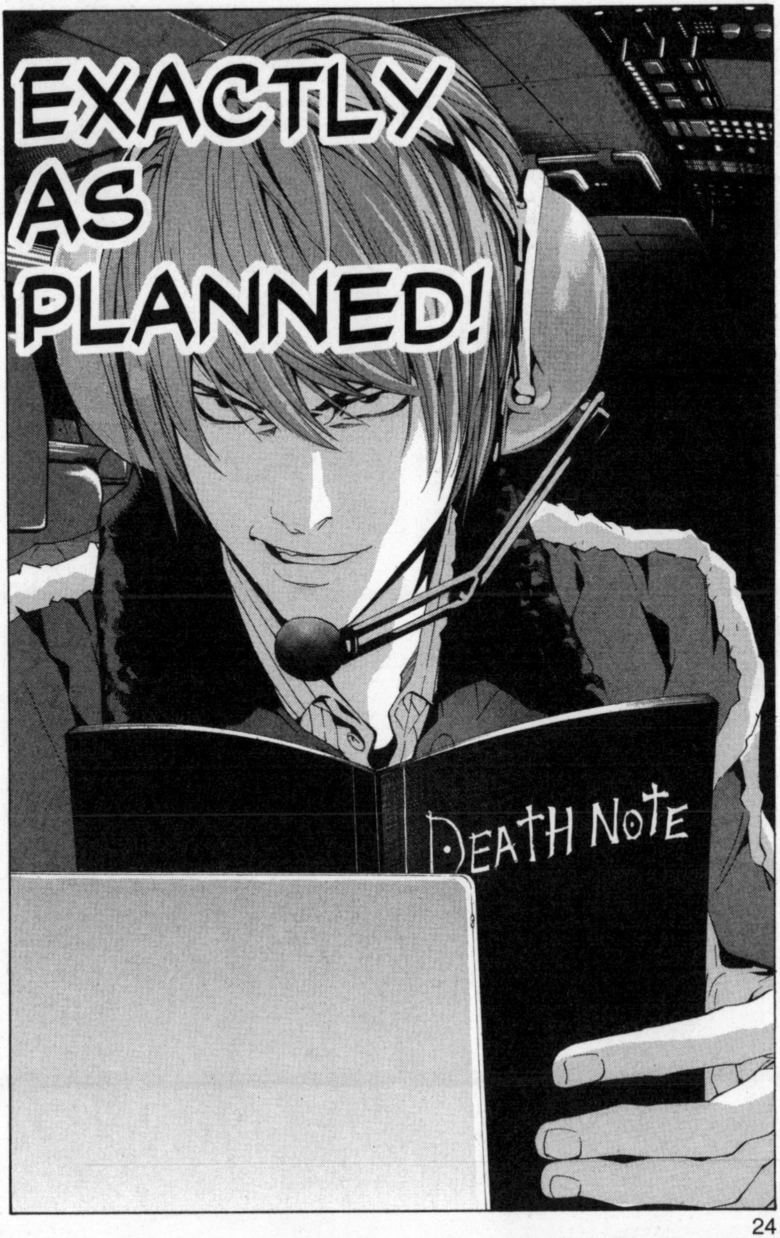
EXACTLY AS PLANNED!
DEATH NOTE

READ THIS WAY

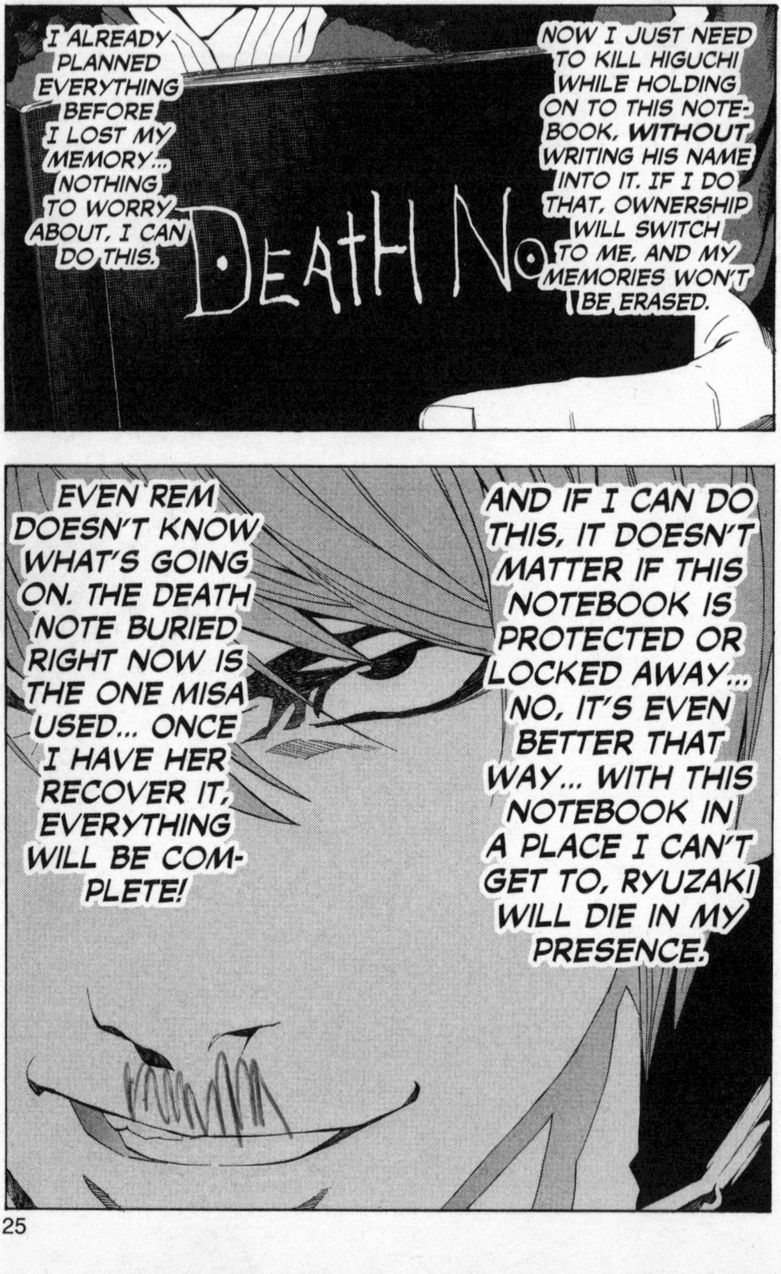
NOW I JUST NEED TO KILL HIGUCHI WHILE HOLDING ON TO THIS NOTE-BOOK, **WITHOUT** WRITING HIS NAME INTO IT. IF I DO THAT, OWNERSHIP WILL SWITCH TO ME, AND MY MEMORIES WON'T BE ERASED.
I ALREADY PLANNED EVERYTHING BEFORE I LOST MY MEMORY... NOTHING TO WORRY ABOUT, I CAN DO THIS.
DEATH NO
AND IF I CAN DO THIS, IT DOESN'T MATTER IF THIS NOTEBOOK IS PROTECTED OR LOCKED AWAY... NO, IT'S EVEN BETTER THAT WAY... WITH THIS NOTEBOOK IN A PLACE I CAN'T GET TO, RYUZAKI WILL DIE IN MY PRESENCE.
EVEN REM DOESN'T KNOW WHAT'S GOING ON. THE DEATH NOTE BURIED RIGHT NOW IS THE ONE MISA USED... ONCE I HAVE HER RECOVER IT, EVERYTHING WILL BE COM-PLETE!

DEATH NOTE
How to use it
XXXVII

- When regaining ownership of the DEATH NOTE, the memories associated with the DEATH NOTE will also return.
  In cases where you were involved with other DEATH NOTEs as well, memories of all the DEATH NOTEs involved will return.

所有権をなくしたノートの所有権を再び得れば、
そのノートに関する記憶が戻る。
万が一、他にも関わったノートがあれば、
関わった全てのノートに関する記憶が戻る。

- Even without obtaining ownership, memories will return just by touching the DEATH NOTE.

また、所有権を得なくとも、ノートに触れていれば、
触れている間のみ記憶は戻る。

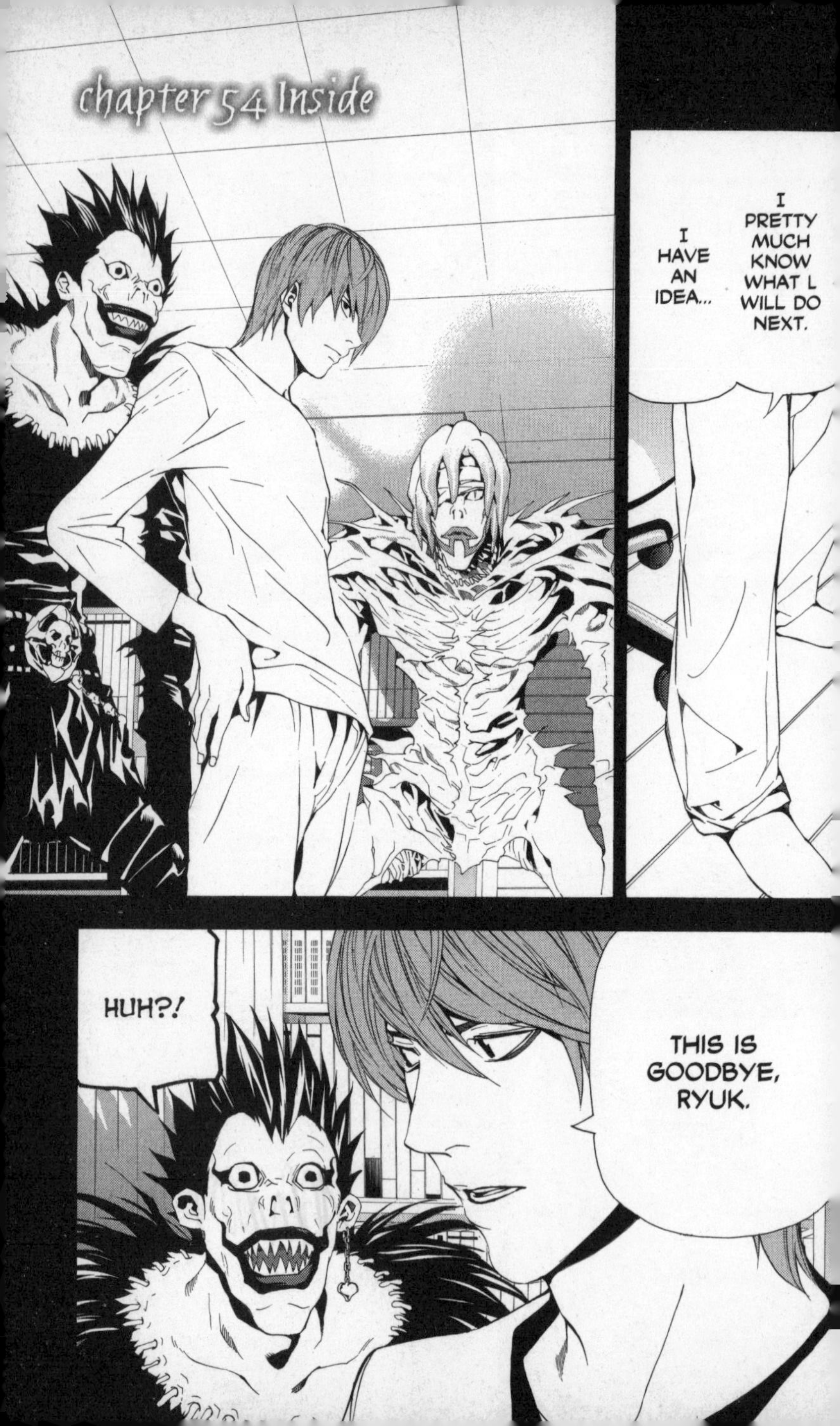
I PRETTY MUCH KNOW WHAT L WILL DO NEXT.
I HAVE AN IDEA...
chapter 54 Inside
THIS IS GOODBYE, RYUK.
HUH?!

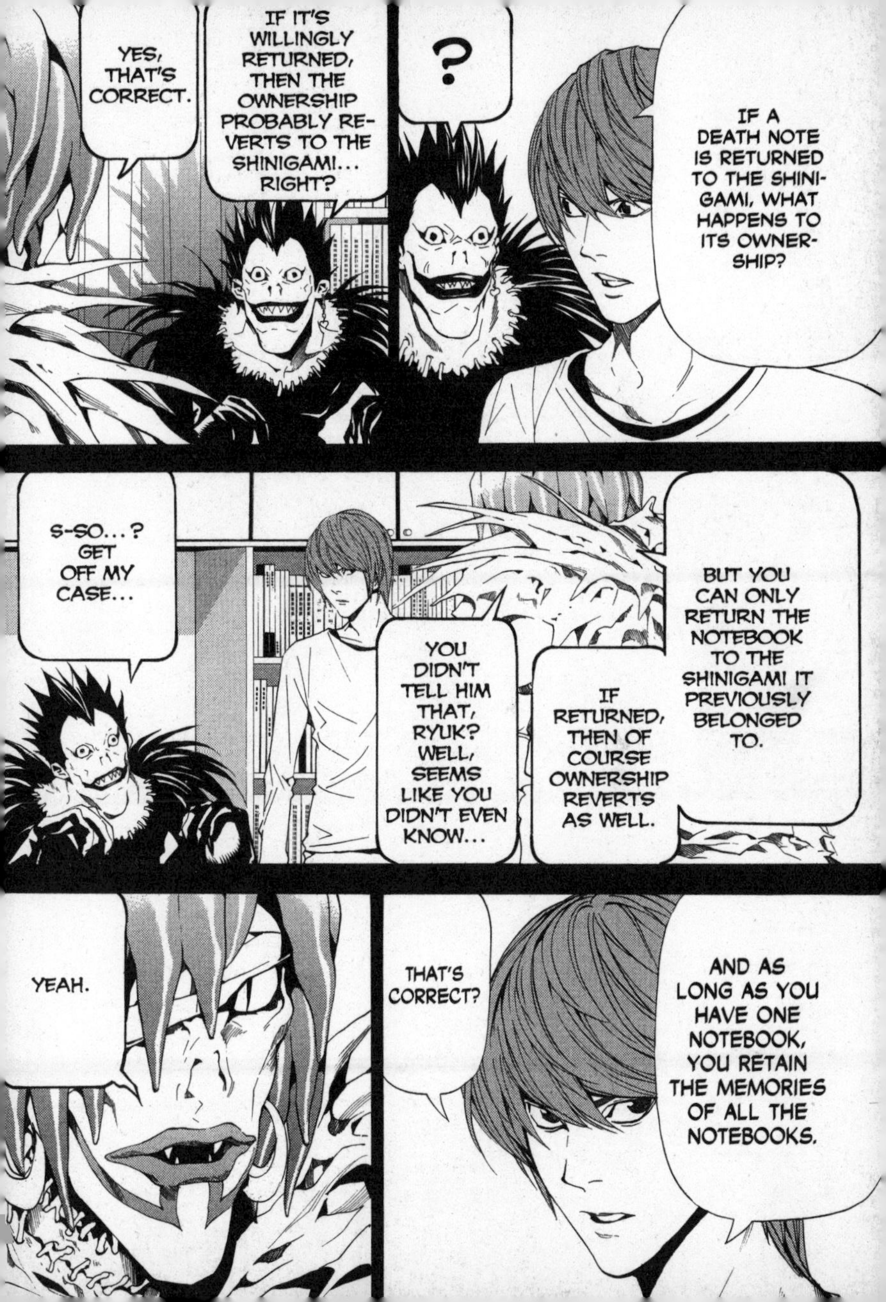
IF A DEATH NOTE IS RETURNED TO THE SHINIGAMI, WHAT HAPPENS TO ITS OWNERSHIP?
?
IF IT'S WILLINGLY RETURNED, THEN THE OWNERSHIP PROBABLY REVERTS TO THE SHINIGAMI... RIGHT?
YES, THAT'S CORRECT.
BUT YOU CAN ONLY RETURN THE NOTEBOOK TO THE SHINIGAMI IT PREVIOUSLY BELONGED TO.
IF RETURNED, THEN OF COURSE OWNERSHIP REVERTS AS WELL.
YOU DIDN'T TELL HIM THAT, RYUK? WELL, SEEMS LIKE YOU DIDN'T EVEN KNOW...
S-SO...? GET OFF MY CASE...
AND AS LONG AS YOU HAVE ONE NOTEBOOK, YOU RETAIN THE MEMORIES OF ALL THE NOTEBOOKS.
THAT'S CORRECT?
YEAH.

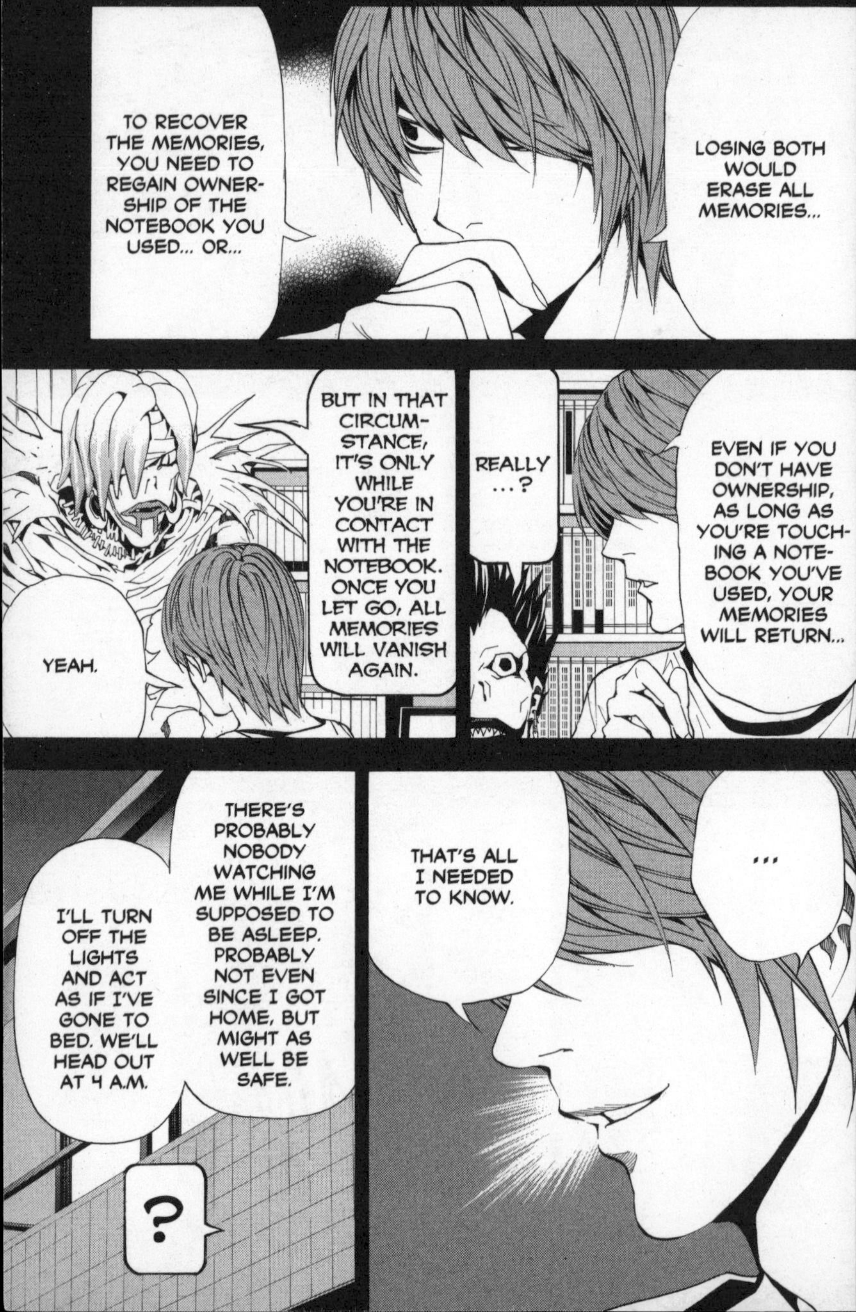
LOSING BOTH WOULD ERASE ALL MEMORIES...
TO RECOVER THE MEMORIES, YOU NEED TO REGAIN OWNERSHIP OF THE NOTEBOOK YOU USED... OR...
EVEN IF YOU DON'T HAVE OWNERSHIP, AS LONG AS YOU'RE TOUCHING A NOTEBOOK YOU'VE USED, YOUR MEMORIES WILL RETURN...
REALLY ...?
BUT IN THAT CIRCUMSTANCE, IT'S ONLY WHILE YOU'RE IN CONTACT WITH THE NOTEBOOK. ONCE YOU LET GO, ALL MEMORIES WILL VANISH AGAIN.
YEAH.
...
THAT'S ALL I NEEDED TO KNOW.
THERE'S PROBABLY NOBODY WATCHING ME WHILE I'M SUPPOSED TO BE ASLEEP. PROBABLY NOT EVEN SINCE I GOT HOME, BUT MIGHT AS WELL BE SAFE.
I'LL TURN OFF THE LIGHTS AND ACT AS IF I'VE GONE TO BED. WE'LL HEAD OUT AT 4 A.M.
?

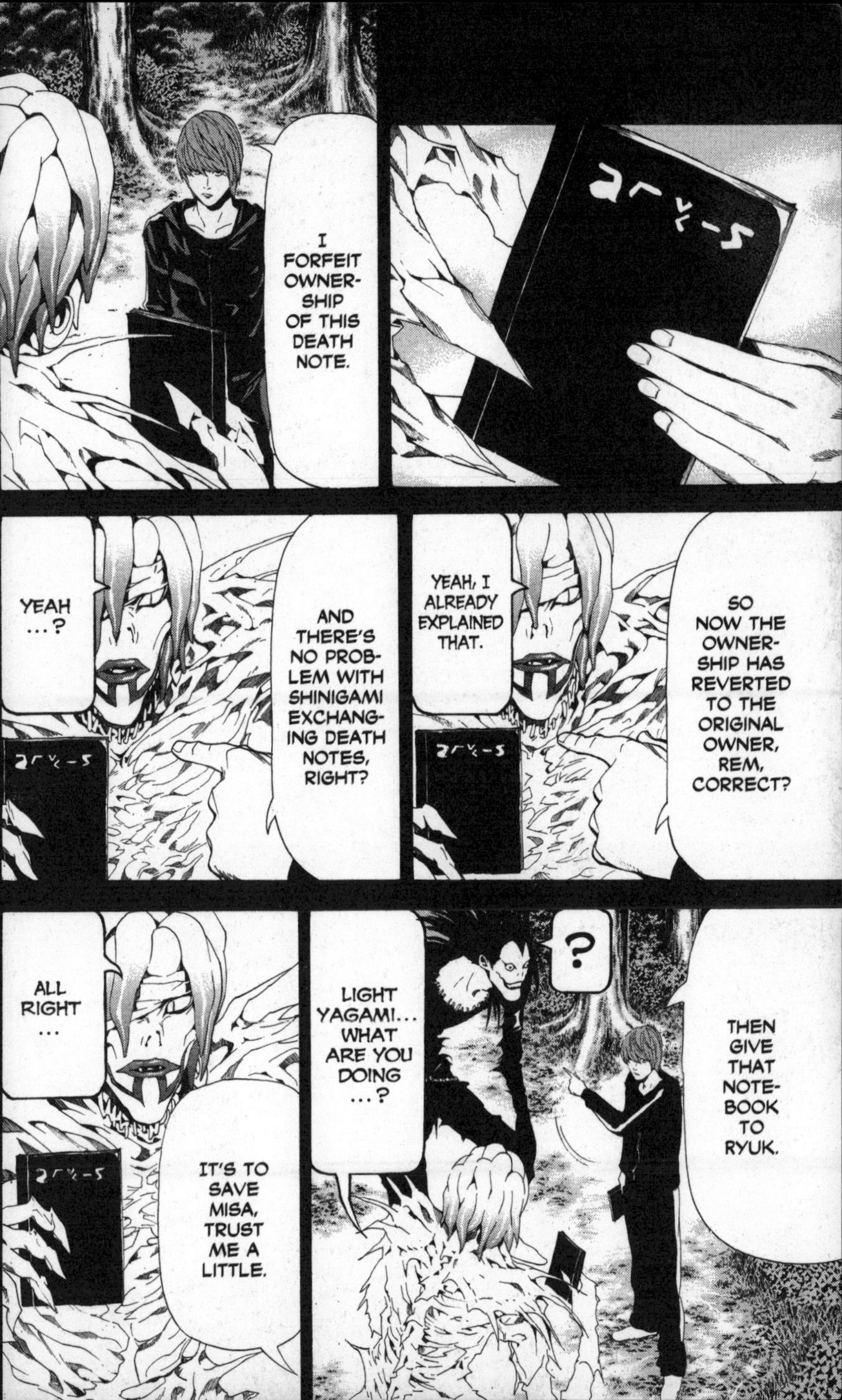
I FORFEIT OWNERSHIP OF THIS DEATH NOTE.
SO NOW THE OWNERSHIP HAS REVERTED TO THE ORIGINAL OWNER, REM, CORRECT?
YEAH, I ALREADY EXPLAINED THAT.
AND THERE'S NO PROBLEM WITH SHINIGAMI EXCHANGING DEATH NOTES, RIGHT?
YEAH ...?
THEN GIVE THAT NOTEBOOK TO RYUK.
?
LIGHT YAGAMI... WHAT ARE YOU DOING ...?
IT'S TO SAVE MISA, TRUST ME A LITTLE.
ALL RIGHT ...

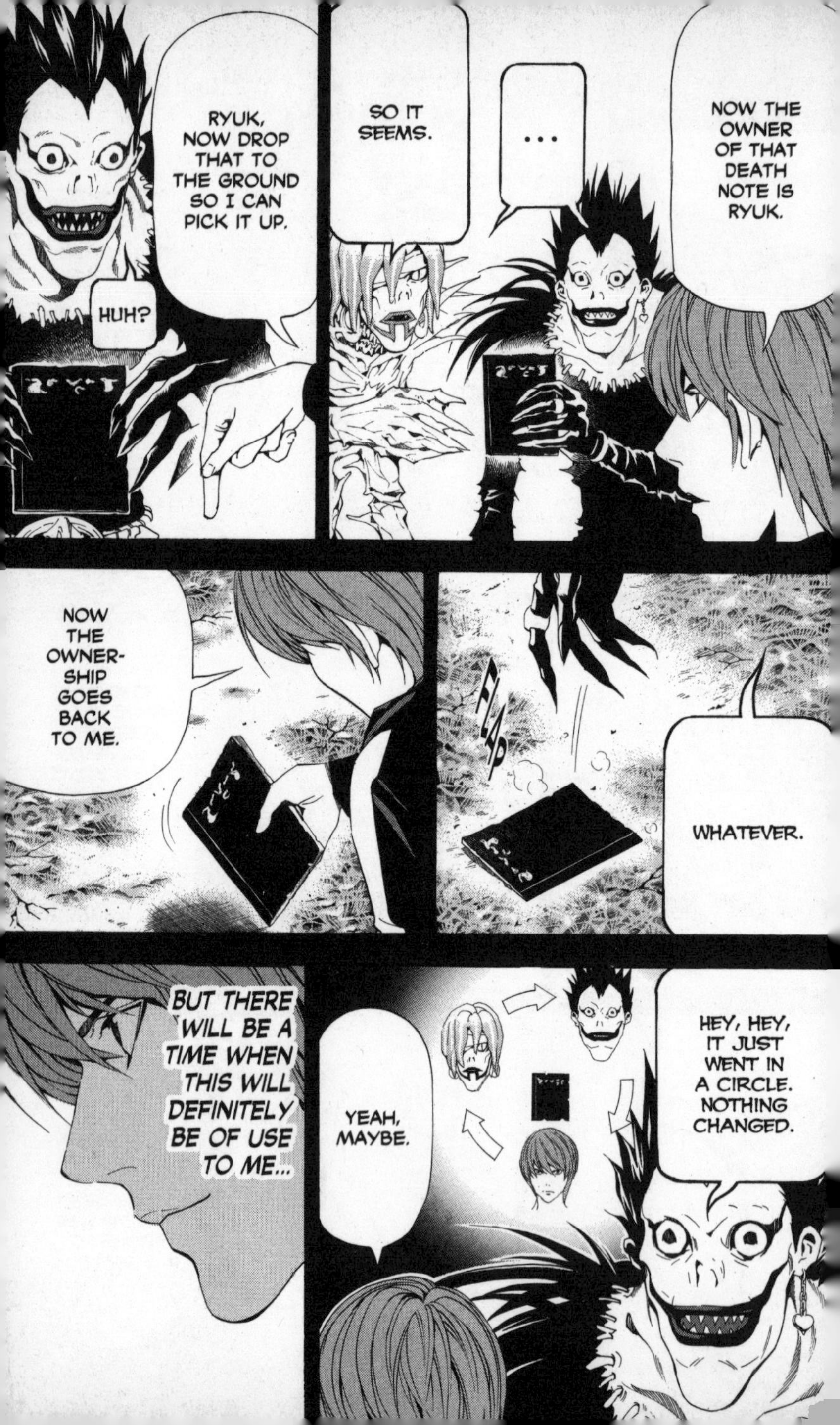
NOW THE OWNER OF THAT DEATH NOTE IS RYUK.
...
SO IT SEEMS.
RYUK, NOW DROP THAT TO THE GROUND SO I CAN PICK IT UP.
HUH?
FLAP
WHATEVER.
NOW THE OWNERSHIP GOES BACK TO ME.
HEY, HEY, IT JUST WENT IN A CIRCLE. NOTHING CHANGED.
YEAH, MAYBE.
BUT THERE WILL BE A TIME WHEN THIS WILL DEFINITELY BE OF USE TO ME...

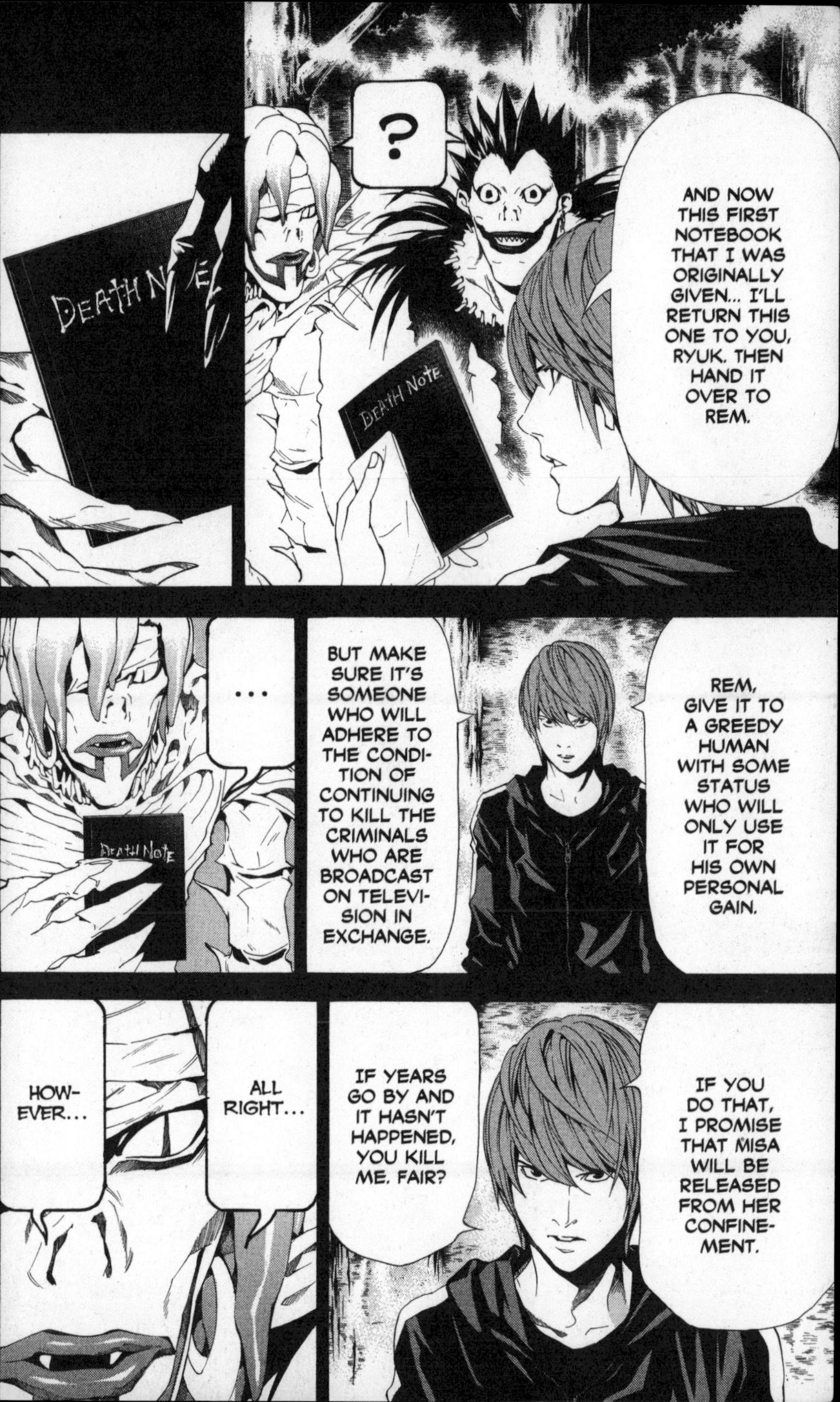
AND NOW THIS FIRST NOTEBOOK THAT I WAS ORIGINALLY GIVEN... I'LL RETURN THIS ONE TO YOU, RYUK. THEN HAND IT OVER TO REM.
?
DEATH NOTE
DEATH NOTE
REM, GIVE IT TO A GREEDY HUMAN WITH SOME STATUS WHO WILL ONLY USE IT FOR HIS OWN PERSONAL GAIN.
BUT MAKE SURE IT'S SOMEONE WHO WILL ADHERE TO THE CONDI-TION OF CONTINUING TO KILL THE CRIMINALS WHO ARE BROADCAST ON TELEVI-SION IN EXCHANGE.
...
DEATH NOTE
IF YOU DO THAT, I PROMISE THAT MISA WILL BE RELEASED FROM HER CONFINE-MENT.
IF YEARS GO BY AND IT HASN'T HAPPENED, YOU KILL ME. FAIR?
ALL RIGHT...
HOW-EVER...

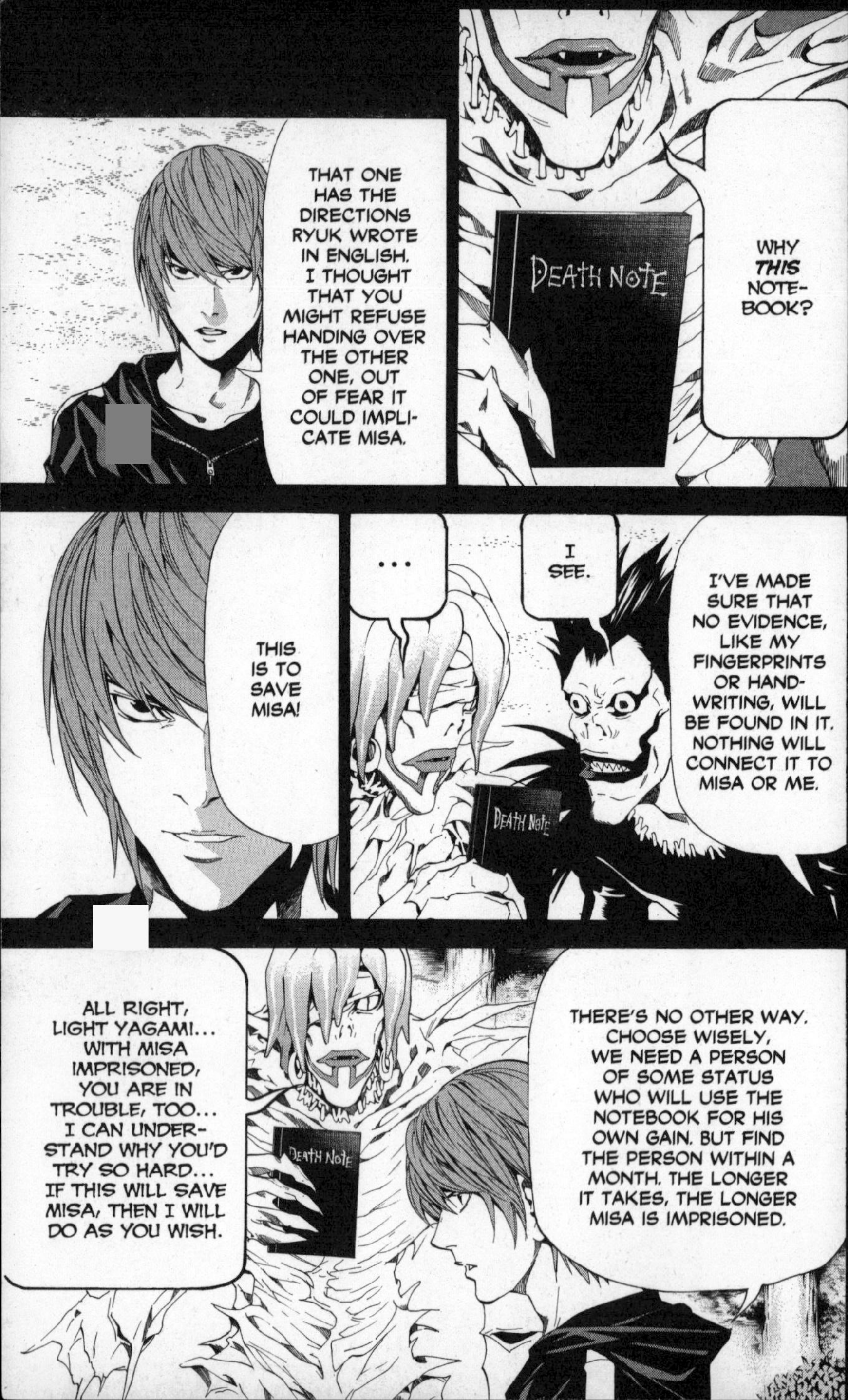
DEATH NOTE
WHY *THIS* NOTEBOOK?
THAT ONE HAS THE DIRECTIONS RYUK WROTE IN ENGLISH. I THOUGHT THAT YOU MIGHT REFUSE HANDING OVER THE OTHER ONE, OUT OF FEAR IT COULD IMPLICATE MISA.
I'VE MADE SURE THAT NO EVIDENCE, LIKE MY FINGERPRINTS OR HANDWRITING, WILL BE FOUND IN IT. NOTHING WILL CONNECT IT TO MISA OR ME.
I SEE.
. . .
DEATH NOTE
THIS IS TO SAVE MISA!
THERE'S NO OTHER WAY. CHOOSE WISELY, WE NEED A PERSON OF SOME STATUS WHO WILL USE THE NOTEBOOK FOR HIS OWN GAIN. BUT FIND THE PERSON WITHIN A MONTH. THE LONGER IT TAKES, THE LONGER MISA IS IMPRISONED.
DEATH NOTE
ALL RIGHT, LIGHT YAGAMI... WITH MISA IMPRISONED, YOU ARE IN TROUBLE, TOO... I CAN UNDERSTAND WHY YOU'D TRY SO HARD... IF THIS WILL SAVE MISA, THEN I WILL DO AS YOU WISH.

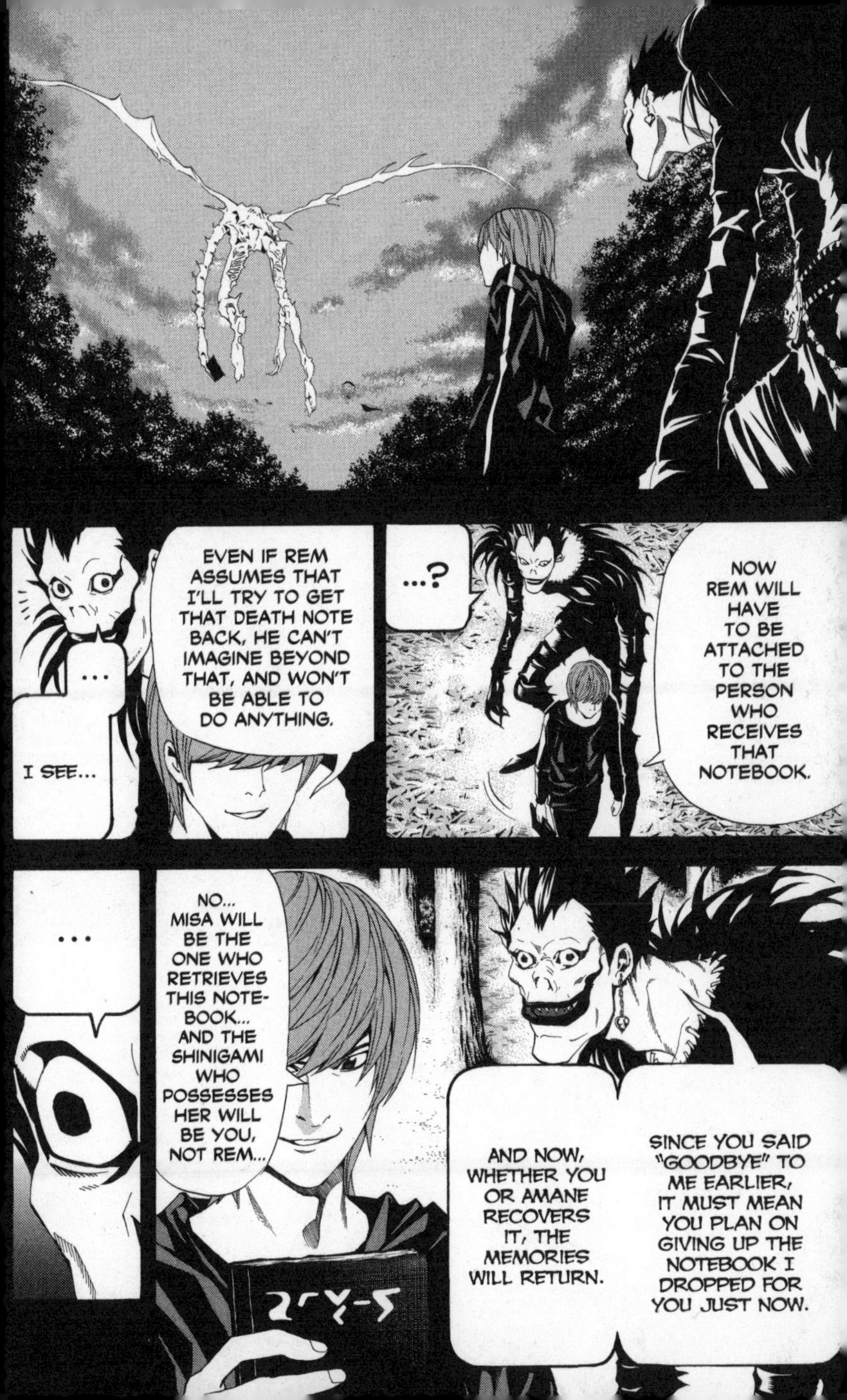
NOW REM WILL HAVE TO BE ATTACHED TO THE PERSON WHO RECEIVES THAT NOTEBOOK.
...?
EVEN IF REM ASSUMES THAT I'LL TRY TO GET THAT DEATH NOTE BACK, HE CAN'T IMAGINE BEYOND THAT, AND WON'T BE ABLE TO DO ANYTHING.
...
I SEE...
SINCE YOU SAID "GOODBYE" TO ME EARLIER, IT MUST MEAN YOU PLAN ON GIVING UP THE NOTEBOOK I DROPPED FOR YOU JUST NOW.
AND NOW, WHETHER YOU OR AMANE RECOVERS IT, THE MEMORIES WILL RETURN.
NO... MISA WILL BE THE ONE WHO RETRIEVES THIS NOTE-BOOK... AND THE SHINIGAMI WHO POSSESSES HER WILL BE YOU, NOT REM...
...

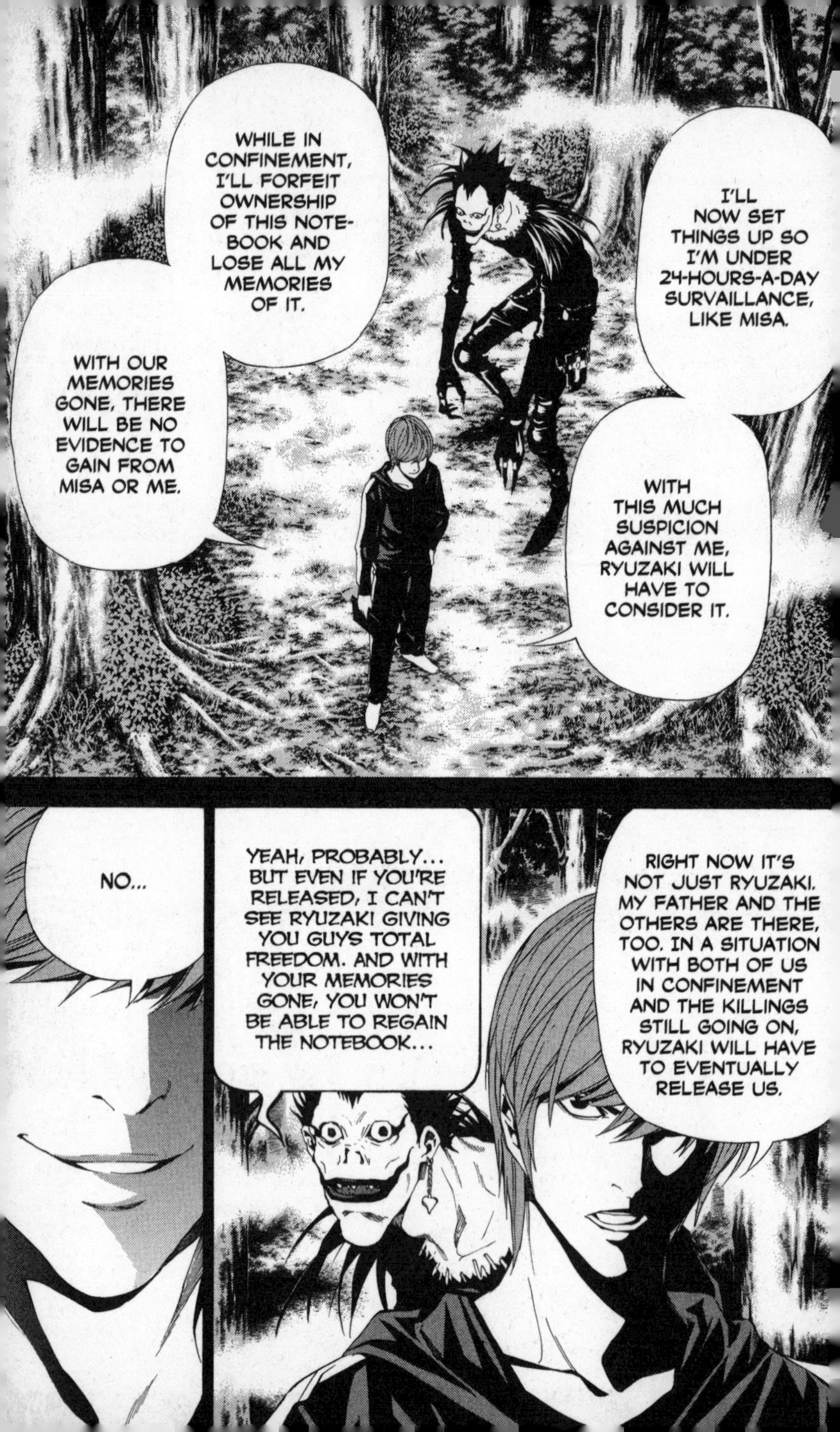
I'LL NOW SET THINGS UP SO I'M UNDER 24-HOURS-A-DAY SURVAILLANCE, LIKE MISA.
WITH THIS MUCH SUSPICION AGAINST ME, RYUZAKI WILL HAVE TO CONSIDER IT.
WHILE IN CONFINEMENT, I'LL FORFEIT OWNERSHIP OF THIS NOTE-BOOK AND LOSE ALL MY MEMORIES OF IT.
WITH OUR MEMORIES GONE, THERE WILL BE NO EVIDENCE TO GAIN FROM MISA OR ME.
RIGHT NOW IT'S NOT JUST RYUZAKI. MY FATHER AND THE OTHERS ARE THERE, TOO. IN A SITUATION WITH BOTH OF US IN CONFINEMENT AND THE KILLINGS STILL GOING ON, RYUZAKI WILL HAVE TO EVENTUALLY RELEASE US.
YEAH, PROBABLY... BUT EVEN IF YOU'RE RELEASED, I CAN'T SEE RYUZAKI GIVING YOU GUYS TOTAL FREEDOM. AND WITH YOUR MEMORIES GONE, YOU WON'T BE ABLE TO REGAIN THE NOTEBOOK...
NO...

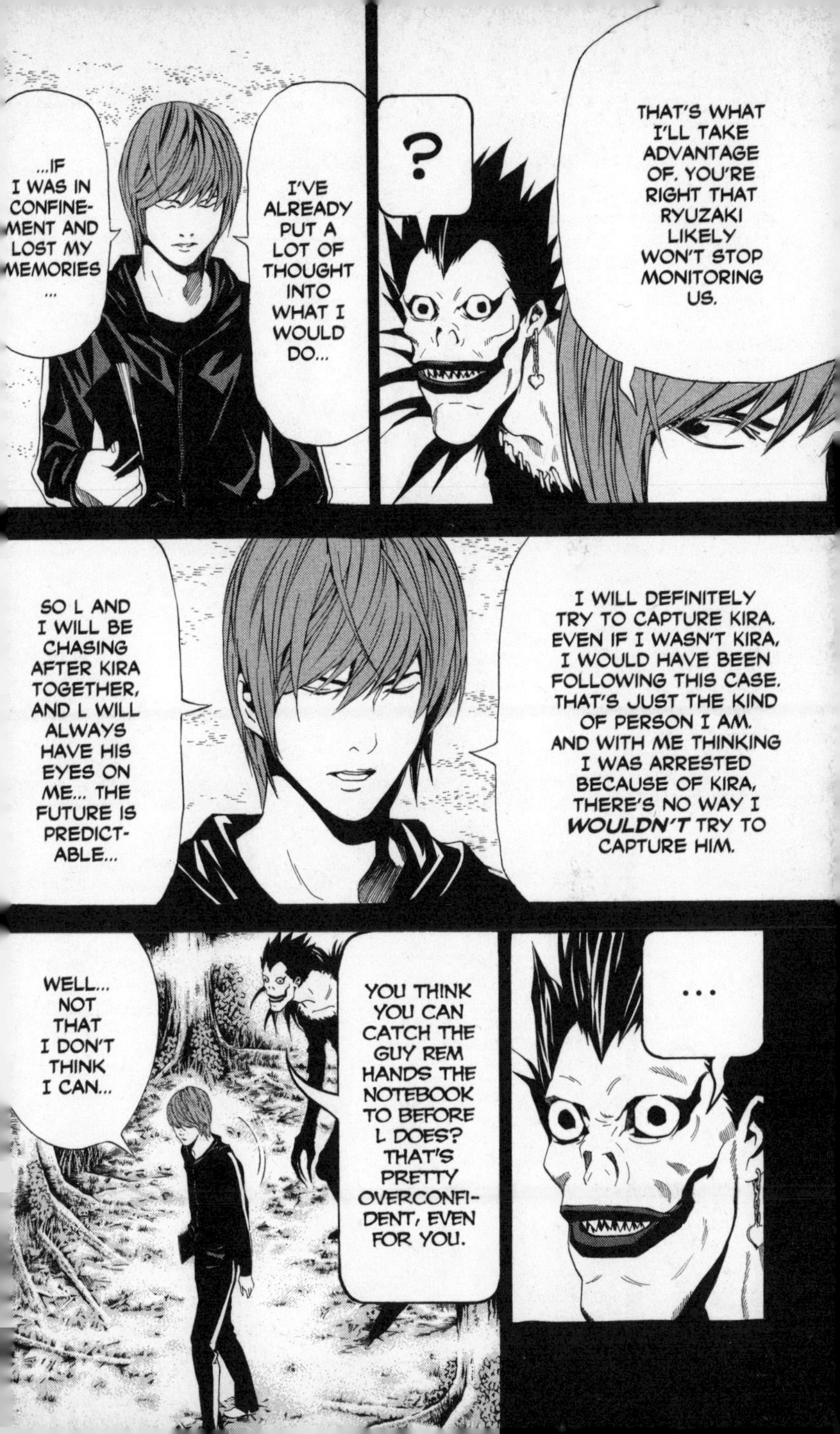
THAT'S WHAT I'LL TAKE ADVANTAGE OF. YOU'RE RIGHT THAT RYUZAKI LIKELY WON'T STOP MONITORING US.
?
I'VE ALREADY PUT A LOT OF THOUGHT INTO WHAT I WOULD DO...
...IF I WAS IN CONFINEMENT AND LOST MY MEMORIES ...
I WILL DEFINITELY TRY TO CAPTURE KIRA. EVEN IF I WASN'T KIRA, I WOULD HAVE BEEN FOLLOWING THIS CASE. THAT'S JUST THE KIND OF PERSON I AM. AND WITH ME THINKING I WAS ARRESTED BECAUSE OF KIRA, THERE'S NO WAY I ***WOULDN'T*** TRY TO CAPTURE HIM.
SO L AND I WILL BE CHASING AFTER KIRA TOGETHER, AND L WILL ALWAYS HAVE HIS EYES ON ME... THE FUTURE IS PREDICTABLE...
...
YOU THINK YOU CAN CATCH THE GUY REM HANDS THE NOTEBOOK TO BEFORE L DOES? THAT'S PRETTY OVERCONFIDENT, EVEN FOR YOU.
WELL... NOT THAT I DON'T THINK I CAN...

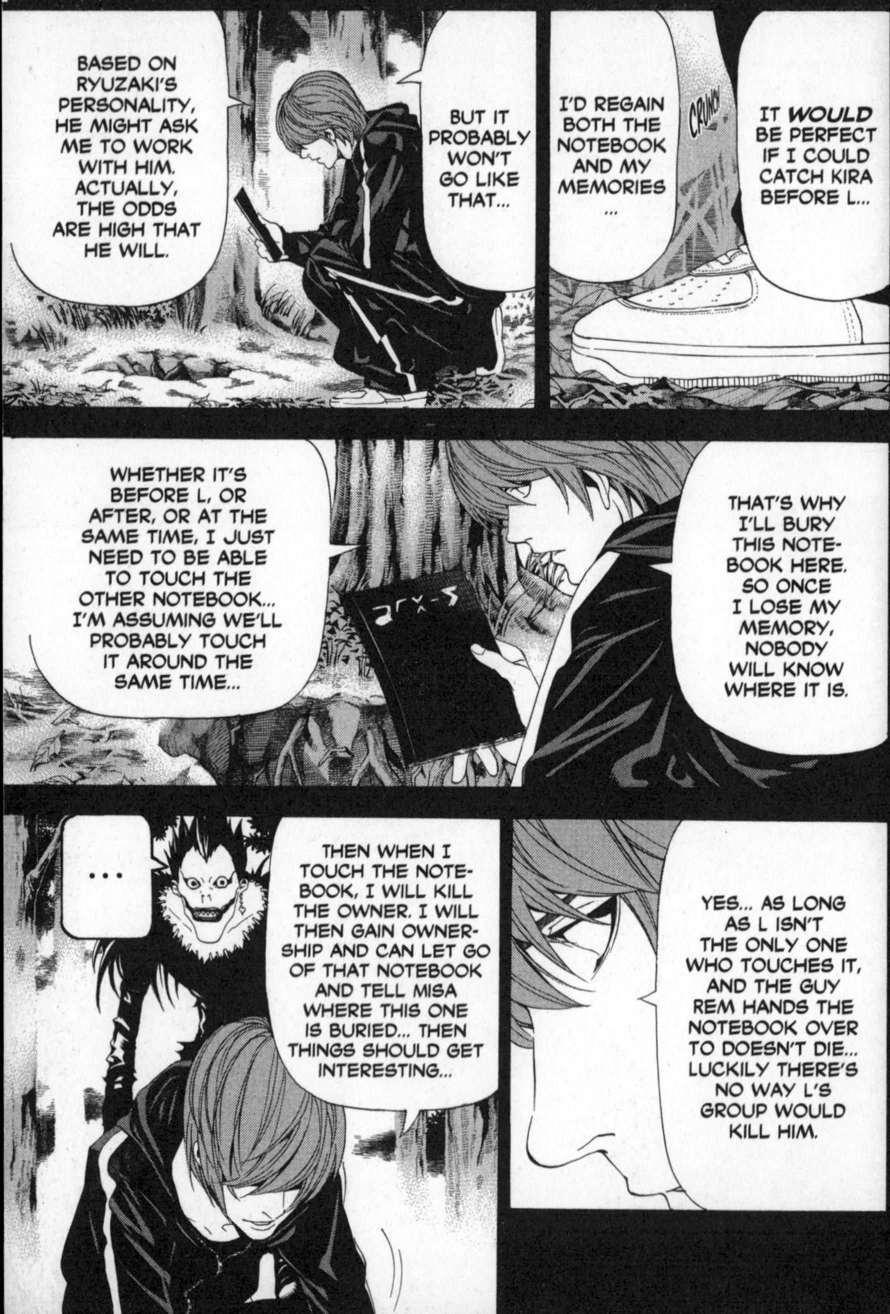
IT *WOULD* BE PERFECT IF I COULD CATCH KIRA BEFORE L...
CRUNCH
I'D REGAIN BOTH THE NOTEBOOK AND MY MEMORIES ...
BUT IT PROBABLY WON'T GO LIKE THAT...
BASED ON RYUZAKI'S PERSONALITY, HE MIGHT ASK ME TO WORK WITH HIM. ACTUALLY, THE ODDS ARE HIGH THAT HE WILL.
THAT'S WHY I'LL BURY THIS NOTE-BOOK HERE. SO ONCE I LOSE MY MEMORY, NOBODY WILL KNOW WHERE IT IS.
WHETHER IT'S BEFORE L, OR AFTER, OR AT THE SAME TIME, I JUST NEED TO BE ABLE TO TOUCH THE OTHER NOTEBOOK... I'M ASSUMING WE'LL PROBABLY TOUCH IT AROUND THE SAME TIME...
YES... AS LONG AS L ISN'T THE ONLY ONE WHO TOUCHES IT, AND THE GUY REM HANDS THE NOTEBOOK OVER TO DOESN'T DIE... LUCKILY THERE'S NO WAY L'S GROUP WOULD KILL HIM.
THEN WHEN I TOUCH THE NOTE-BOOK, I WILL KILL THE OWNER. I WILL THEN GAIN OWNER-SHIP AND CAN LET GO OF THAT NOTEBOOK AND TELL MISA WHERE THIS ONE IS BURIED... THEN THINGS SHOULD GET INTERESTING...
...

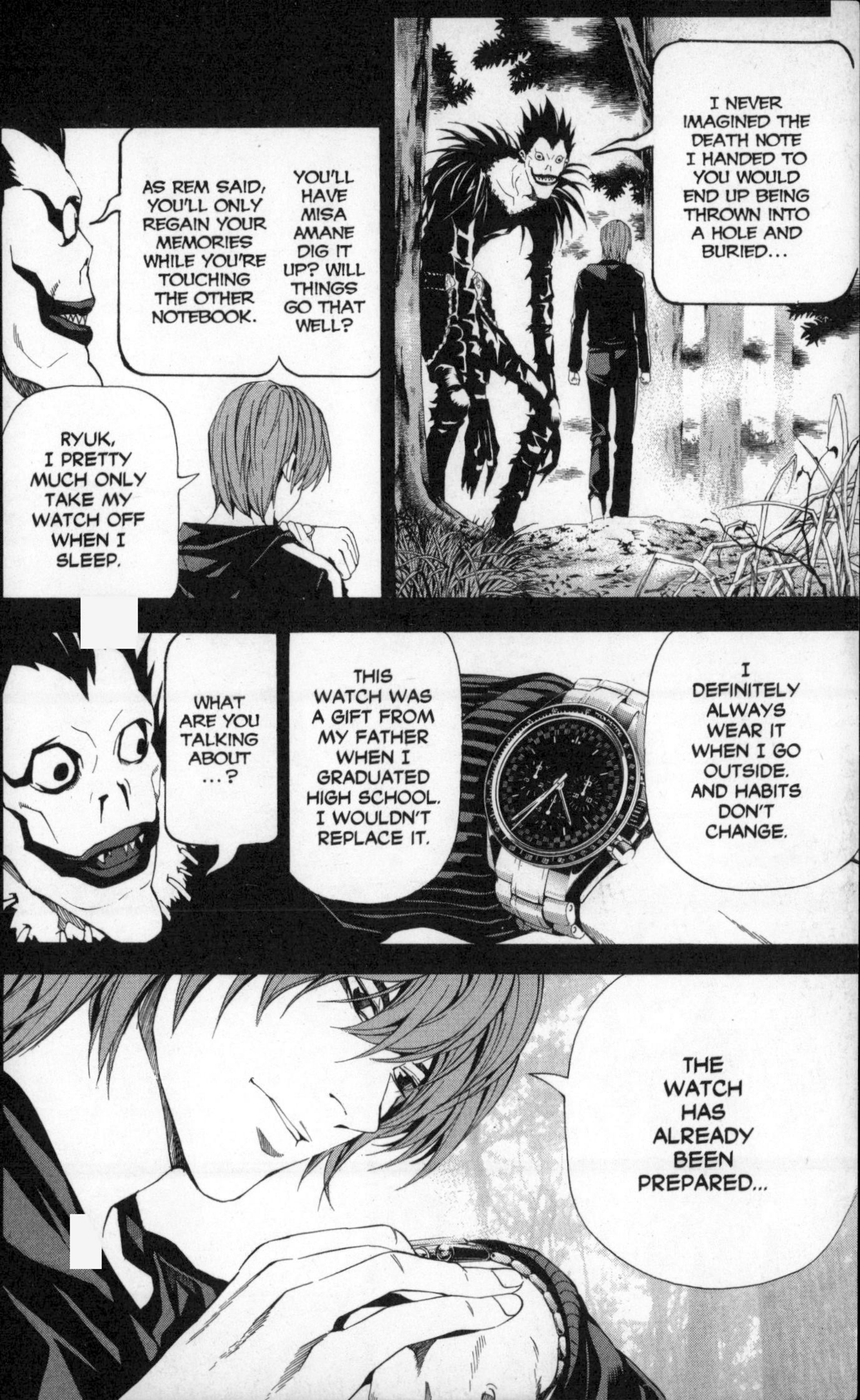
I NEVER IMAGINED THE DEATH NOTE I HANDED TO YOU WOULD END UP BEING THROWN INTO A HOLE AND BURIED...
YOU'LL HAVE MISA AMANE DIG IT UP? WILL THINGS GO THAT WELL?
AS REM SAID, YOU'LL ONLY REGAIN YOUR MEMORIES WHILE YOU'RE TOUCHING THE OTHER NOTEBOOK.
RYUK, I PRETTY MUCH ONLY TAKE MY WATCH OFF WHEN I SLEEP.
I DEFINITELY ALWAYS WEAR IT WHEN I GO OUTSIDE. AND HABITS DON'T CHANGE.
THIS WATCH WAS A GIFT FROM MY FATHER WHEN I GRADUATED HIGH SCHOOL. I WOULDN'T REPLACE IT.
WHAT ARE YOU TALKING ABOUT ...?
THE WATCH HAS ALREADY BEEN PREPARED...

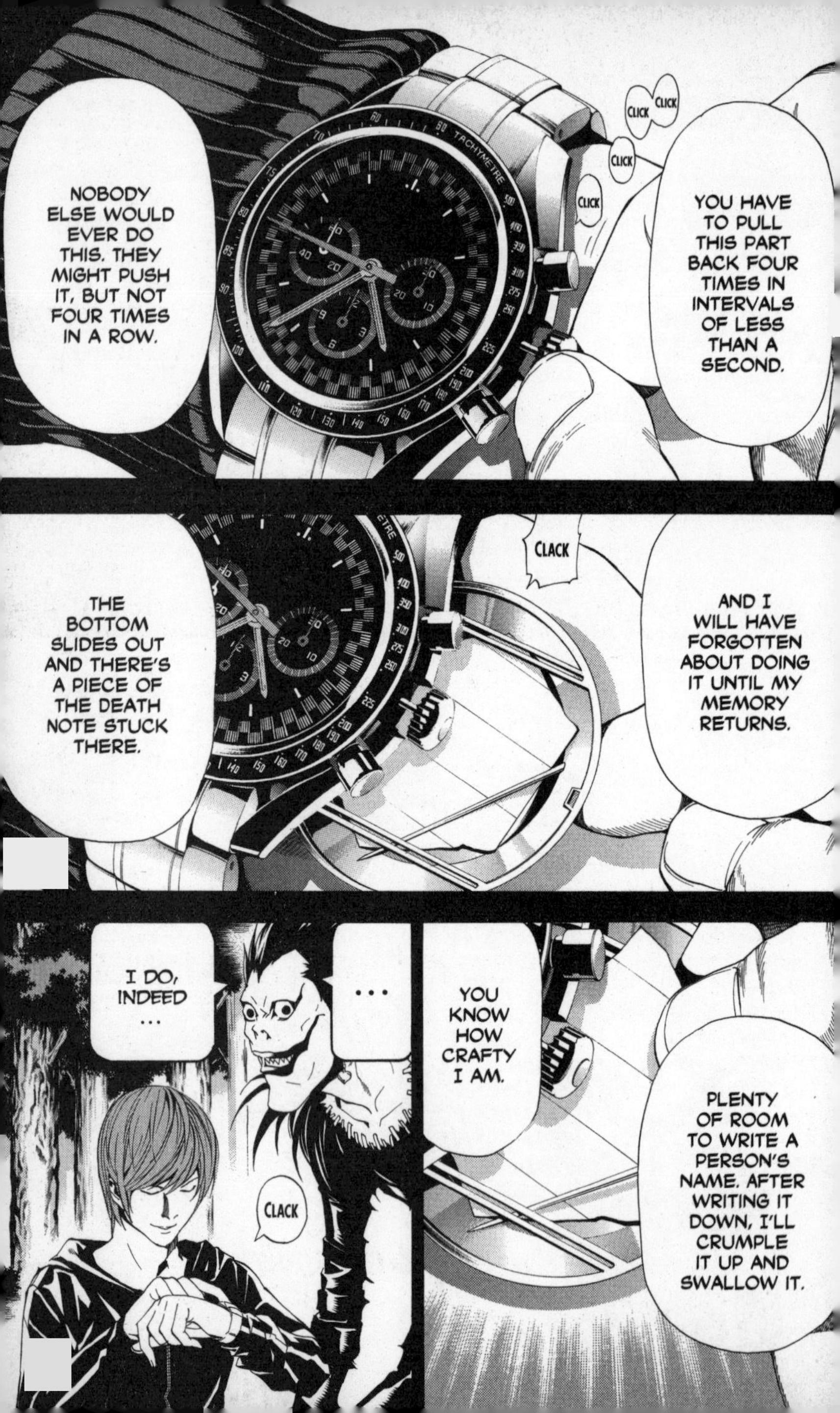
CLICK
CLICK
CLICK
CLICK
YOU HAVE TO PULL THIS PART BACK FOUR TIMES IN INTERVALS OF LESS THAN A SECOND.
NOBODY ELSE WOULD EVER DO THIS. THEY MIGHT PUSH IT, BUT NOT FOUR TIMES IN A ROW.
CLACK
AND I WILL HAVE FORGOTTEN ABOUT DOING IT UNTIL MY MEMORY RETURNS.
THE BOTTOM SLIDES OUT AND THERE'S A PIECE OF THE DEATH NOTE STUCK THERE.
PLENTY OF ROOM TO WRITE A PERSON'S NAME. AFTER WRITING IT DOWN, I'LL CRUMPLE IT UP AND SWALLOW IT.
YOU KNOW HOW CRAFTY I AM.
...
I DO, INDEED ...
CLACK

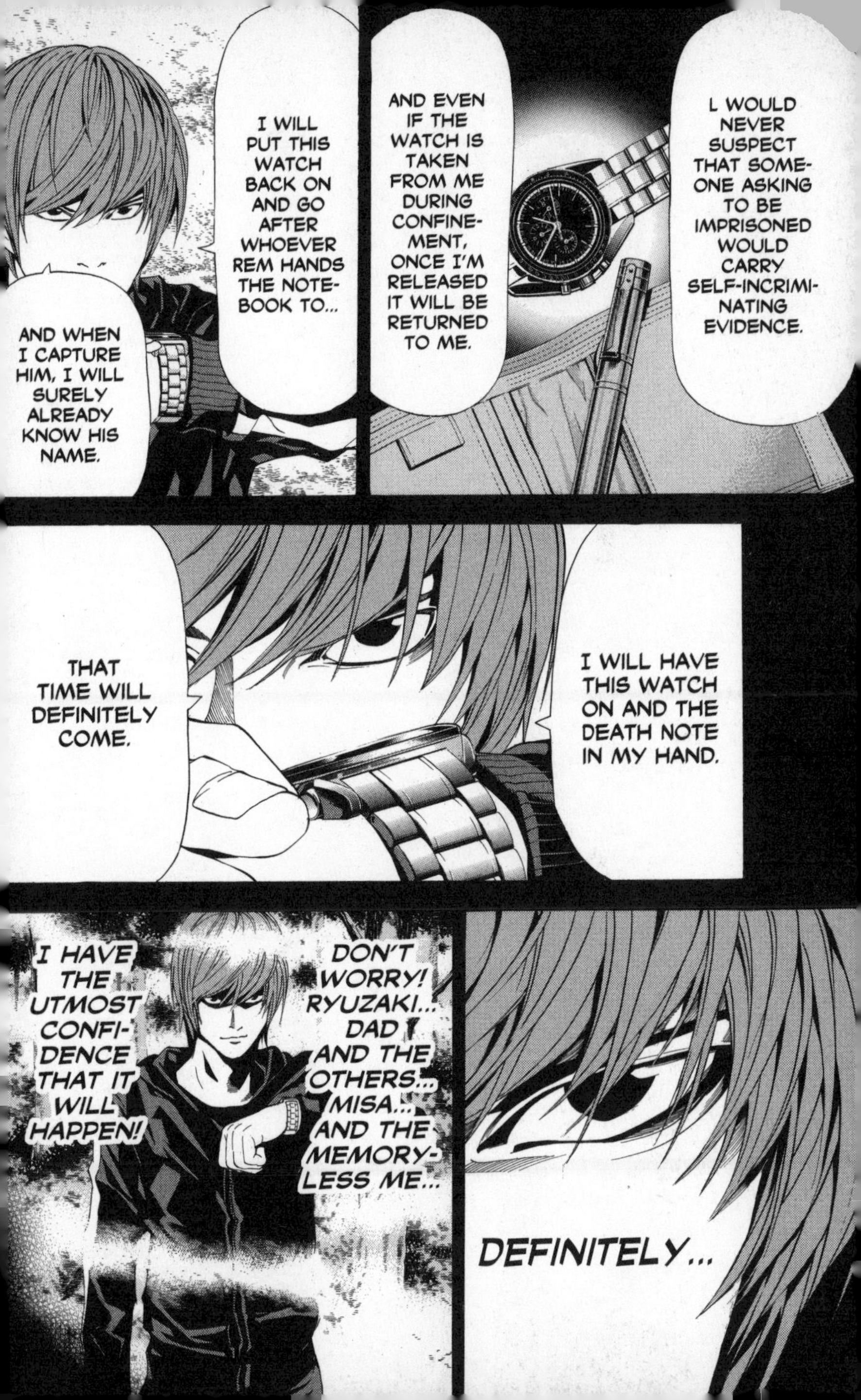
L WOULD NEVER SUSPECT THAT SOMEONE ASKING TO BE IMPRISONED WOULD CARRY SELF-INCRIMINATING EVIDENCE.
AND EVEN IF THE WATCH IS TAKEN FROM ME DURING CONFINEMENT, ONCE I'M RELEASED IT WILL BE RETURNED TO ME.
I WILL PUT THIS WATCH BACK ON AND GO AFTER WHOEVER REM HANDS THE NOTEBOOK TO...
AND WHEN I CAPTURE HIM, I WILL SURELY ALREADY KNOW HIS NAME.
I WILL HAVE THIS WATCH ON AND THE DEATH NOTE IN MY HAND.
THAT TIME WILL DEFINITELY COME.
DEFINITELY...
DON'T WORRY! RYUZAKI... DAD AND THE OTHERS... MISA... AND THE MEMORY-LESS ME...
I HAVE THE UTMOST CONFIDENCE THAT IT WILL HAPPEN!

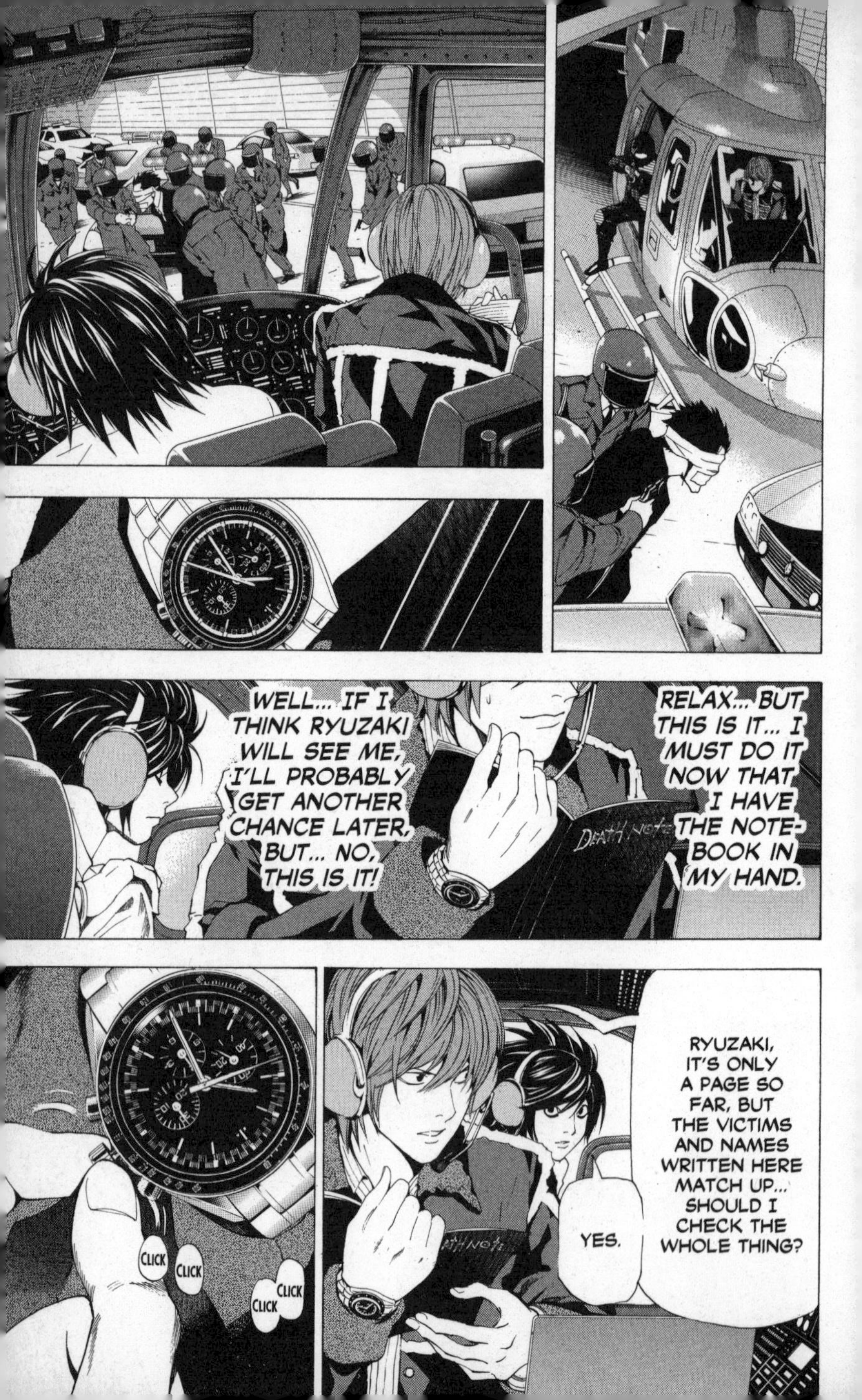
RELAX... BUT THIS IS IT... I MUST DO IT NOW THAT I HAVE THE NOTE-BOOK IN MY HAND.
WELL... IF I THINK RYUZAKI WILL SEE ME, I'LL PROBABLY GET ANOTHER CHANCE LATER, BUT... NO, THIS IS IT!
DEATH Note
RYUZAKI, IT'S ONLY A PAGE SO FAR, BUT THE VICTIMS AND NAMES WRITTEN HERE MATCH UP... SHOULD I CHECK THE WHOLE THING?
YES.
CLICK
CLICK
CLICK
CLICK

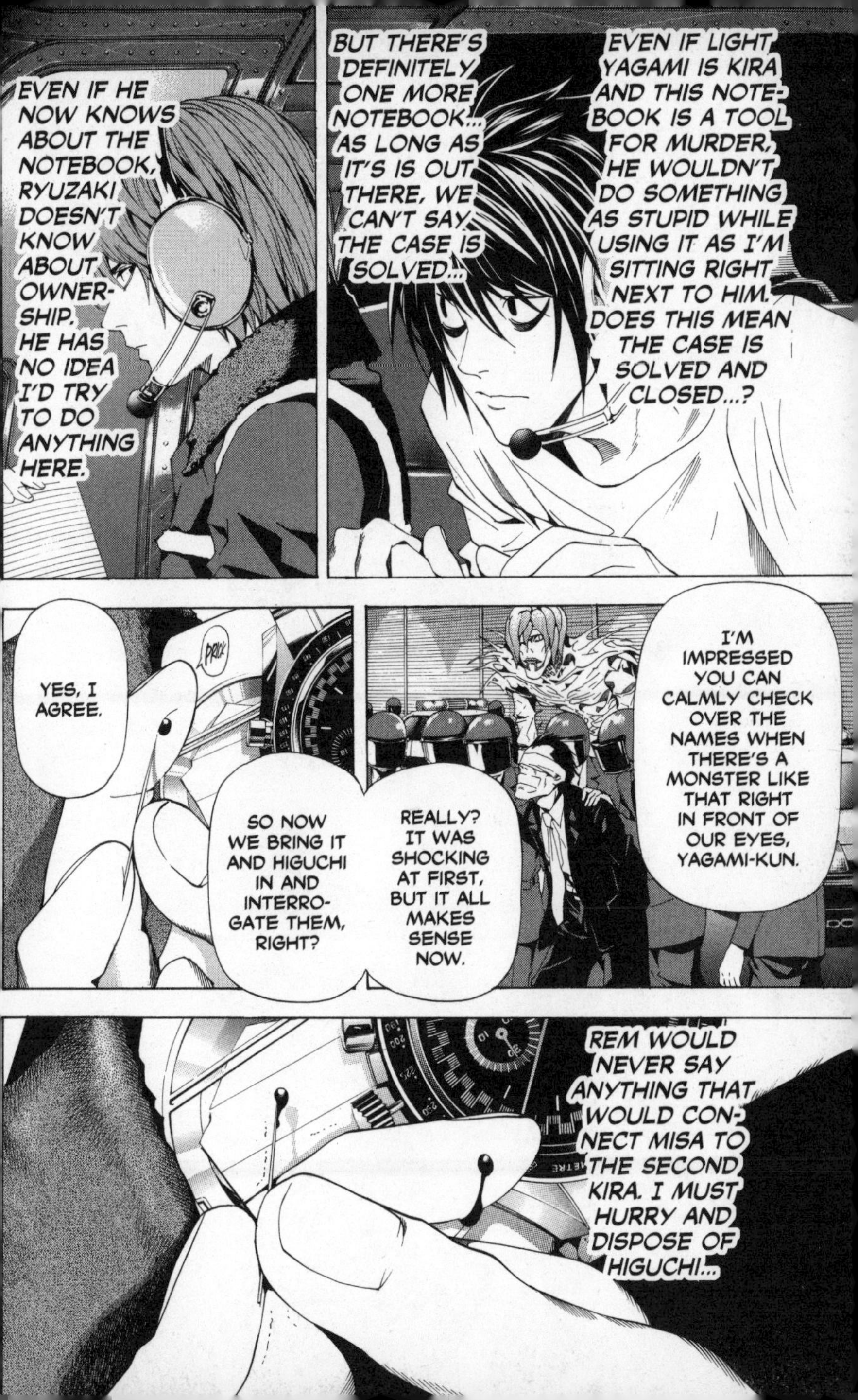
EVEN IF LIGHT YAGAMI IS KIRA AND THIS NOTE-BOOK IS A TOOL FOR MURDER, HE WOULDN'T DO SOMETHING AS STUPID WHILE USING IT AS I'M SITTING RIGHT NEXT TO HIM. DOES THIS MEAN THE CASE IS SOLVED AND CLOSED...?
BUT THERE'S DEFINITELY ONE MORE NOTEBOOK... AS LONG AS IT'S IS OUT THERE, WE CAN'T SAY THE CASE IS SOLVED...
EVEN IF HE NOW KNOWS ABOUT THE NOTEBOOK, RYUZAKI DOESN'T KNOW ABOUT OWNERSHIP. HE HAS NO IDEA I'D TRY TO DO ANYTHING HERE.
I'M IMPRESSED YOU CAN CALMLY CHECK OVER THE NAMES WHEN THERE'S A MONSTER LIKE THAT RIGHT IN FRONT OF OUR EYES, YAGAMI-KUN.
REALLY? IT WAS SHOCKING AT FIRST, BUT IT ALL MAKES SENSE NOW.
SO NOW WE BRING IT AND HIGUCHI IN AND INTERRO-GATE THEM, RIGHT?
PRICK
YES, I AGREE.
REM WOULD NEVER SAY ANYTHING THAT WOULD CON-NECT MISA TO THE SECOND KIRA. I MUST HURRY AND DISPOSE OF HIGUCHI...

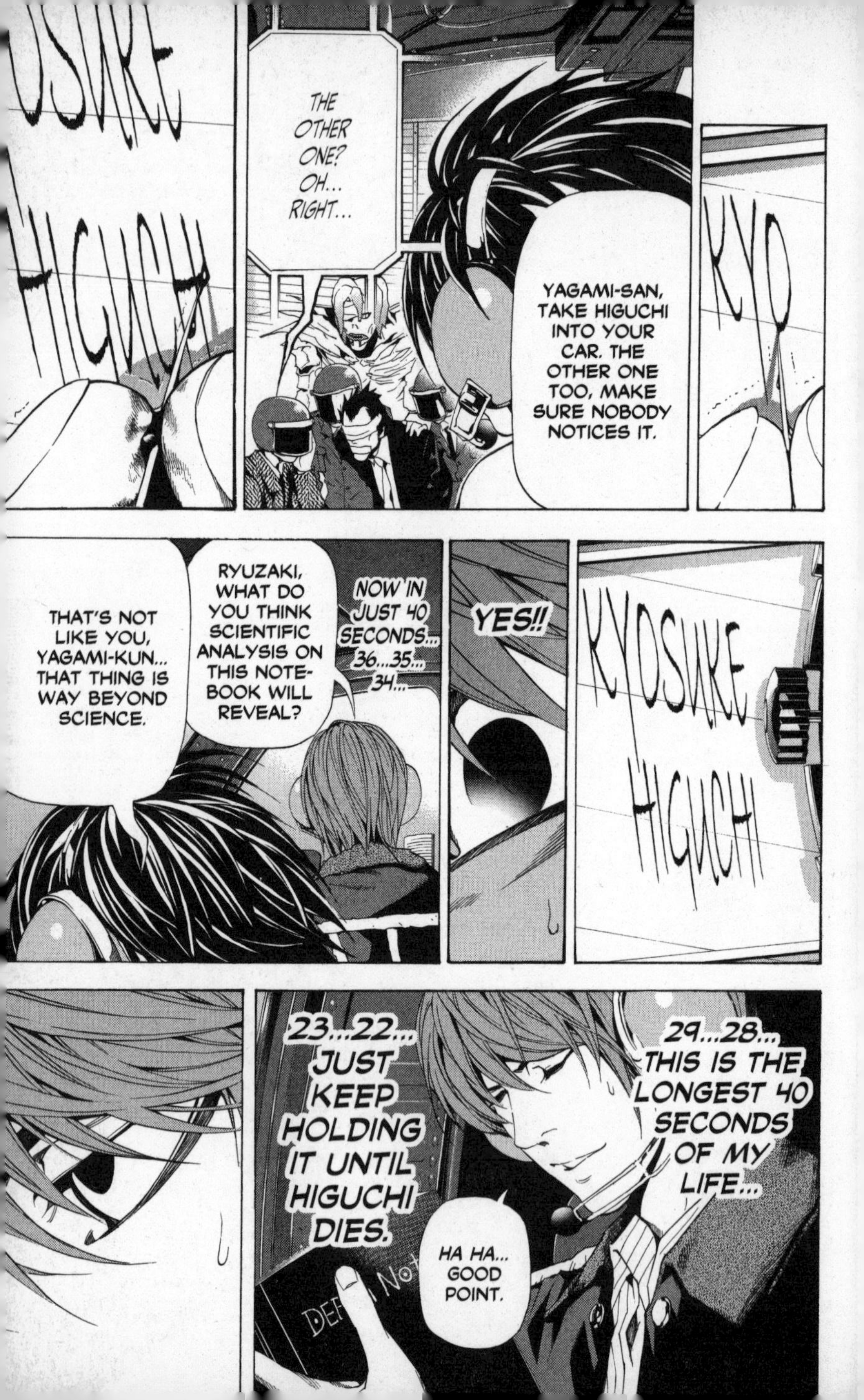
KYO
YAGAMI-SAN, TAKE HIGUCHI INTO YOUR CAR. THE OTHER ONE TOO, MAKE SURE NOBODY NOTICES IT.
THE OTHER ONE? OH... RIGHT...
OSUKE
HIGUCH
KYOSUKE HIGUCHI
YES!!
NOW IN JUST 40 SECONDS... 36...35... 34...
RYUZAKI, WHAT DO YOU THINK SCIENTIFIC ANALYSIS ON THIS NOTE-BOOK WILL REVEAL?
THAT'S NOT LIKE YOU, YAGAMI-KUN... THAT THING IS WAY BEYOND SCIENCE.
29...28... THIS IS THE LONGEST 40 SECONDS OF MY LIFE...
23...22... JUST KEEP HOLDING IT UNTIL HIGUCHI DIES.
HA HA... GOOD POINT.

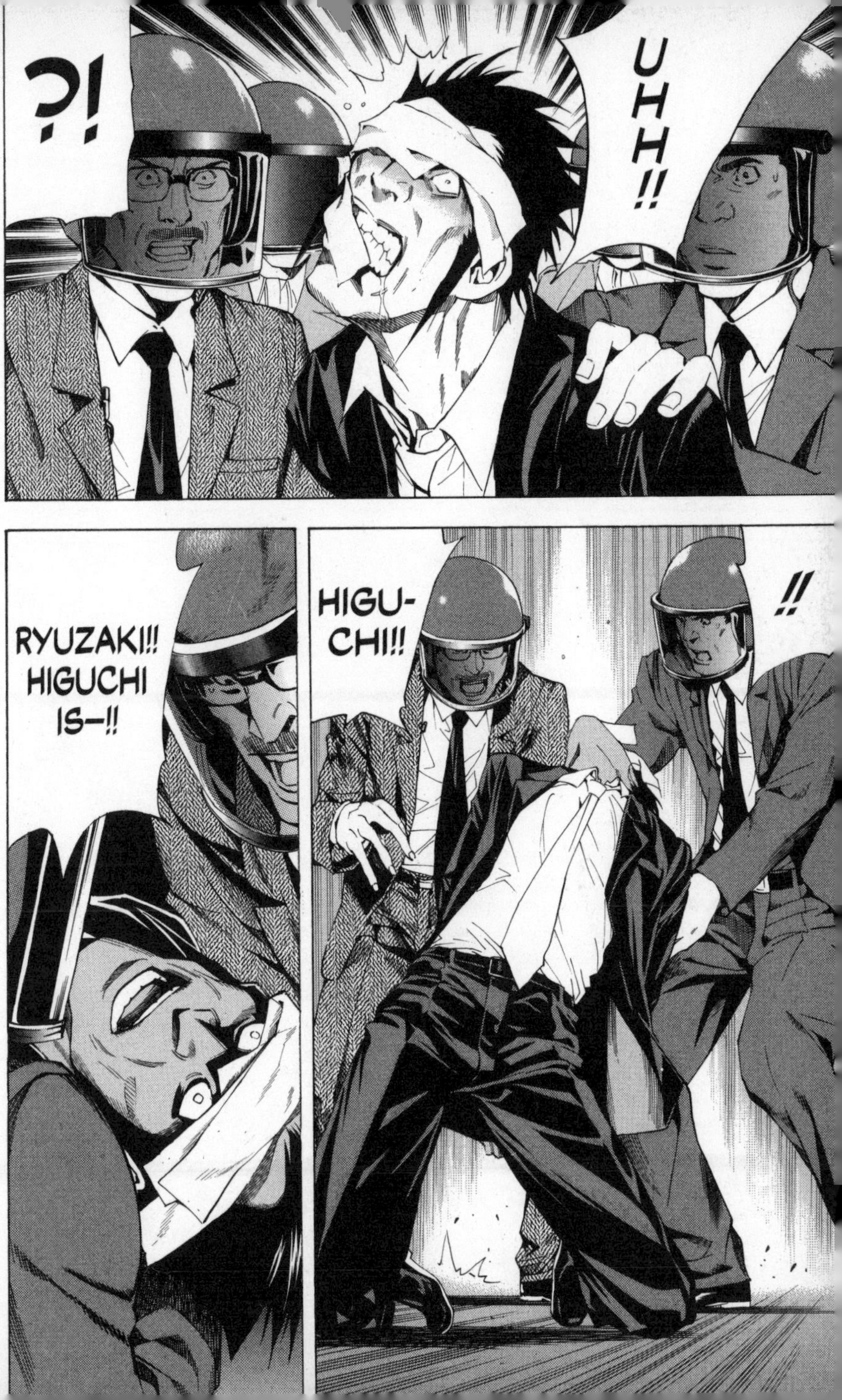
UHH!!
?!
!!
HIGU-CHI!!
RYUZAKI!!! HIGUCHI IS--!!

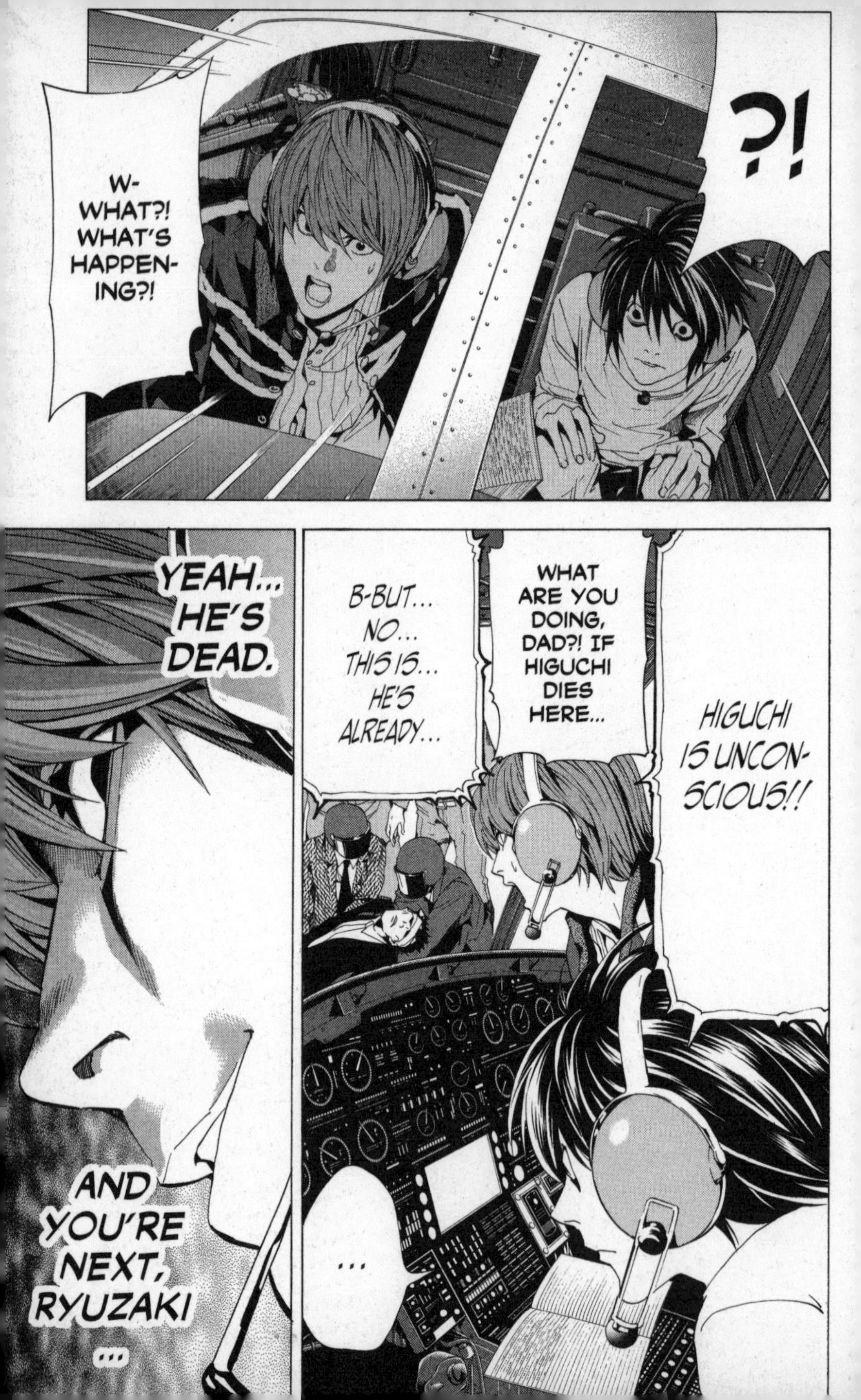
?!
W-WHAT?! WHAT'S HAPPENING?!
HIGUCHI IS UNCONSCIOUS!!
WHAT ARE YOU DOING, DAD?! IF HIGUCHI DIES HERE...
B-BUT... NO... THIS IS... HE'S ALREADY...
...
YEAH... HE'S DEAD.
AND YOU'RE NEXT, RYUZAKI...

DEATH NOTE
How to use it
XXXVIII

- You will lose memory of the DEATH NOTE when losing its ownership. But you can regain this memory by either obtaining the ownership once again or by touching the DEATH NOTE. This can be done up to 6 times per DEATH NOTE.

デスノートの所有権をなくした事で、そのノートに関する記憶がなくなり、再び所有権を得る事か触れる事で記憶が戻るのは、一冊のノートで6回まで。

- If the 6 times are exceeded, the person's memory of the DEATH NOTE will not return and they will have to use it without any previous memory of it.

よって、触れたり所有権を得る事で6回記憶を戻し、さらに同じノートを手にした場合、それを使うならば、記憶は戻らない状態で新たに使用する事になる。

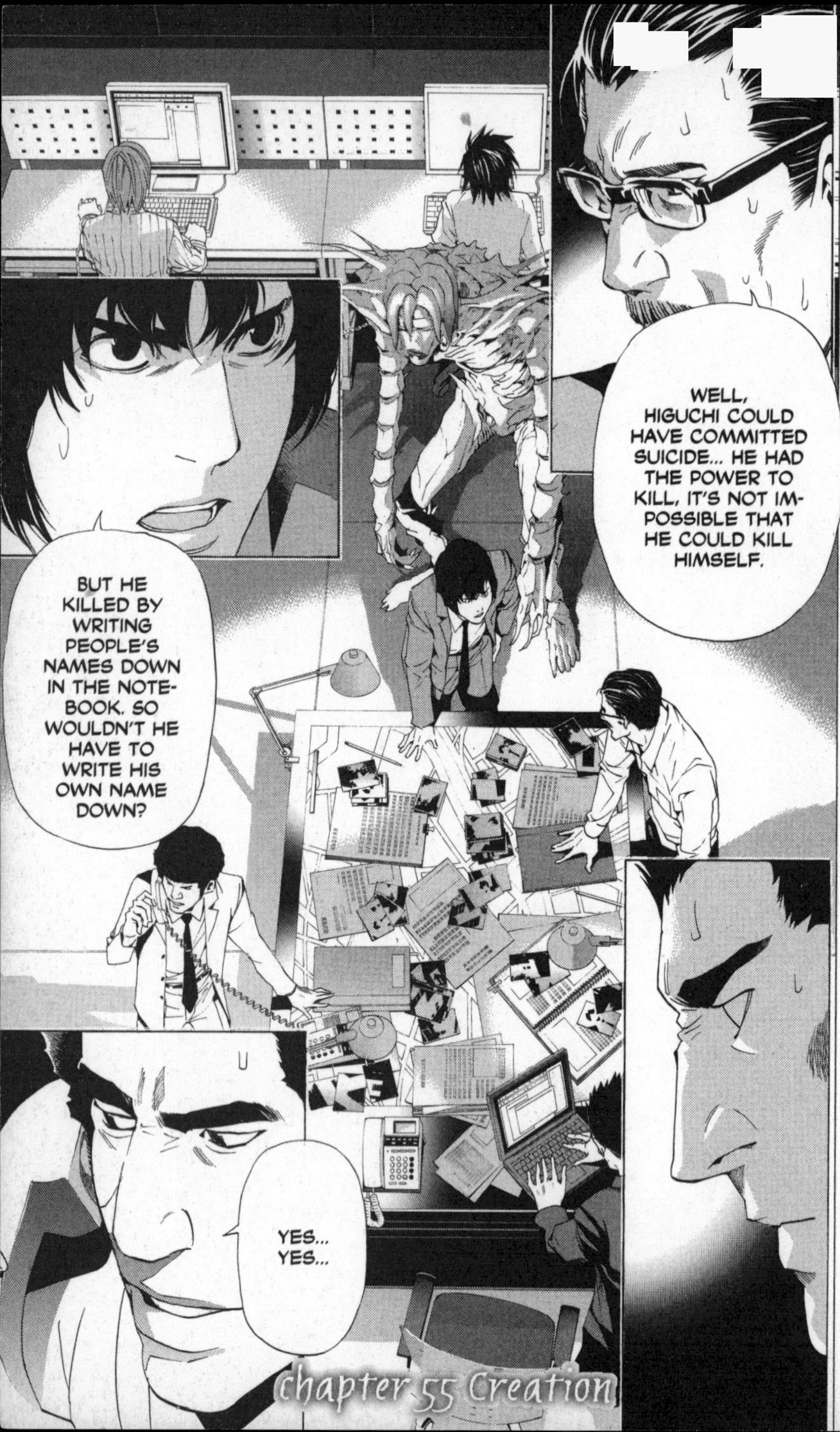
WELL, HIGUCHI COULD HAVE COMMITTED SUICIDE... HE HAD THE POWER TO KILL, IT'S NOT IM-POSSIBLE THAT HE COULD KILL HIMSELF.
BUT HE KILLED BY WRITING PEOPLE'S NAMES DOWN IN THE NOTE-BOOK. SO WOULDN'T HE HAVE TO WRITE HIS OWN NAME DOWN?
YES... YES...
chapter 55 Creation

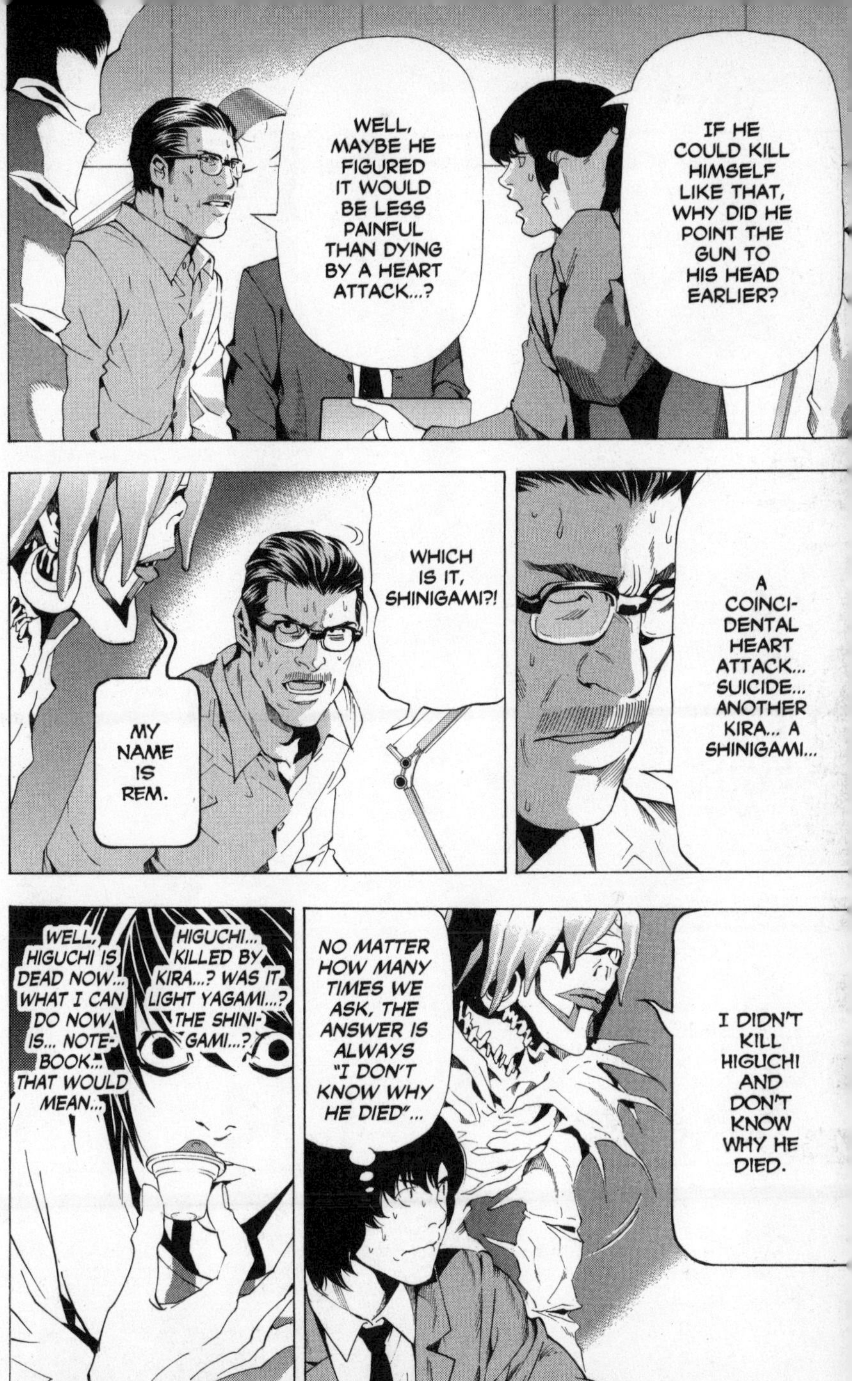
IF HE COULD KILL HIMSELF LIKE THAT, WHY DID HE POINT THE GUN TO HIS HEAD EARLIER?
WELL, MAYBE HE FIGURED IT WOULD BE LESS PAINFUL THAN DYING BY A HEART ATTACK...?
A COINCIDENTAL HEART ATTACK... SUICIDE... ANOTHER KIRA... A SHINIGAMI...
WHICH IS IT, SHINIGAMI?!
MY NAME IS REM.
I DIDN'T KILL HIGUCHI AND DON'T KNOW WHY HE DIED.
NO MATTER HOW MANY TIMES WE ASK, THE ANSWER IS ALWAYS "I DON'T KNOW WHY HE DIED"...
HIGUCHI... KILLED BY KIRA...? WAS IT LIGHT YAGAMI...? THE SHINIGAMI...?
WELL, HIGUCHI IS DEAD NOW... WHAT I CAN DO NOW IS... NOTEBOOK... THAT WOULD MEAN...

READ THIS WAY

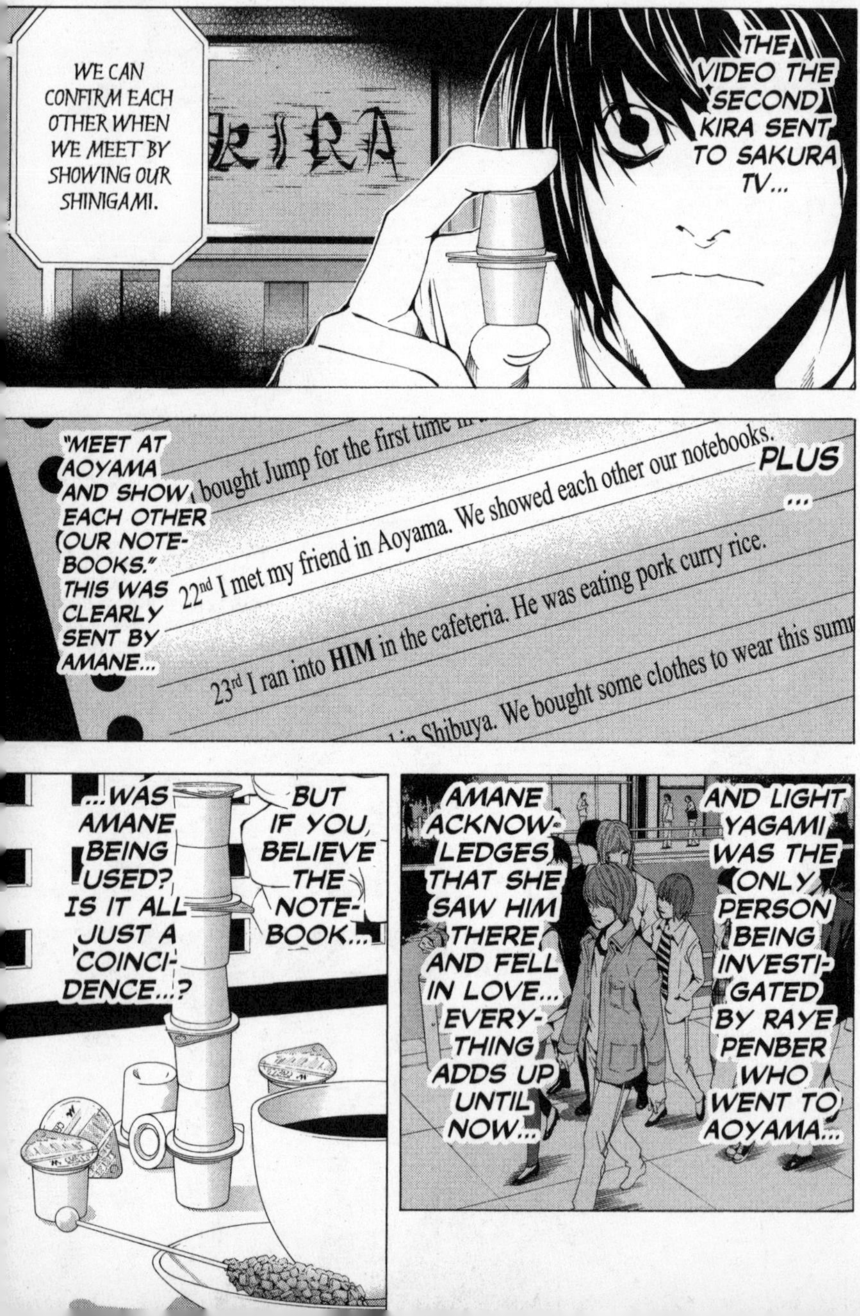
THE VIDEO THE SECOND KIRA SENT TO SAKURA TV...
WE CAN CONFIRM EACH OTHER WHEN WE MEET BY SHOWING OUR SHINIGAMI.
KIRA
PLUS...
bought Jump for the first time
22nd I met my friend in Aoyama. We showed each other our notebooks.
23rd I ran into HIM in the cafeteria. He was eating pork curry rice.
Shibuya. We bought some clothes to wear this sum
"MEET AT AOYAMA AND SHOW EACH OTHER OUR NOTEBOOKS." THIS WAS CLEARLY SENT BY AMANE...
AND LIGHT YAGAMI WAS THE ONLY PERSON BEING INVESTIGATED BY RAYE PENBER WHO WENT TO AOYAMA...
AMANE ACKNOWLEDGES THAT SHE SAW HIM THERE AND FELL IN LOVE... EVERYTHING ADDS UP UNTIL NOW...
BUT IF YOU BELIEVE THE NOTEBOOK...
...WAS AMANE BEING USED? IS IT ALL JUST A COINCIDENCE...?

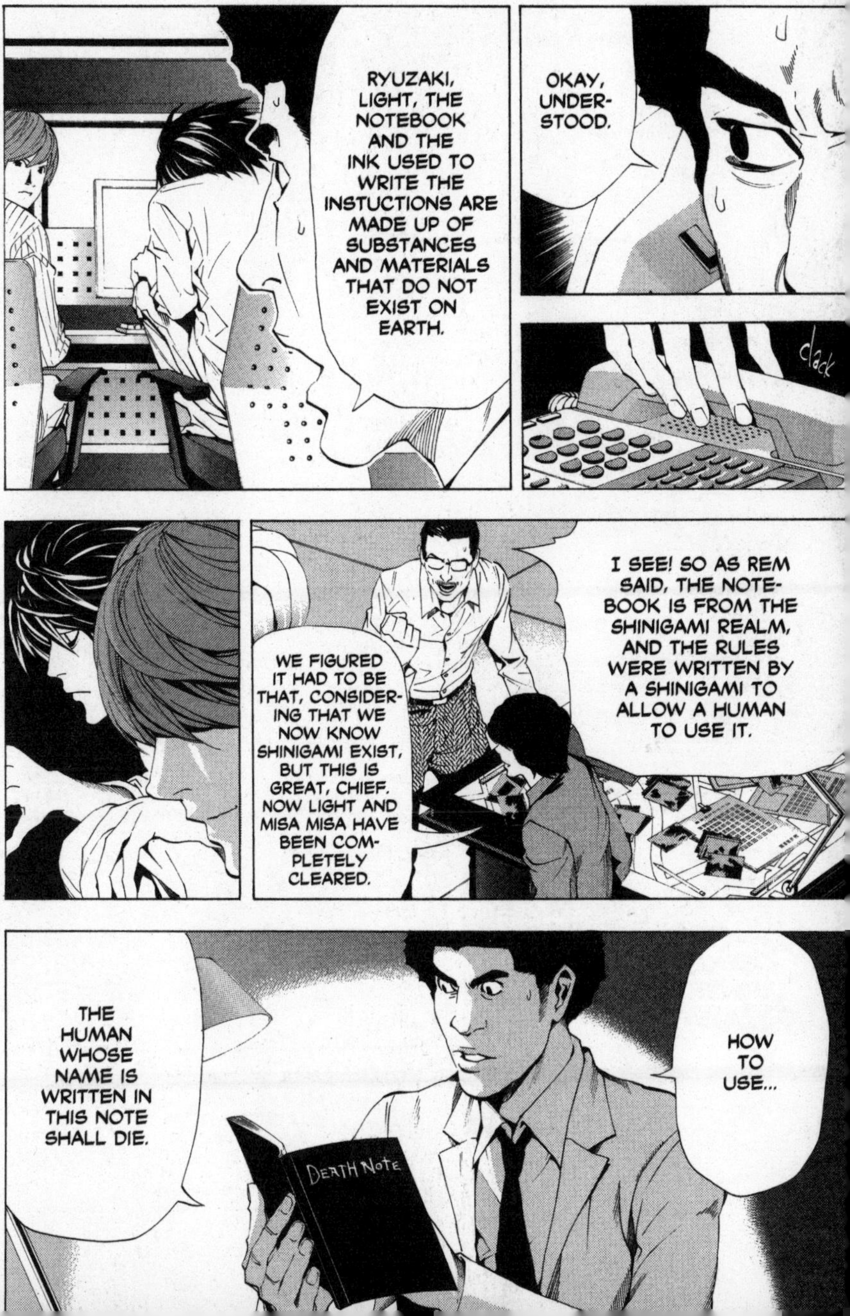
OKAY, UNDER-STOOD.
clack
RYUZAKI, LIGHT, THE NOTEBOOK AND THE INK USED TO WRITE THE INSTUCTIONS ARE MADE UP OF SUBSTANCES AND MATERIALS THAT DO NOT EXIST ON EARTH.
I SEE! SO AS REM SAID, THE NOTE-BOOK IS FROM THE SHINIGAMI REALM, AND THE RULES WERE WRITTEN BY A SHINIGAMI TO ALLOW A HUMAN TO USE IT.
WE FIGURED IT HAD TO BE THAT, CONSIDER-ING THAT WE NOW KNOW SHINIGAMI EXIST, BUT THIS IS GREAT, CHIEF. NOW LIGHT AND MISA MISA HAVE BEEN COM-PLETELY CLEARED.
HOW TO USE...
DEATH NOTE
THE HUMAN WHOSE NAME IS WRITTEN IN THIS NOTE SHALL DIE.

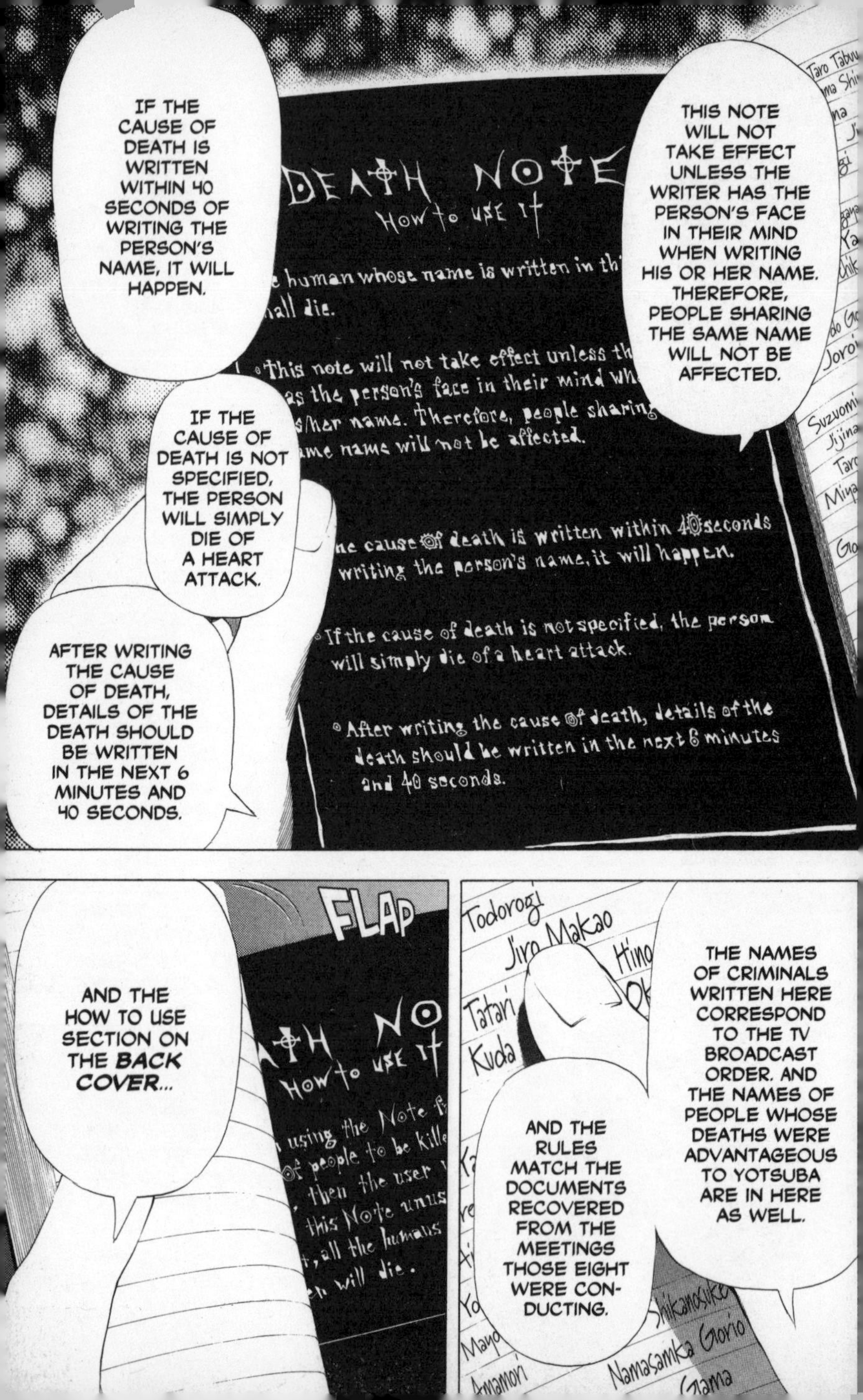

THIS NOTE WILL NOT TAKE EFFECT UNLESS THE WRITER HAS THE PERSON'S FACE IN THEIR MIND WHEN WRITING HIS OR HER NAME. THEREFORE, PEOPLE SHARING THE SAME NAME WILL NOT BE AFFECTED.
DEATH NOTE
How to use it
human whose name is written in th
hall die.
This note will not take effect unless th
as the person's face in their mind wh
s/her name. Therefore, people sharin
ame name will not be affected.
ne cause of death is written within 40 seconds
writing the person's name, it will happen.
If the cause of death is not specified, the person
will simply die of a heart attack.
After writing the cause of death, details of the
death should be written in the next 6 minutes
and 40 seconds.
IF THE CAUSE OF DEATH IS WRITTEN WITHIN 40 SECONDS OF WRITING THE PERSON'S NAME, IT WILL HAPPEN.
IF THE CAUSE OF DEATH IS NOT SPECIFIED, THE PERSON WILL SIMPLY DIE OF A HEART ATTACK.
AFTER WRITING THE CAUSE OF DEATH, DETAILS OF THE DEATH SHOULD BE WRITTEN IN THE NEXT 6 MINUTES AND 40 SECONDS.
THE NAMES OF CRIMINALS WRITTEN HERE CORRESPOND TO THE TV BROADCAST ORDER. AND THE NAMES OF PEOPLE WHOSE DEATHS WERE ADVANTAGEOUS TO YOTSUBA ARE IN HERE AS WELL.
Todorogi
Jiro Makao
Tatari
Kuda
AND THE RULES MATCH THE DOCUMENTS RECOVERED FROM THE MEETINGS THOSE EIGHT WERE CON-DUCTING.
Shikanosuke
Namasamka Gorio
Amamori
FLAP
How to use it
AND THE HOW TO USE SECTION ON THE *BACK COVER*...

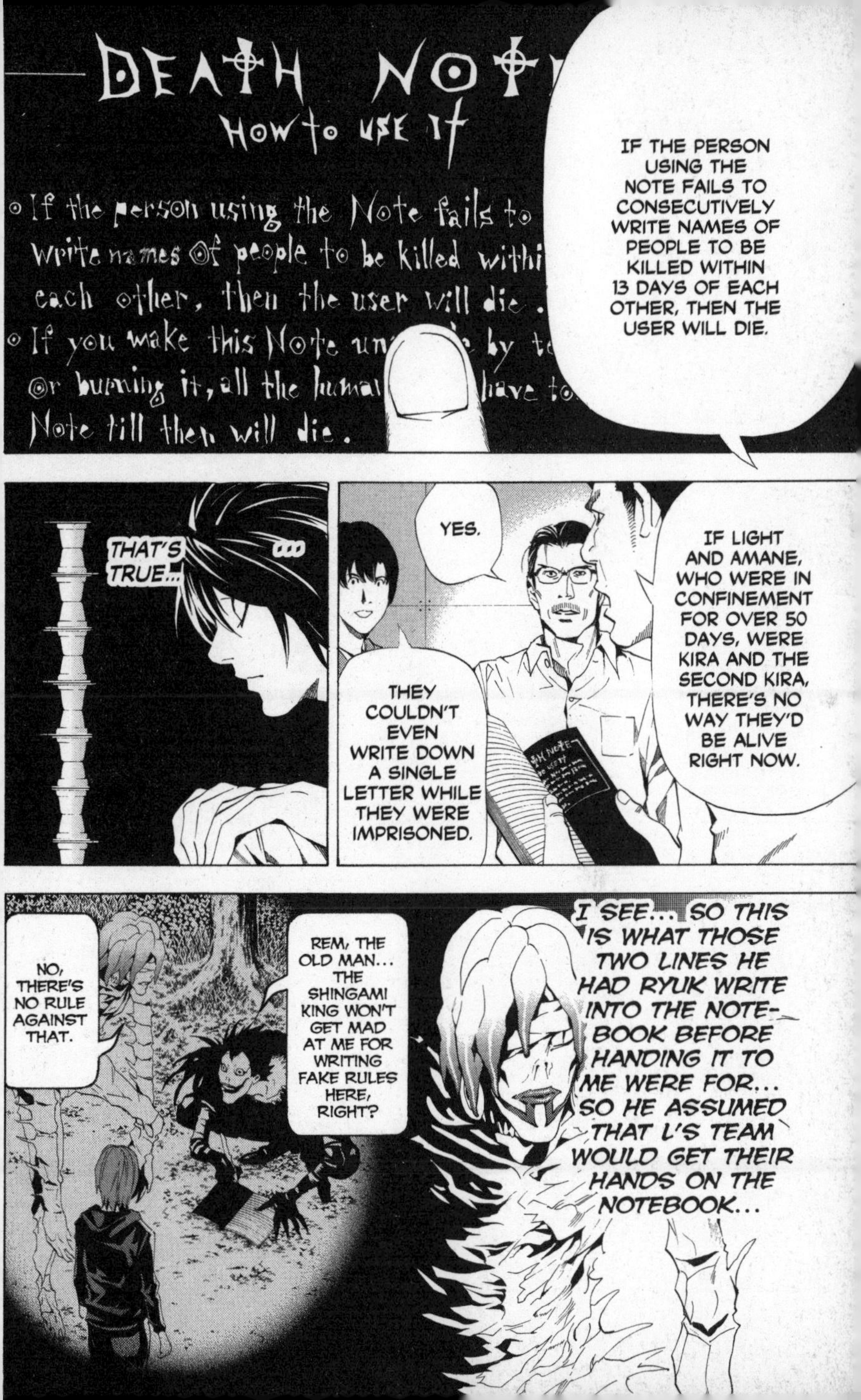
IF THE PERSON USING THE NOTE FAILS TO CONSECUTIVELY WRITE NAMES OF PEOPLE TO BE KILLED WITHIN 13 DAYS OF EACH OTHER, THEN THE USER WILL DIE.
DEATH NOTE
How to use it
If the person using the Note fails to
write names of people to be killed withi
each other, then the user will die.
If you make this Note un
by te
or burning it, all the huma
have to
Note till then will die.
IF LIGHT AND AMANE, WHO WERE IN CONFINEMENT FOR OVER 50 DAYS, WERE KIRA AND THE SECOND KIRA, THERE'S NO WAY THEY'D BE ALIVE RIGHT NOW.
YES.
THEY COULDN'T EVEN WRITE DOWN A SINGLE LETTER WHILE THEY WERE IMPRISONED.
...
THAT'S TRUE...
I SEE... SO THIS IS WHAT THOSE TWO LINES HE HAD RYUK WRITE INTO THE NOTEBOOK BEFORE HANDING IT TO ME WERE FOR... SO HE ASSUMED THAT L'S TEAM WOULD GET THEIR HANDS ON THE NOTEBOOK...
REM, THE OLD MAN... THE SHINGAMI KING WON'T GET MAD AT ME FOR WRITING FAKE RULES HERE, RIGHT?
NO, THERE'S NO RULE AGAINST THAT.

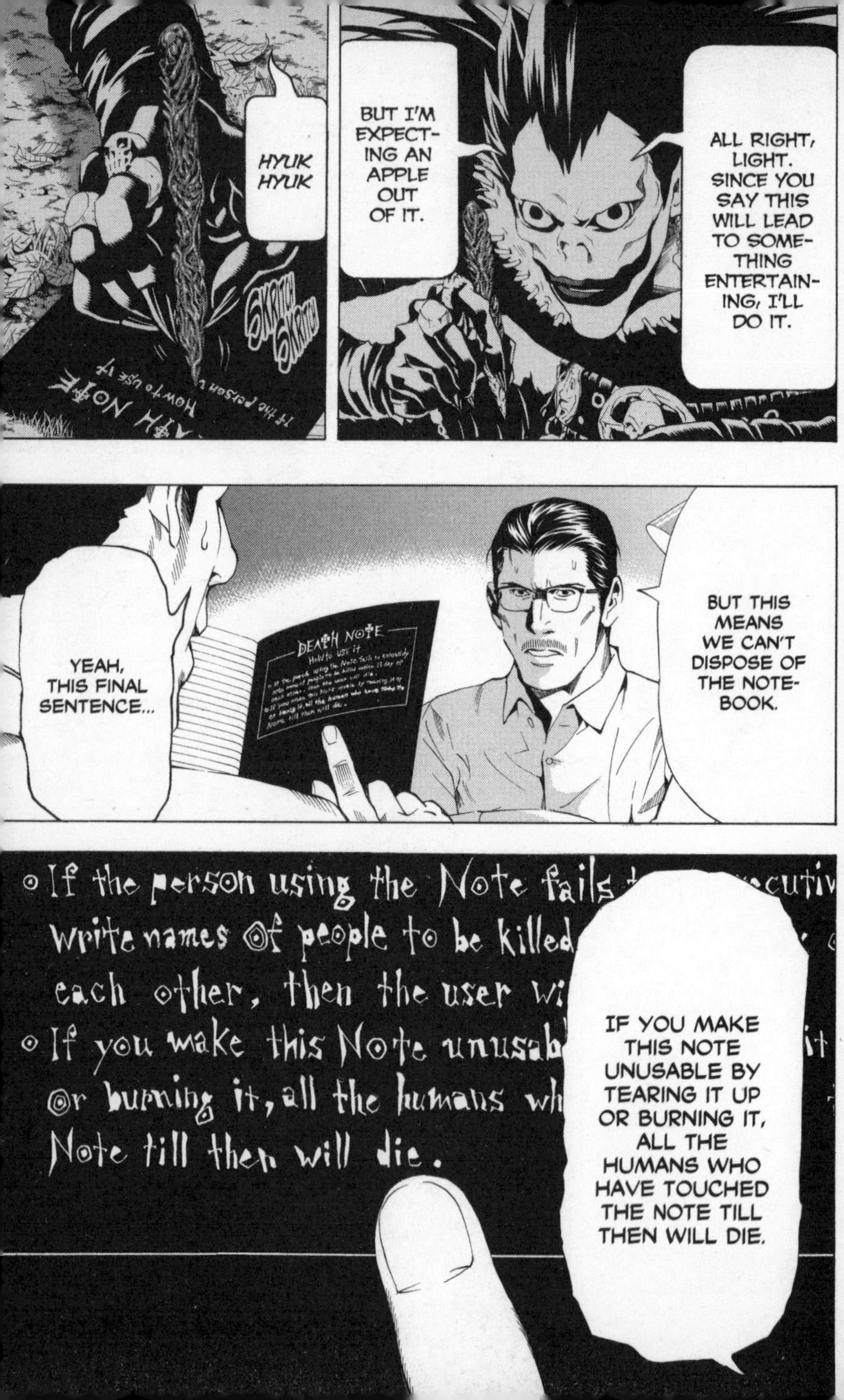
ALL RIGHT, LIGHT. SINCE YOU SAY THIS WILL LEAD TO SOMETHING ENTERTAINING, I'LL DO IT.
BUT I'M EXPECTING AN APPLE OUT OF IT.
HYUK HYUK
SKRITCH SKRITCH
BUT THIS MEANS WE CAN'T DISPOSE OF THE NOTEBOOK.
YEAH, THIS FINAL SENTENCE...
DEATH NOTE
How to use it
IF YOU MAKE THIS NOTE UNUSABLE BY TEARING IT UP OR BURNING IT, ALL THE HUMANS WHO HAVE TOUCHED THE NOTE TILL THEN WILL DIE.
If the person using the Note fails
write names of people to be killed
each other, then the user
If you make this Note
or burning it, all the humans
Note till then will die.

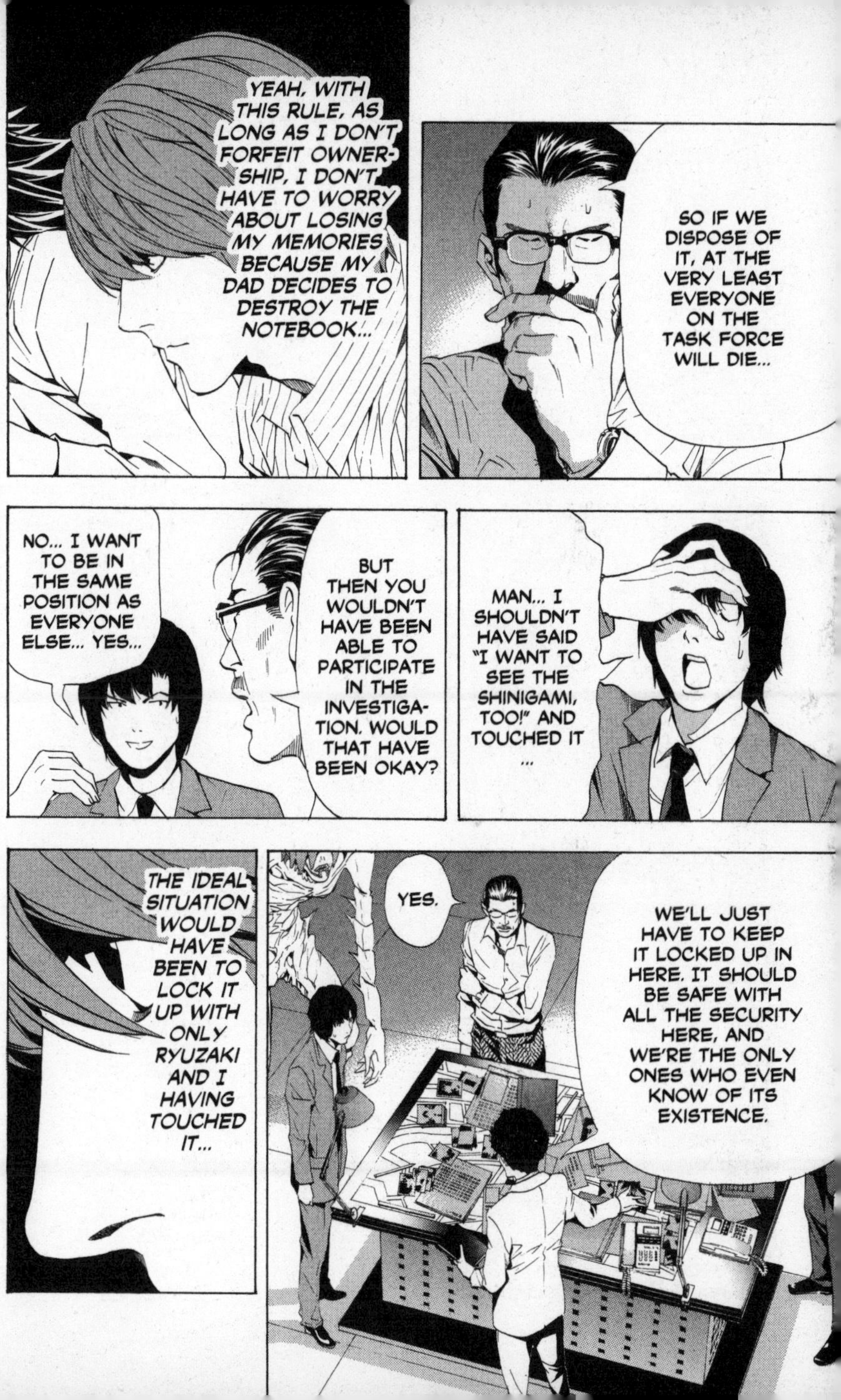
SO IF WE DISPOSE OF IT, AT THE VERY LEAST EVERYONE ON THE TASK FORCE WILL DIE...
YEAH, WITH THIS RULE, AS LONG AS I DON'T FORFEIT OWNERSHIP, I DON'T HAVE TO WORRY ABOUT LOSING MY MEMORIES BECAUSE MY DAD DECIDES TO DESTROY THE NOTEBOOK...
MAN... I SHOULDN'T HAVE SAID "I WANT TO SEE THE SHINIGAMI, TOO!" AND TOUCHED IT ...
BUT THEN YOU WOULDN'T HAVE BEEN ABLE TO PARTICIPATE IN THE INVESTIGATION. WOULD THAT HAVE BEEN OKAY?
NO... I WANT TO BE IN THE SAME POSITION AS EVERYONE ELSE... YES...
WE'LL JUST HAVE TO KEEP IT LOCKED UP IN HERE. IT SHOULD BE SAFE WITH ALL THE SECURITY HERE, AND WE'RE THE ONLY ONES WHO EVEN KNOW OF ITS EXISTENCE.
YES.
THE IDEAL SITUATION WOULD HAVE BEEN TO LOCK IT UP WITH ONLY RYUZAKI AND I HAVING TOUCHED IT...

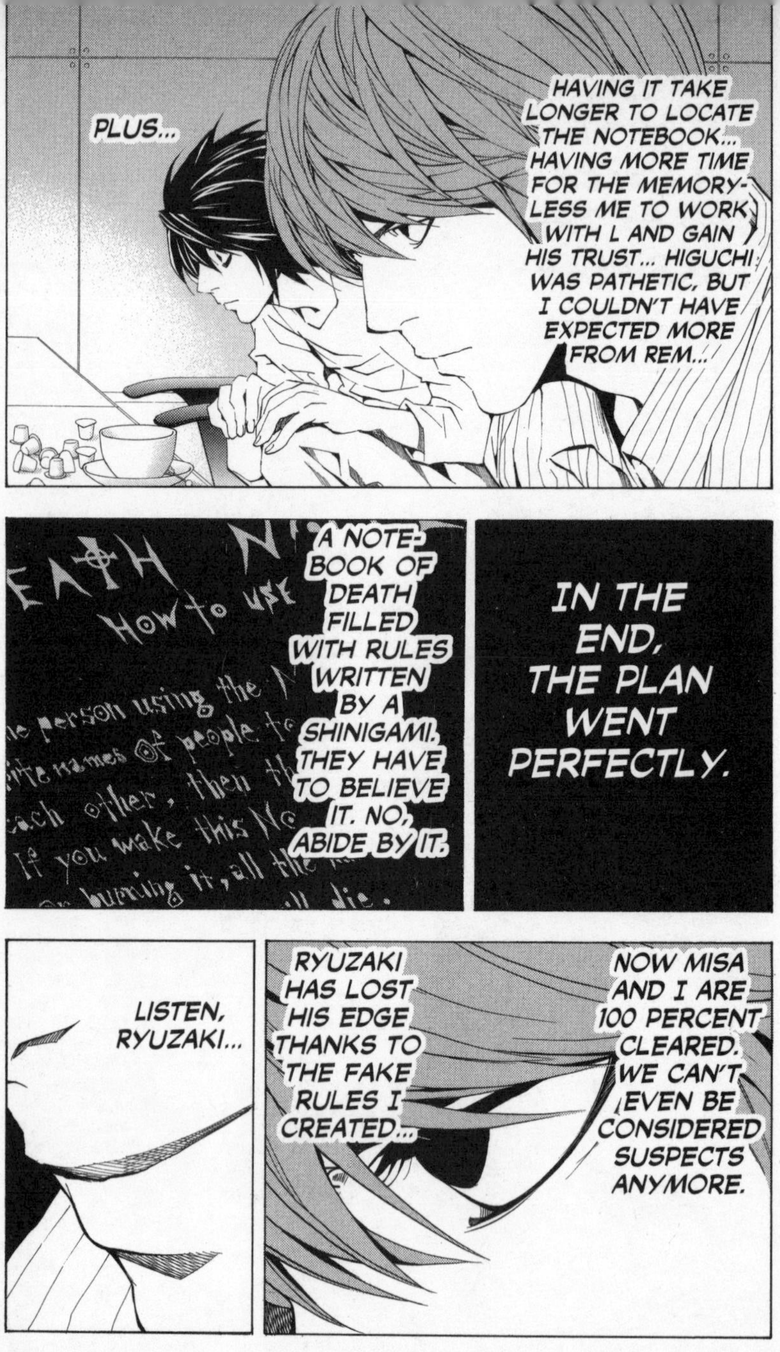
HAVING IT TAKE LONGER TO LOCATE THE NOTEBOOK... HAVING MORE TIME FOR THE MEMORY-LESS ME TO WORK WITH L AND GAIN HIS TRUST... HIGUCHI WAS PATHETIC, BUT I COULDN'T HAVE EXPECTED MORE FROM REM...
PLUS...
IN THE END, THE PLAN WENT PERFECTLY.
A NOTE-BOOK OF DEATH FILLED WITH RULES WRITTEN BY A SHINIGAMI. THEY HAVE TO BELIEVE IT. NO, ABIDE BY IT.
NOW MISA AND I ARE 100 PERCENT CLEARED. WE CAN'T EVEN BE CONSIDERED SUSPECTS ANYMORE.
RYUZAKI HAS LOST HIS EDGE THANKS TO THE FAKE RULES I CREATED...
LISTEN, RYUZAKI...

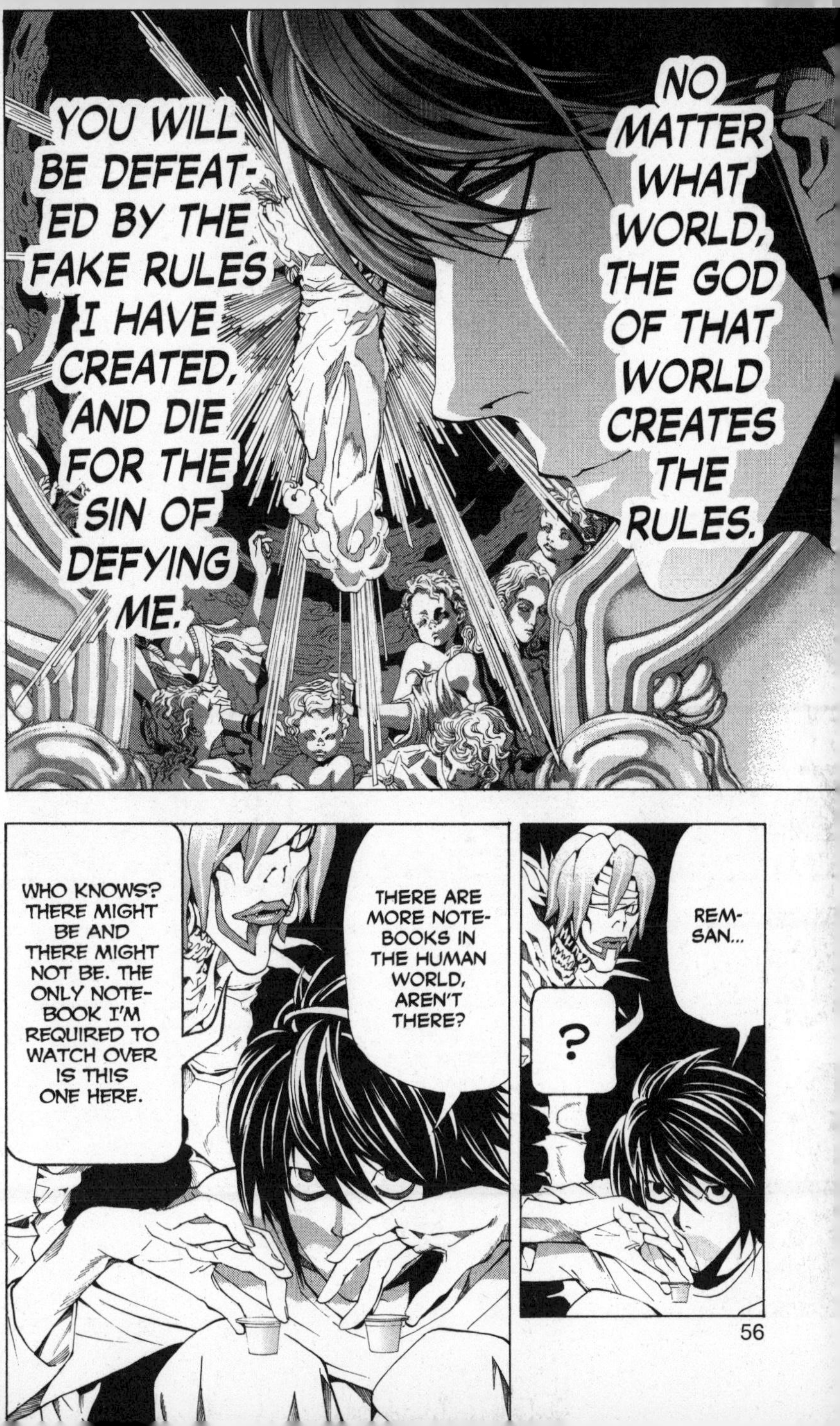
NO MATTER WHAT WORLD, THE GOD OF THAT WORLD CREATES THE RULES.
YOU WILL BE DEFEAT-ED BY THE FAKE RULES I HAVE CREATED, AND DIE FOR THE SIN OF DEFYING ME.
REM-SAN...
?
THERE ARE MORE NOTE-BOOKS IN THE HUMAN WORLD, AREN'T THERE?
WHO KNOWS? THERE MIGHT BE AND THERE MIGHT NOT BE. THE ONLY NOTE-BOOK I'M REQUIRED TO WATCH OVER IS THIS ONE HERE.

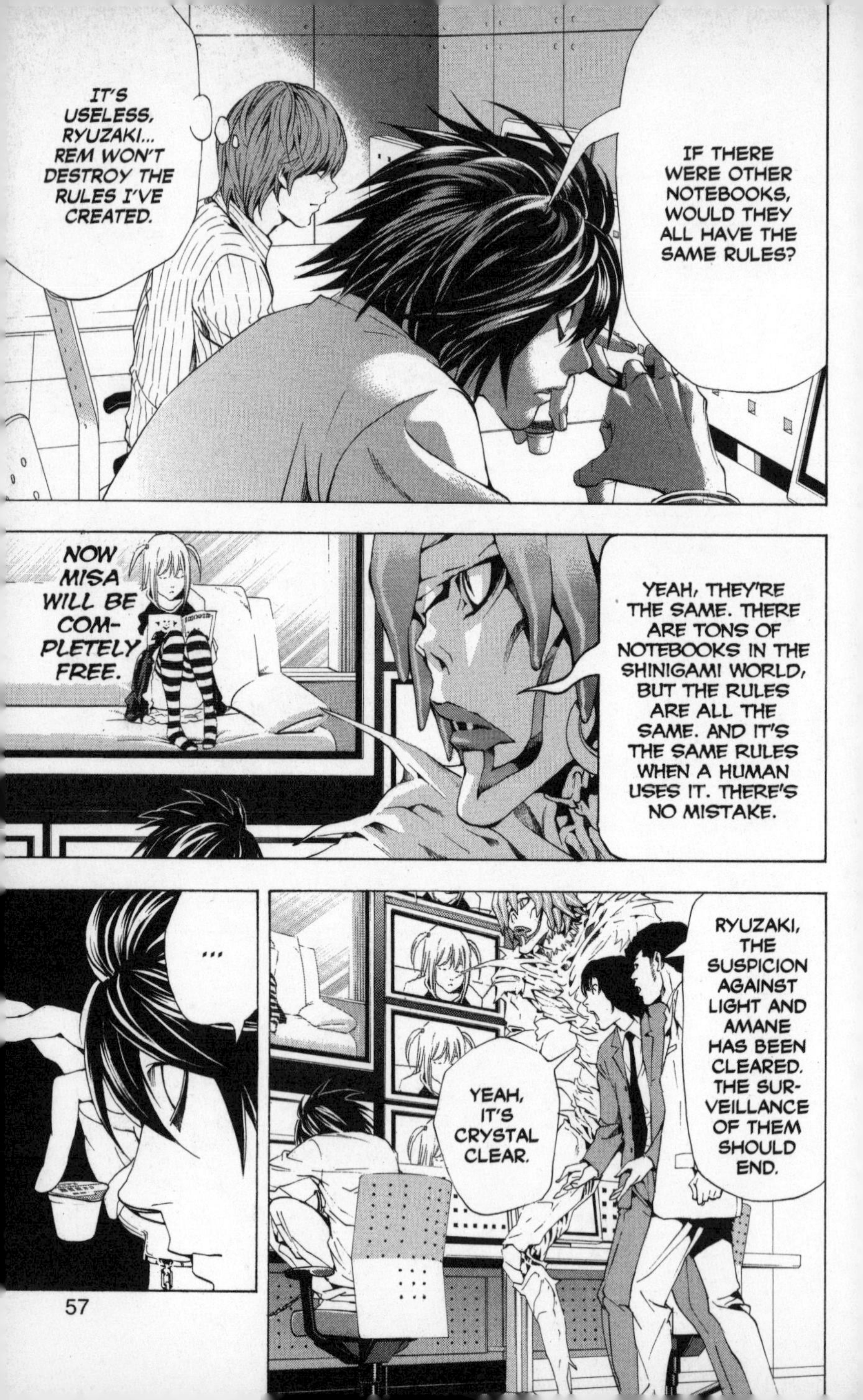
IF THERE WERE OTHER NOTEBOOKS, WOULD THEY ALL HAVE THE SAME RULES?
IT'S USELESS, RYUZAKI... REM WON'T DESTROY THE RULES I'VE CREATED.
YEAH, THEY'RE THE SAME. THERE ARE TONS OF NOTEBOOKS IN THE SHINIGAMI WORLD, BUT THE RULES ARE ALL THE SAME. AND IT'S THE SAME RULES WHEN A HUMAN USES IT. THERE'S NO MISTAKE.
NOW MISA WILL BE COMPLETELY FREE.
RYUZAKI, THE SUSPICION AGAINST LIGHT AND AMANE HAS BEEN CLEARED. THE SURVEILLANCE OF THEM SHOULD END.
YEAH, IT'S CRYSTAL CLEAR.
...

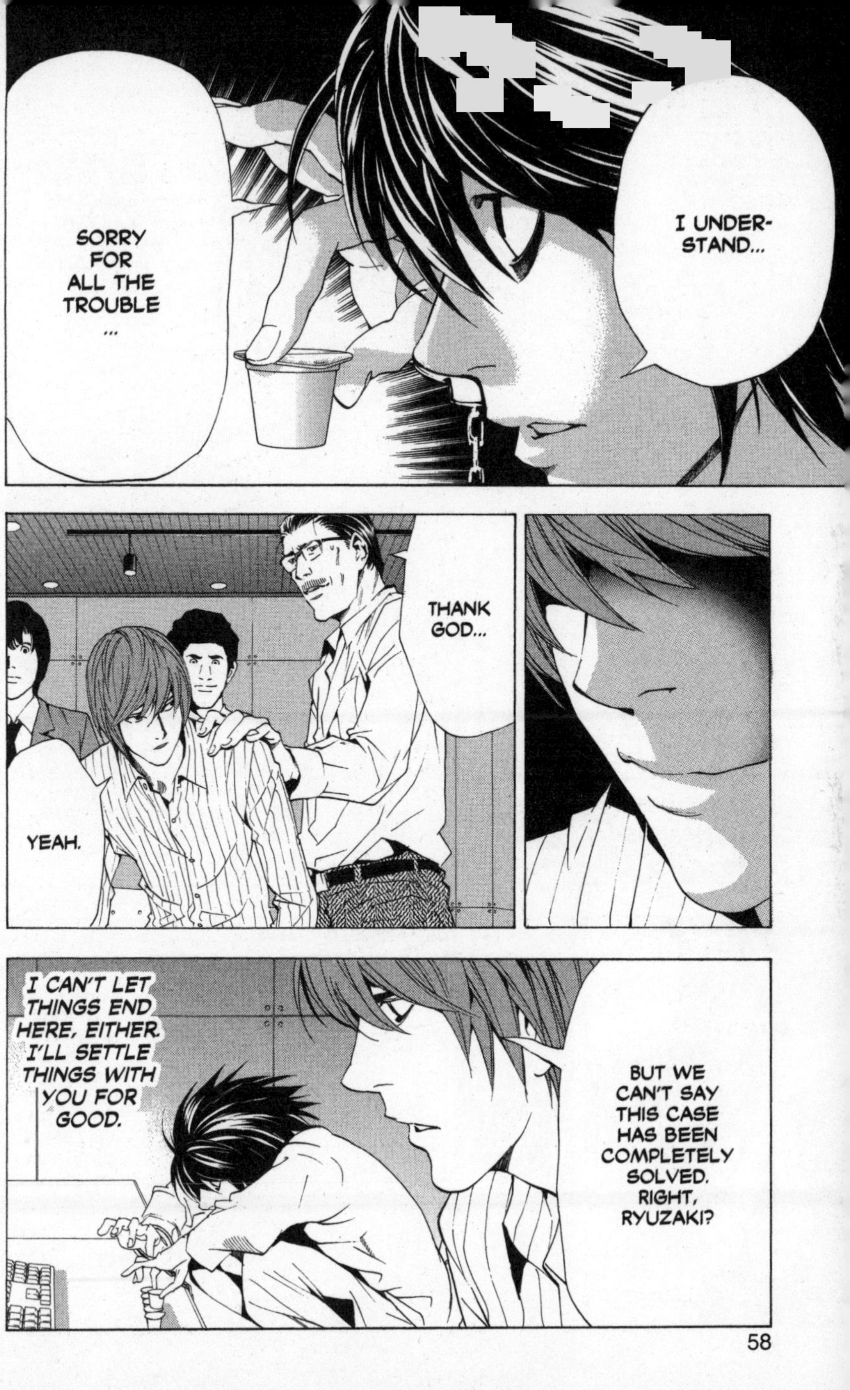
I UNDER-STAND...
SORRY FOR ALL THE TROUBLE ...
THANK GOD...
YEAH.
BUT WE CAN'T SAY THIS CASE HAS BEEN COMPLETELY SOLVED. RIGHT, RYUZAKI?
I CAN'T LET THINGS END HERE, EITHER. I'LL SETTLE THINGS WITH YOU FOR GOOD.

READ THIS WAY

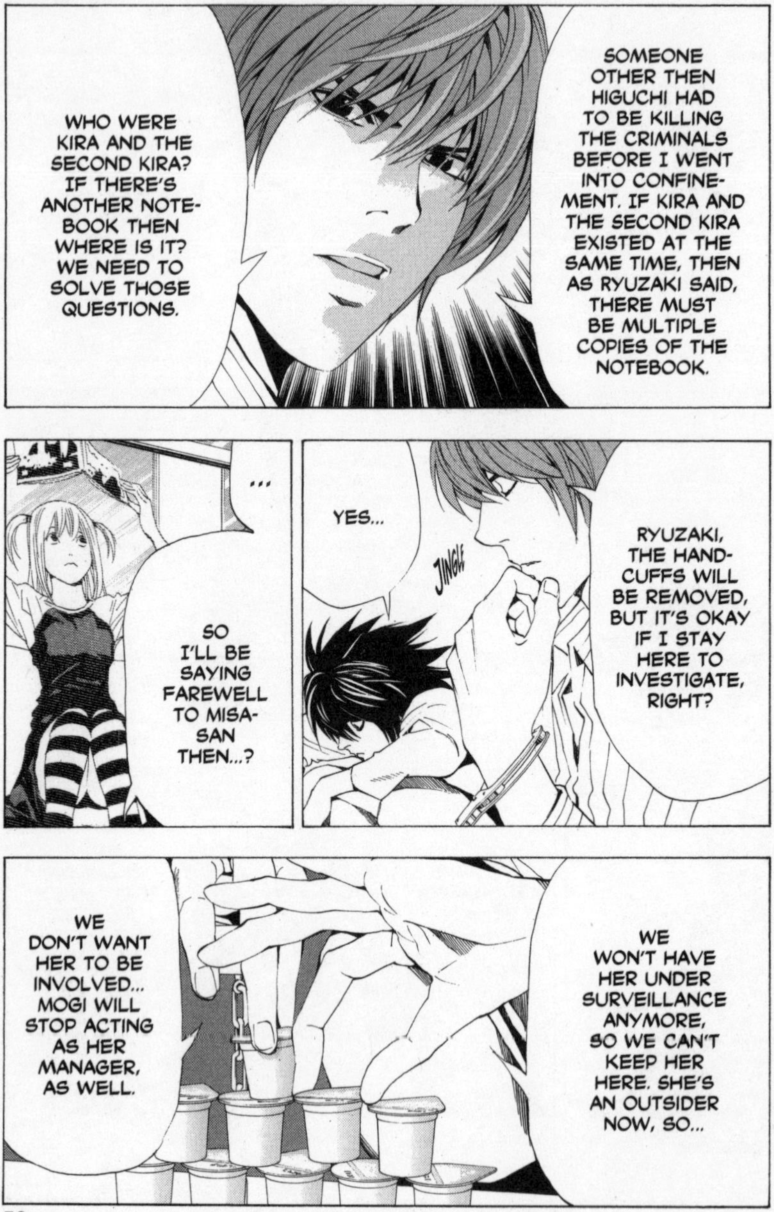
SOMEONE OTHER THEN HIGUCHI HAD TO BE KILLING THE CRIMINALS BEFORE I WENT INTO CONFINEMENT. IF KIRA AND THE SECOND KIRA EXISTED AT THE SAME TIME, THEN AS RYUZAKI SAID, THERE MUST BE MULTIPLE COPIES OF THE NOTEBOOK.
WHO WERE KIRA AND THE SECOND KIRA? IF THERE'S ANOTHER NOTEBOOK THEN WHERE IS IT? WE NEED TO SOLVE THOSE QUESTIONS.
RYUZAKI, THE HANDCUFFS WILL BE REMOVED, BUT IT'S OKAY IF I STAY HERE TO INVESTIGATE, RIGHT?
JINGLE
YES...
...
SO I'LL BE SAYING FAREWELL TO MISA-SAN THEN...?
WE WON'T HAVE HER UNDER SURVEILLANCE ANYMORE, SO WE CAN'T KEEP HER HERE. SHE'S AN OUTSIDER NOW, SO...
WE DON'T WANT HER TO BE INVOLVED... MOGI WILL STOP ACTING AS HER MANAGER, AS WELL.

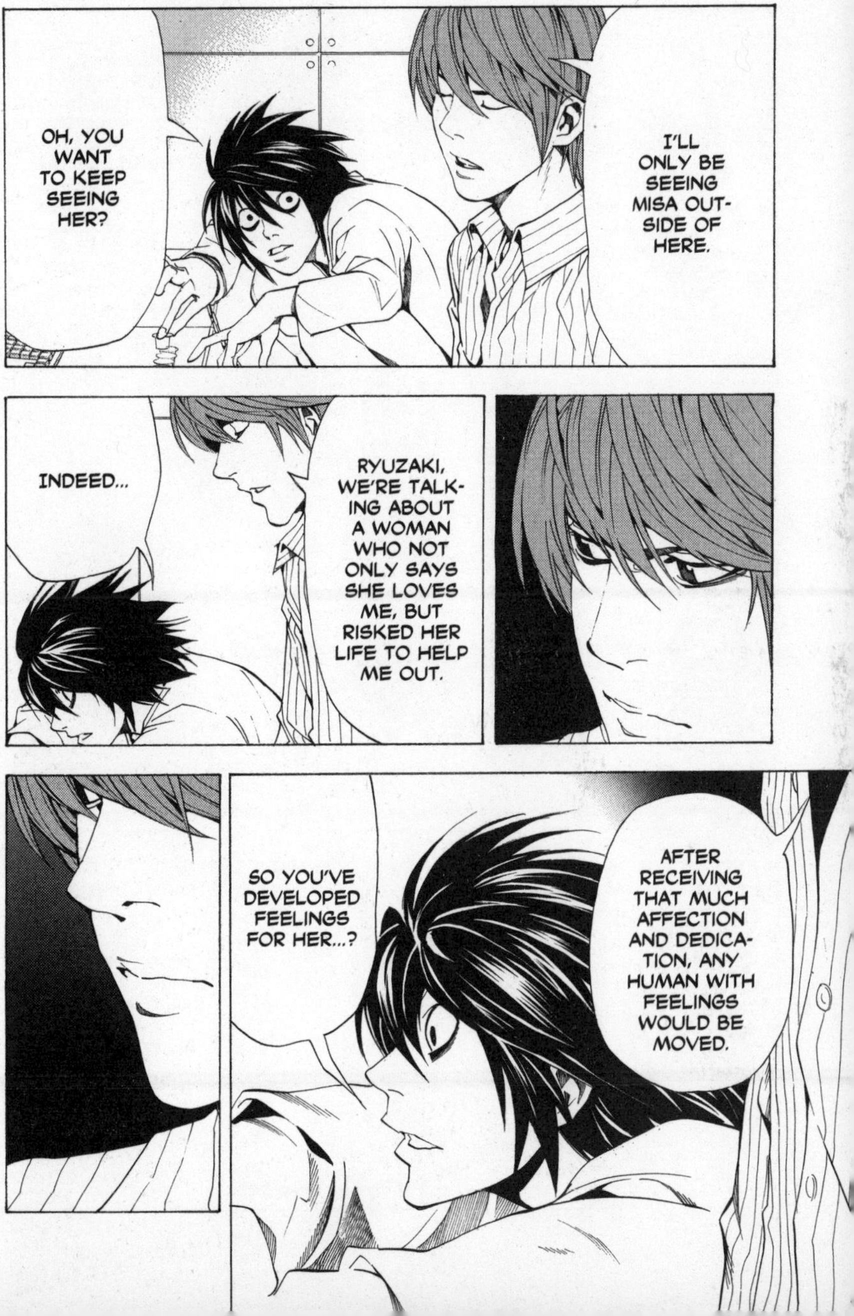
I'LL ONLY BE SEEING MISA OUTSIDE OF HERE.
OH, YOU WANT TO KEEP SEEING HER?
RYUZAKI, WE'RE TALKING ABOUT A WOMAN WHO NOT ONLY SAYS SHE LOVES ME, BUT RISKED HER LIFE TO HELP ME OUT.
INDEED...
SO YOU'VE DEVELOPED FEELINGS FOR HER...?
AFTER RECEIVING THAT MUCH AFFECTION AND DEDICATION, ANY HUMAN WITH FEELINGS WOULD BE MOVED.

READ THIS WAY

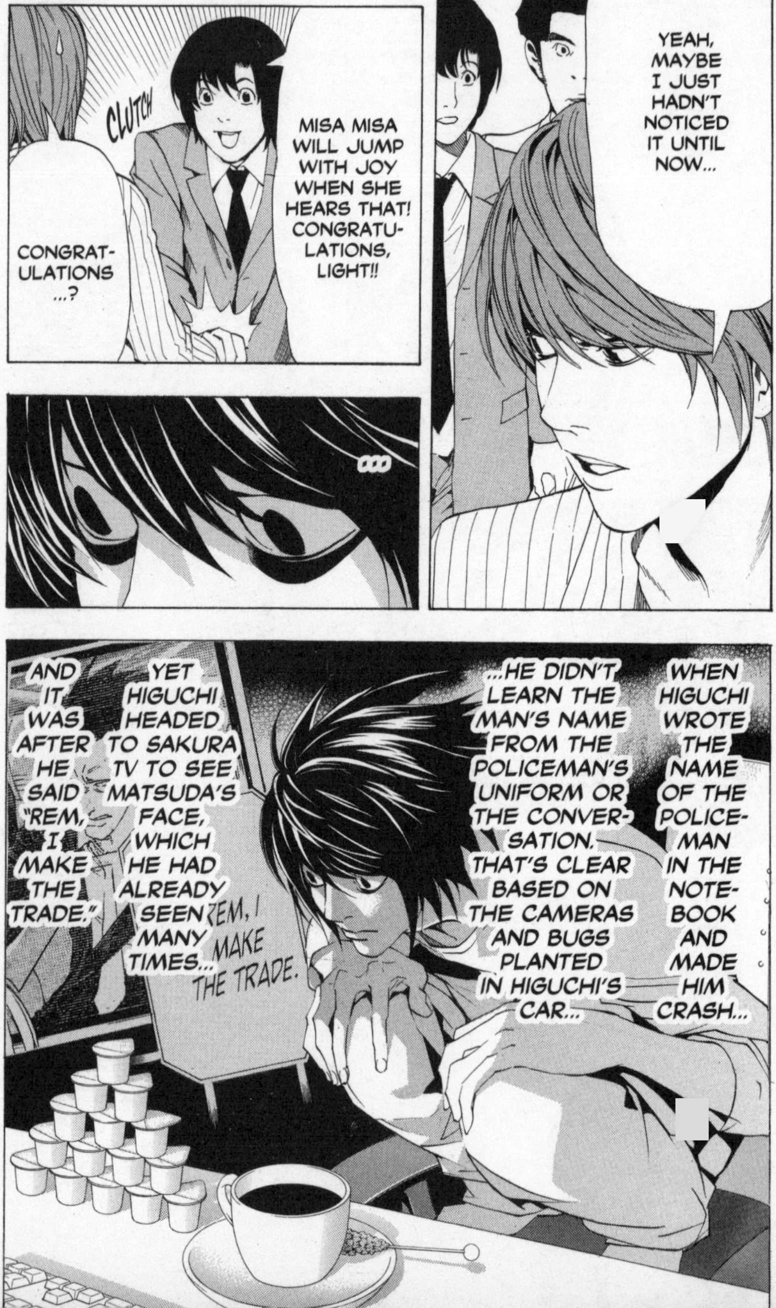
YEAH, MAYBE I JUST HADN'T NOTICED IT UNTIL NOW...
MISA MISA WILL JUMP WITH JOY WHEN SHE HEARS THAT! CONGRATULATIONS, LIGHT!!
CLUTCH
CONGRATULATIONS...?
...
WHEN HIGUCHI WROTE THE NAME OF THE POLICEMAN IN THE NOTEBOOK AND MADE HIM CRASH...
...HE DIDN'T LEARN THE MAN'S NAME FROM THE POLICEMAN'S UNIFORM OR THE CONVERSATION. THAT'S CLEAR BASED ON THE CAMERAS AND BUGS PLANTED IN HIGUCHI'S CAR...
YET HIGUCHI HEADED TO SAKURA TV TO SEE MATSUDA'S FACE, WHICH HE HAD ALREADY SEEN MANY TIMES...
AND IT WAS AFTER HE SAID "REM, I MAKE THE TRADE."
REM, I MAKE THE TRADE.

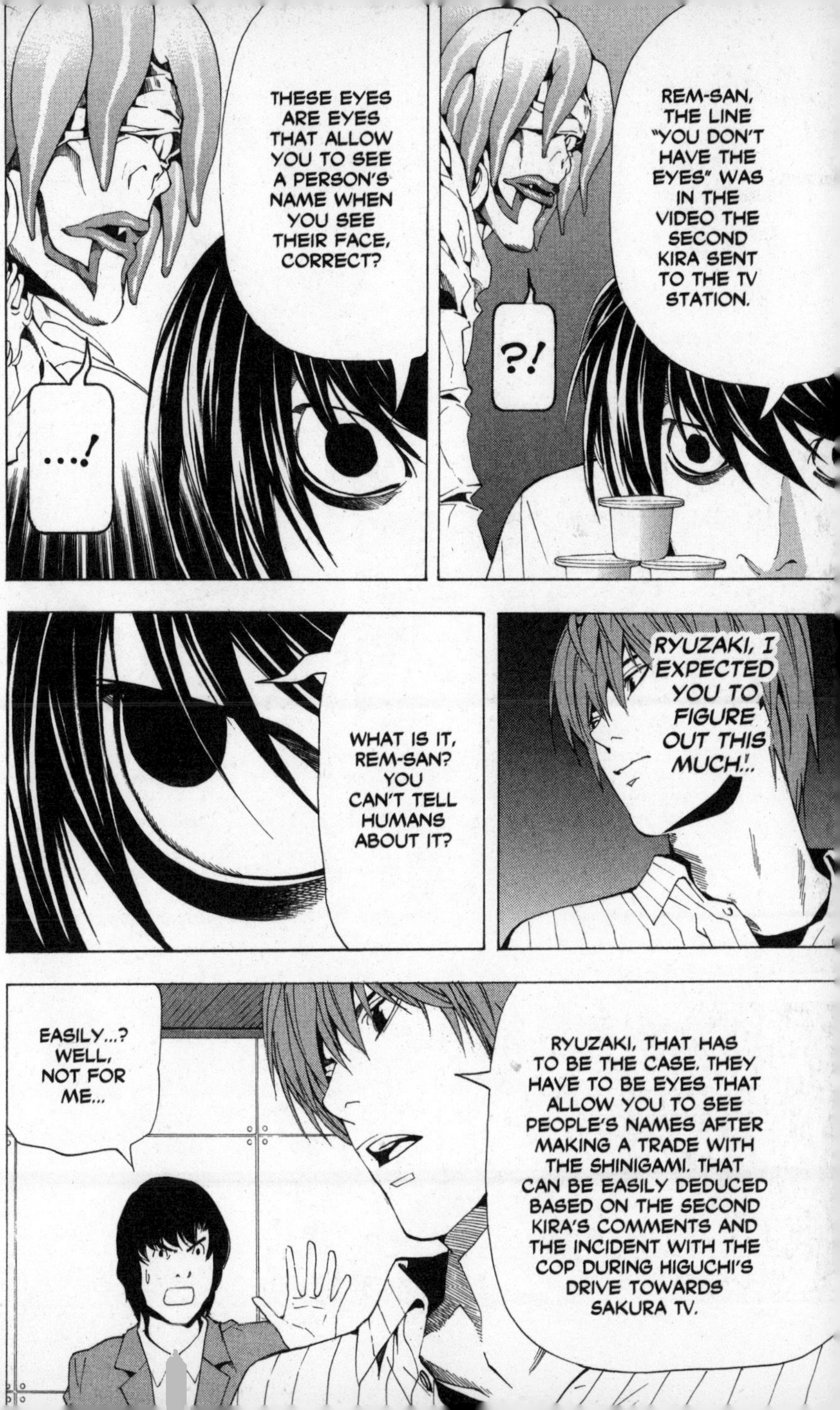
REM-SAN, THE LINE "YOU DON'T HAVE THE EYES" WAS IN THE VIDEO THE SECOND KIRA SENT TO THE TV STATION.
?!
THESE EYES ARE EYES THAT ALLOW YOU TO SEE A PERSON'S NAME WHEN YOU SEE THEIR FACE, CORRECT?
...!
RYUZAKI, I EXPECTED YOU TO FIGURE OUT THIS MUCH...
WHAT IS IT, REM-SAN? YOU CAN'T TELL HUMANS ABOUT IT?
RYUZAKI, THAT HAS TO BE THE CASE. THEY HAVE TO BE EYES THAT ALLOW YOU TO SEE PEOPLE'S NAMES AFTER MAKING A TRADE WITH THE SHINIGAMI. THAT CAN BE EASILY DEDUCED BASED ON THE SECOND KIRA'S COMMENTS AND THE INCIDENT WITH THE COP DURING HIGUCHI'S DRIVE TOWARDS SAKURA TV.
EASILY...? WELL, NOT FOR ME...

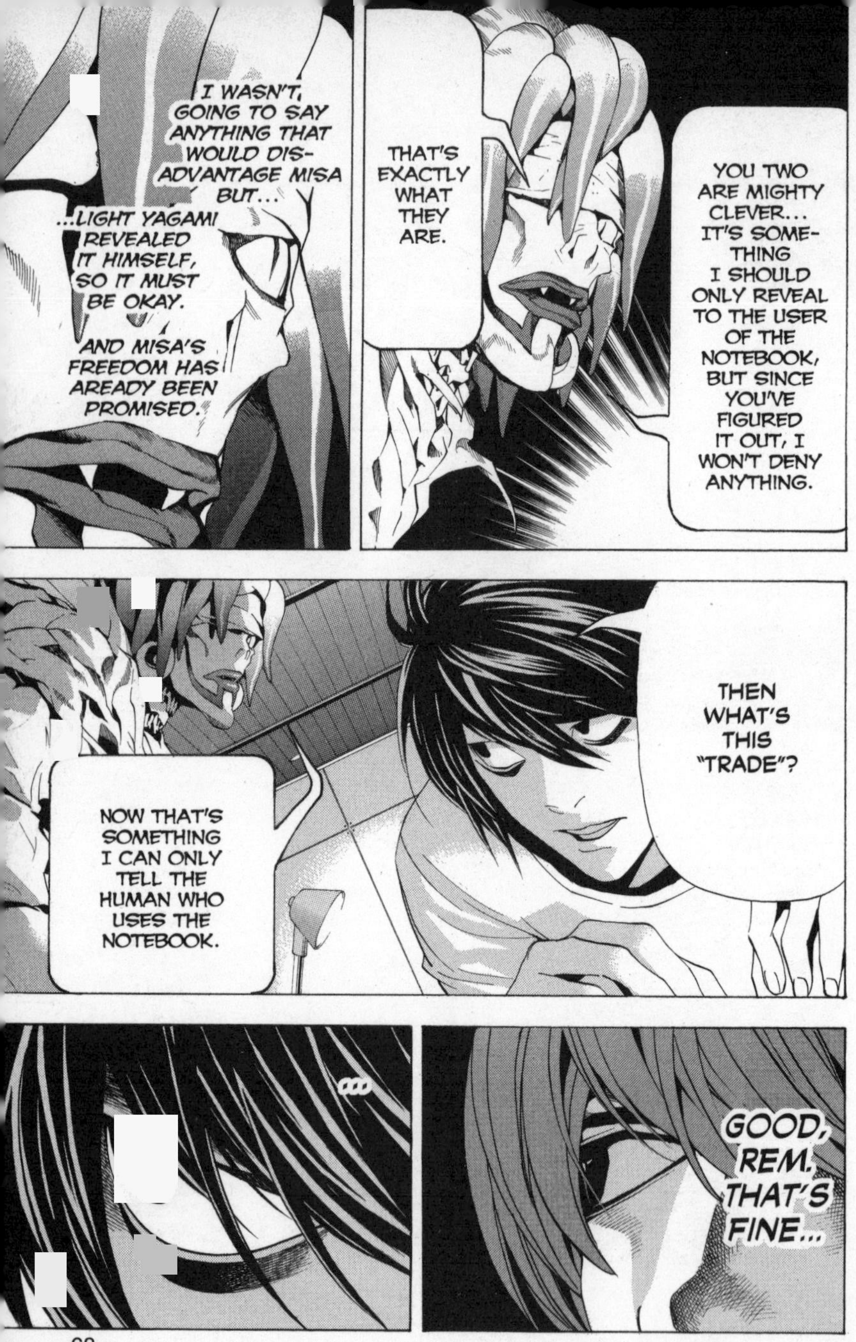
YOU TWO ARE MIGHTY CLEVER... IT'S SOMETHING I SHOULD ONLY REVEAL TO THE USER OF THE NOTEBOOK, BUT SINCE YOU'VE FIGURED IT OUT, I WON'T DENY ANYTHING.
THAT'S EXACTLY WHAT THEY ARE.
I WASN'T GOING TO SAY ANYTHING THAT WOULD DIS-ADVANTAGE MISA BUT...
...LIGHT YAGAMI REVEALED IT HIMSELF, SO IT MUST BE OKAY.
AND MISA'S FREEDOM HAS AREADY BEEN PROMISED.
THEN WHAT'S THIS "TRADE"?
NOW THAT'S SOMETHING I CAN ONLY TELL THE HUMAN WHO USES THE NOTEBOOK.
GOOD, REM. THAT'S FINE...
...

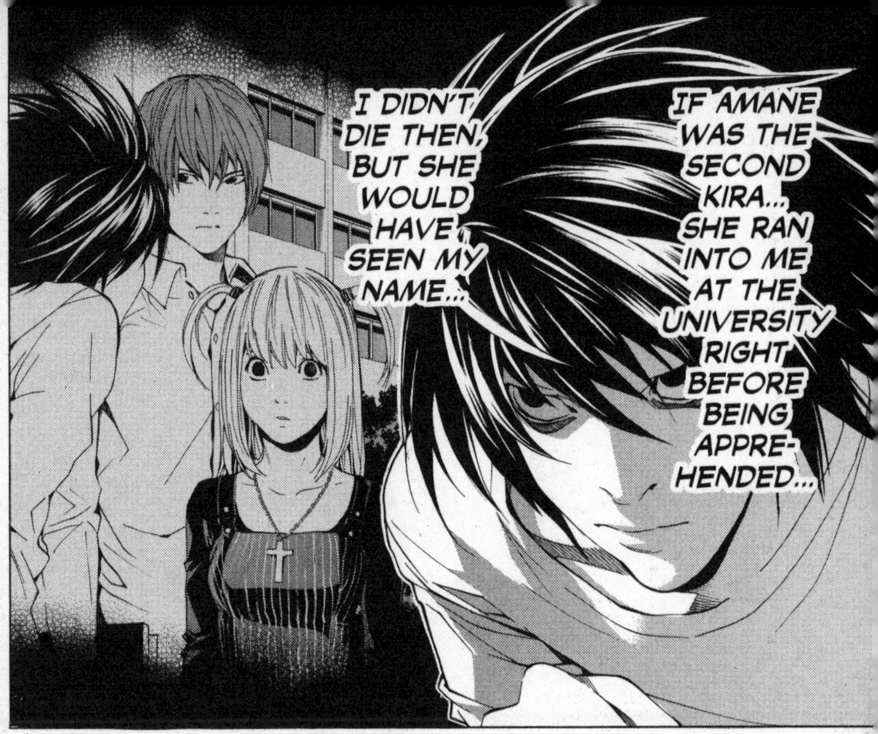
IF AMANE WAS THE SECOND KIRA... SHE RAN INTO ME AT THE UNIVERSITY RIGHT BEFORE BEING APPRE-HENDED...
I DIDN'T DIE THEN, BUT SHE WOULD HAVE SEEN MY NAME...
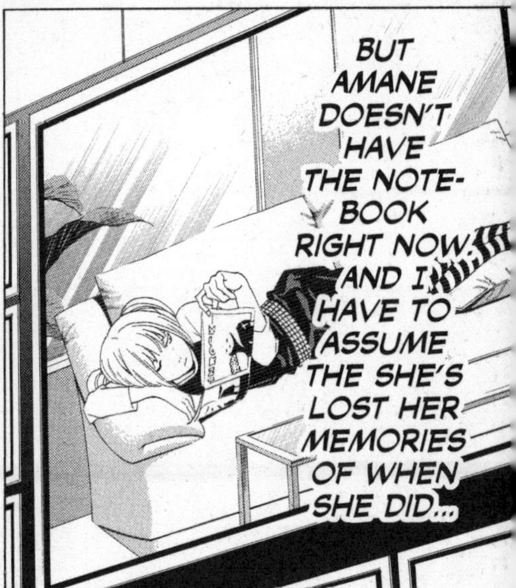
BUT AMANE DOESN'T HAVE THE NOTE-BOOK RIGHT NOW AND I HAVE TO ASSUME THE SHE'S LOST HER MEMORIES OF WHEN SHE DID...
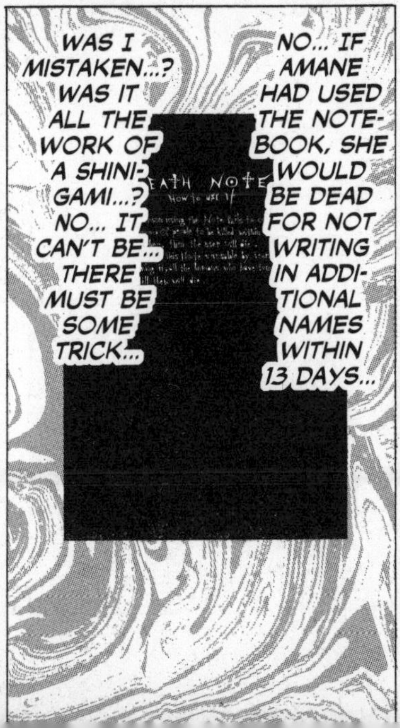
NO... IF AMANE HAD USED THE NOTE-BOOK, SHE WOULD BE DEAD FOR NOT WRITING IN ADDI-TIONAL NAMES WITHIN 13 DAYS...
WAS I MISTAKEN...? WAS IT ALL THE WORK OF A SHINI-GAMI...? NO... IT CAN'T BE... THERE MUST BE SOME TRICK...

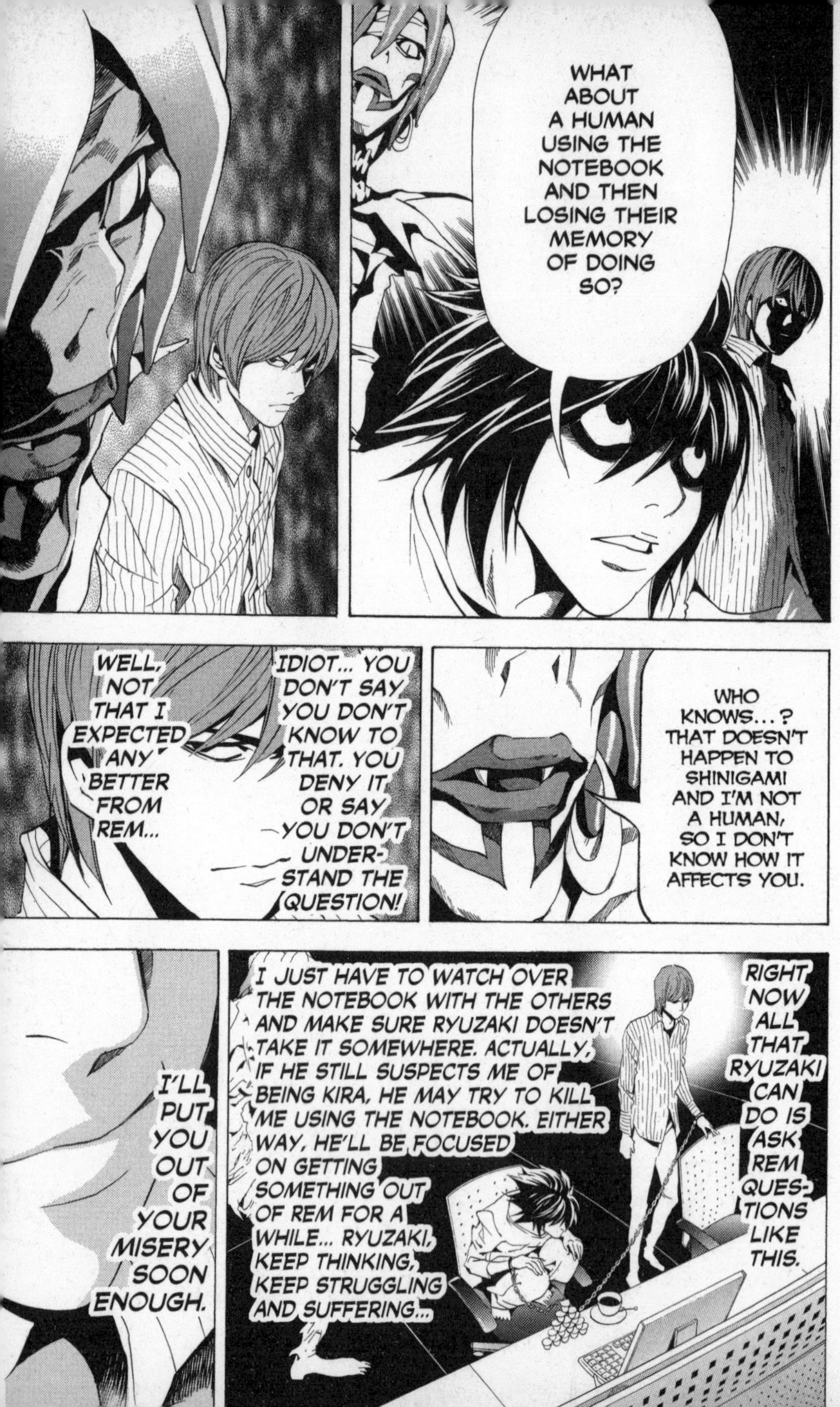
WHAT ABOUT A HUMAN USING THE NOTEBOOK AND THEN LOSING THEIR MEMORY OF DOING SO?
WHO KNOWS...? THAT DOESN'T HAPPEN TO SHINIGAMI AND I'M NOT A HUMAN, SO I DON'T KNOW HOW IT AFFECTS YOU.
IDIOT... YOU DON'T SAY YOU DON'T KNOW TO THAT. YOU DENY IT OR SAY YOU DON'T UNDERSTAND THE QUESTION!
WELL, NOT THAT I EXPECTED ANY BETTER FROM REM...
RIGHT NOW ALL THAT RYUZAKI CAN DO IS ASK REM QUESTIONS LIKE THIS.
I JUST HAVE TO WATCH OVER THE NOTEBOOK WITH THE OTHERS AND MAKE SURE RYUZAKI DOESN'T TAKE IT SOMEWHERE. ACTUALLY, IF HE STILL SUSPECTS ME OF BEING KIRA, HE MAY TRY TO KILL ME USING THE NOTEBOOK. EITHER WAY, HE'LL BE FOCUSED ON GETTING SOMETHING OUT OF REM FOR A WHILE... RYUZAKI, KEEP THINKING, KEEP STRUGGLING AND SUFFERING...
I'LL PUT YOU OUT OF YOUR MISERY SOON ENOUGH.

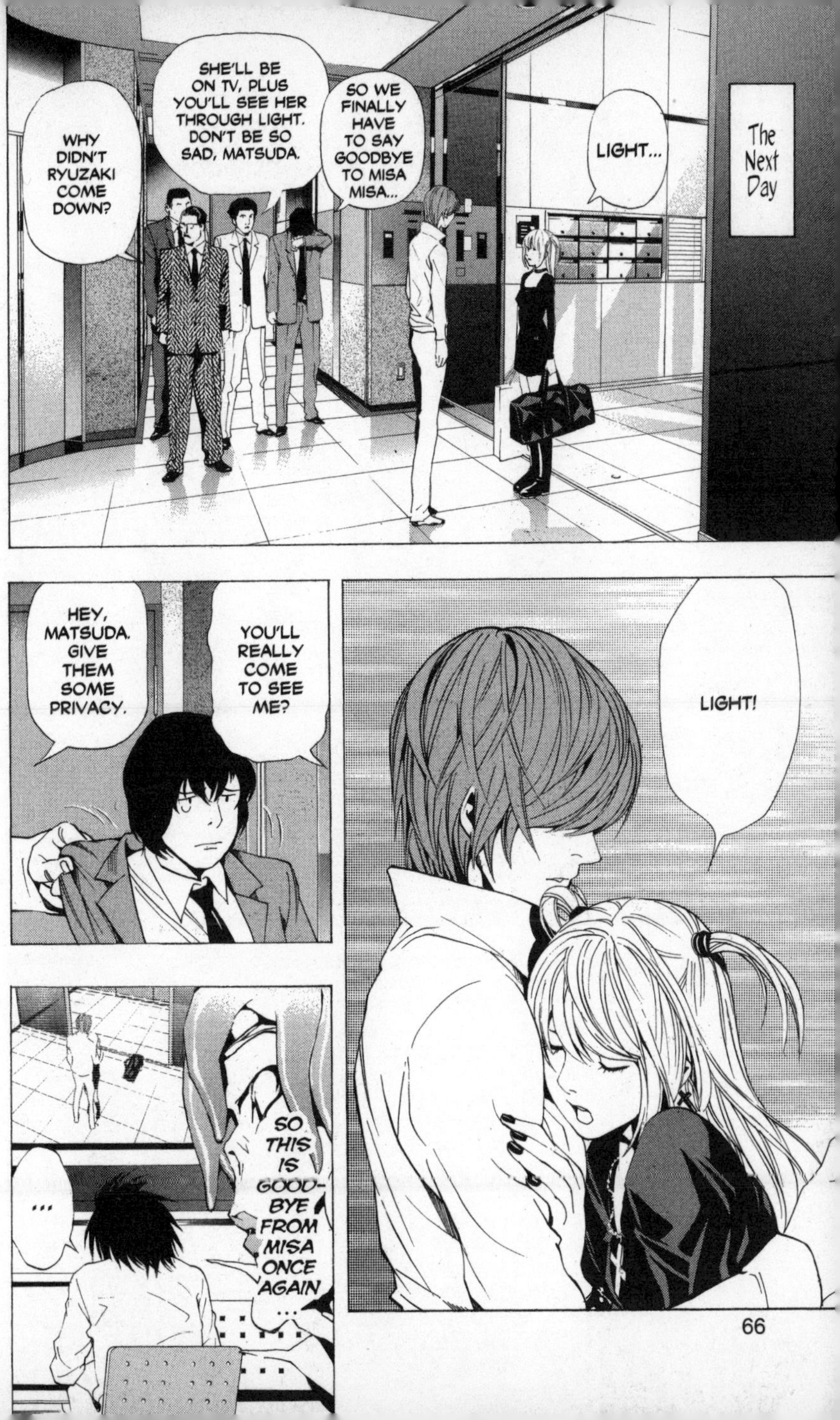
The Next Day
LIGHT...
SO WE FINALLY HAVE TO SAY GOODBYE TO MISA MISA...
SHE'LL BE ON TV, PLUS YOU'LL SEE HER THROUGH LIGHT. DON'T BE SO SAD, MATSUDA.
WHY DIDN'T RYUZAKI COME DOWN?
LIGHT!
YOU'LL REALLY COME TO SEE ME?
HEY, MATSUDA. GIVE THEM SOME PRIVACY.
SO THIS IS GOOD-BYE FROM MISA ONCE AGAIN...
...

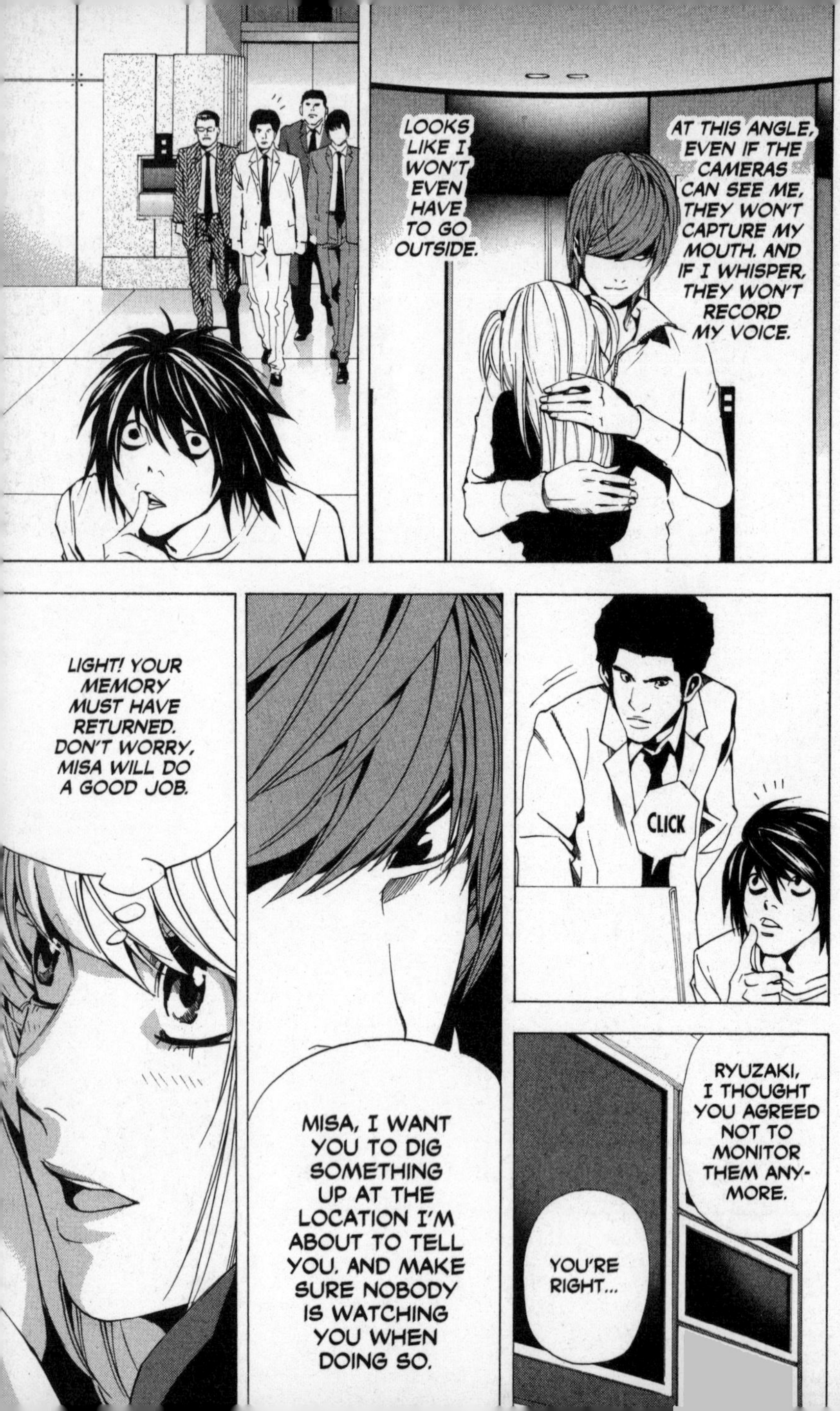
AT THIS ANGLE, EVEN IF THE CAMERAS CAN SEE ME, THEY WON'T CAPTURE MY MOUTH. AND IF I WHISPER, THEY WON'T RECORD MY VOICE.
LOOKS LIKE I WON'T EVEN HAVE TO GO OUTSIDE.
CLICK
RYUZAKI, I THOUGHT YOU AGREED NOT TO MONITOR THEM ANY-MORE.
YOU'RE RIGHT...
MISA, I WANT YOU TO DIG SOMETHING UP AT THE LOCATION I'M ABOUT TO TELL YOU. AND MAKE SURE NOBODY IS WATCHING YOU WHEN DOING SO.
LIGHT! YOUR MEMORY MUST HAVE RETURNED. DON'T WORRY, MISA WILL DO A GOOD JOB.

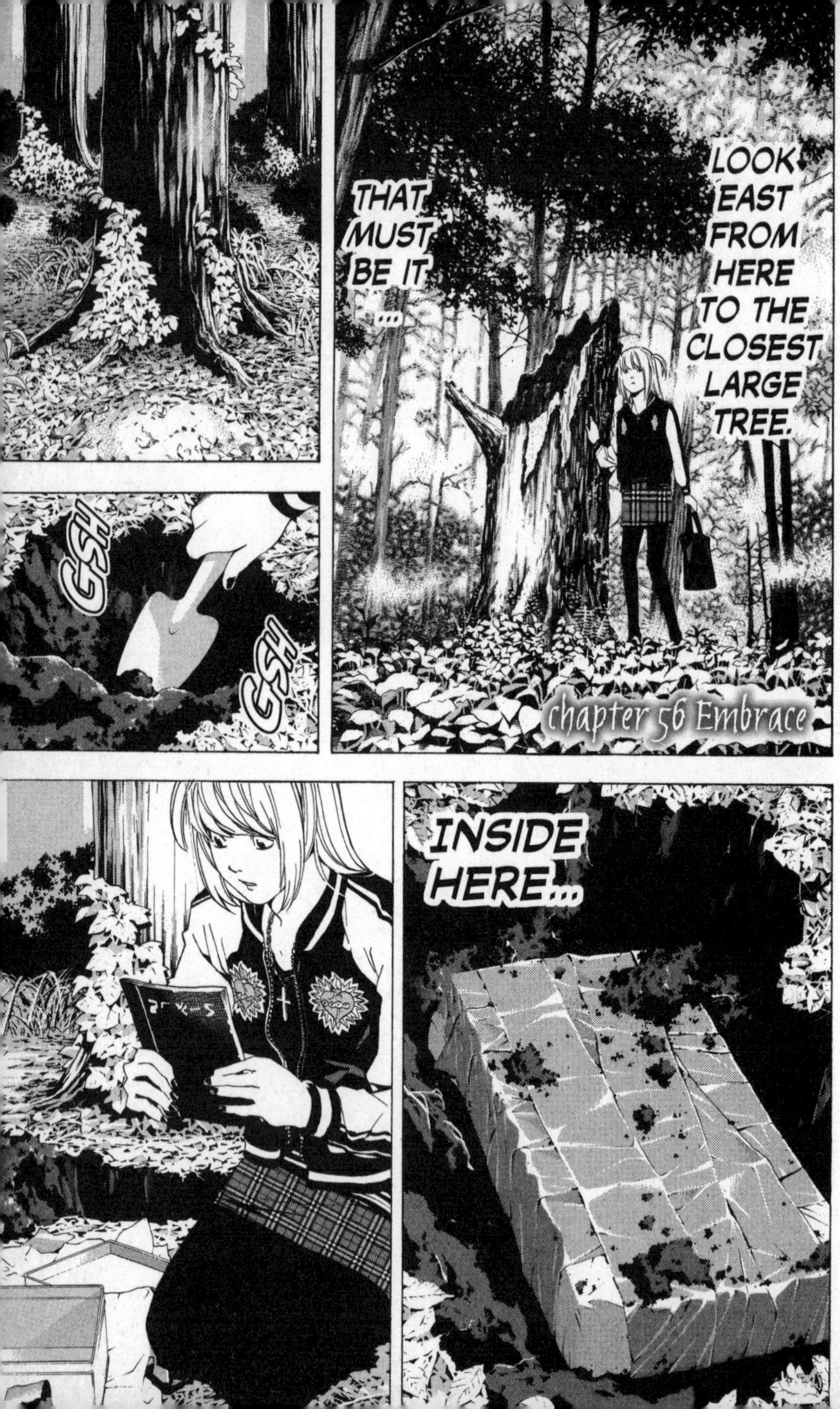
LOOK EAST FROM HERE TO THE CLOSEST LARGE TREE.
THAT MUST BE IT ...
chapter 56 Embrace
GSH
GSH
INSIDE HERE...

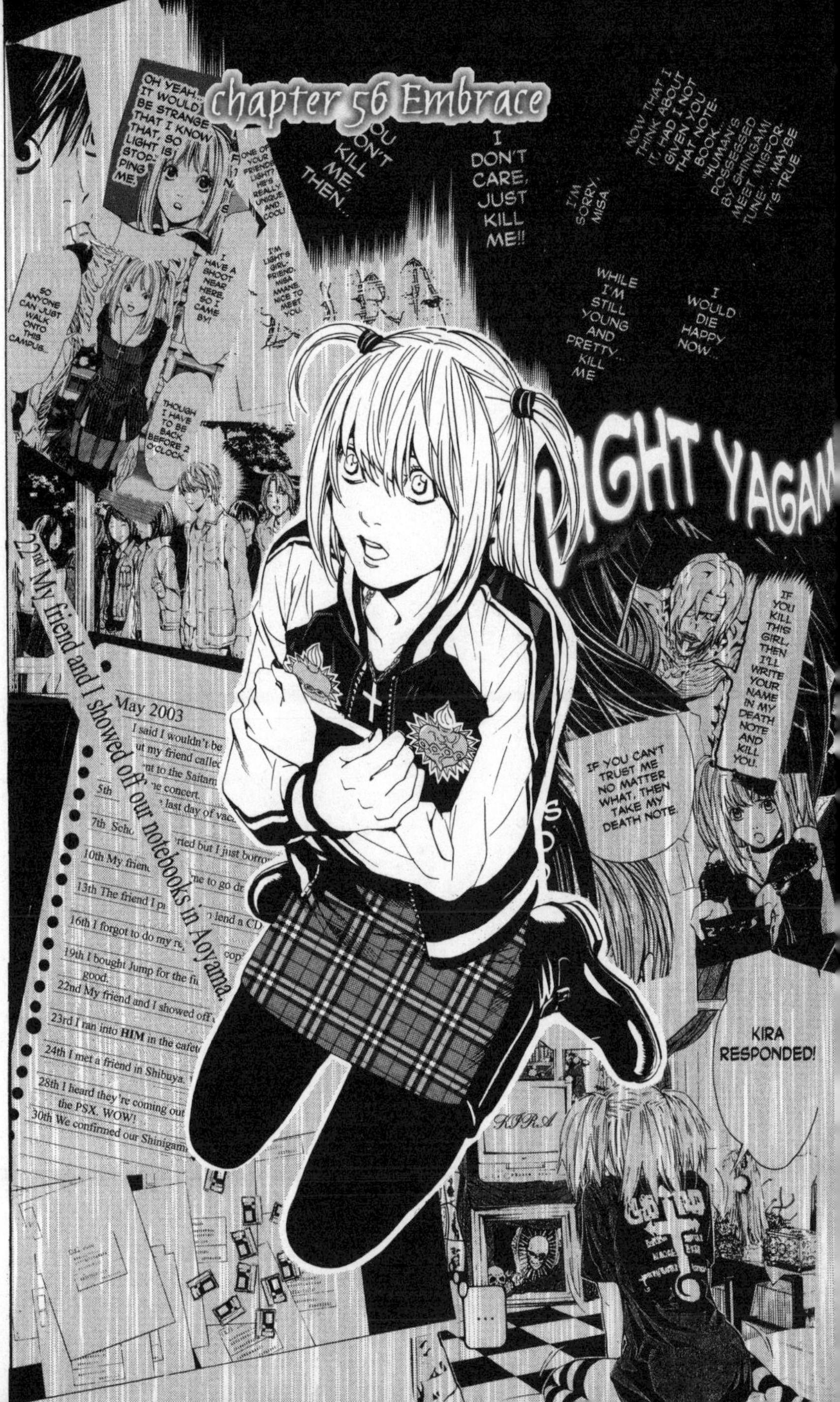
chapter 56 Embrace
NOW THAT I THINK ABOUT IT, HAD I NOT GIVEN YOU THAT NOTE-BOOK... "HUMAN'S POSSESSED BY SHINIGAMI MEET MISFOR-TUNE"... MAYBE IT'S TRUE.
I'M SORRY, MISA
I DON'T CARE, JUST KILL ME!!
YOU DON'T KILL ME, THEN...
I WOULD DIE HAPPY NOW...
WHILE I'M STILL YOUNG AND PRETTY... KILL ME
ONE OF YOUR FRIENDS LIGHT? HE'S REALLY UNIQUE AND COOL!
OH YEAH... IT WOULD BE STRANGE THAT I KNOW THAT, SO LIGHT IS STOP-PING ME.
I'M LIGHT'S GIRL-FRIEND, MISA AMANE NICE TO MEET YOU.
I HAVE A SHOOT NEAR HERE, SO I CAME BY!
SO ANYONE CAN JUST WALK ONTO THIS CAMPUS...
THOUGH I HAVE TO BE BACK BEFORE 2 O'CLOCK.
LIGHT YAGAMI
IF YOU KILL THIS GIRL, THEN I'LL WRITE YOUR NAME IN MY DEATH NOTE AND KILL YOU.
IF YOU CAN'T TRUST ME NO MATTER WHAT, THEN TAKE MY DEATH NOTE.
22nd My friend and I showed off our notebooks in Aoyama.
May 2003
I said I wouldn't be
ut my friend callec
nt to the Saitam
5th
ne concert.
last day of vac
7th Scho
rted but I just borro
10th My frien
me to go dr
13th The friend I p
lend a CD
16th I forgot to do my r
cop
19th I bought Jump for the fi
good.
22nd My friend and I showed off
23rd I ran into HIM in the cafet
24th I met a friend in Shibuya.
28th I heard they're coming out
the PSX. WOW!
30th We confirmed our Shinigam
KIRA RESPONDED!
KIRA

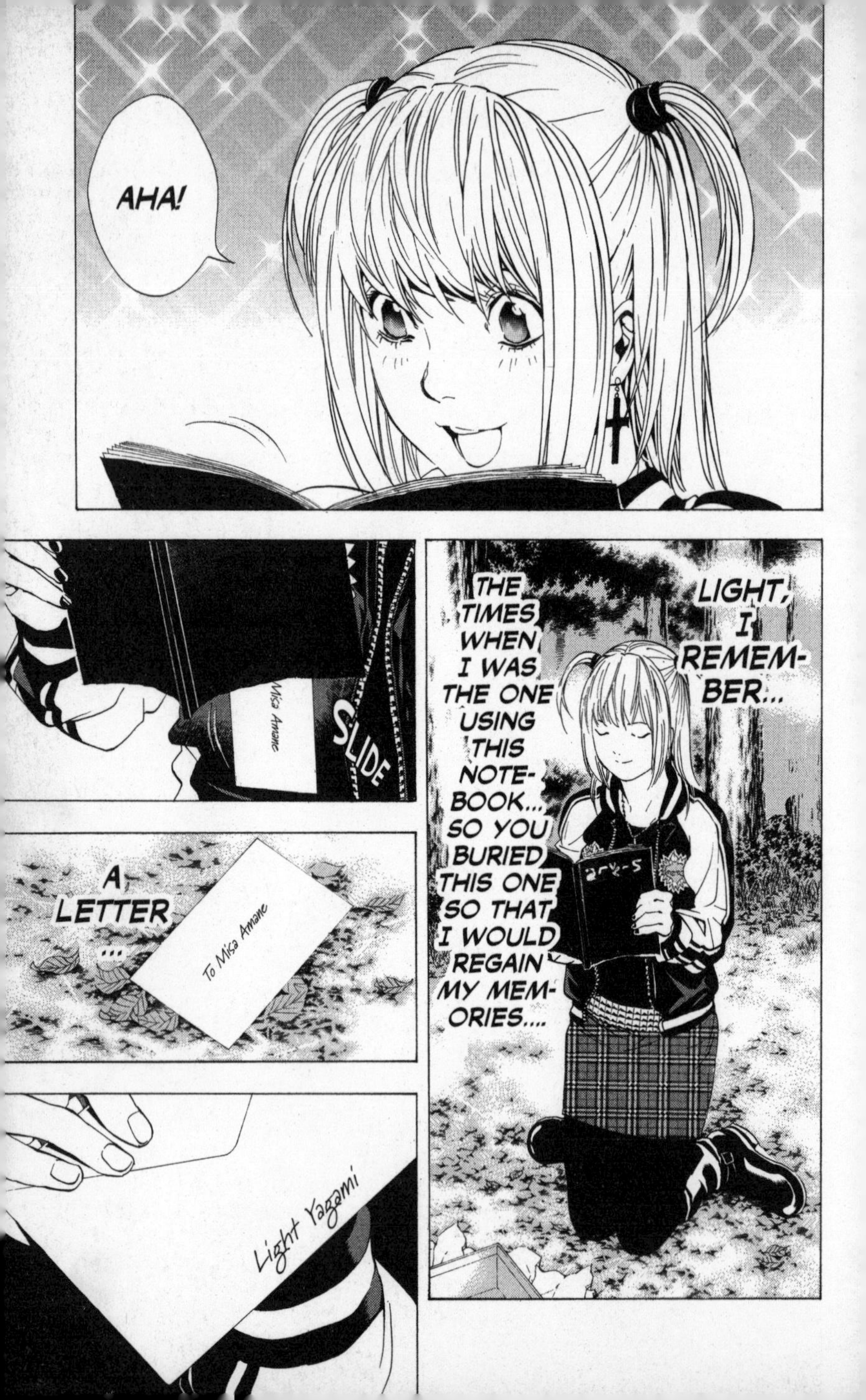
AHA!
LIGHT, I REMEMBER...
THE TIMES WHEN I WAS THE ONE USING THIS NOTEBOOK... SO YOU BURIED THIS ONE SO THAT I WOULD REGAIN MY MEMORIES....
Misa Amane
SLIDE
A LETTER ...
To Misa Amane
Light Yagami

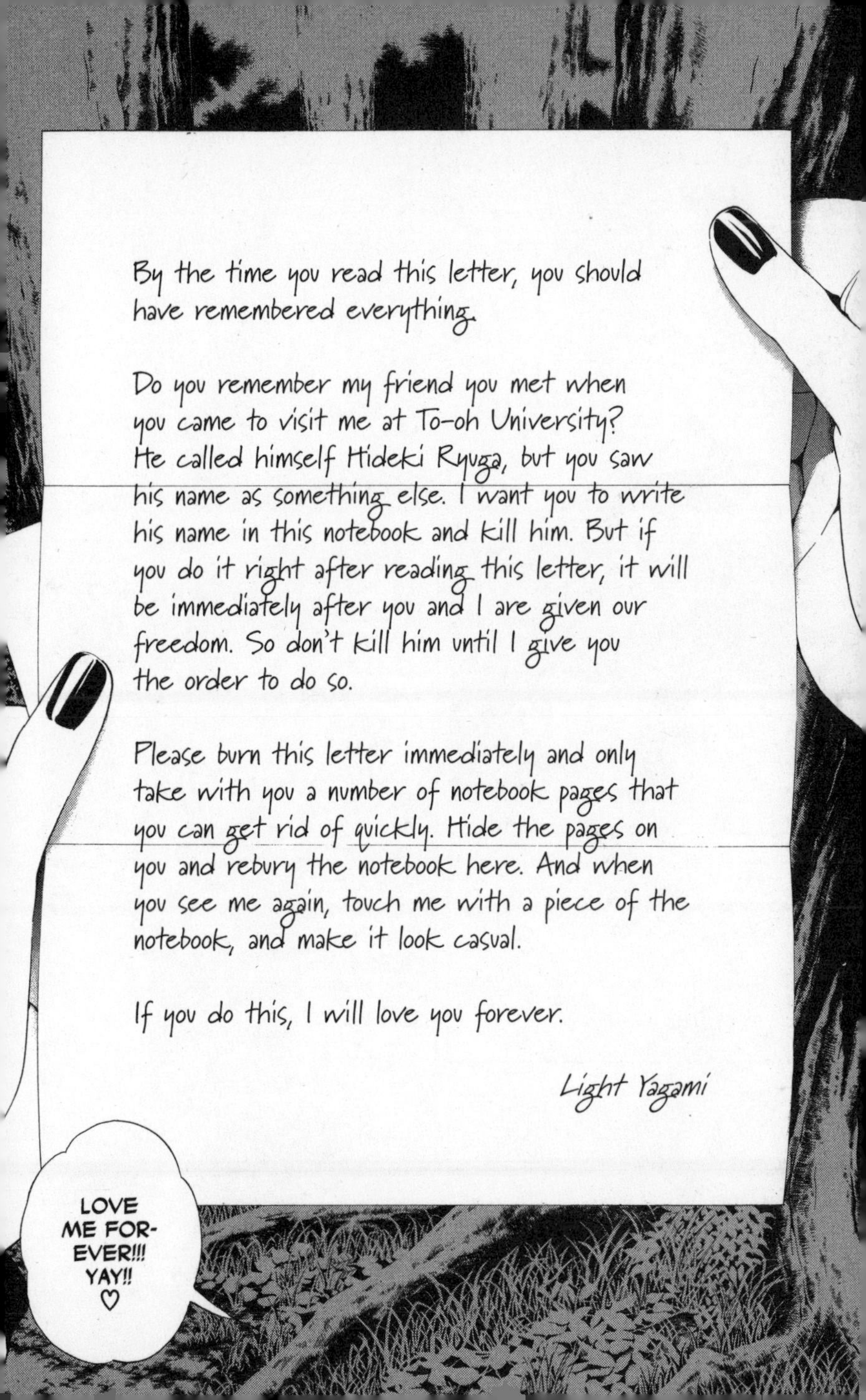
By the time you read this letter, you should have remembered everything.
Do you remember my friend you met when you came to visit me at To-oh University? He called himself Hideki Ryuga, but you saw his name as something else. I want you to write his name in this notebook and kill him. But if you do it right after reading this letter, it will be immediately after you and I are given our freedom. So don't kill him until I give you the order to do so.
Please burn this letter immediately and only take with you a number of notebook pages that you can get rid of quickly. Hide the pages on you and rebury the notebook here. And when you see me again, touch me with a piece of the notebook, and make it look casual.
If you do this, I will love you forever.
Light Yagami
LOVE ME FOR-EVER!!! YAY!! ♡

READ THIS WAY

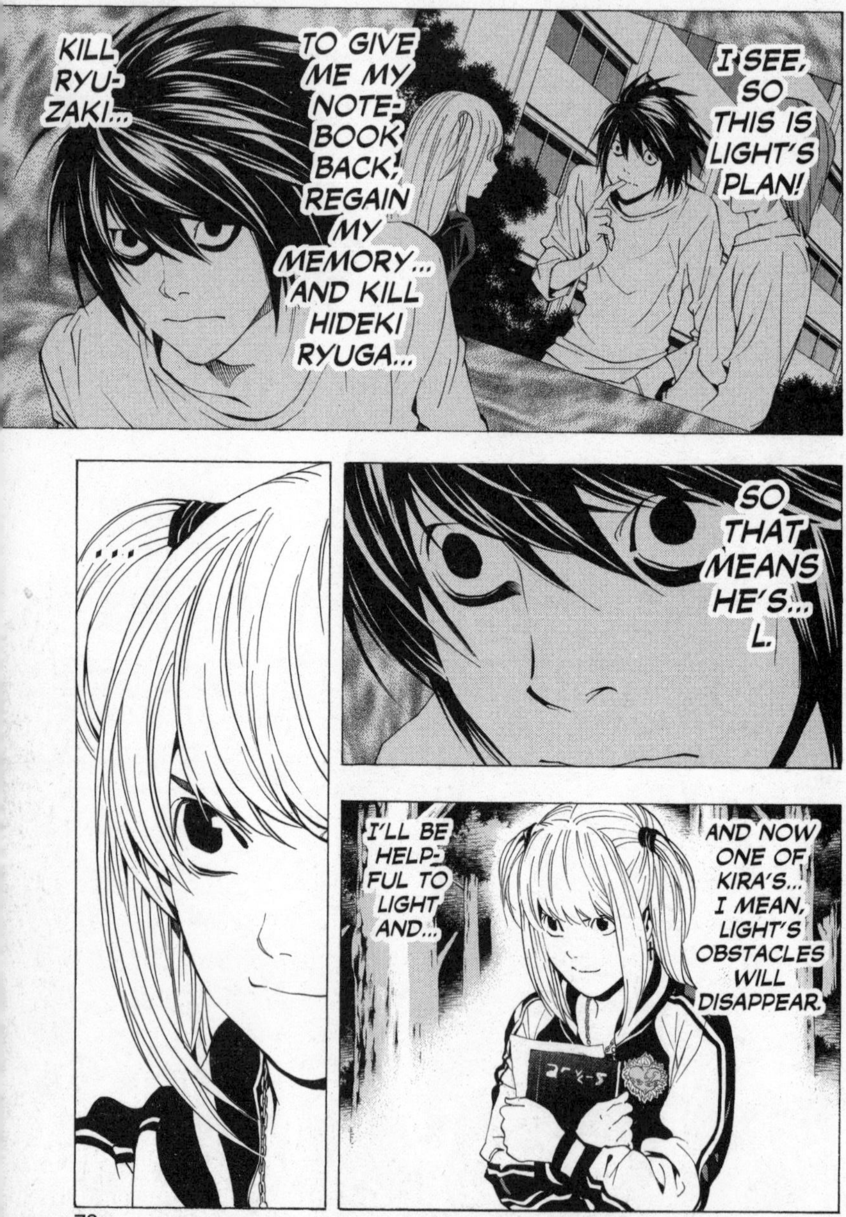
I SEE, SO THIS IS LIGHT'S PLAN!
TO GIVE ME MY NOTE-BOOK BACK, REGAIN MY MEMORY... AND KILL HIDEKI RYUGA...
KILL RYU-ZAKI...
SO THAT MEANS HE'S... L.
AND NOW ONE OF KIRA'S... I MEAN, LIGHT'S OBSTACLES WILL DISAPPEAR.
I'LL BE HELP-FUL TO LIGHT AND...
...

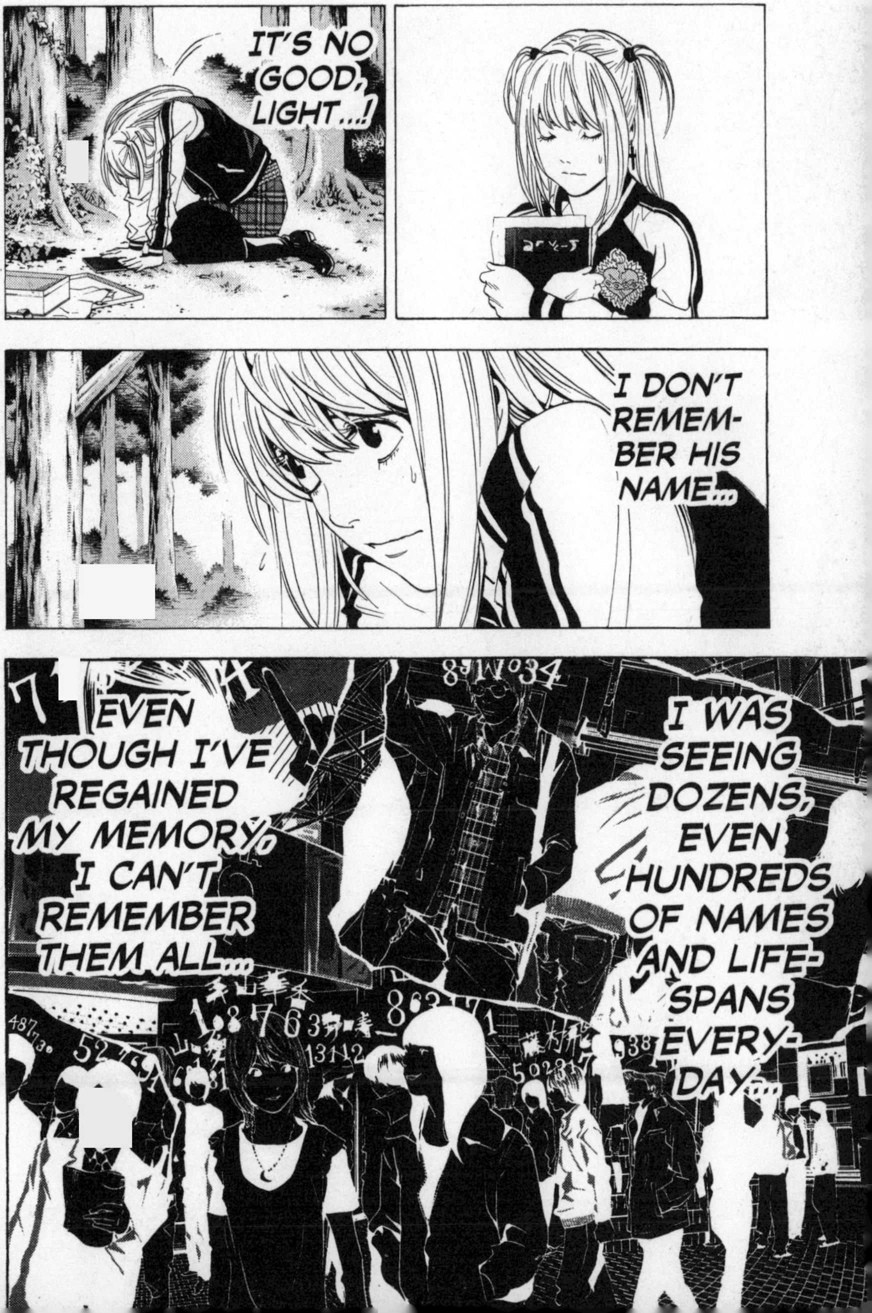
IT'S NO GOOD, LIGHT...!
I DON'T REMEMBER HIS NAME...
I WAS SEEING DOZENS, EVEN HUNDREDS OF NAMES AND LIFESPANS EVERYDAY...
EVEN THOUGH I'VE REGAINED MY MEMORY, I CAN'T REMEMBER THEM ALL...

READ THIS WAY

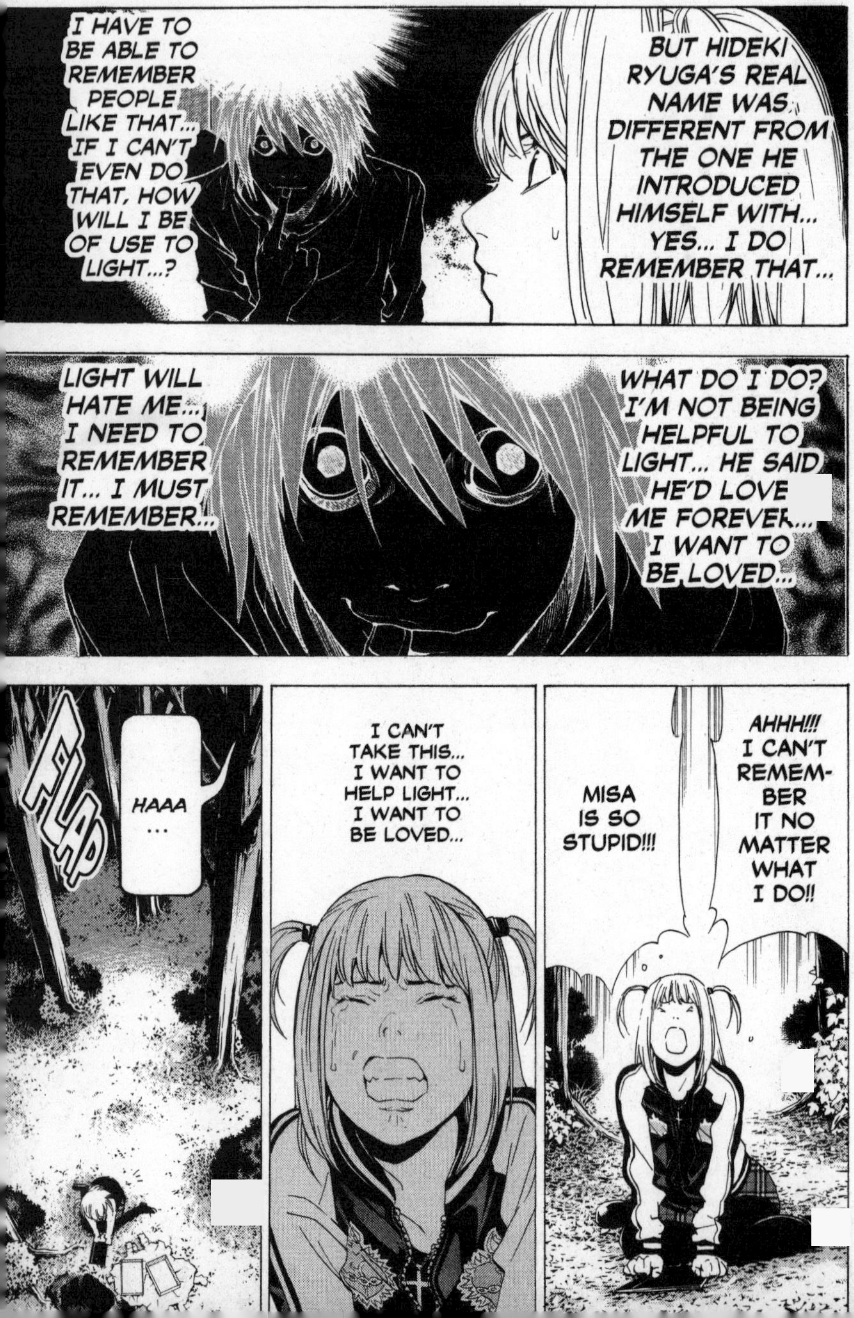
BUT HIDEKI RYUGA'S REAL NAME WAS DIFFERENT FROM THE ONE HE INTRODUCED HIMSELF WITH... YES... I DO REMEMBER THAT...
I HAVE TO BE ABLE TO REMEMBER PEOPLE LIKE THAT... IF I CAN'T EVEN DO THAT, HOW WILL I BE OF USE TO LIGHT...?
WHAT DO I DO? I'M NOT BEING HELPFUL TO LIGHT... HE SAID HE'D LOVE ME FOREVER... I WANT TO BE LOVED...
LIGHT WILL HATE ME... I NEED TO REMEMBER IT... I MUST REMEMBER...
AHHH!!! I CAN'T REMEM-BER IT NO MATTER WHAT I DO!!
MISA IS SO STUPID!!!
I CAN'T TAKE THIS... I WANT TO HELP LIGHT... I WANT TO BE LOVED...
HAAA ...
FLAP

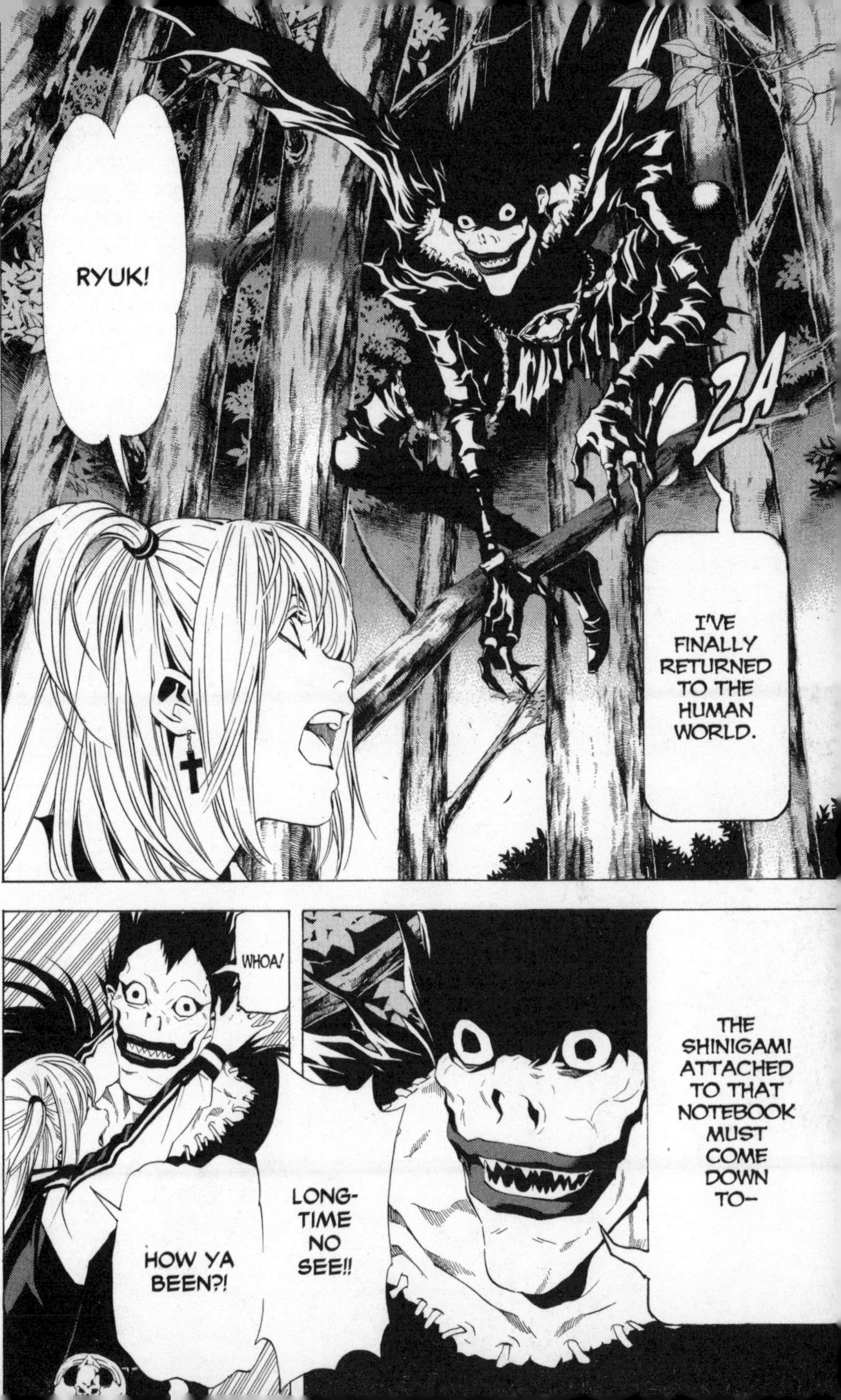
ZA
I'VE FINALLY RETURNED TO THE HUMAN WORLD.
RYUK!
THE SHINIGAMI ATTACHED TO THAT NOTEBOOK MUST COME DOWN TO–
LONG-TIME NO SEE!!
HOW YA BEEN?!
WHOA!

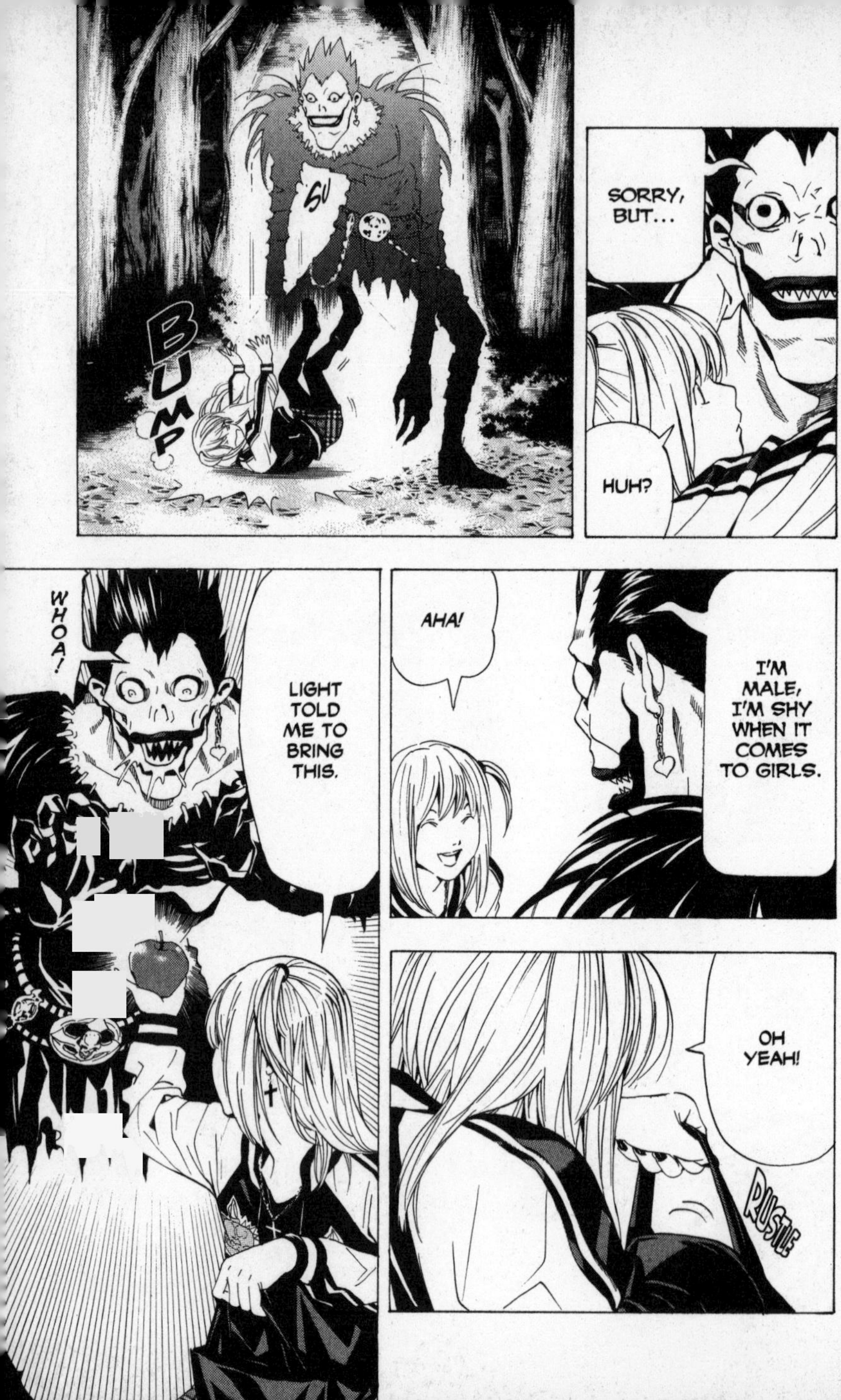
SORRY, BUT...
HUH?
BUMP
I'M MALE, I'M SHY WHEN IT COMES TO GIRLS.
AHA!
OH YEAH!
RUSTLE
LIGHT TOLD ME TO BRING THIS.
WHOA!

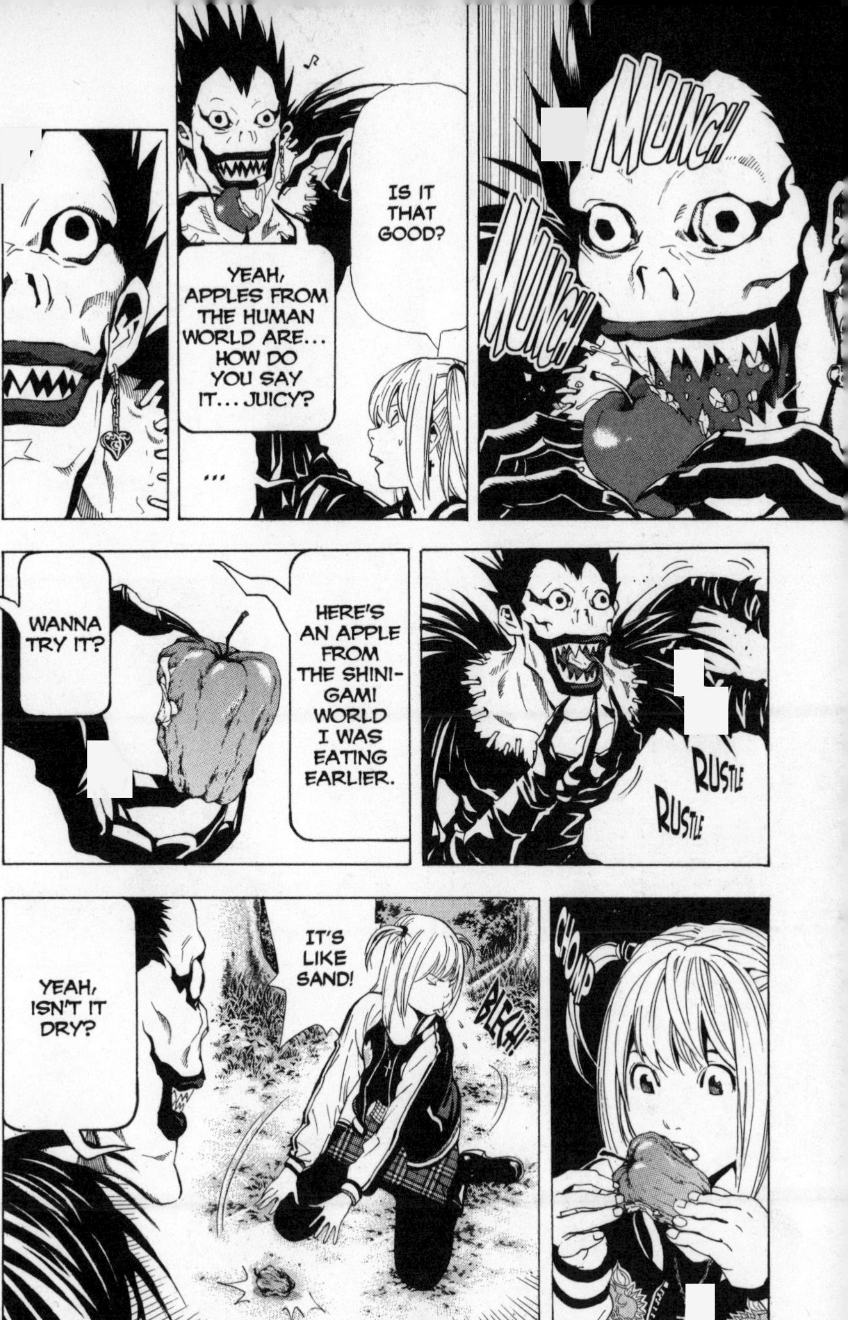
MUNCH
MUNCH
IS IT THAT GOOD?
YEAH, APPLES FROM THE HUMAN WORLD ARE... HOW DO YOU SAY IT... JUICY?
...
RUSTLE
RUSTLE
HERE'S AN APPLE FROM THE SHINIGAMI WORLD I WAS EATING EARLIER.
WANNA TRY IT?
CHOMP
BLEH!
IT'S LIKE SAND!
YEAH, ISN'T IT DRY?

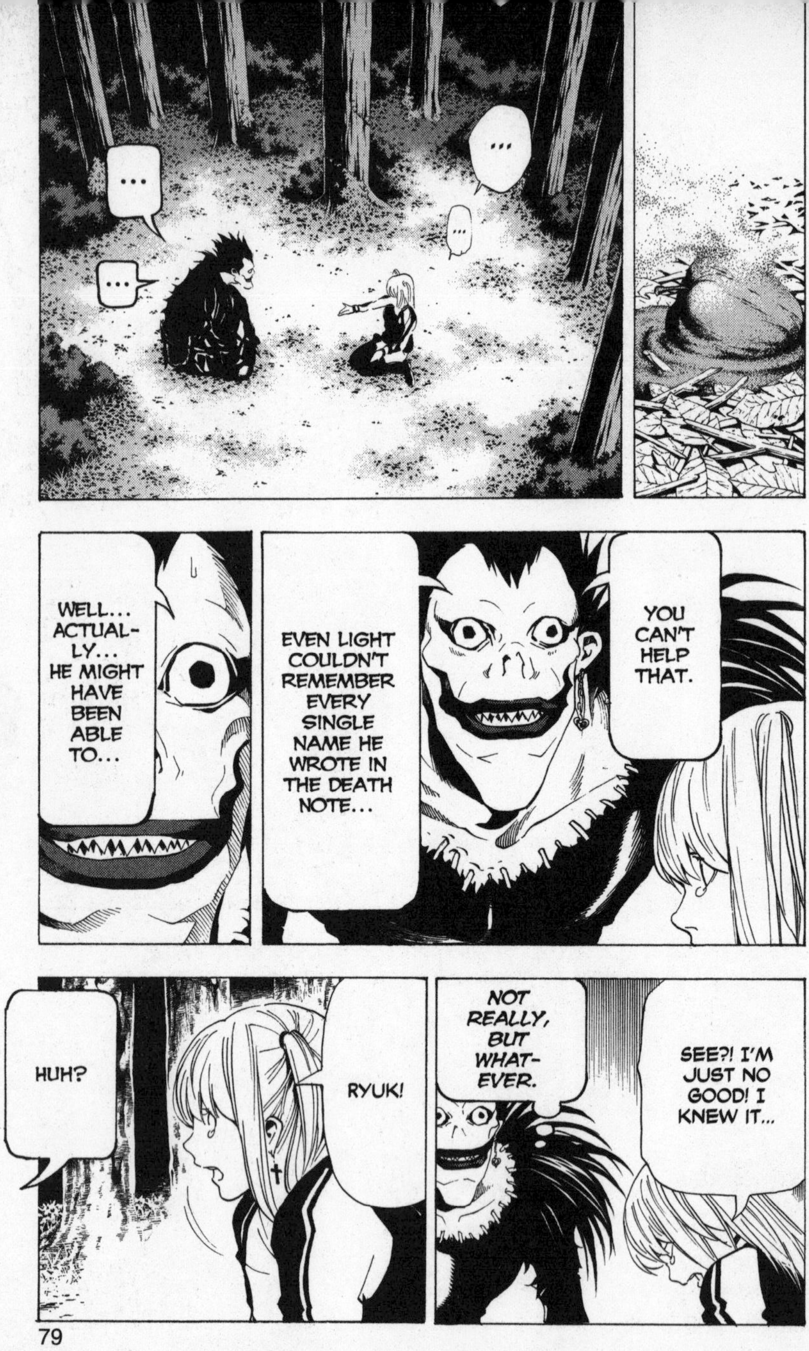
...
...
...
...
YOU CAN'T HELP THAT.
EVEN LIGHT COULDN'T REMEMBER EVERY SINGLE NAME HE WROTE IN THE DEATH NOTE...
WELL... ACTUAL-LY... HE MIGHT HAVE BEEN ABLE TO...
SEE?! I'M JUST NO GOOD! I KNEW IT...
NOT REALLY, BUT WHAT-EVER.
RYUK!
HUH?

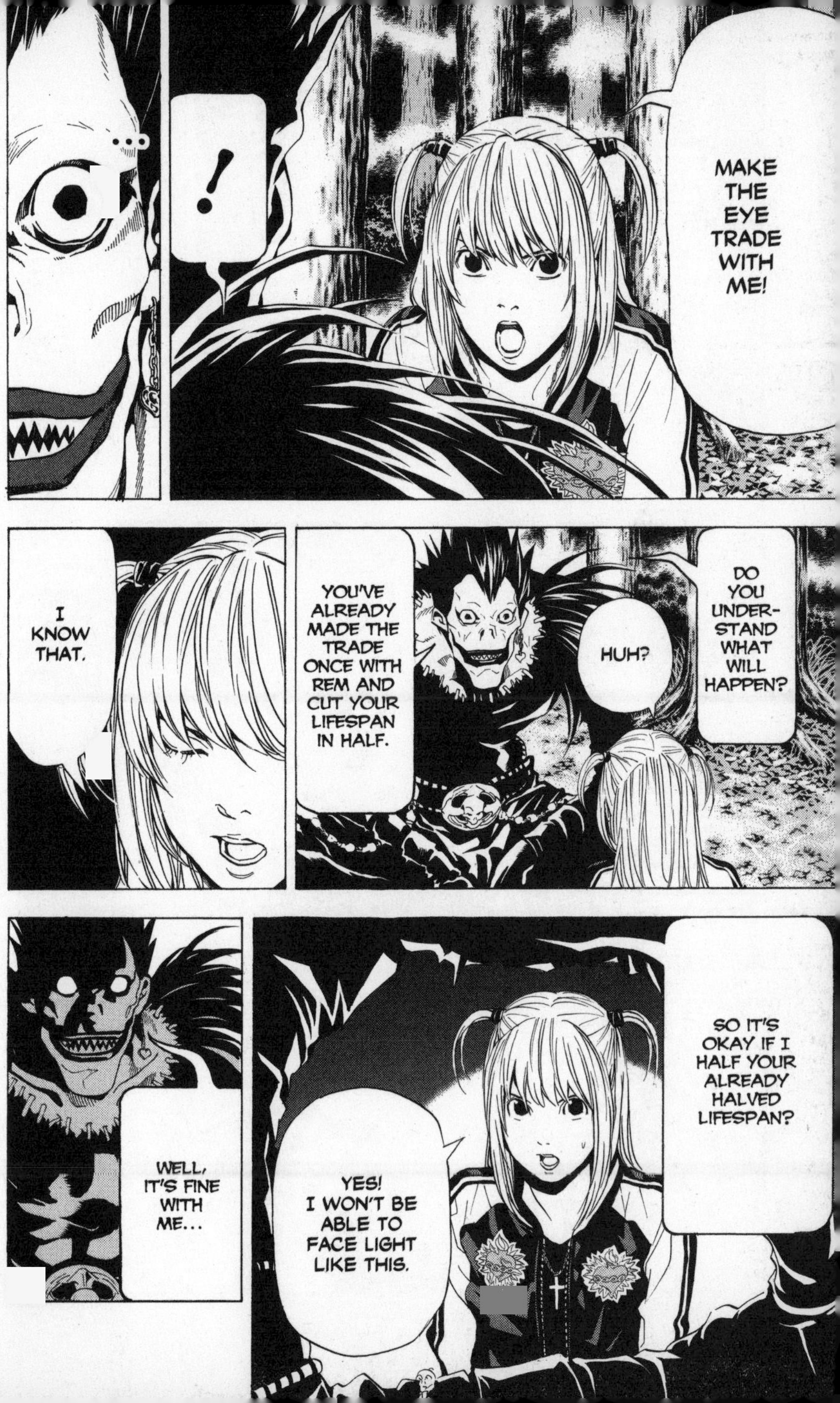
MAKE THE EYE TRADE WITH ME!
!
...
DO YOU UNDER-STAND WHAT WILL HAPPEN?
HUH?
YOU'VE ALREADY MADE THE TRADE ONCE WITH REM AND CUT YOUR LIFESPAN IN HALF.
I KNOW THAT.
SO IT'S OKAY IF I HALF YOUR ALREADY HALVED LIFESPAN?
YES! I WON'T BE ABLE TO FACE LIGHT LIKE THIS.
WELL, IT'S FINE WITH ME...

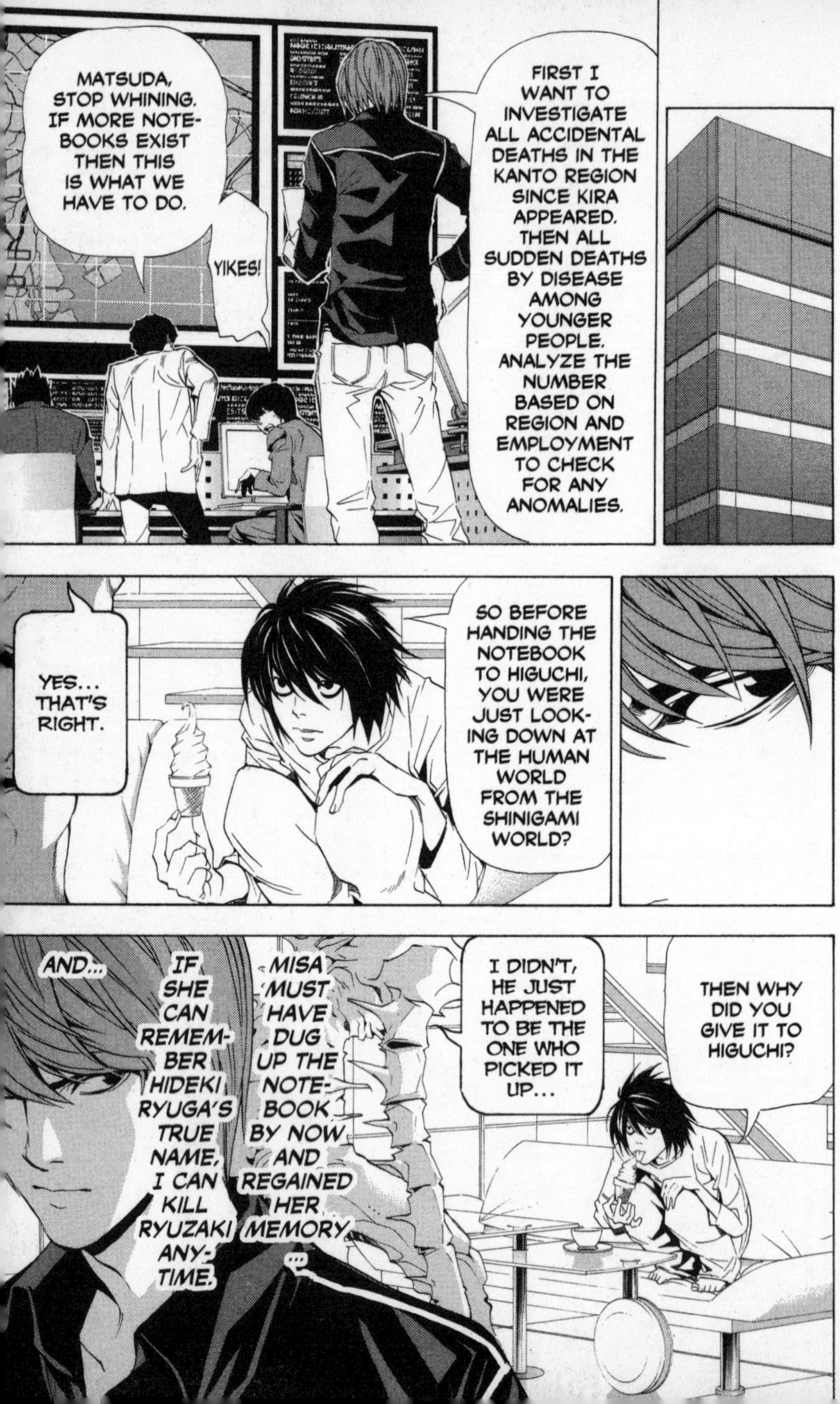
FIRST I WANT TO INVESTIGATE ALL ACCIDENTAL DEATHS IN THE KANTO REGION SINCE KIRA APPEARED. THEN ALL SUDDEN DEATHS BY DISEASE AMONG YOUNGER PEOPLE. ANALYZE THE NUMBER BASED ON REGION AND EMPLOYMENT TO CHECK FOR ANY ANOMALIES.
YIKES!
MATSUDA, STOP WHINING. IF MORE NOTE-BOOKS EXIST THEN THIS IS WHAT WE HAVE TO DO.
SO BEFORE HANDING THE NOTEBOOK TO HIGUCHI, YOU WERE JUST LOOK-ING DOWN AT THE HUMAN WORLD FROM THE SHINIGAMI WORLD?
YES... THAT'S RIGHT.
THEN WHY DID YOU GIVE IT TO HIGUCHI?
I DIDN'T, HE JUST HAPPENED TO BE THE ONE WHO PICKED IT UP...
MISA MUST HAVE DUG UP THE NOTE-BOOK BY NOW AND REGAINED HER MEMORY...
AND...
IF SHE CAN REMEM-BER HIDEKI RYUGA'S TRUE NAME, I CAN KILL RYUZAKI ANY-TIME.

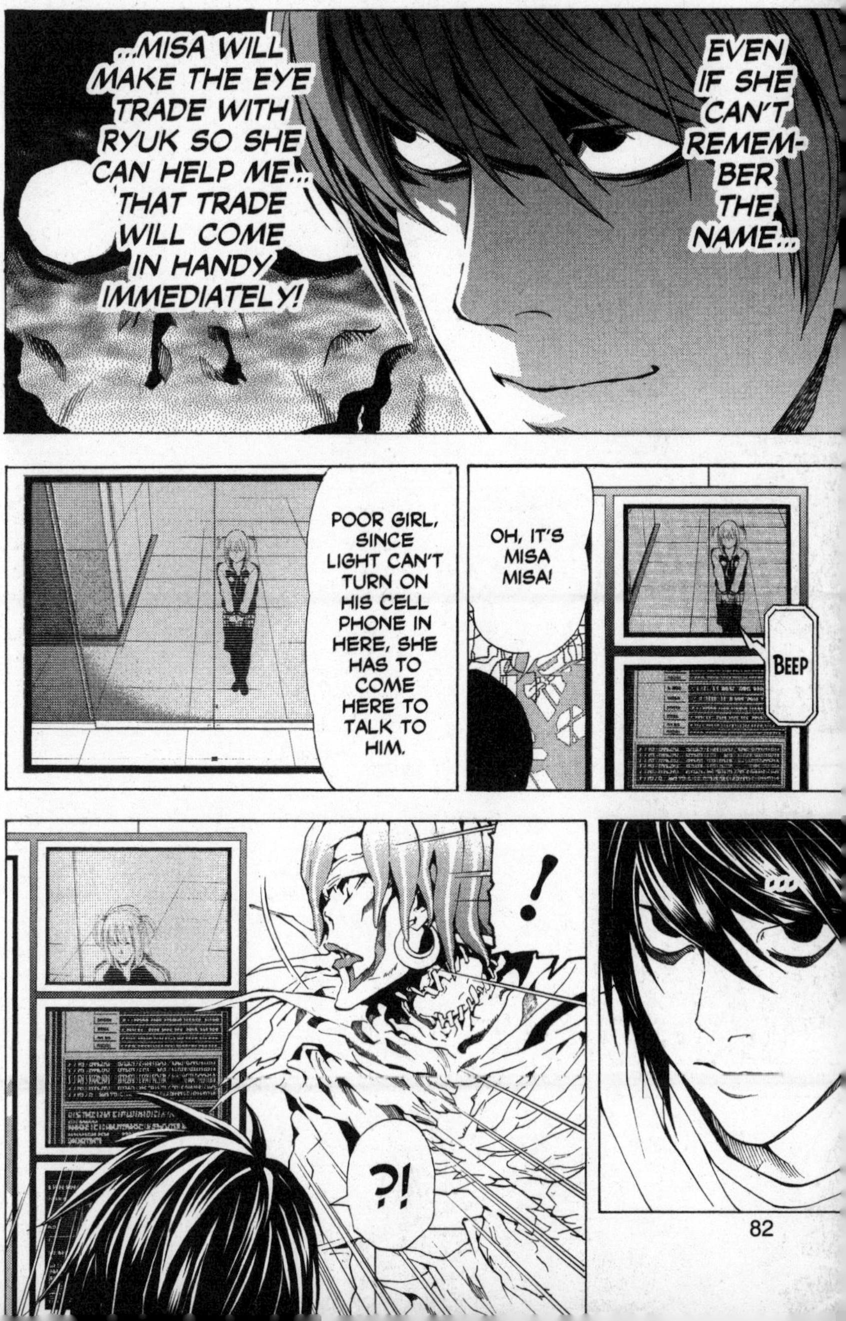
EVEN IF SHE CAN'T REMEMBER THE NAME...
...MISA WILL MAKE THE EYE TRADE WITH RYUK SO SHE CAN HELP ME... THAT TRADE WILL COME IN HANDY IMMEDIATELY!
BEEP
OH, IT'S MISA MISA!
POOR GIRL, SINCE LIGHT CAN'T TURN ON HIS CELL PHONE IN HERE, SHE HAS TO COME HERE TO TALK TO HIM.
...
!
?!

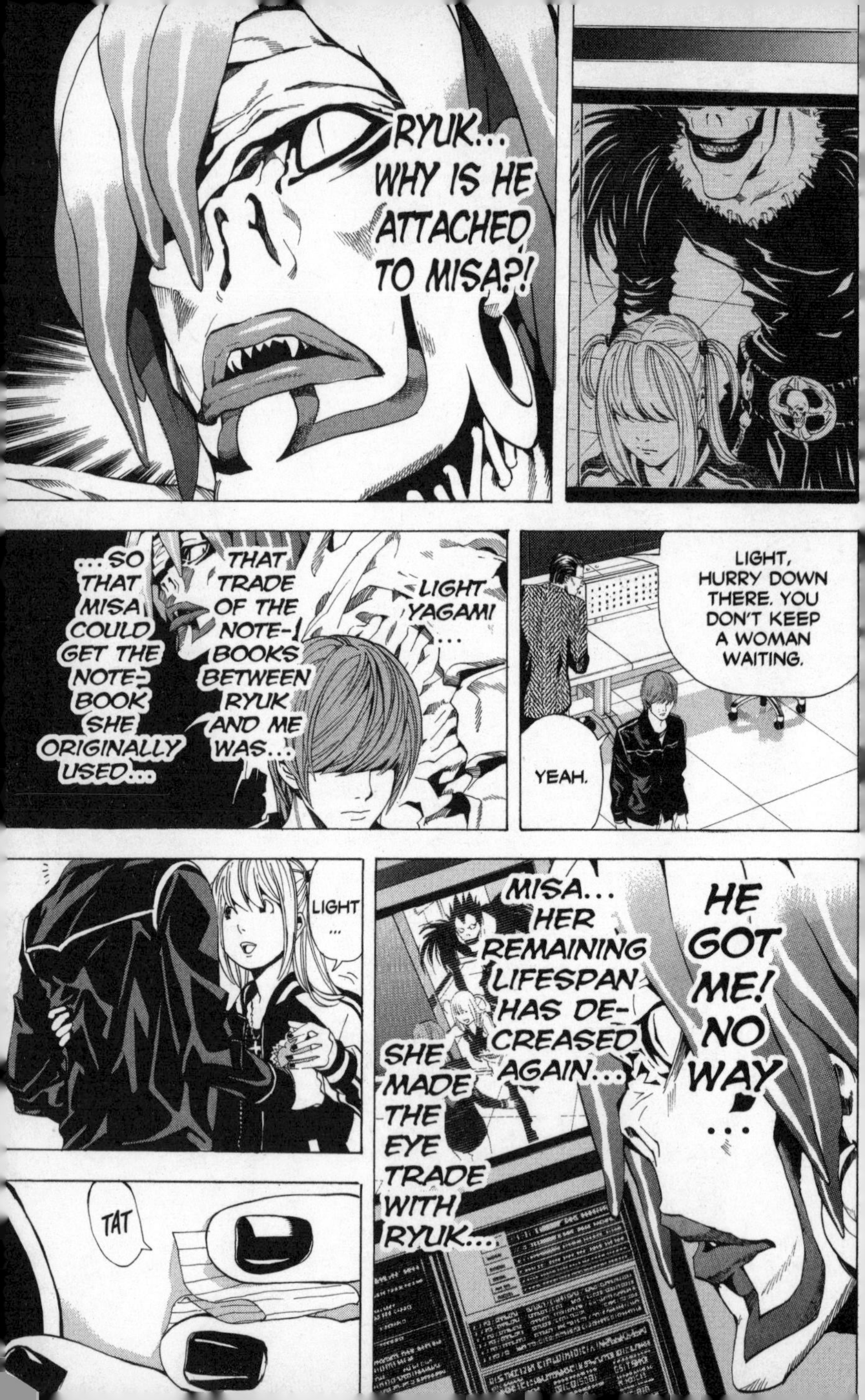
RYUK... WHY IS HE ATTACHED TO MISA?!
LIGHT, HURRY DOWN THERE. YOU DON'T KEEP A WOMAN WAITING.
YEAH.
LIGHT YAGAMI...
THAT TRADE OF THE NOTE-BOOKS BETWEEN RYUK AND ME WAS...
...SO THAT MISA COULD GET THE NOTE-BOOK SHE ORIGINALLY USED...
HE GOT ME! NO WAY...
MISA... HER REMAINING LIFESPAN HAS DE-CREASED AGAIN...
SHE MADE THE EYE TRADE WITH RYUK...
LIGHT...
TAT

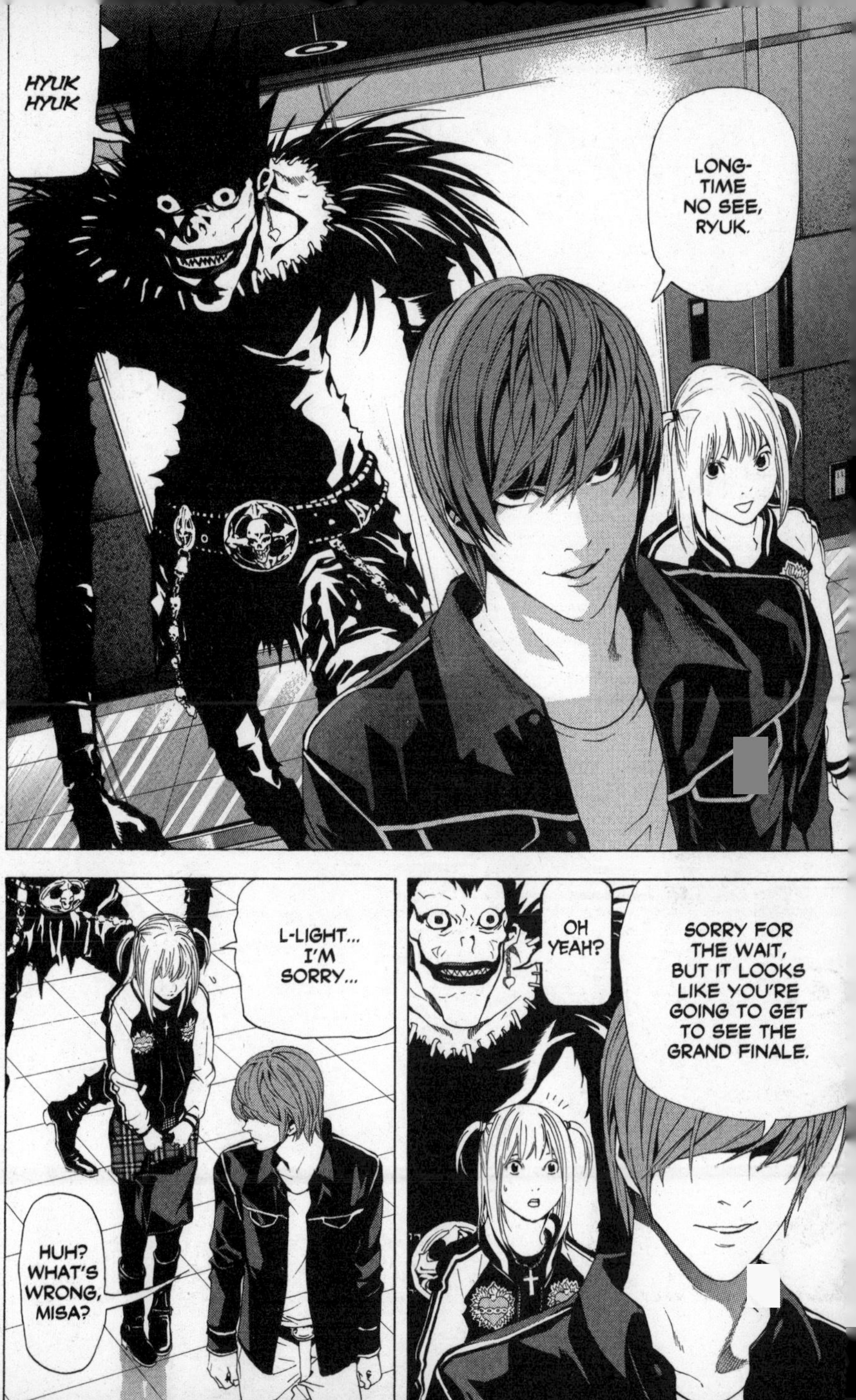
LONG-TIME NO SEE, RYUK.
HYUK HYUK
SORRY FOR THE WAIT, BUT IT LOOKS LIKE YOU'RE GOING TO GET TO SEE THE GRAND FINALE.
OH YEAH?
L-LIGHT... I'M SORRY...
HUH? WHAT'S WRONG, MISA?

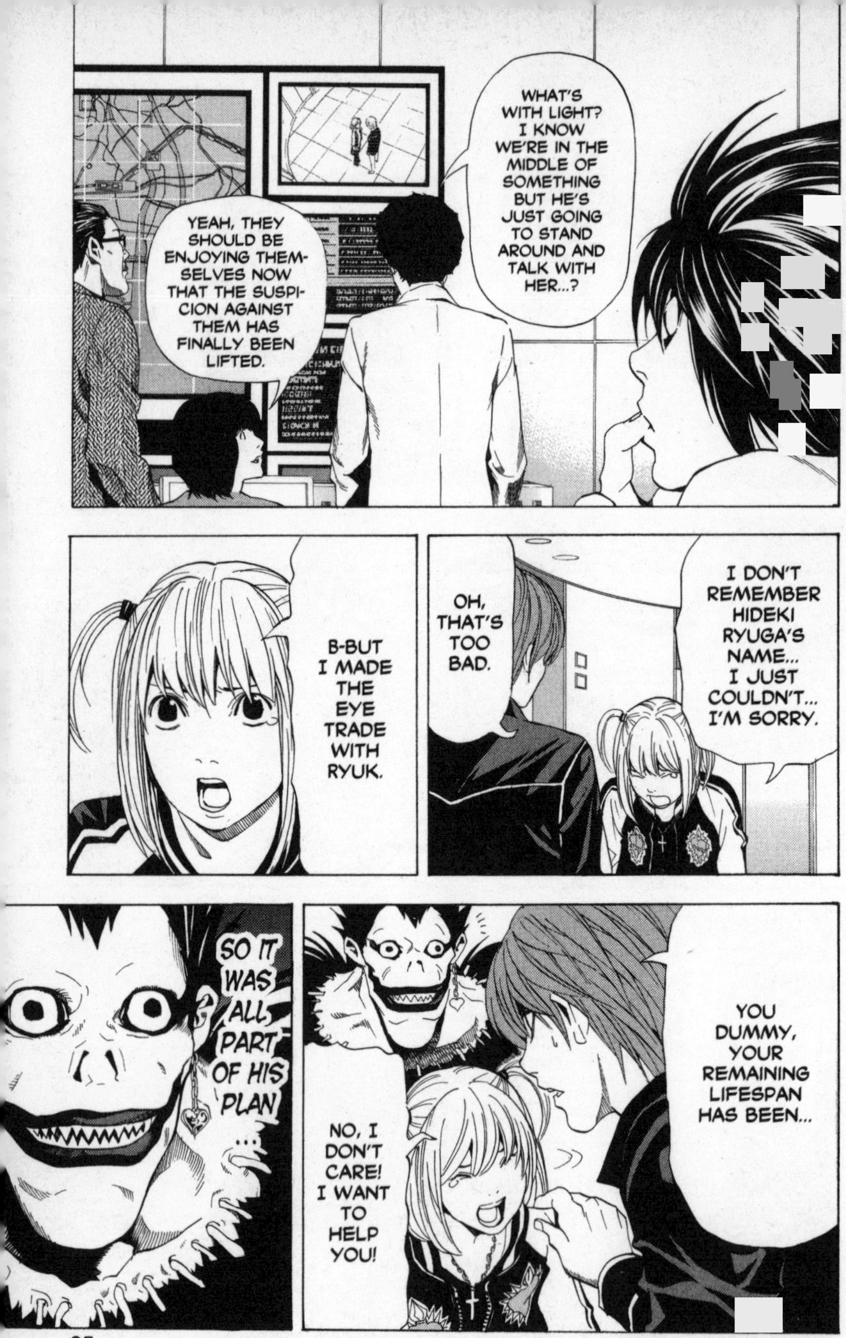
WHAT'S WITH LIGHT? I KNOW WE'RE IN THE MIDDLE OF SOMETHING BUT HE'S JUST GOING TO STAND AROUND AND TALK WITH HER...?
YEAH, THEY SHOULD BE ENJOYING THEM-SELVES NOW THAT THE SUSPI-CION AGAINST THEM HAS FINALLY BEEN LIFTED.
I DON'T REMEMBER HIDEKI RYUGA'S NAME... I JUST COULDN'T... I'M SORRY.
OH, THAT'S TOO BAD.
B-BUT I MADE THE EYE TRADE WITH RYUK.
YOU DUMMY, YOUR REMAINING LIFESPAN HAS BEEN...
NO, I DON'T CARE! I WANT TO HELP YOU!
SO IT WAS ALL PART OF HIS PLAN...

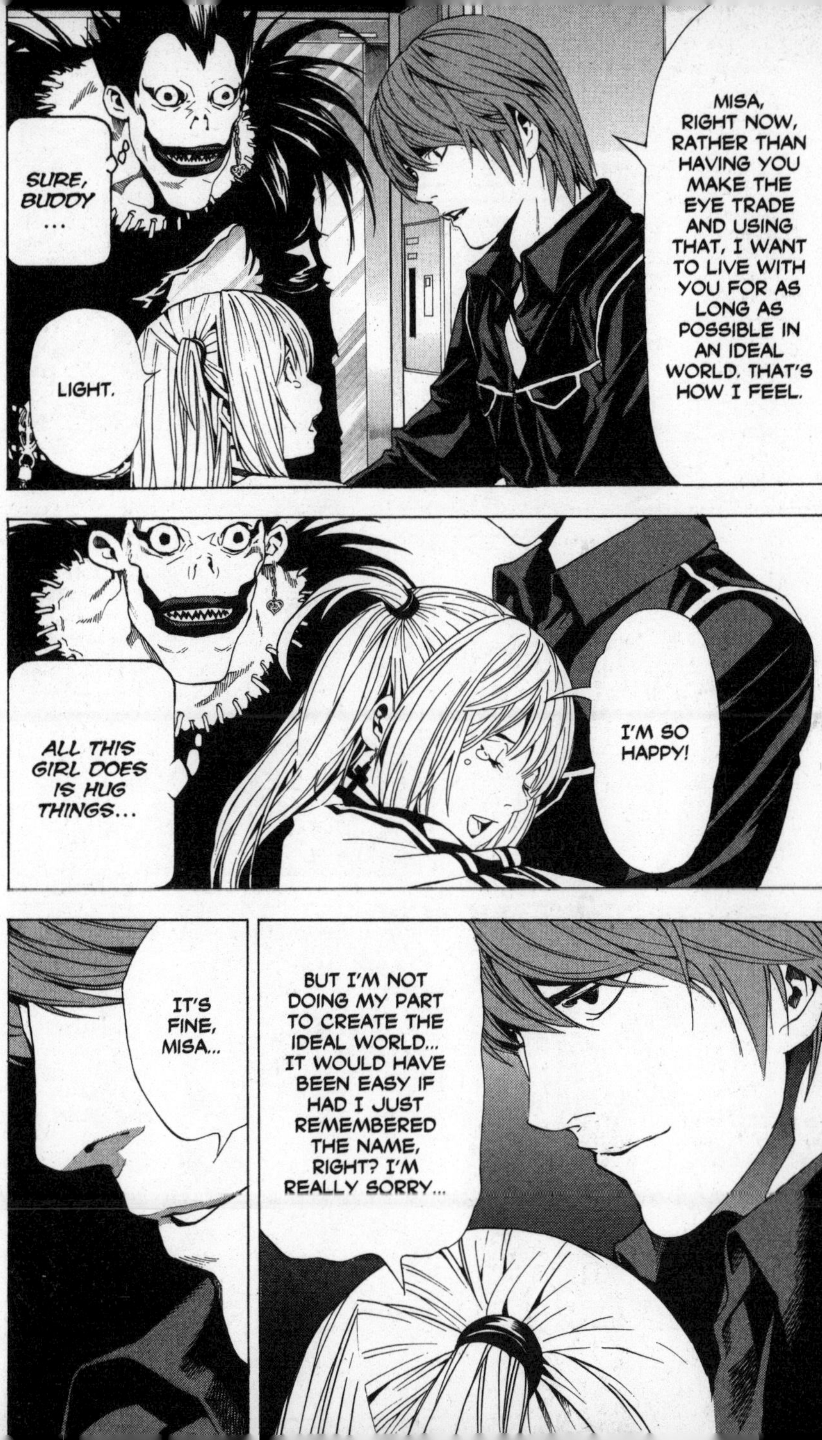
MISA, RIGHT NOW, RATHER THAN HAVING YOU MAKE THE EYE TRADE AND USING THAT, I WANT TO LIVE WITH YOU FOR AS LONG AS POSSIBLE IN AN IDEAL WORLD. THAT'S HOW I FEEL.
SURE, BUDDY ...
LIGHT.
I'M SO HAPPY!
ALL THIS GIRL DOES IS HUG THINGS...
BUT I'M NOT DOING MY PART TO CREATE THE IDEAL WORLD... IT WOULD HAVE BEEN EASY IF HAD I JUST REMEMBERED THE NAME, RIGHT? I'M REALLY SORRY...
IT'S FINE, MISA...

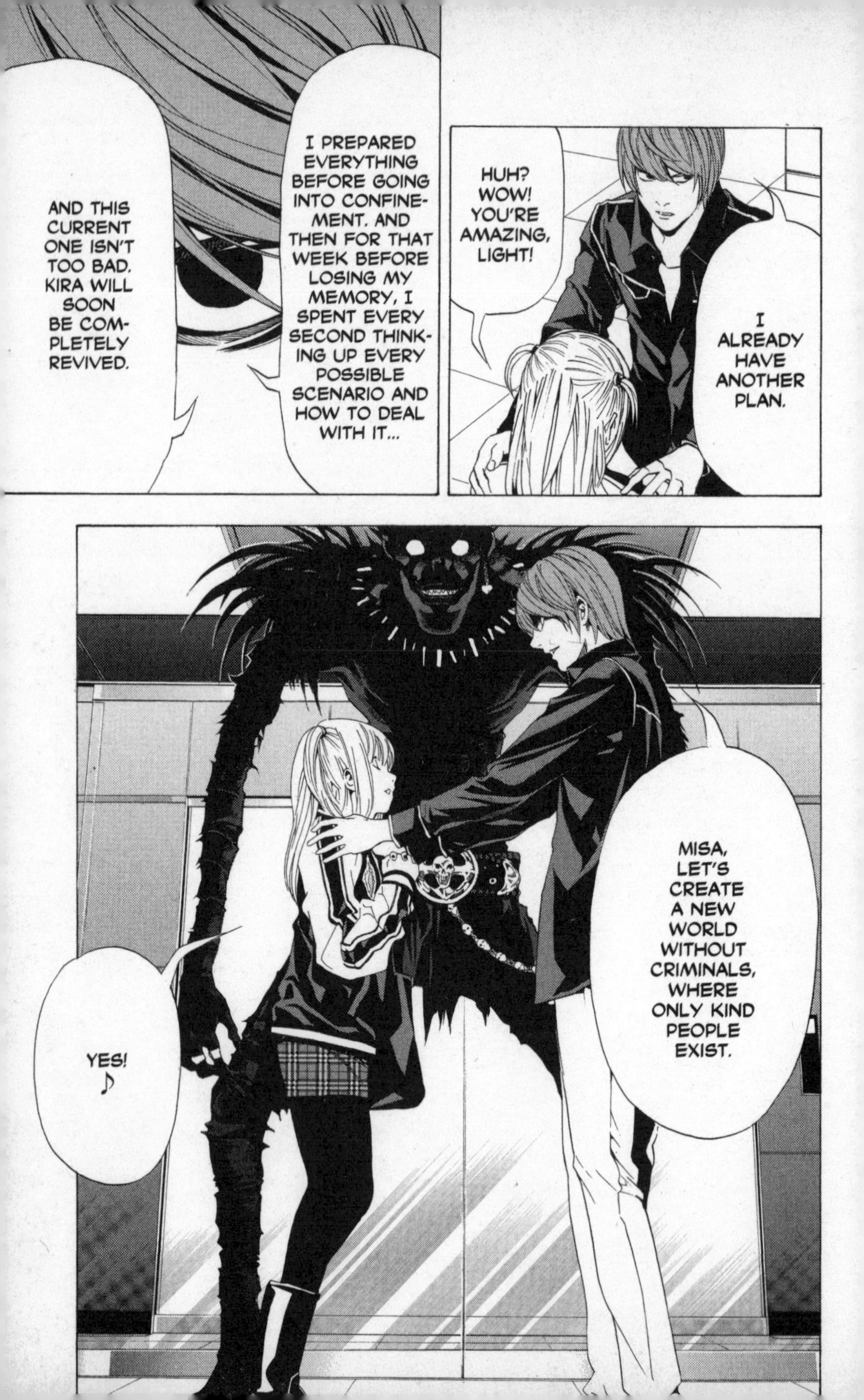
I ALREADY HAVE ANOTHER PLAN.
HUH? WOW! YOU'RE AMAZING, LIGHT!
I PREPARED EVERYTHING BEFORE GOING INTO CONFINEMENT. AND THEN FOR THAT WEEK BEFORE LOSING MY MEMORY, I SPENT EVERY SECOND THINKING UP EVERY POSSIBLE SCENARIO AND HOW TO DEAL WITH IT...
AND THIS CURRENT ONE ISN'T TOO BAD. KIRA WILL SOON BE COMPLETELY REVIVED.
MISA, LET'S CREATE A NEW WORLD WITHOUT CRIMINALS, WHERE ONLY KIND PEOPLE EXIST.
YES! ♪

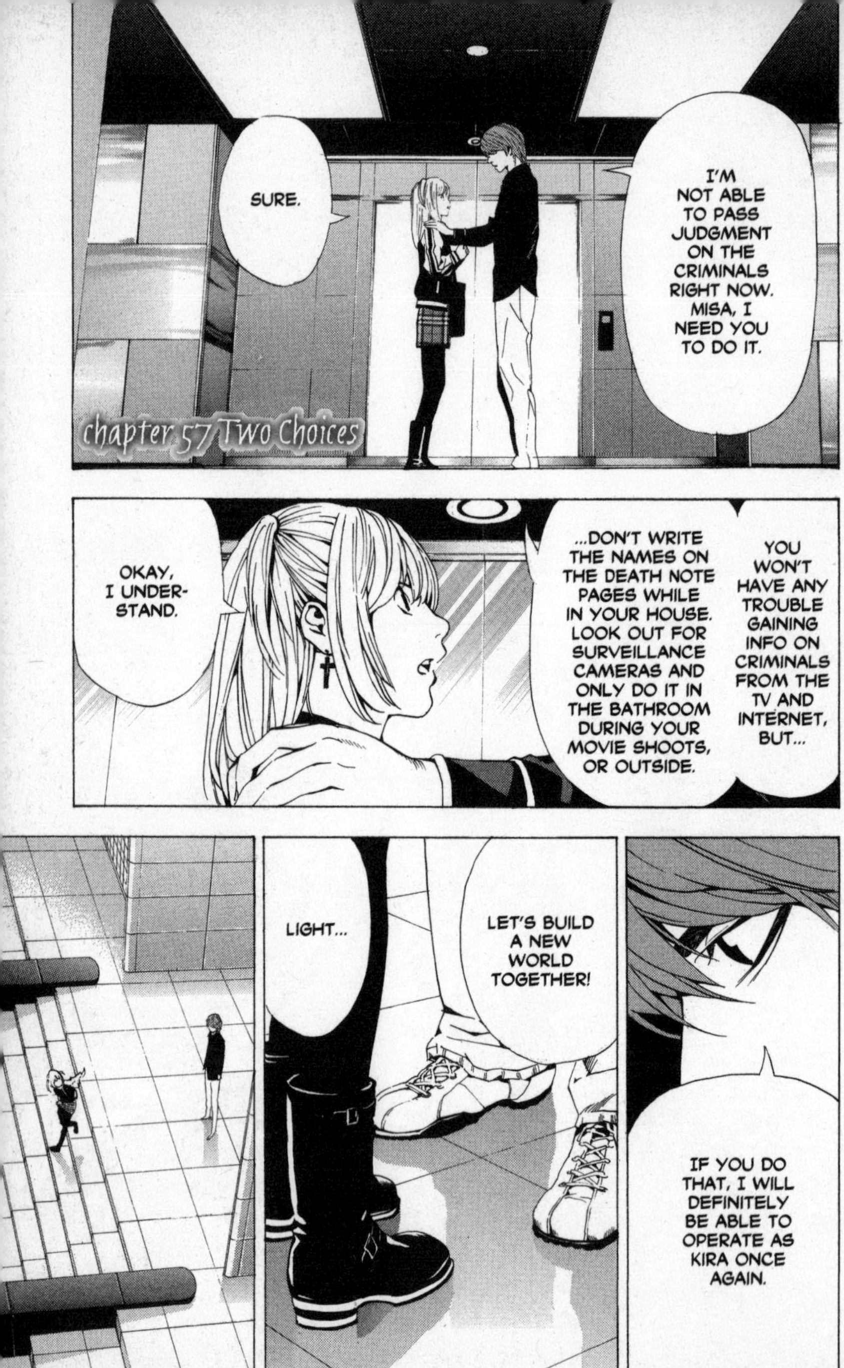
chapter 57 Two Choices
I'M NOT ABLE TO PASS JUDGMENT ON THE CRIMINALS RIGHT NOW. MISA, I NEED YOU TO DO IT.
SURE.
YOU WON'T HAVE ANY TROUBLE GAINING INFO ON CRIMINALS FROM THE TV AND INTERNET, BUT...
...DON'T WRITE THE NAMES ON THE DEATH NOTE PAGES WHILE IN YOUR HOUSE. LOOK OUT FOR SURVEILLANCE CAMERAS AND ONLY DO IT IN THE BATHROOM DURING YOUR MOVIE SHOOTS, OR OUTSIDE.
OKAY, I UNDERSTAND.
IF YOU DO THAT, I WILL DEFINITELY BE ABLE TO OPERATE AS KIRA ONCE AGAIN.
LET'S BUILD A NEW WORLD TOGETHER!
LIGHT...

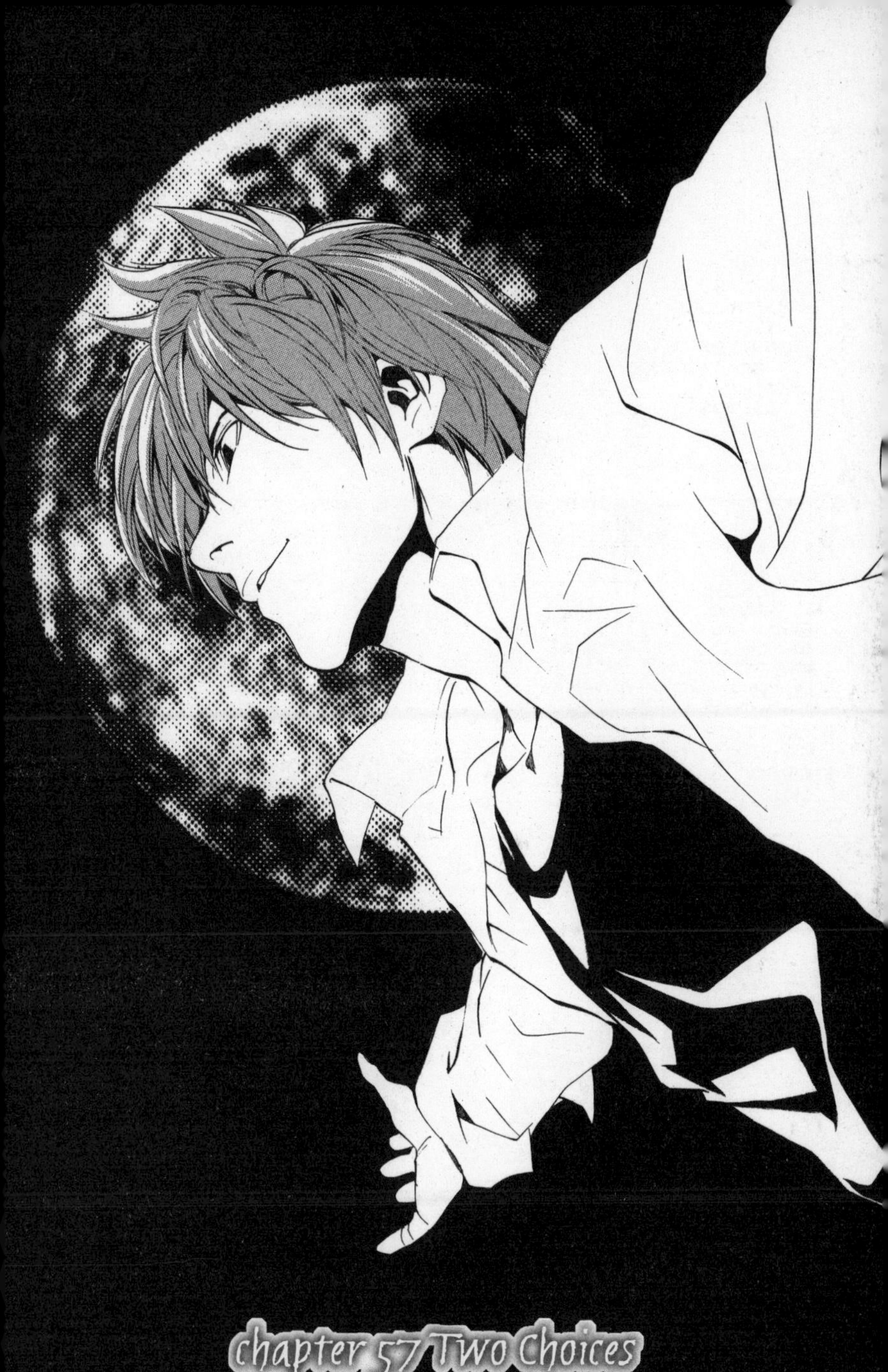

chapter 57 Two Choices

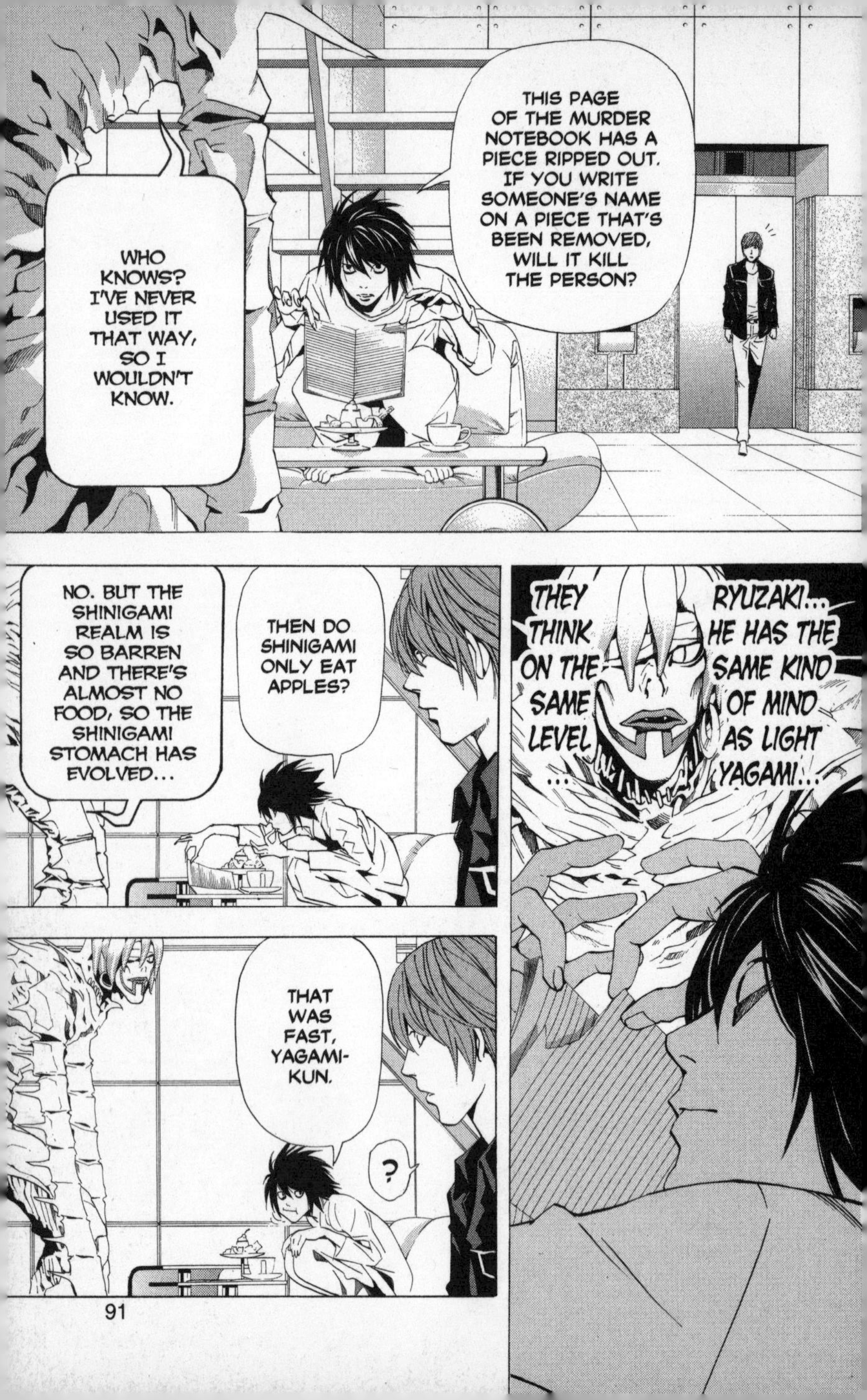
THIS PAGE OF THE MURDER NOTEBOOK HAS A PIECE RIPPED OUT. IF YOU WRITE SOMEONE'S NAME ON A PIECE THAT'S BEEN REMOVED, WILL IT KILL THE PERSON?
WHO KNOWS? I'VE NEVER USED IT THAT WAY, SO I WOULDN'T KNOW.
RYUZAKI... HE HAS THE SAME KIND OF MIND AS LIGHT YAGAMI...
THEY THINK ON THE SAME LEVEL...
THEN DO SHINIGAMI ONLY EAT APPLES?
NO. BUT THE SHINIGAMI REALM IS SO BARREN AND THERE'S ALMOST NO FOOD, SO THE SHINIGAMI STOMACH HAS EVOLVED...
THAT WAS FAST, YAGAMI-KUN.
?

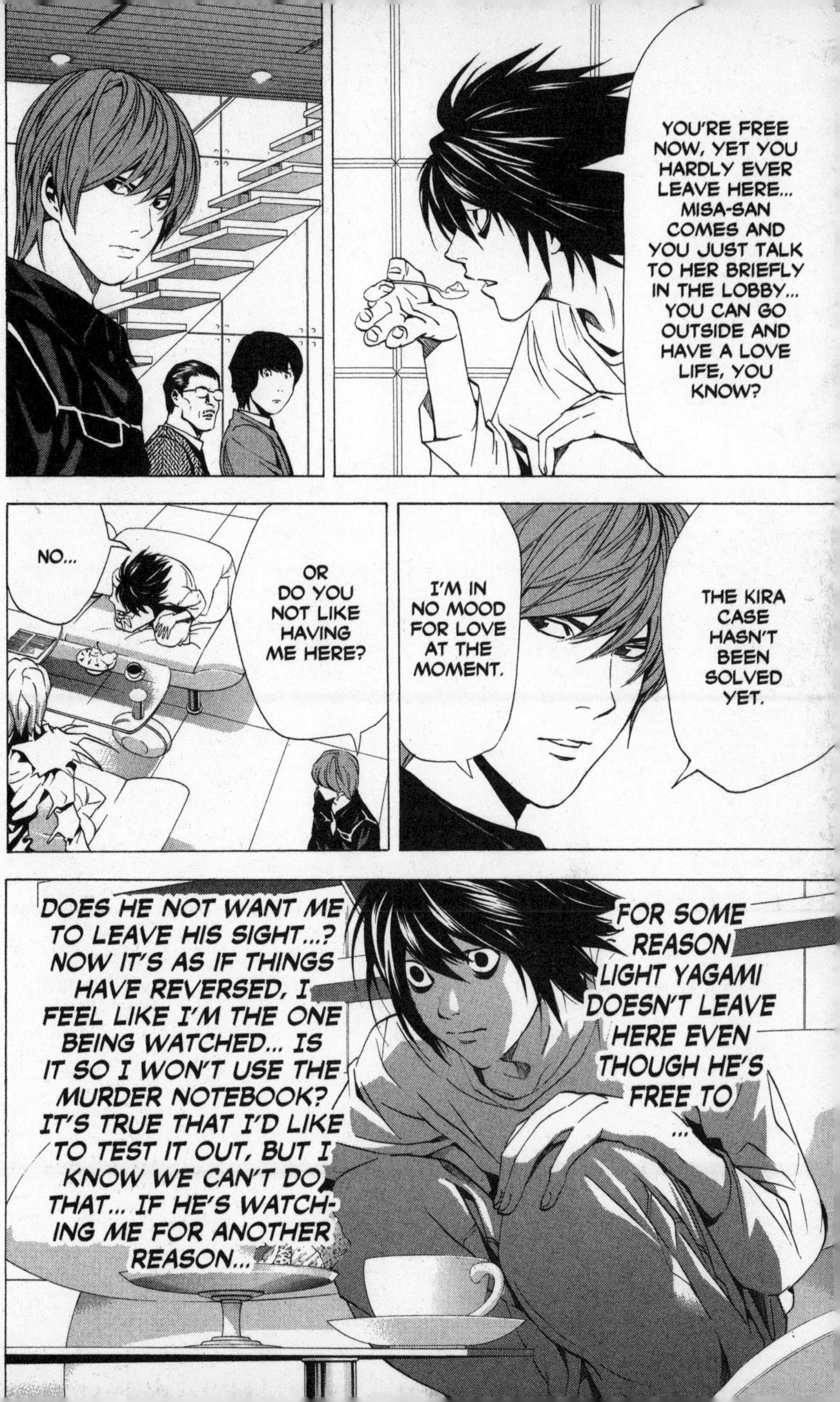
YOU'RE FREE NOW, YET YOU HARDLY EVER LEAVE HERE... MISA-SAN COMES AND YOU JUST TALK TO HER BRIEFLY IN THE LOBBY... YOU CAN GO OUTSIDE AND HAVE A LOVE LIFE, YOU KNOW?
THE KIRA CASE HASN'T BEEN SOLVED YET.
I'M IN NO MOOD FOR LOVE AT THE MOMENT.
OR DO YOU NOT LIKE HAVING ME HERE?
NO...
FOR SOME REASON LIGHT YAGAMI DOESN'T LEAVE HERE EVEN THOUGH HE'S FREE TO ...
DOES HE NOT WANT ME TO LEAVE HIS SIGHT...? NOW IT'S AS IF THINGS HAVE REVERSED, I FEEL LIKE I'M THE ONE BEING WATCHED... IS IT SO I WON'T USE THE MURDER NOTEBOOK? IT'S TRUE THAT I'D LIKE TO TEST IT OUT, BUT I KNOW WE CAN'T DO THAT... IF HE'S WATCHING ME FOR ANOTHER REASON...

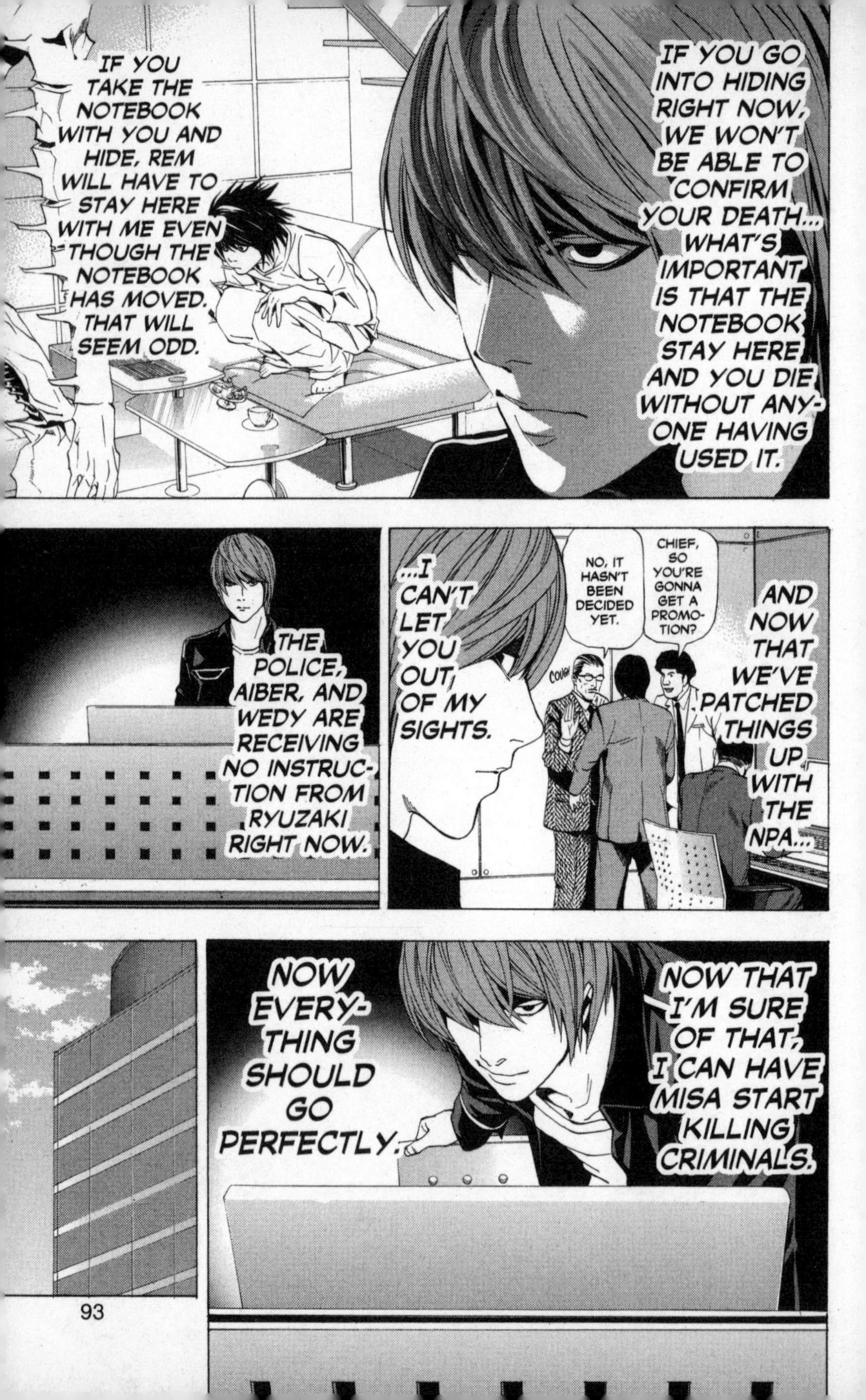
IF YOU GO INTO HIDING RIGHT NOW, WE WON'T BE ABLE TO CONFIRM YOUR DEATH... WHAT'S IMPORTANT IS THAT THE NOTEBOOK STAY HERE AND YOU DIE WITHOUT ANYONE HAVING USED IT.
IF YOU TAKE THE NOTEBOOK WITH YOU AND HIDE, REM WILL HAVE TO STAY HERE WITH ME EVEN THOUGH THE NOTEBOOK HAS MOVED. THAT WILL SEEM ODD.
AND NOW THAT WE'VE PATCHED THINGS UP WITH THE NPA...
CHIEF, SO YOU'RE GONNA GET A PROMOTION?
NO, IT HASN'T BEEN DECIDED YET.
COUGH
...I CAN'T LET YOU OUT OF MY SIGHTS.
THE POLICE, AIBER, AND WEDY ARE RECEIVING NO INSTRUCTION FROM RYUZAKI RIGHT NOW.
NOW THAT I'M SURE OF THAT, I CAN HAVE MISA START KILLING CRIMINALS.
NOW EVERYTHING SHOULD GO PERFECTLY.

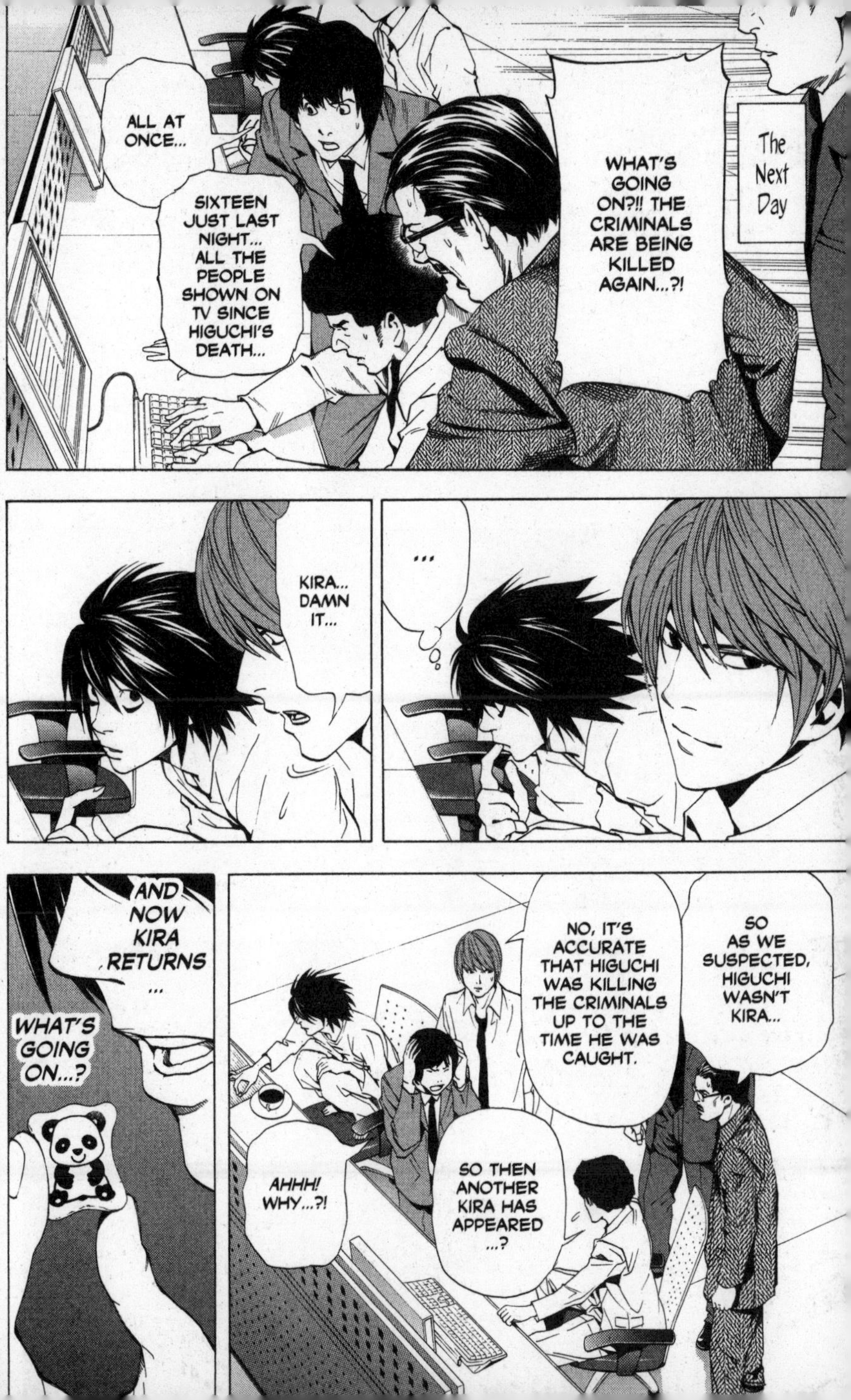
The Next Day
WHAT'S GOING ON?!! THE CRIMINALS ARE BEING KILLED AGAIN...?!
SIXTEEN JUST LAST NIGHT... ALL THE PEOPLE SHOWN ON TV SINCE HIGUCHI'S DEATH...
ALL AT ONCE...
...
KIRA... DAMN IT...
SO AS WE SUSPECTED, HIGUCHI WASN'T KIRA...
NO, IT'S ACCURATE THAT HIGUCHI WAS KILLING THE CRIMINALS UP TO THE TIME HE WAS CAUGHT.
SO THEN ANOTHER KIRA HAS APPEARED ...?
AHHH! WHY...?!
AND NOW KIRA RETURNS ...
WHAT'S GOING ON...?

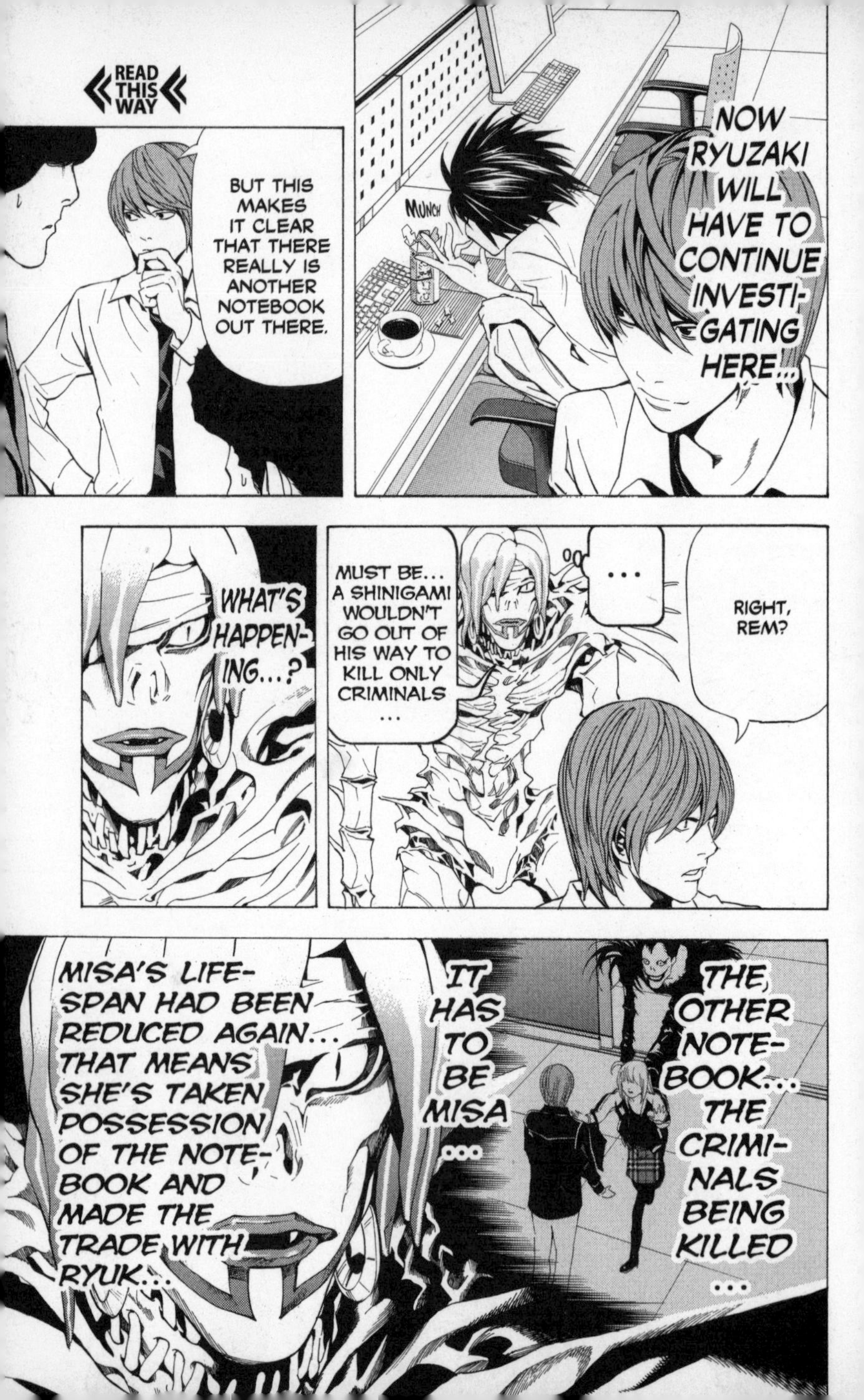
READ THIS WAY
NOW RYUZAKI WILL HAVE TO CONTINUE INVESTI-GATING HERE...
MUNCH
BUT THIS MAKES IT CLEAR THAT THERE REALLY IS ANOTHER NOTEBOOK OUT THERE.
RIGHT, REM?
...
MUST BE... A SHINIGAMI WOULDN'T GO OUT OF HIS WAY TO KILL ONLY CRIMINALS ...
WHAT'S HAPPEN-ING...?
THE OTHER NOTE-BOOK... THE CRIMI-NALS BEING KILLED ...
IT HAS TO BE MISA ...
MISA'S LIFE-SPAN HAD BEEN REDUCED AGAIN... THAT MEANS SHE'S TAKEN POSSESSION OF THE NOTE-BOOK AND MADE THE TRADE WITH RYUK...

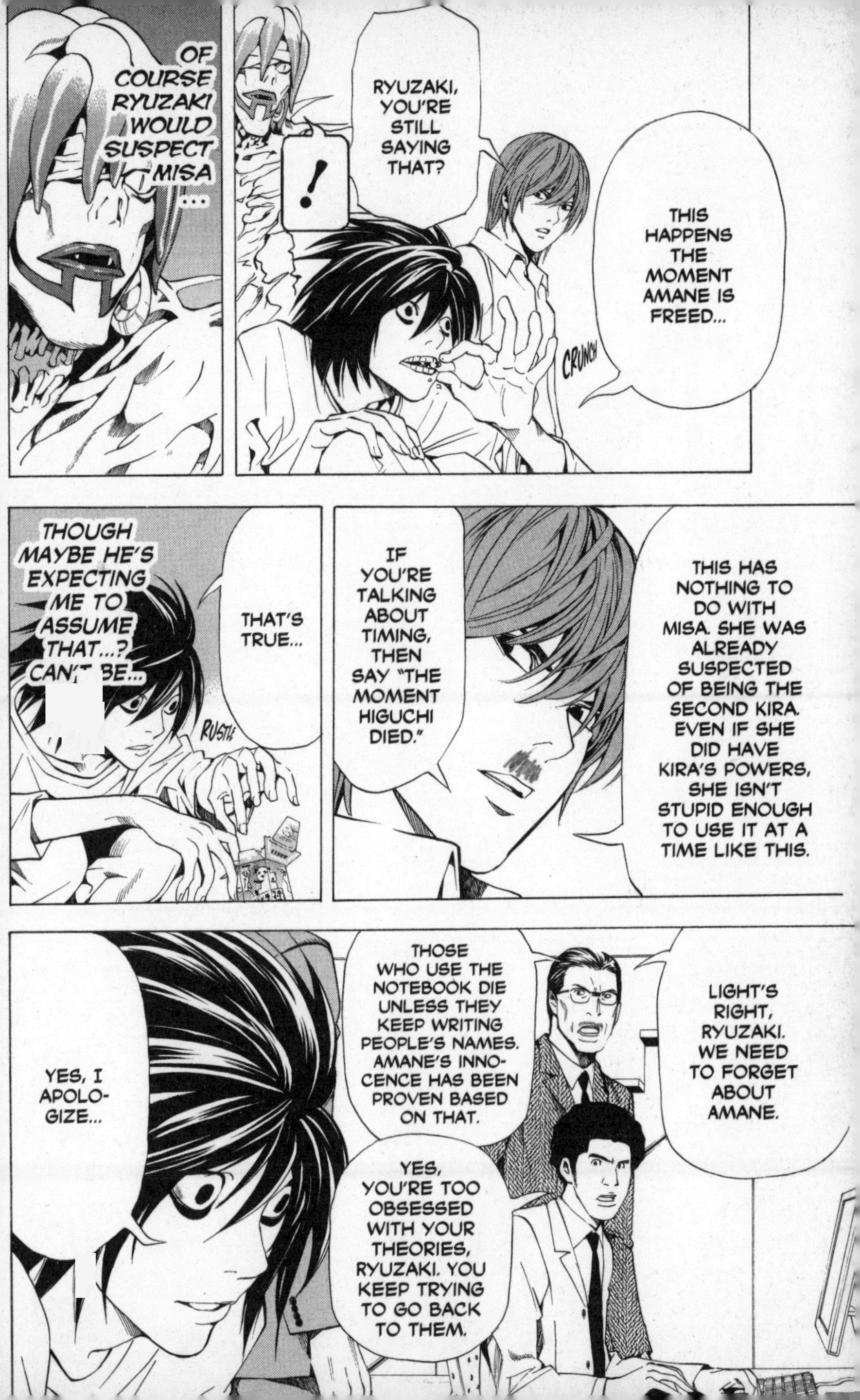
THIS HAPPENS THE MOMENT AMANE IS FREED...
RYUZAKI, YOU'RE STILL SAYING THAT?
!
CRUNCH
OF COURSE RYUZAKI WOULD SUSPECT MISA...
THIS HAS NOTHING TO DO WITH MISA. SHE WAS ALREADY SUSPECTED OF BEING THE SECOND KIRA. EVEN IF SHE DID HAVE KIRA'S POWERS, SHE ISN'T STUPID ENOUGH TO USE IT AT A TIME LIKE THIS.
IF YOU'RE TALKING ABOUT TIMING, THEN SAY "THE MOMENT HIGUCHI DIED."
THAT'S TRUE...
RUSTLE
THOUGH MAYBE HE'S EXPECTING ME TO ASSUME THAT...? CAN'T BE...
LIGHT'S RIGHT, RYUZAKI. WE NEED TO FORGET ABOUT AMANE.
THOSE WHO USE THE NOTEBOOK DIE UNLESS THEY KEEP WRITING PEOPLE'S NAMES. AMANE'S INNOCENCE HAS BEEN PROVEN BASED ON THAT.
YES, YOU'RE TOO OBSESSED WITH YOUR THEORIES, RYUZAKI. YOU KEEP TRYING TO GO BACK TO THEM.
YES, I APOLOGIZE...

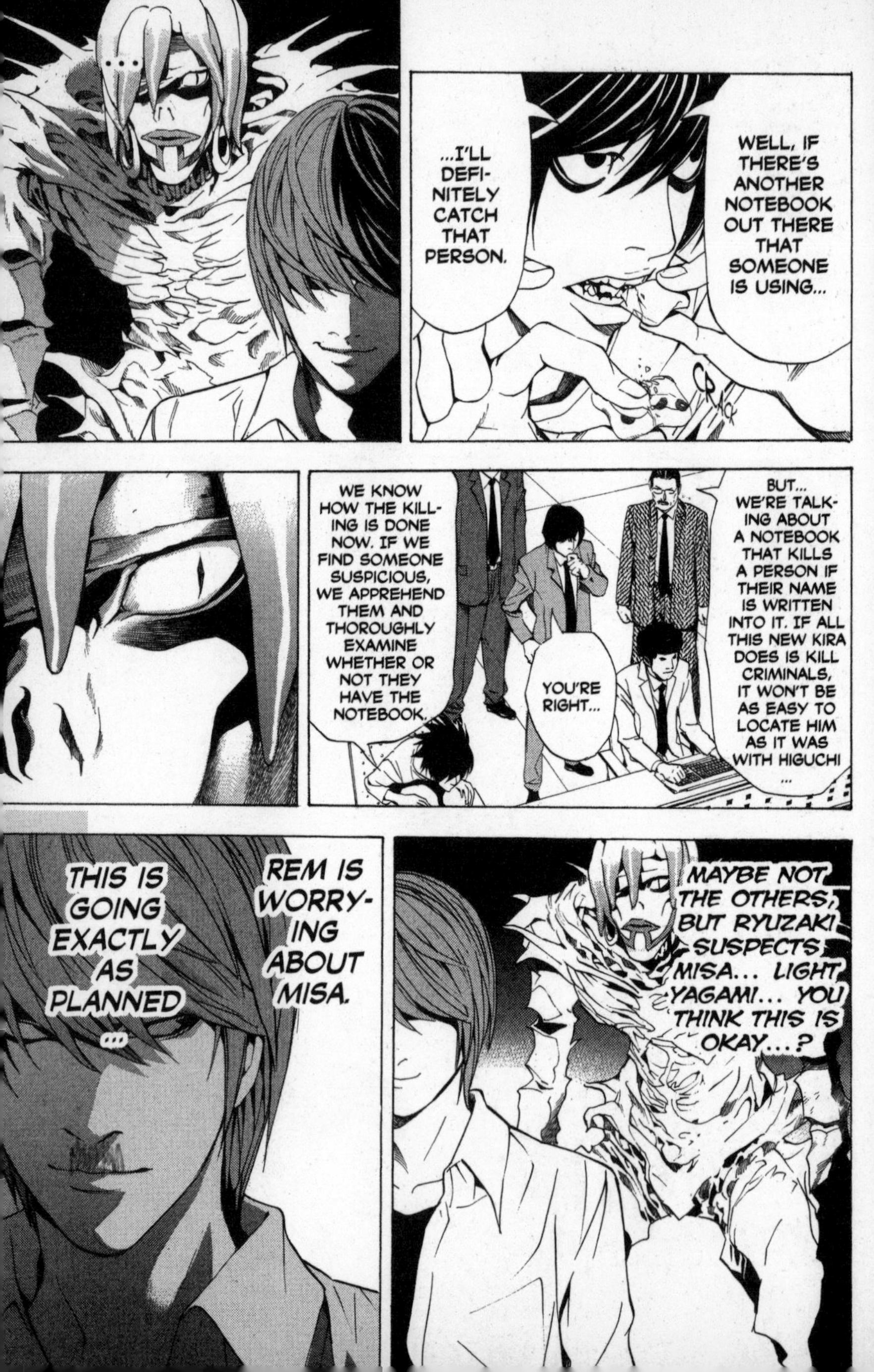
WELL, IF THERE'S ANOTHER NOTEBOOK OUT THERE THAT SOMEONE IS USING...
...I'LL DEFINITELY CATCH THAT PERSON.
CRACK
...
BUT... WE'RE TALKING ABOUT A NOTEBOOK THAT KILLS A PERSON IF THEIR NAME IS WRITTEN INTO IT. IF ALL THIS NEW KIRA DOES IS KILL CRIMINALS, IT WON'T BE AS EASY TO LOCATE HIM AS IT WAS WITH HIGUCHI ...
YOU'RE RIGHT...
WE KNOW HOW THE KILLING IS DONE NOW. IF WE FIND SOMEONE SUSPICIOUS, WE APPREHEND THEM AND THOROUGHLY EXAMINE WHETHER OR NOT THEY HAVE THE NOTEBOOK.
MAYBE NOT THE OTHERS, BUT RYUZAKI SUSPECTS MISA... LIGHT YAGAMI... YOU THINK THIS IS OKAY...?
REM IS WORRYING ABOUT MISA.
THIS IS GOING EXACTLY AS PLANNED ...

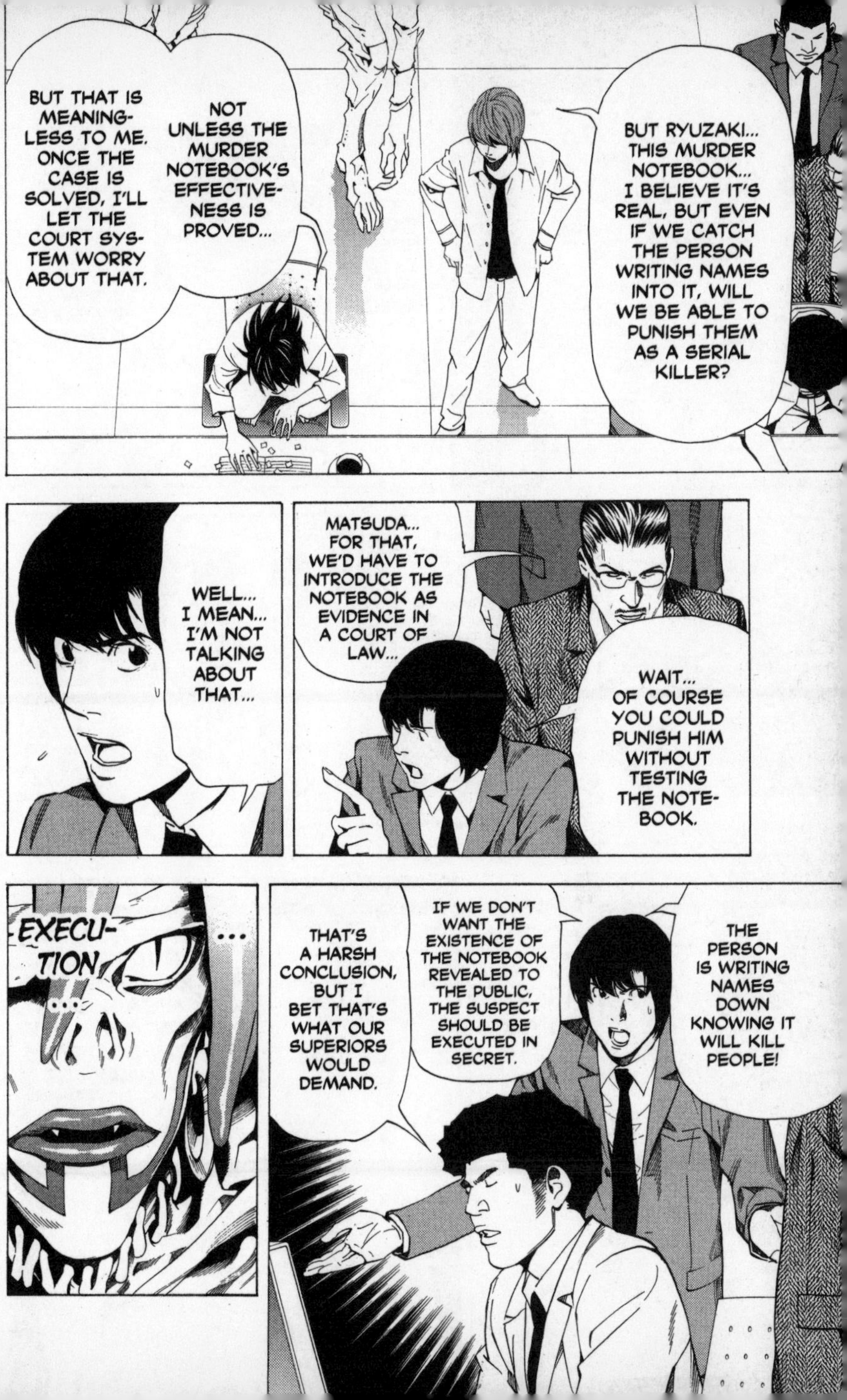
BUT RYUZAKI... THIS MURDER NOTEBOOK... I BELIEVE IT'S REAL, BUT EVEN IF WE CATCH THE PERSON WRITING NAMES INTO IT, WILL WE BE ABLE TO PUNISH THEM AS A SERIAL KILLER?
NOT UNLESS THE MURDER NOTEBOOK'S EFFECTIVENESS IS PROVED...
BUT THAT IS MEANINGLESS TO ME. ONCE THE CASE IS SOLVED, I'LL LET THE COURT SYSTEM WORRY ABOUT THAT.
MATSUDA... FOR THAT, WE'D HAVE TO INTRODUCE THE NOTEBOOK AS EVIDENCE IN A COURT OF LAW...
WAIT... OF COURSE YOU COULD PUNISH HIM WITHOUT TESTING THE NOTEBOOK.
WELL... I MEAN... I'M NOT TALKING ABOUT THAT...
THE PERSON IS WRITING NAMES DOWN KNOWING IT WILL KILL PEOPLE!
IF WE DON'T WANT THE EXISTENCE OF THE NOTEBOOK REVEALED TO THE PUBLIC, THE SUSPECT SHOULD BE EXECUTED IN SECRET.
THAT'S A HARSH CONCLUSION, BUT I BET THAT'S WHAT OUR SUPERIORS WOULD DEMAND.
EXECUTION
...
...

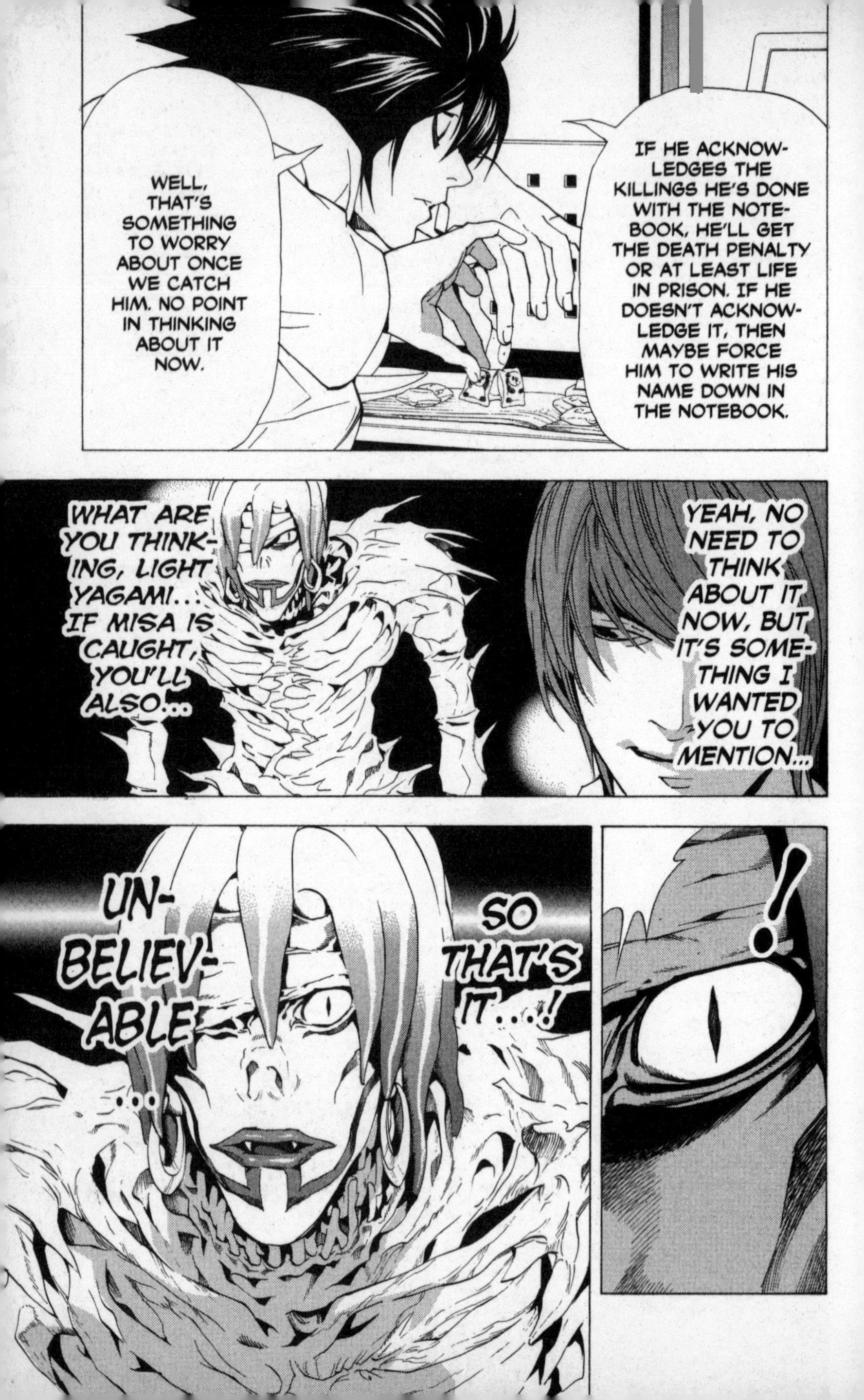
IF HE ACKNOWLEDGES THE KILLINGS HE'S DONE WITH THE NOTEBOOK, HE'LL GET THE DEATH PENALTY OR AT LEAST LIFE IN PRISON. IF HE DOESN'T ACKNOWLEDGE IT, THEN MAYBE FORCE HIM TO WRITE HIS NAME DOWN IN THE NOTEBOOK.
WELL, THAT'S SOMETHING TO WORRY ABOUT ONCE WE CATCH HIM. NO POINT IN THINKING ABOUT IT NOW.
YEAH, NO NEED TO THINK ABOUT IT NOW, BUT IT'S SOMETHING I WANTED YOU TO MENTION...
WHAT ARE YOU THINKING, LIGHT YAGAMI... IF MISA IS CAUGHT, YOU'LL ALSO...
!
SO THAT'S IT...!
UNBELIEVABLE...

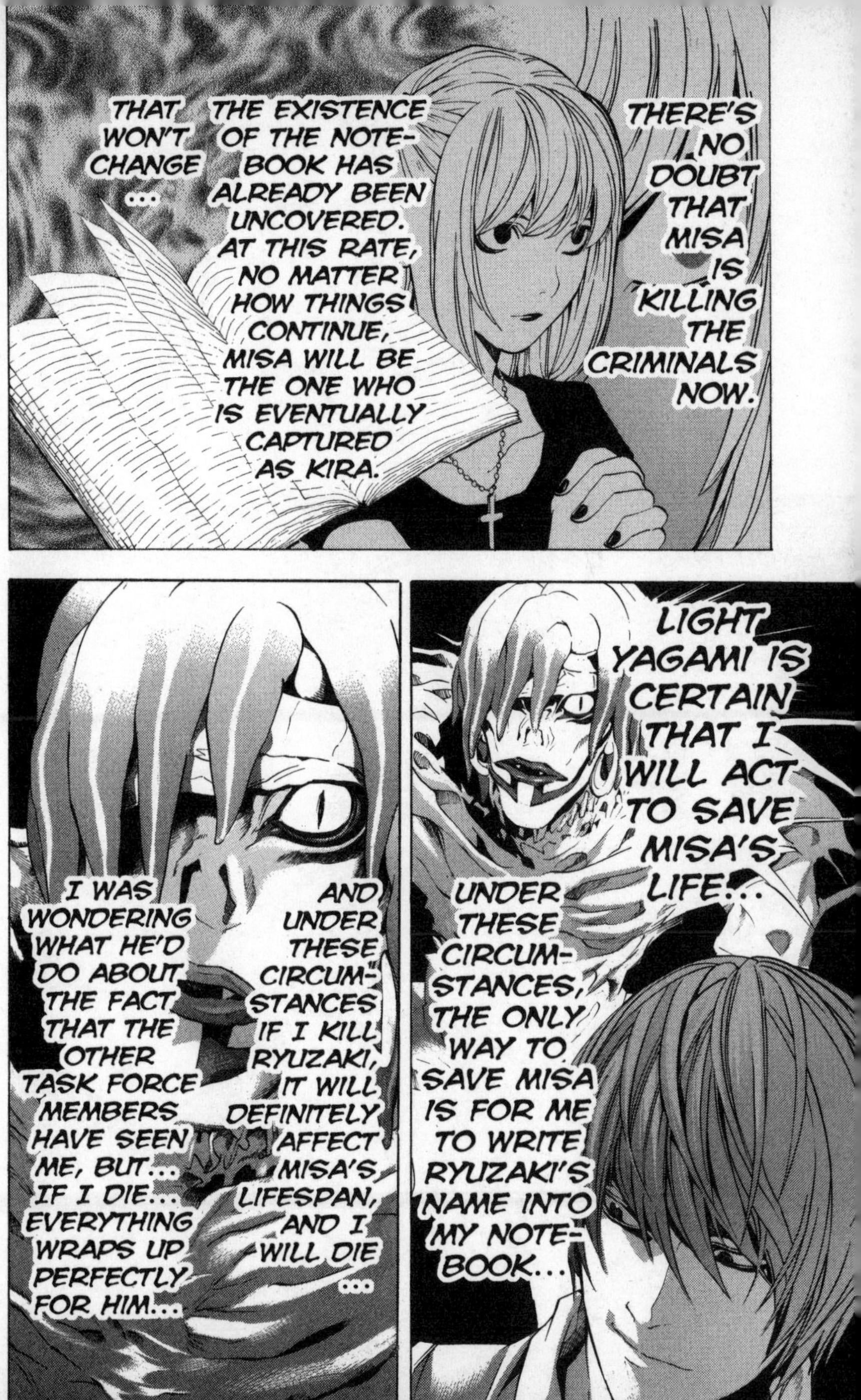
THERE'S NO DOUBT THAT MISA IS KILLING THE CRIMINALS NOW.
THE EXISTENCE OF THE NOTE-BOOK HAS ALREADY BEEN UNCOVERED. AT THIS RATE, NO MATTER HOW THINGS CONTINUE, MISA WILL BE THE ONE WHO IS EVENTUALLY CAPTURED AS KIRA.
THAT WON'T CHANGE...
LIGHT YAGAMI IS CERTAIN THAT I WILL ACT TO SAVE MISA'S LIFE...
UNDER THESE CIRCUM-STANCES, THE ONLY WAY TO SAVE MISA IS FOR ME TO WRITE RYUZAKI'S NAME INTO MY NOTE-BOOK...
AND UNDER THESE CIRCUM-STANCES IF I KILL RYUZAKI, IT WILL DEFINITELY AFFECT MISA'S LIFESPAN, AND I WILL DIE...
I WAS WONDERING WHAT HE'D DO ABOUT THE FACT THAT THE OTHER TASK FORCE MEMBERS HAVE SEEN ME, BUT... IF I DIE... EVERYTHING WRAPS UP PERFECTLY FOR HIM...

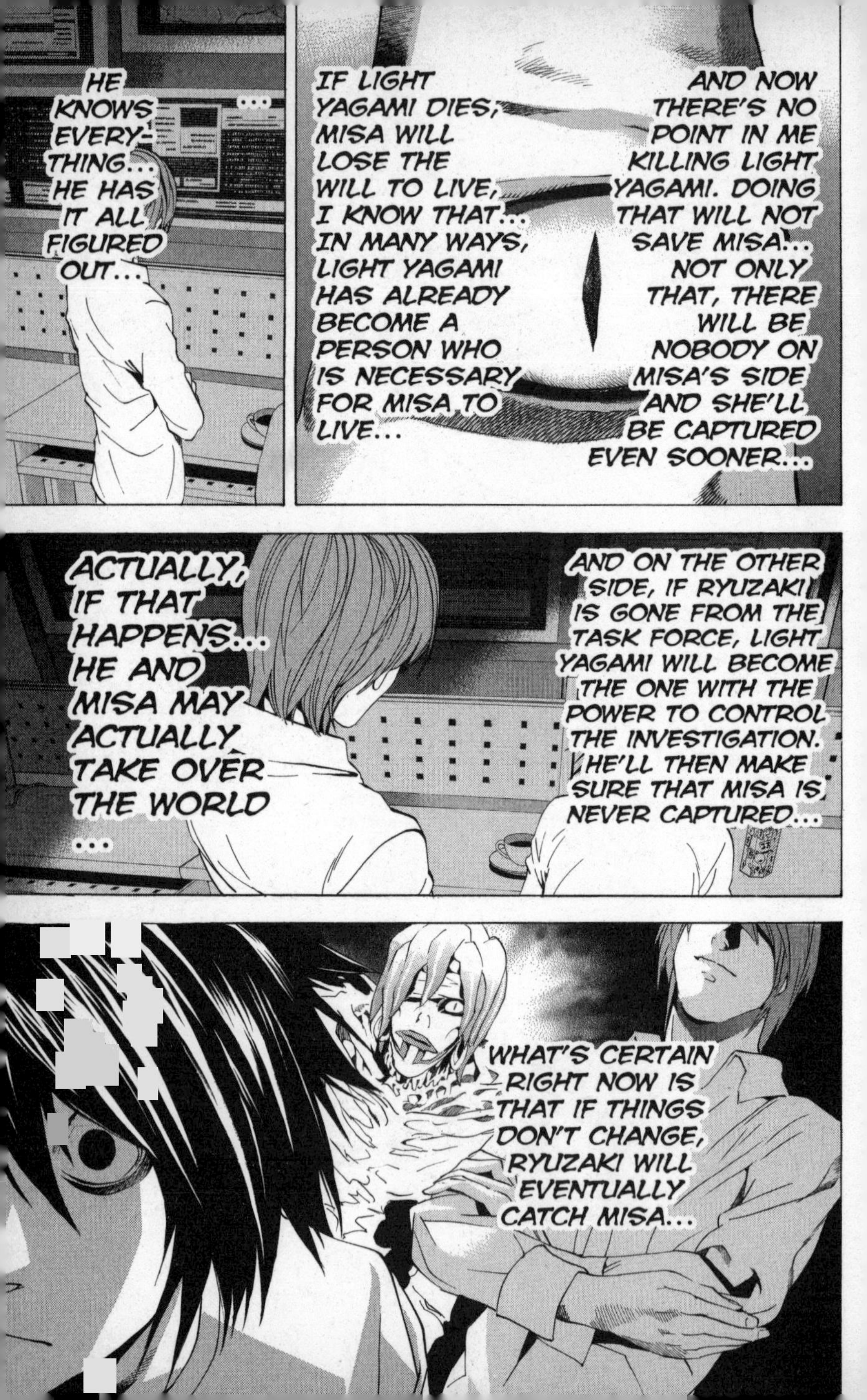
AND NOW THERE'S NO POINT IN ME KILLING LIGHT YAGAMI. DOING THAT WILL NOT SAVE MISA... NOT ONLY THAT, THERE WILL BE NOBODY ON MISA'S SIDE AND SHE'LL BE CAPTURED EVEN SOONER...
IF LIGHT YAGAMI DIES, MISA WILL LOSE THE WILL TO LIVE, I KNOW THAT... IN MANY WAYS, LIGHT YAGAMI HAS ALREADY BECOME A PERSON WHO IS NECESSARY FOR MISA TO LIVE...
...
HE KNOWS EVERY-THING... HE HAS IT ALL FIGURED OUT...
AND ON THE OTHER SIDE, IF RYUZAKI IS GONE FROM THE TASK FORCE, LIGHT YAGAMI WILL BECOME THE ONE WITH THE POWER TO CONTROL THE INVESTIGATION. HE'LL THEN MAKE SURE THAT MISA IS NEVER CAPTURED...
ACTUALLY, IF THAT HAPPENS... HE AND MISA MAY ACTUALLY TAKE OVER THE WORLD
...
WHAT'S CERTAIN RIGHT NOW IS THAT IF THINGS DON'T CHANGE, RYUZAKI WILL EVENTUALLY CATCH MISA...

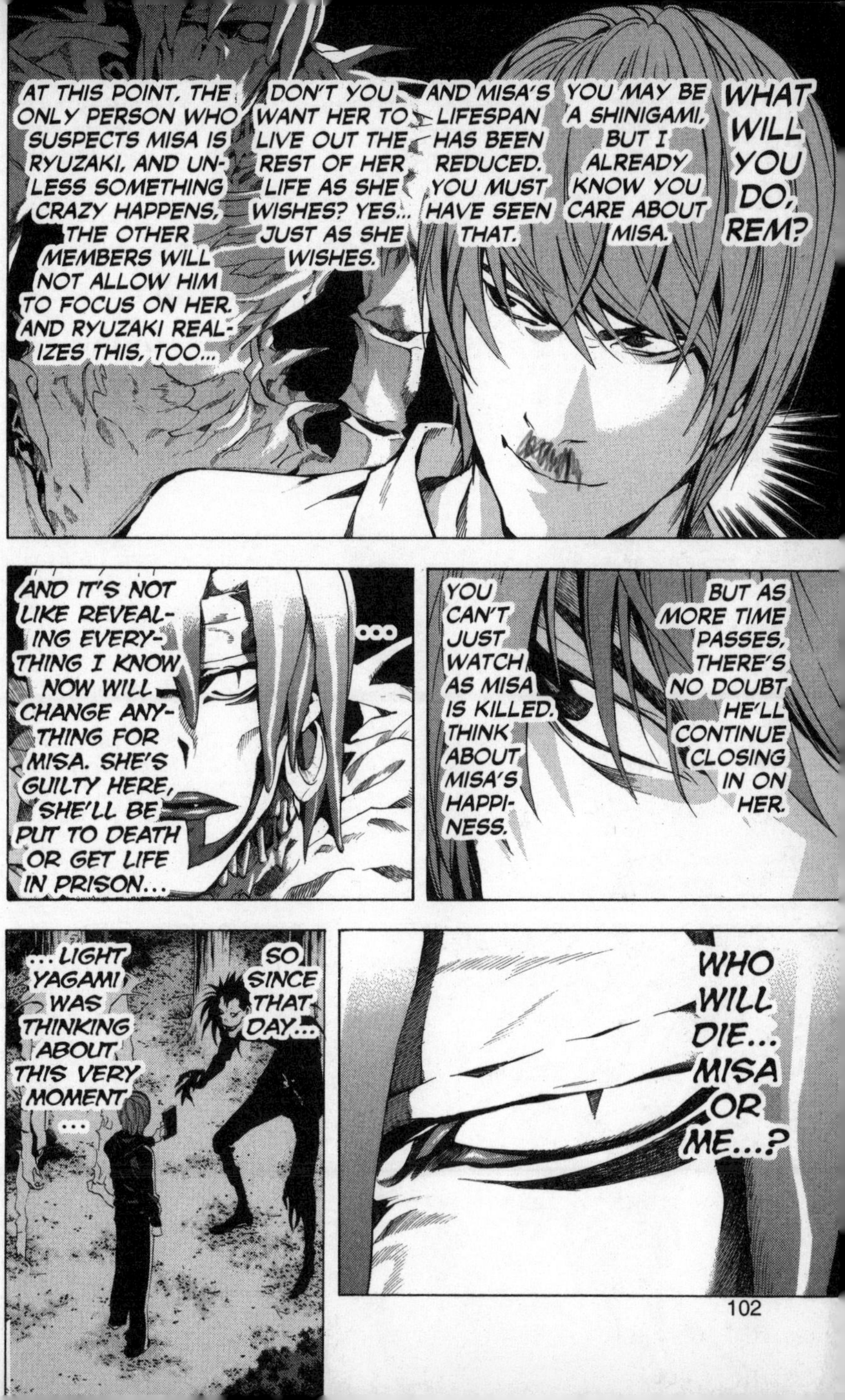
WHAT WILL YOU DO, REM?
YOU MAY BE A SHINIGAMI, BUT I ALREADY KNOW YOU CARE ABOUT MISA.
AND MISA'S LIFESPAN HAS BEEN REDUCED. YOU MUST HAVE SEEN THAT.
DON'T YOU WANT HER TO LIVE OUT THE REST OF HER LIFE AS SHE WISHES? YES... JUST AS SHE WISHES.
AT THIS POINT, THE ONLY PERSON WHO SUSPECTS MISA IS RYUZAKI, AND UNLESS SOMETHING CRAZY HAPPENS, THE OTHER MEMBERS WILL NOT ALLOW HIM TO FOCUS ON HER. AND RYUZAKI REALIZES THIS, TOO...
BUT AS MORE TIME PASSES, THERE'S NO DOUBT HE'LL CONTINUE CLOSING IN ON HER.
YOU CAN'T JUST WATCH AS MISA IS KILLED. THINK ABOUT MISA'S HAPPINESS.
...
AND IT'S NOT LIKE REVEALING EVERYTHING I KNOW NOW WILL CHANGE ANYTHING FOR MISA. SHE'S GUILTY HERE, SHE'LL BE PUT TO DEATH OR GET LIFE IN PRISON...
WHO WILL DIE... MISA OR ME...?
SO SINCE THAT DAY...
...LIGHT YAGAMI WAS THINKING ABOUT THIS VERY MOMENT...

READ THIS WAY

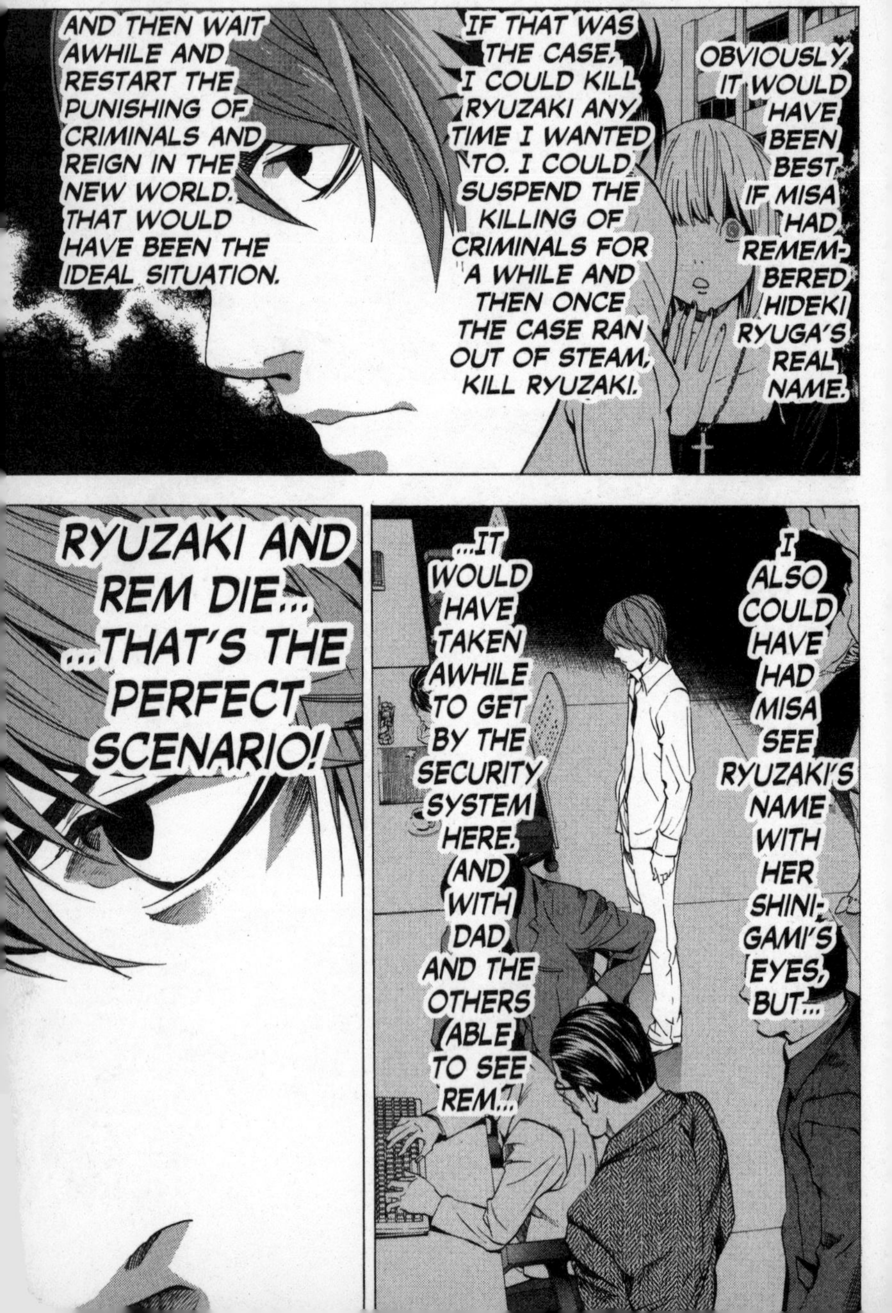
OBVIOUSLY IT WOULD HAVE BEEN BEST IF MISA HAD REMEMBERED HIDEKI RYUGA'S REAL NAME.
IF THAT WAS THE CASE, I COULD KILL RYUZAKI ANY TIME I WANTED TO. I COULD SUSPEND THE KILLING OF CRIMINALS FOR A WHILE AND THEN ONCE THE CASE RAN OUT OF STEAM, KILL RYUZAKI.
AND THEN WAIT AWHILE AND RESTART THE PUNISHING OF CRIMINALS AND REIGN IN THE NEW WORLD. THAT WOULD HAVE BEEN THE IDEAL SITUATION.
I ALSO COULD HAVE HAD MISA SEE RYUZAKI'S NAME WITH HER SHINIGAMI'S EYES, BUT...
...IT WOULD HAVE TAKEN AWHILE TO GET BY THE SECURITY SYSTEM HERE. AND WITH DAD AND THE OTHERS ABLE TO SEE REM...
RYUZAKI AND REM DIE... ...THAT'S THE PERFECT SCENARIO!

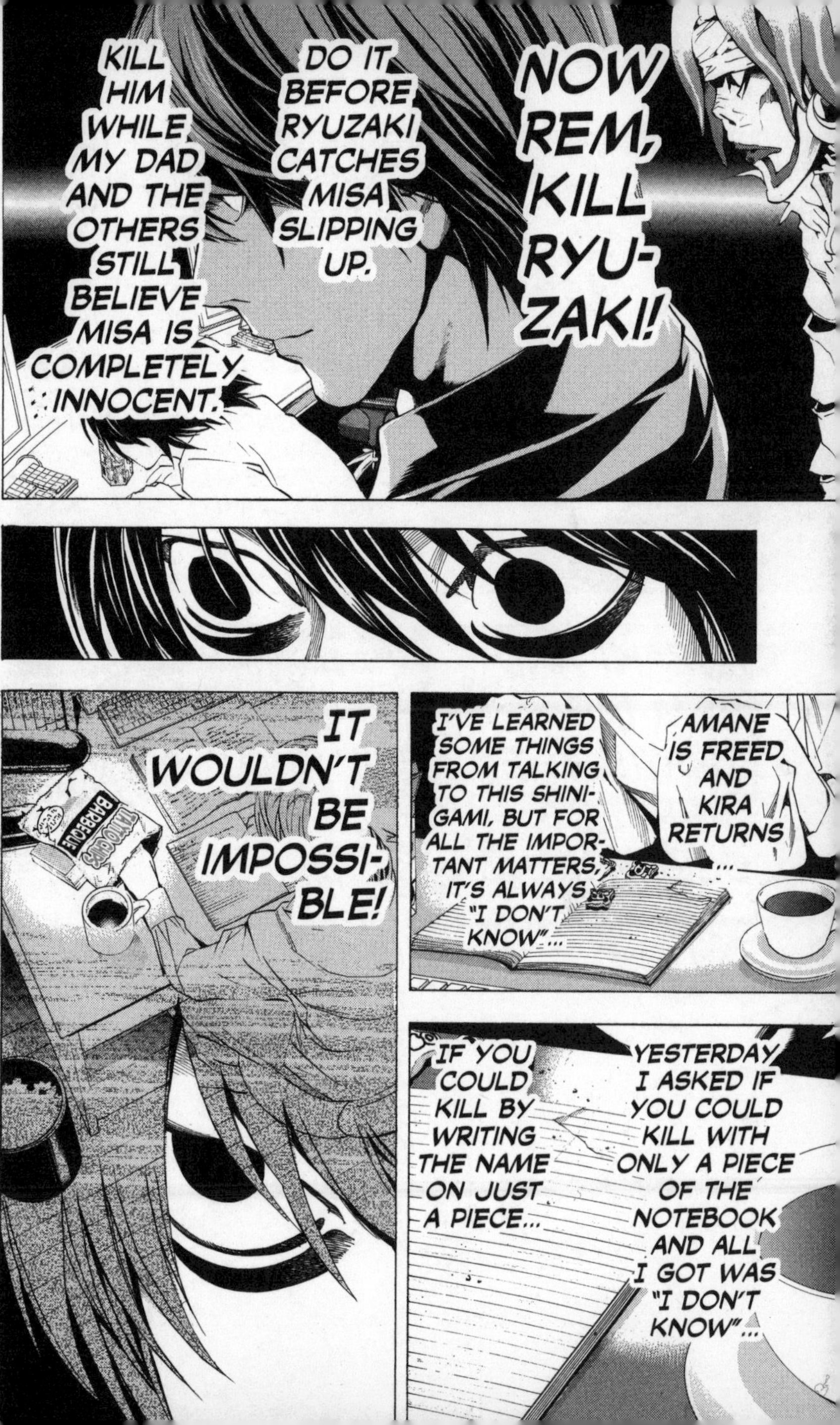
NOW REM, KILL RYU-ZAKI!
DO IT BEFORE RYUZAKI CATCHES MISA SLIPPING UP.
KILL HIM WHILE MY DAD AND THE OTHERS STILL BELIEVE MISA IS COMPLETELY INNOCENT.
AMANE IS FREED AND KIRA RETURNS...
I'VE LEARNED SOME THINGS FROM TALKING TO THIS SHINI-GAMI, BUT FOR ALL THE IMPOR-TANT MATTERS, IT'S ALWAYS "I DON'T KNOW"...
YESTERDAY I ASKED IF YOU COULD KILL WITH ONLY A PIECE OF THE NOTEBOOK AND ALL I GOT WAS "I DON'T KNOW"...
IF YOU COULD KILL BY WRITING THE NAME ON JUST A PIECE...
IT WOULDN'T BE IMPOSSI-BLE!

READ THIS WAY

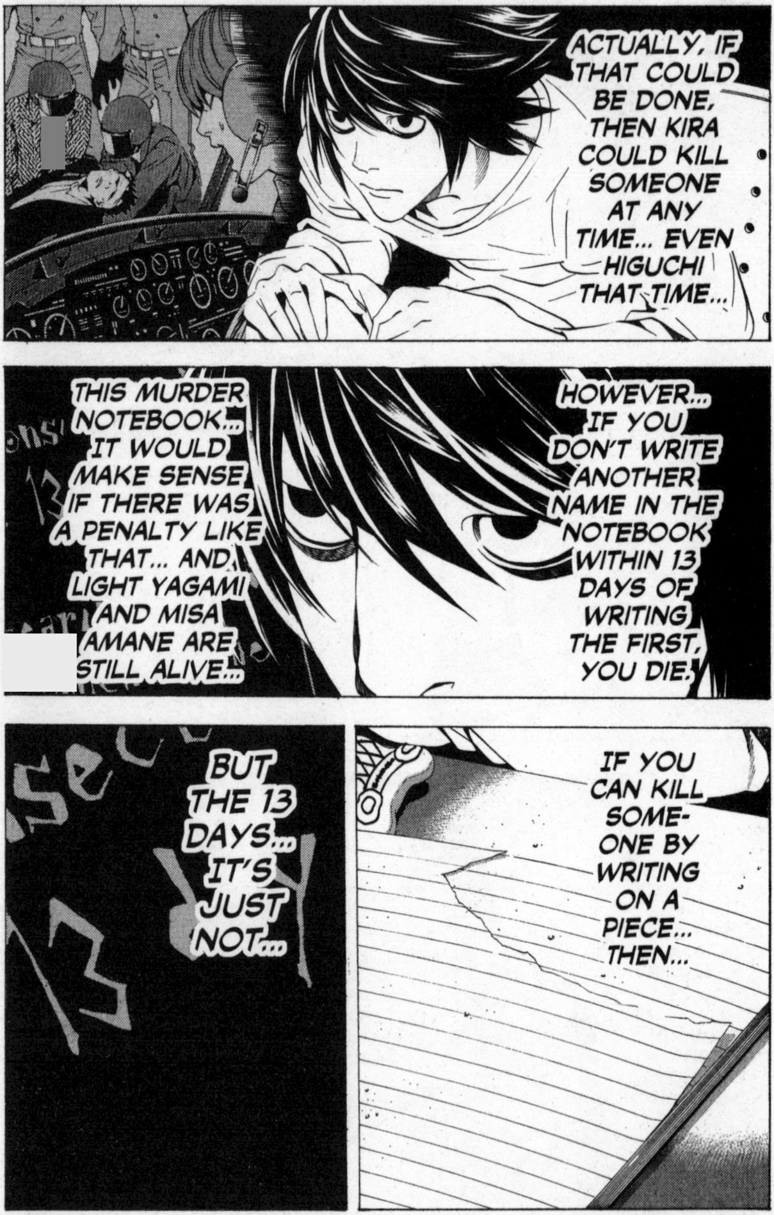
ACTUALLY, IF THAT COULD BE DONE, THEN KIRA COULD KILL SOMEONE AT ANY TIME... EVEN HIGUCHI THAT TIME...
HOWEVER... IF YOU DON'T WRITE ANOTHER NAME IN THE NOTEBOOK WITHIN 13 DAYS OF WRITING THE FIRST, YOU DIE.
THIS MURDER NOTEBOOK... IT WOULD MAKE SENSE IF THERE WAS A PENALTY LIKE THAT... AND LIGHT YAGAMI AND MISA AMANE ARE STILL ALIVE...
IF YOU CAN KILL SOME-ONE BY WRITING ON A PIECE... THEN...
BUT THE 13 DAYS... IT'S JUST NOT...

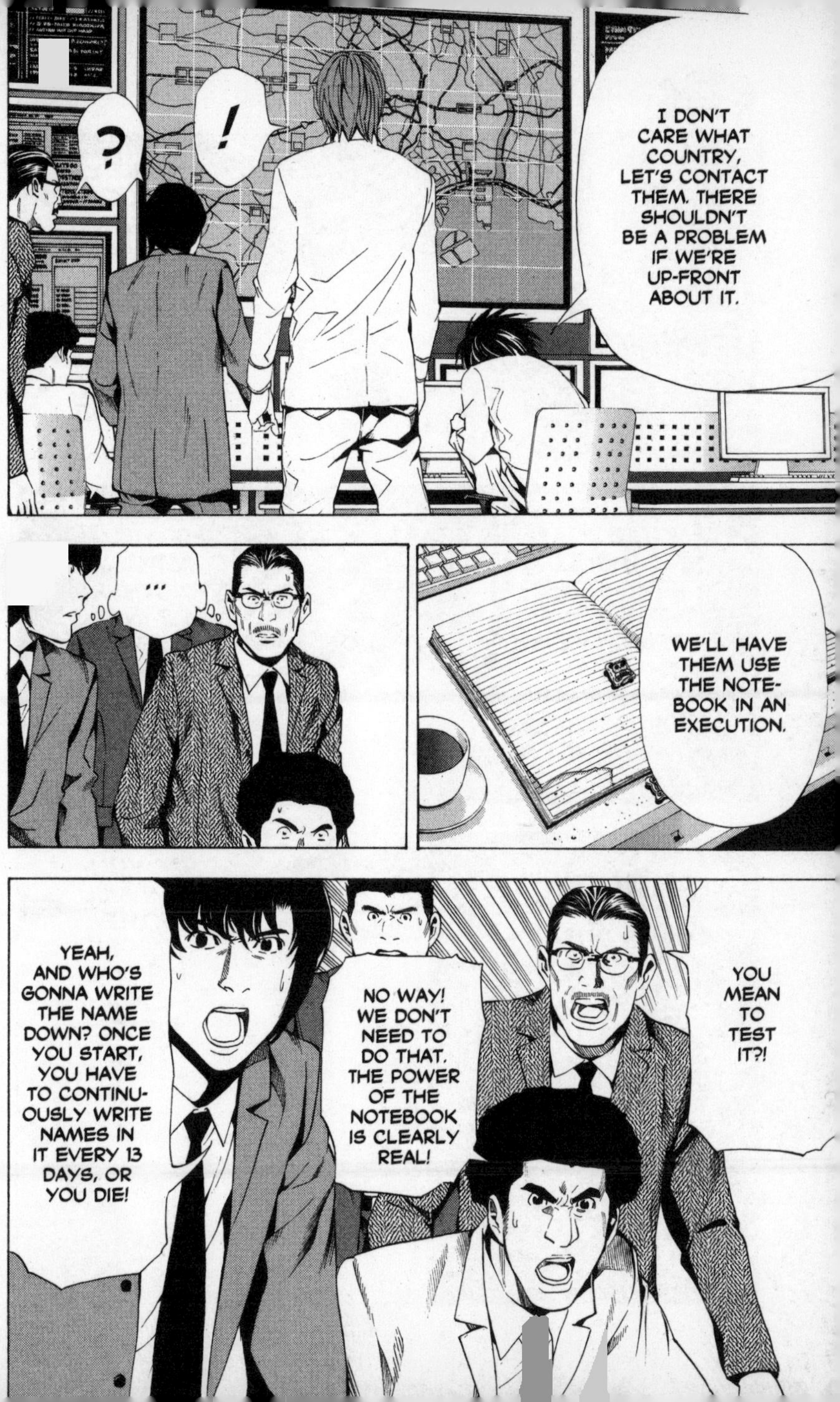
I DON'T CARE WHAT COUNTRY, LET'S CONTACT THEM. THERE SHOULDN'T BE A PROBLEM IF WE'RE UP-FRONT ABOUT IT.
!
?
WE'LL HAVE THEM USE THE NOTE-BOOK IN AN EXECUTION.
...
YOU MEAN TO TEST IT?!
NO WAY! WE DON'T NEED TO DO THAT. THE POWER OF THE NOTEBOOK IS CLEARLY REAL!
YEAH, AND WHO'S GONNA WRITE THE NAME DOWN? ONCE YOU START, YOU HAVE TO CONTINU-OUSLY WRITE NAMES IN IT EVERY 13 DAYS, OR YOU DIE!

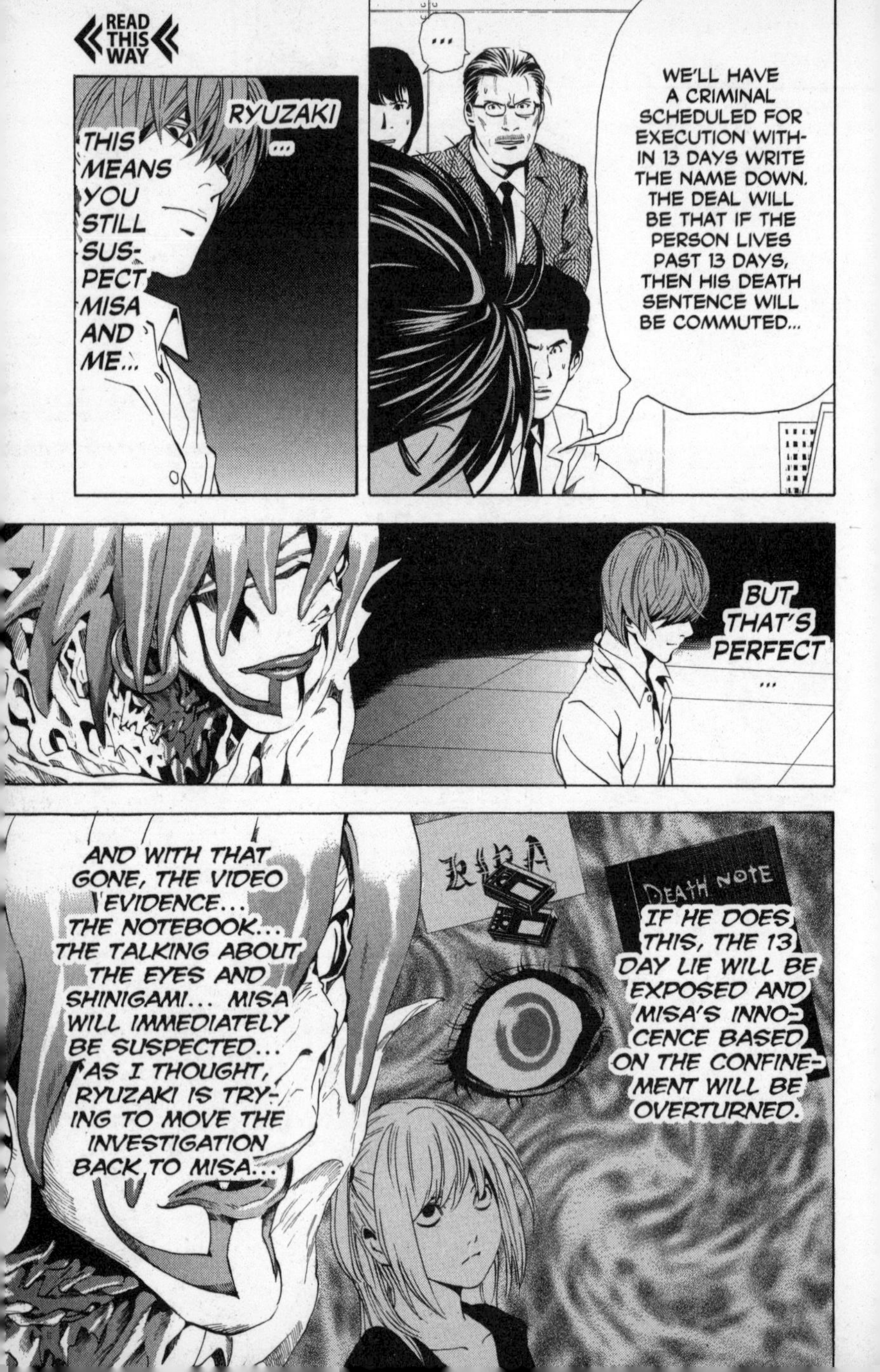
READ THIS WAY
WE'LL HAVE A CRIMINAL SCHEDULED FOR EXECUTION WITH-IN 13 DAYS WRITE THE NAME DOWN. THE DEAL WILL BE THAT IF THE PERSON LIVES PAST 13 DAYS, THEN HIS DEATH SENTENCE WILL BE COMMUTED...
...
RYUZAKI ...
THIS MEANS YOU STILL SUS-PECT MISA AND ME...
BUT THAT'S PERFECT ...
DEATH NOTE
IF HE DOES THIS, THE 13 DAY LIE WILL BE EXPOSED AND MISA'S INNO-CENCE BASED ON THE CONFINE-MENT WILL BE OVERTURNED.
AND WITH THAT GONE, THE VIDEO EVIDENCE... THE NOTEBOOK... THE TALKING ABOUT THE EYES AND SHINIGAMI... MISA WILL IMMEDIATELY BE SUSPECTED... AS I THOUGHT, RYUZAKI IS TRY-ING TO MOVE THE INVESTIGATION BACK TO MISA...

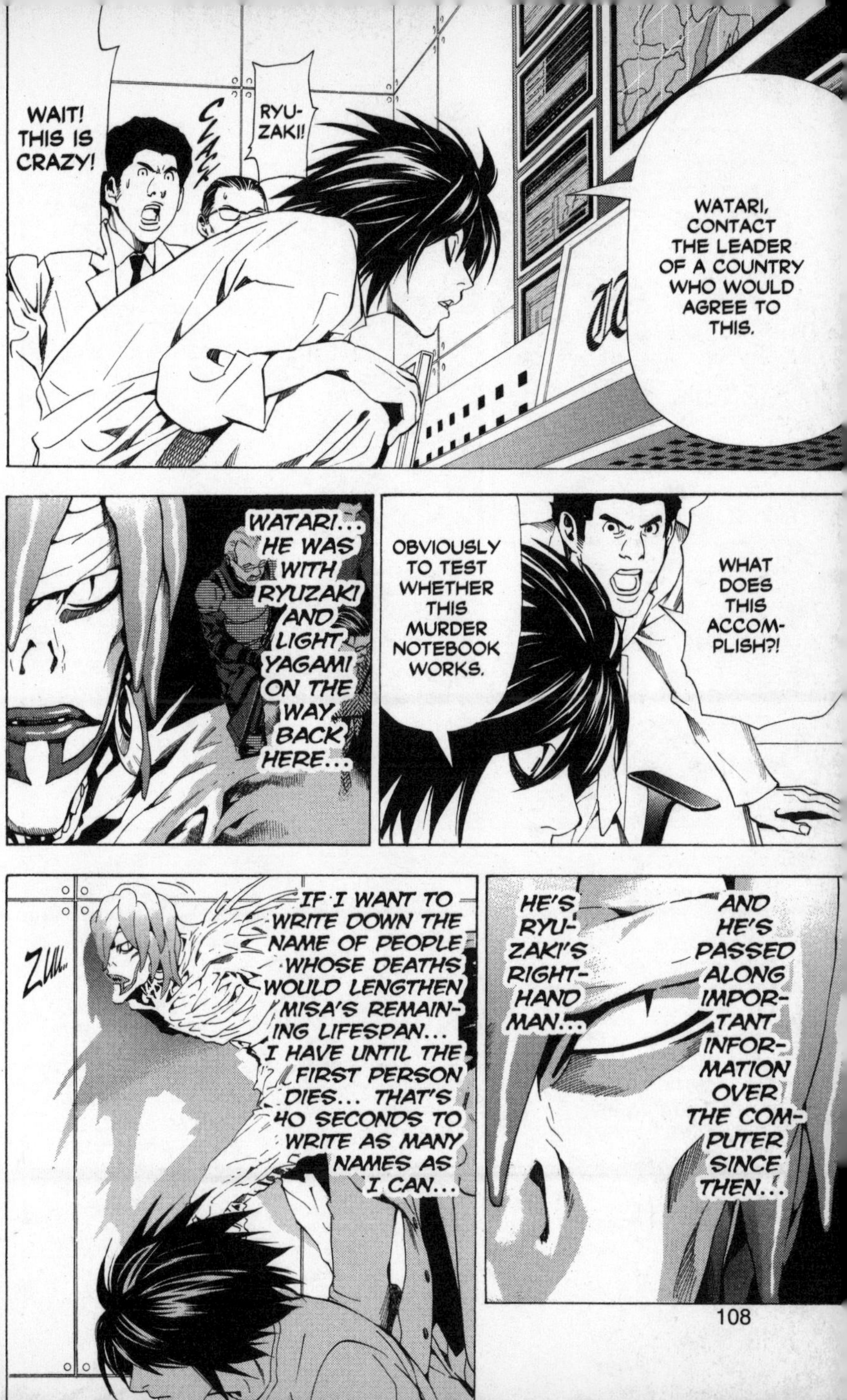
WATARI, CONTACT THE LEADER OF A COUNTRY WHO WOULD AGREE TO THIS.
RYU-ZAKI!
CLACK
WAIT! THIS IS CRAZY!
WHAT DOES THIS ACCOM-PLISH?!
OBVIOUSLY TO TEST WHETHER THIS MURDER NOTEBOOK WORKS.
WATARI... HE WAS WITH RYUZAKI AND LIGHT YAGAMI ON THE WAY BACK HERE...
HE'S RYU-ZAKI'S RIGHT-HAND MAN...
AND HE'S PASSED ALONG IMPOR-TANT INFOR-MATION OVER THE COM-PUTER SINCE THEN...
IF I WANT TO WRITE DOWN THE NAME OF PEOPLE WHOSE DEATHS WOULD LENGTHEN MISA'S REMAIN-ING LIFESPAN... I HAVE UNTIL THE FIRST PERSON DIES... THAT'S 40 SECONDS TO WRITE AS MANY NAMES AS I CAN...
ZUU...

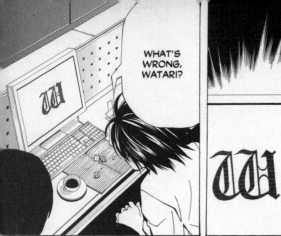

WHAT'S WRONG, WATARI?

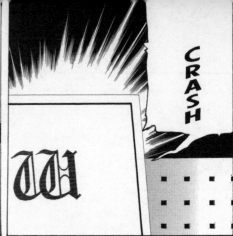

CRASH

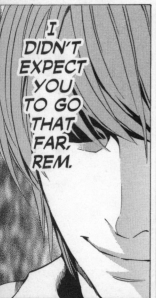

I DIDN'T EXPECT YOU TO GO THAT FAR, REM.

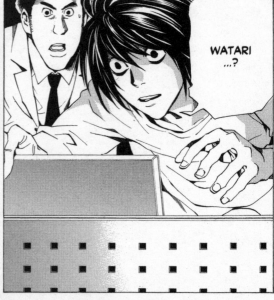

WATARI...?

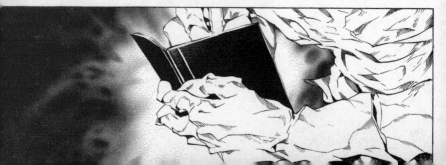

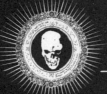

DEATH NOTE
How to Use It
XXXIX

- Humans that have traded for the eye power of a god of death cannot see the name or life-span of humans who have already passed away by looking at their photos.

死神の目を取引した人間は、写真等で既に死んでいる人間の顔を見ても、名前も寿命も見えない。

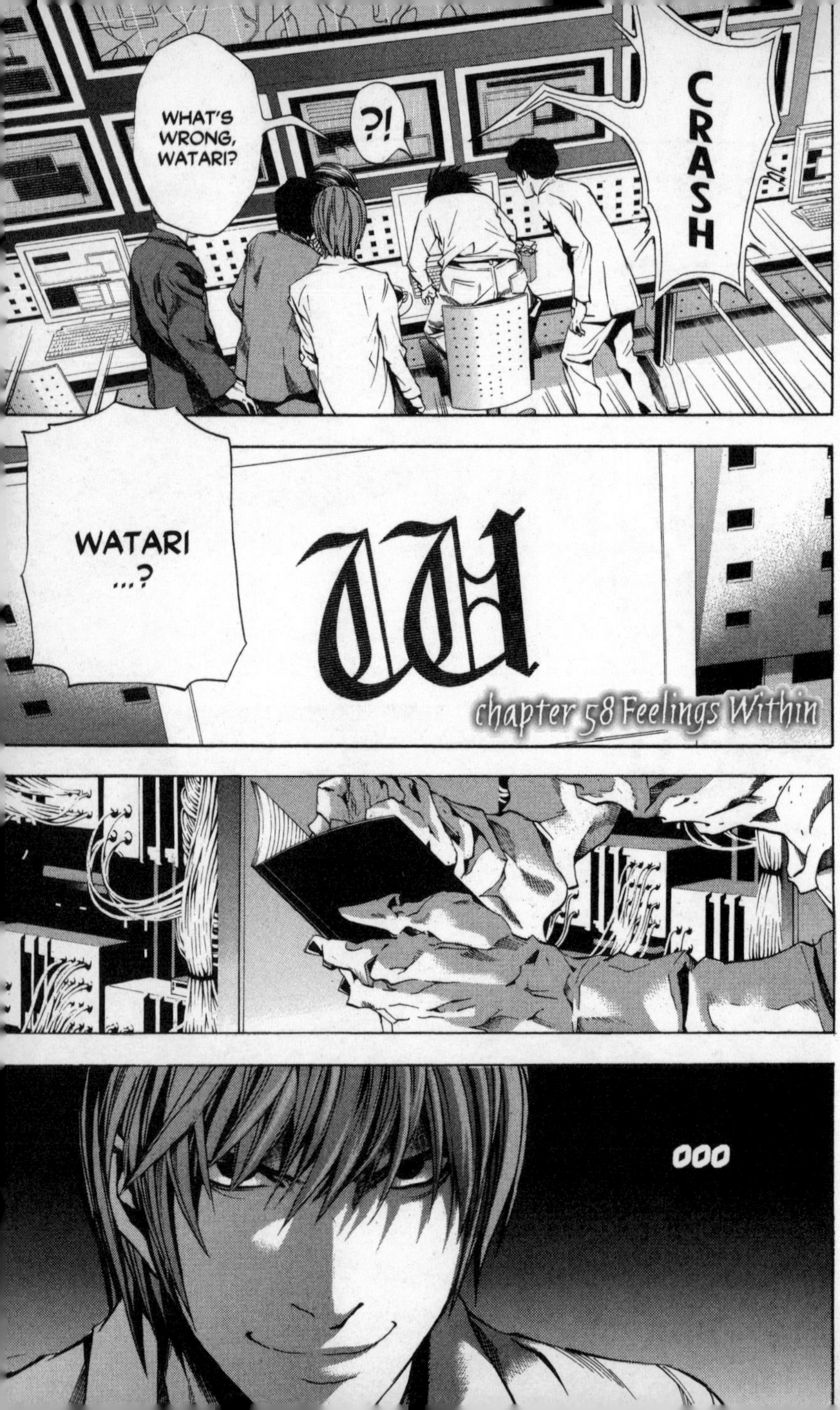
CRASH
?!
WHAT'S WRONG, WATARI?
W
chapter 58 Feelings Within
WATARI ...?
ooo

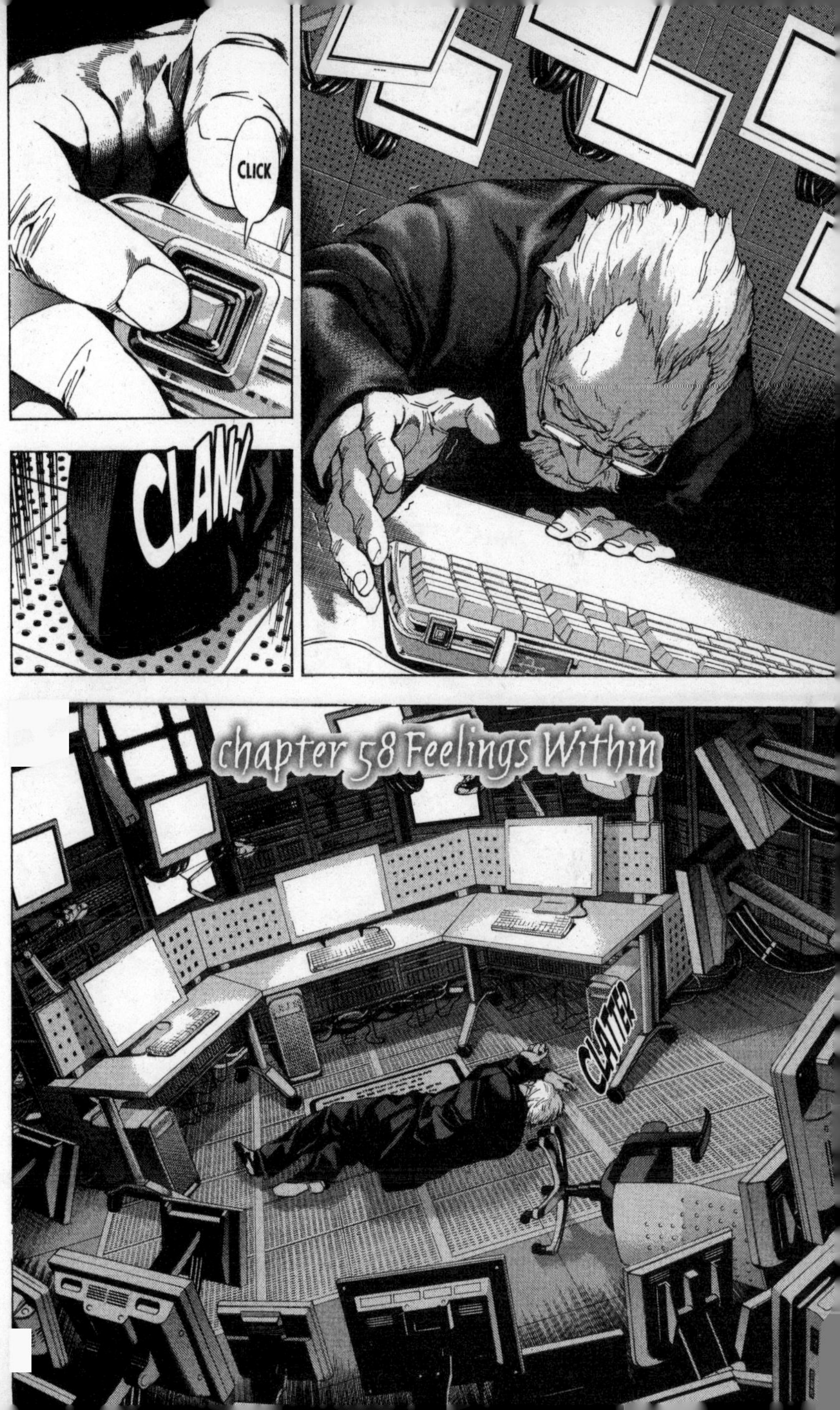
CLICK
CLANK
chapter 58 Feelings Within
CLATTER

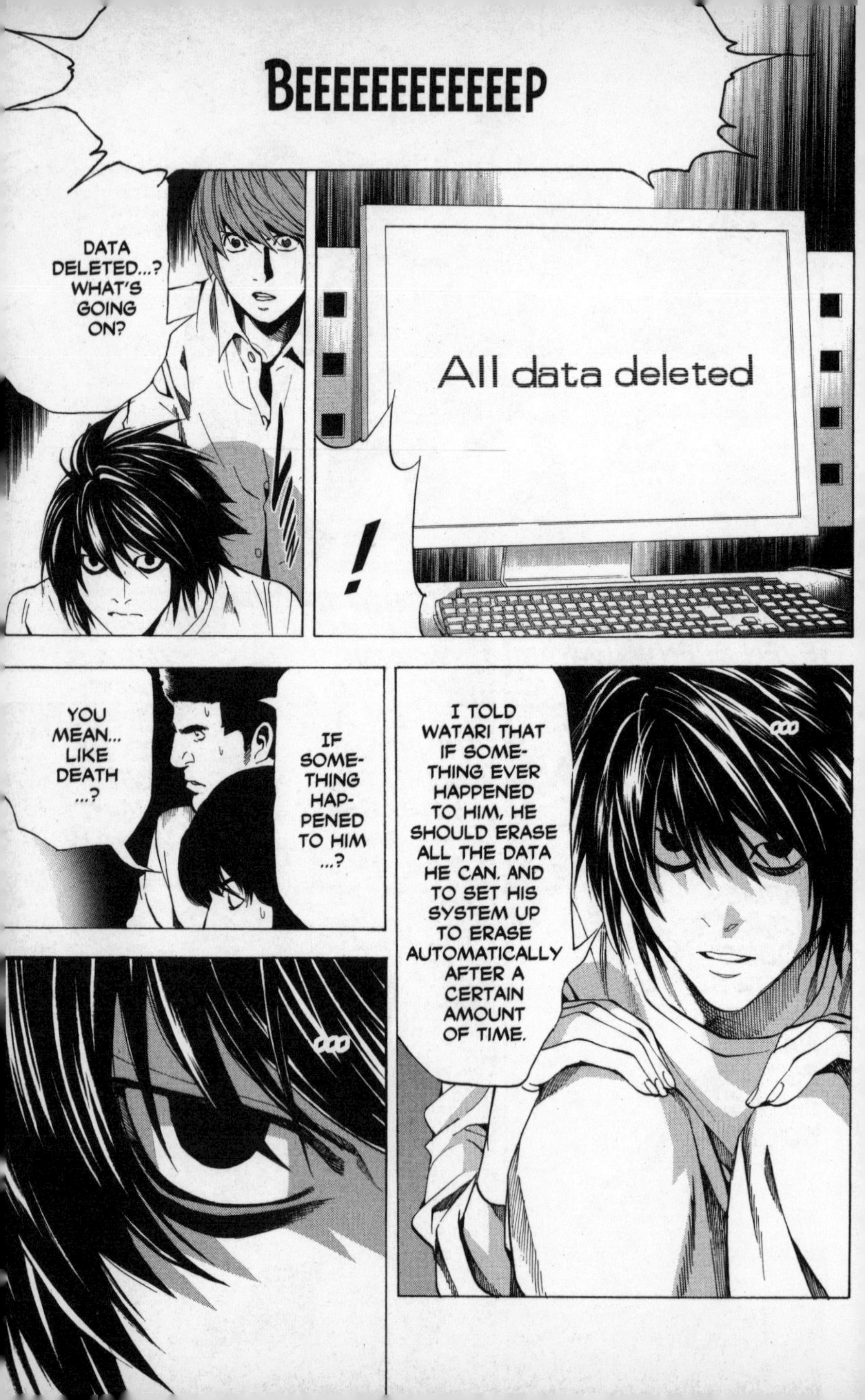
BEEEEEEEEEEEEP
All data deleted
!
DATA DELETED...? WHAT'S GOING ON?
I TOLD WATARI THAT IF SOME-THING EVER HAPPENED TO HIM, HE SHOULD ERASE ALL THE DATA HE CAN. AND TO SET HIS SYSTEM UP TO ERASE AUTOMATICALLY AFTER A CERTAIN AMOUNT OF TIME.
IF SOME-THING HAP-PENED TO HIM ...?
YOU MEAN... LIKE DEATH ...?

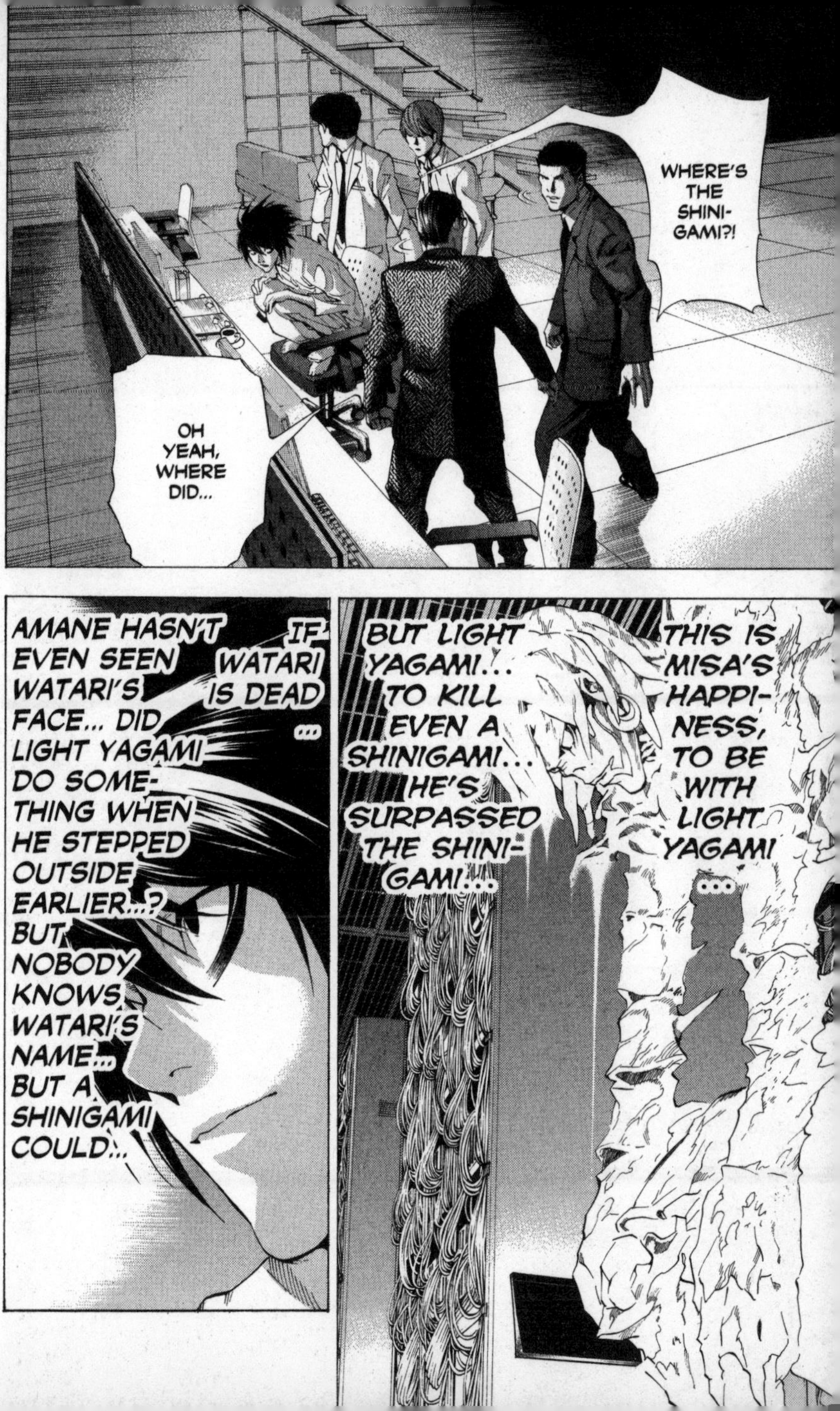
WHERE'S THE SHINIGAMI?!
OH YEAH, WHERE DID...
THIS IS MISA'S HAPPINESS, TO BE WITH LIGHT YAGAMI...
BUT LIGHT YAGAMI... TO KILL EVEN A SHINIGAMI... HE'S SURPASSED THE SHINIGAMI...
IF WATARI IS DEAD...
AMANE HASN'T EVEN SEEN WATARI'S FACE... DID LIGHT YAGAMI DO SOMETHING WHEN HE STEPPED OUTSIDE EARLIER...? BUT NOBODY KNOWS WATARI'S NAME... BUT A SHINIGAMI COULD...

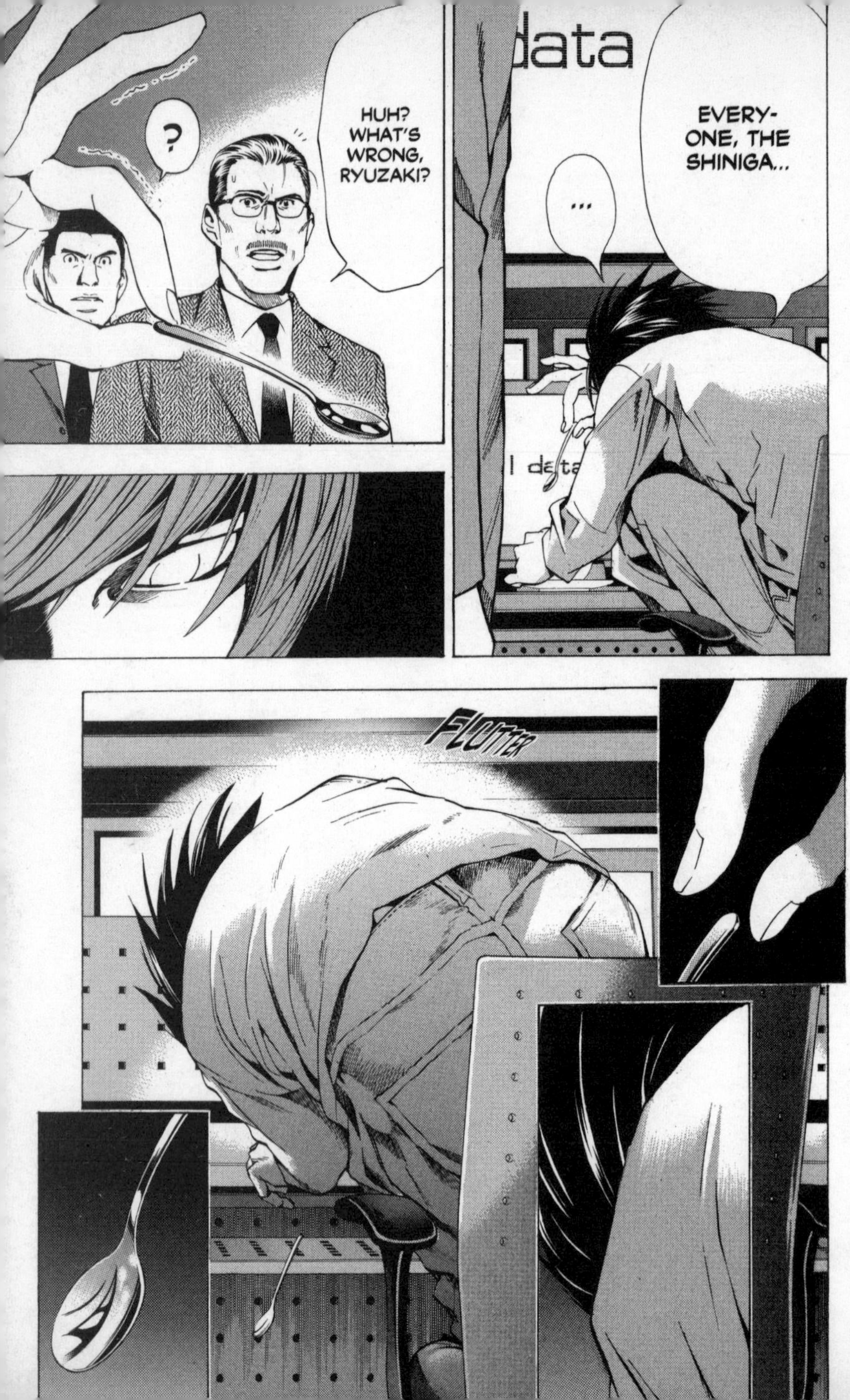
data
EVERY-ONE, THE SHINIGA...
...
HUH? WHAT'S WRONG, RYUZAKI?
?
FLUTTER

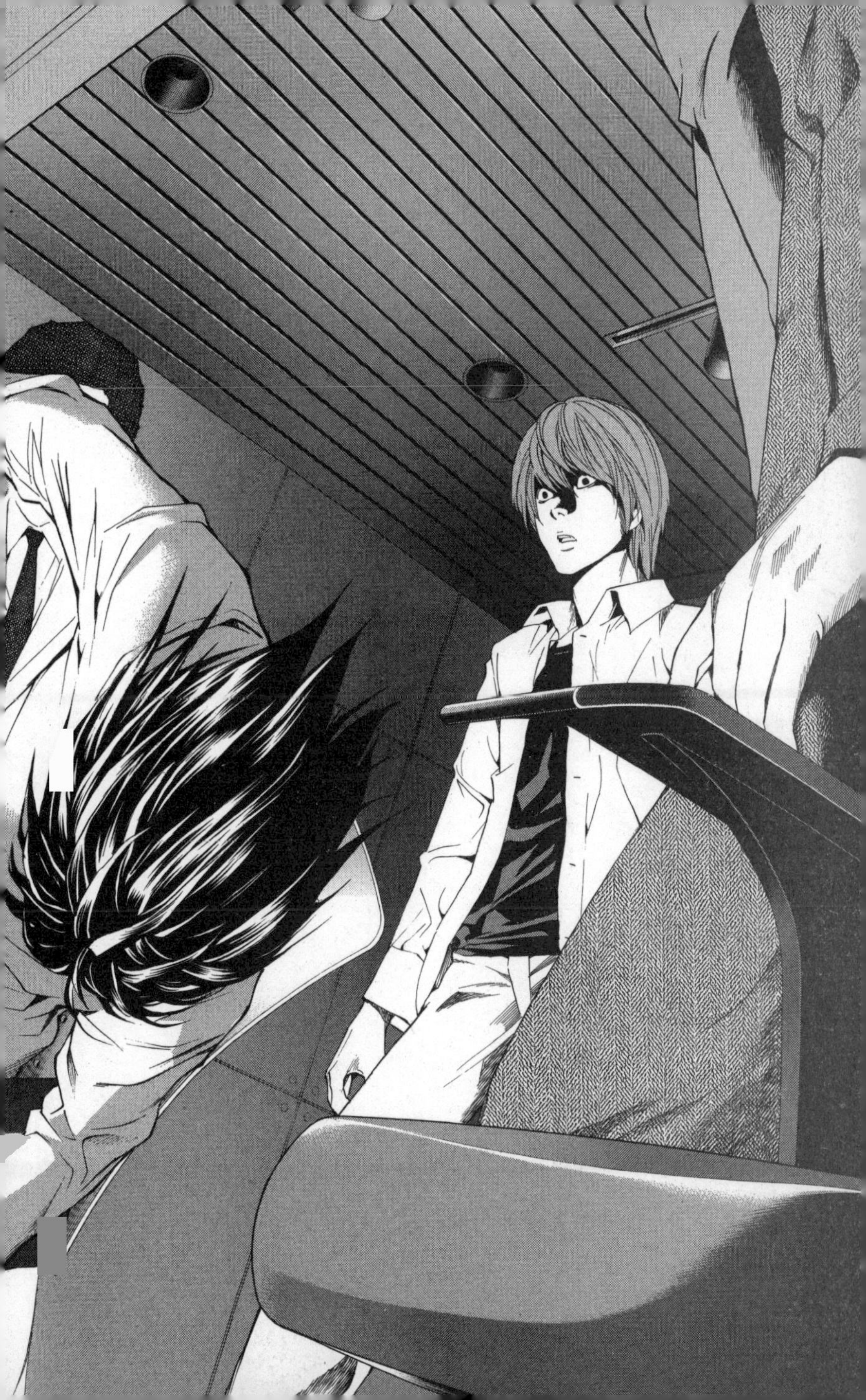

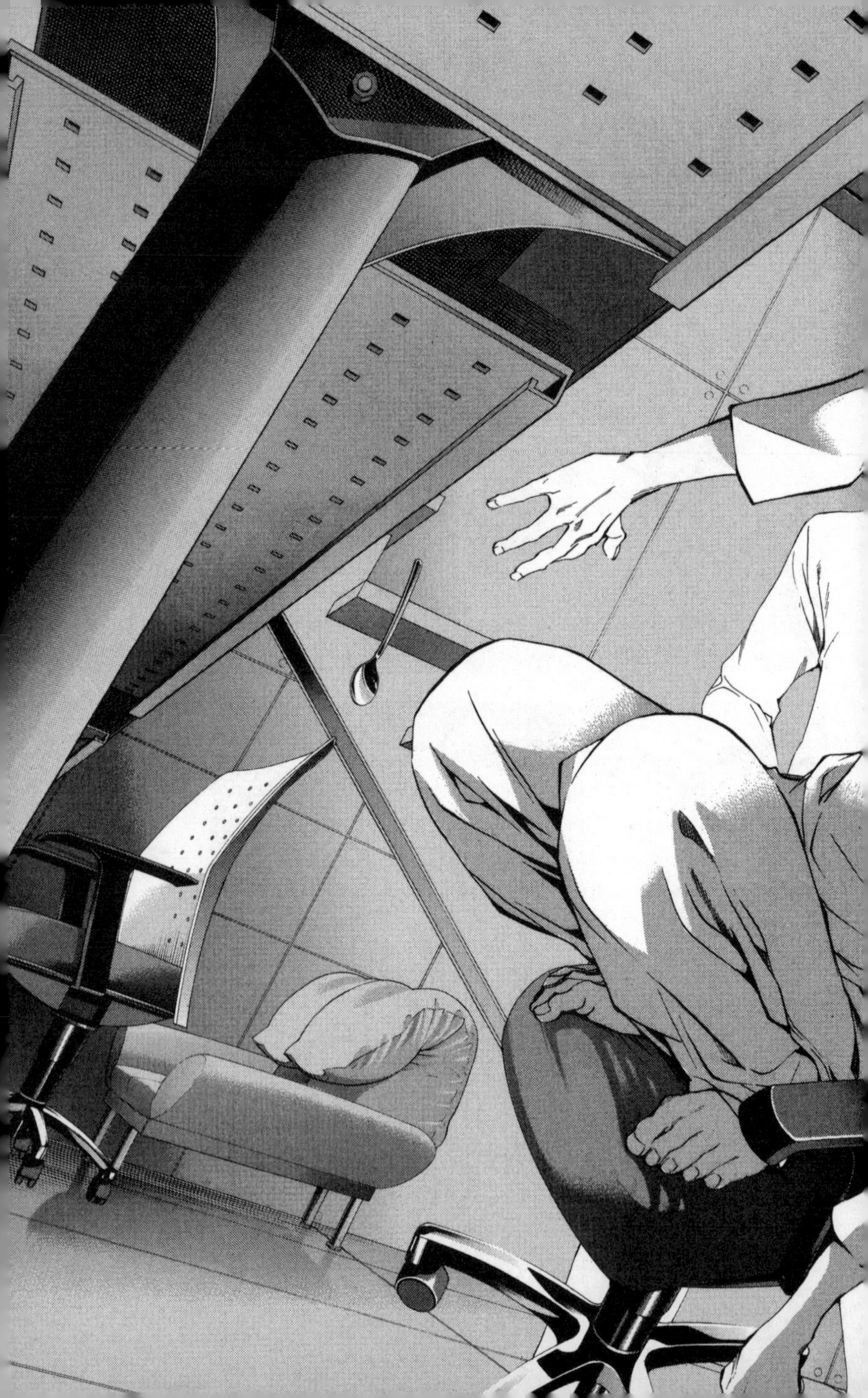

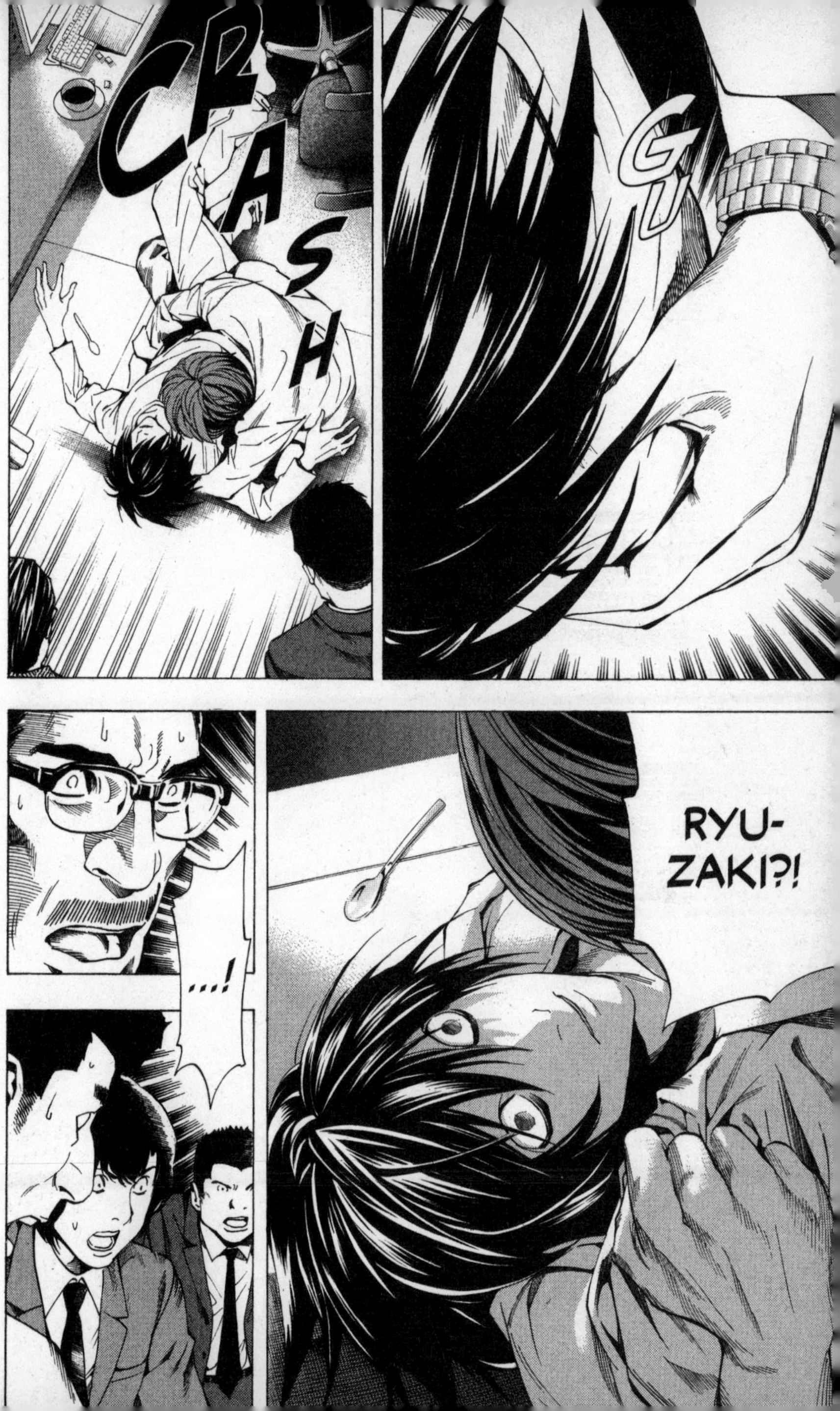
GU
CRASH
RYU-ZAKI?!
...!

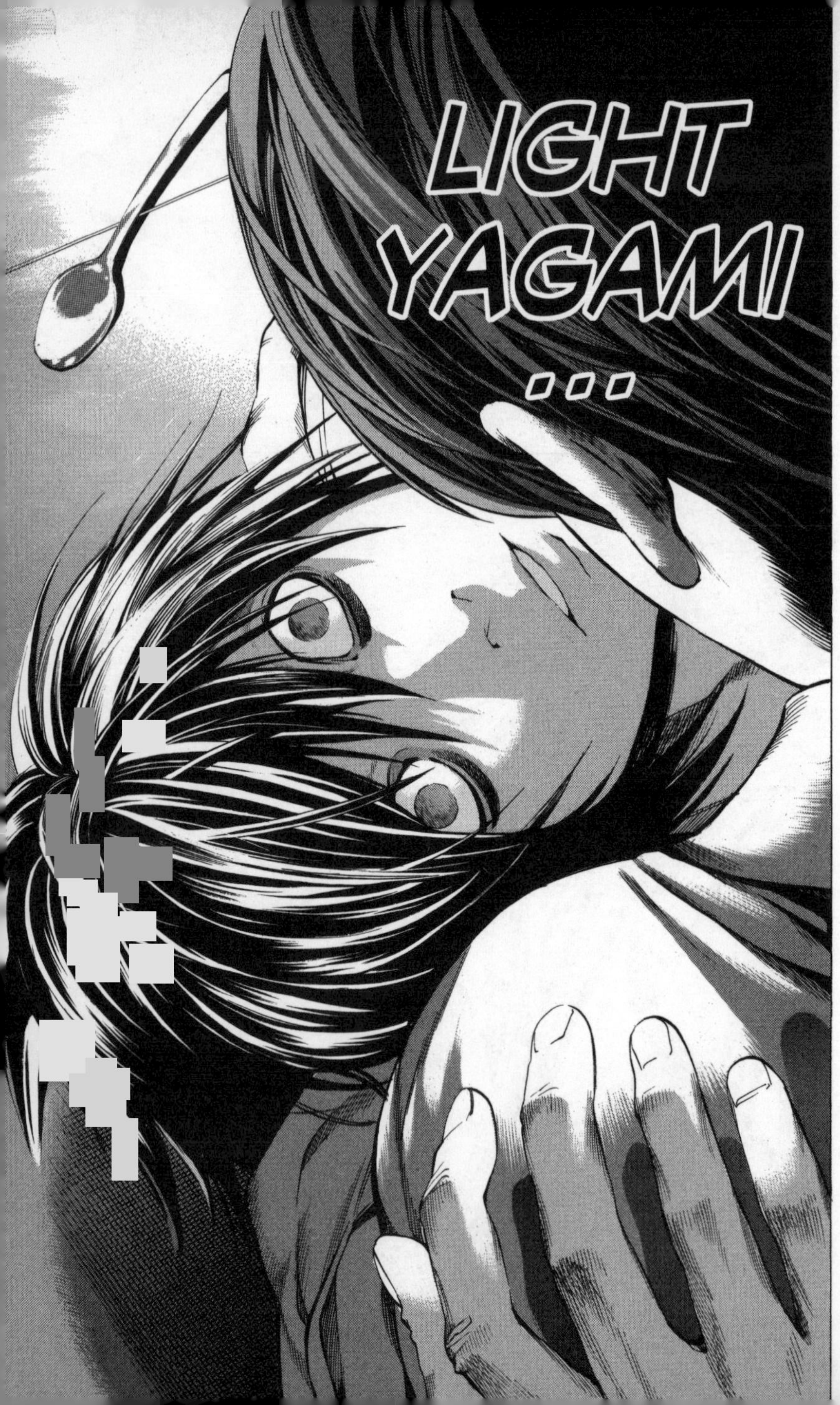
LIGHT YAGAMI ...

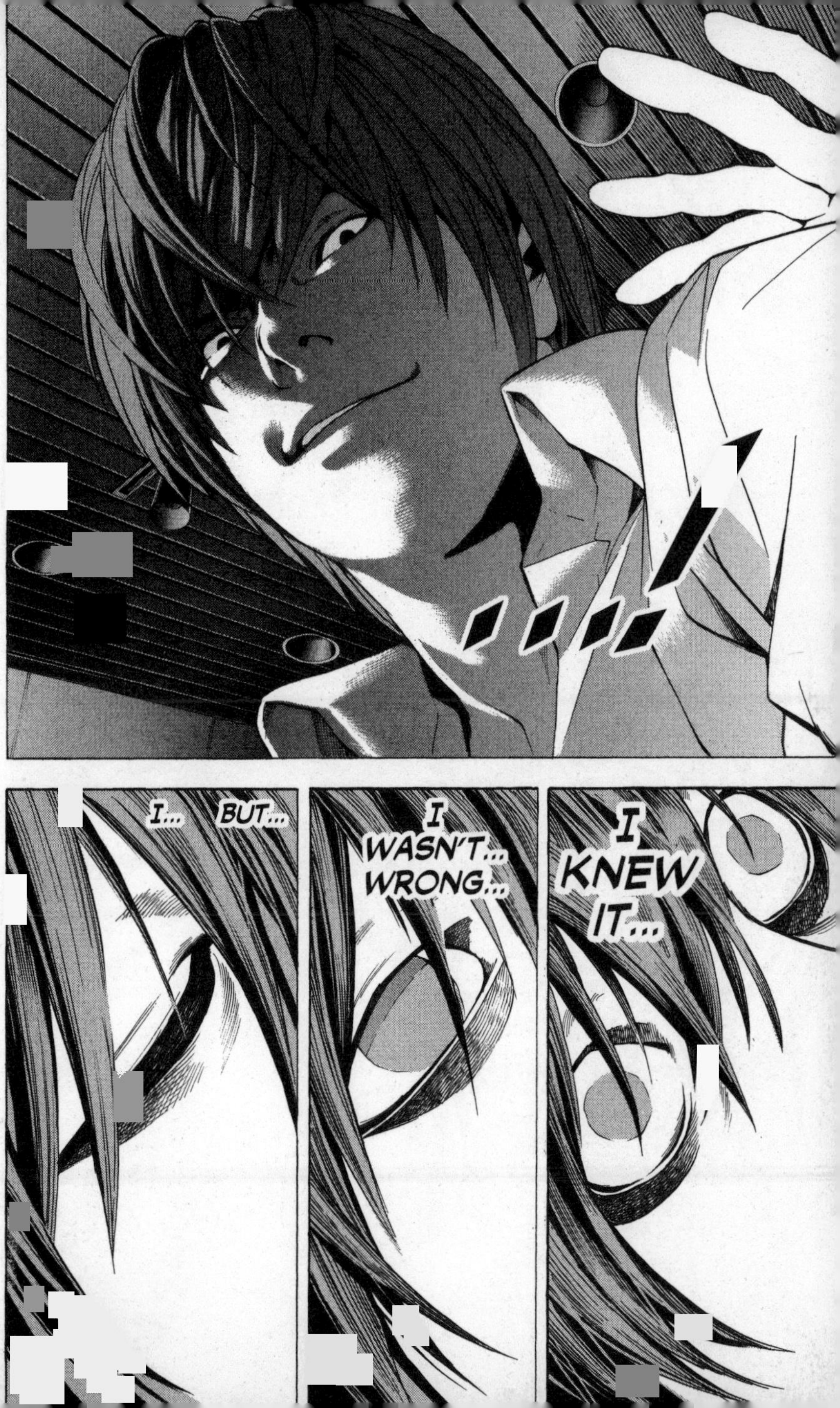
I KNEW IT...
I WASN'T... WRONG...
BUT...
I...

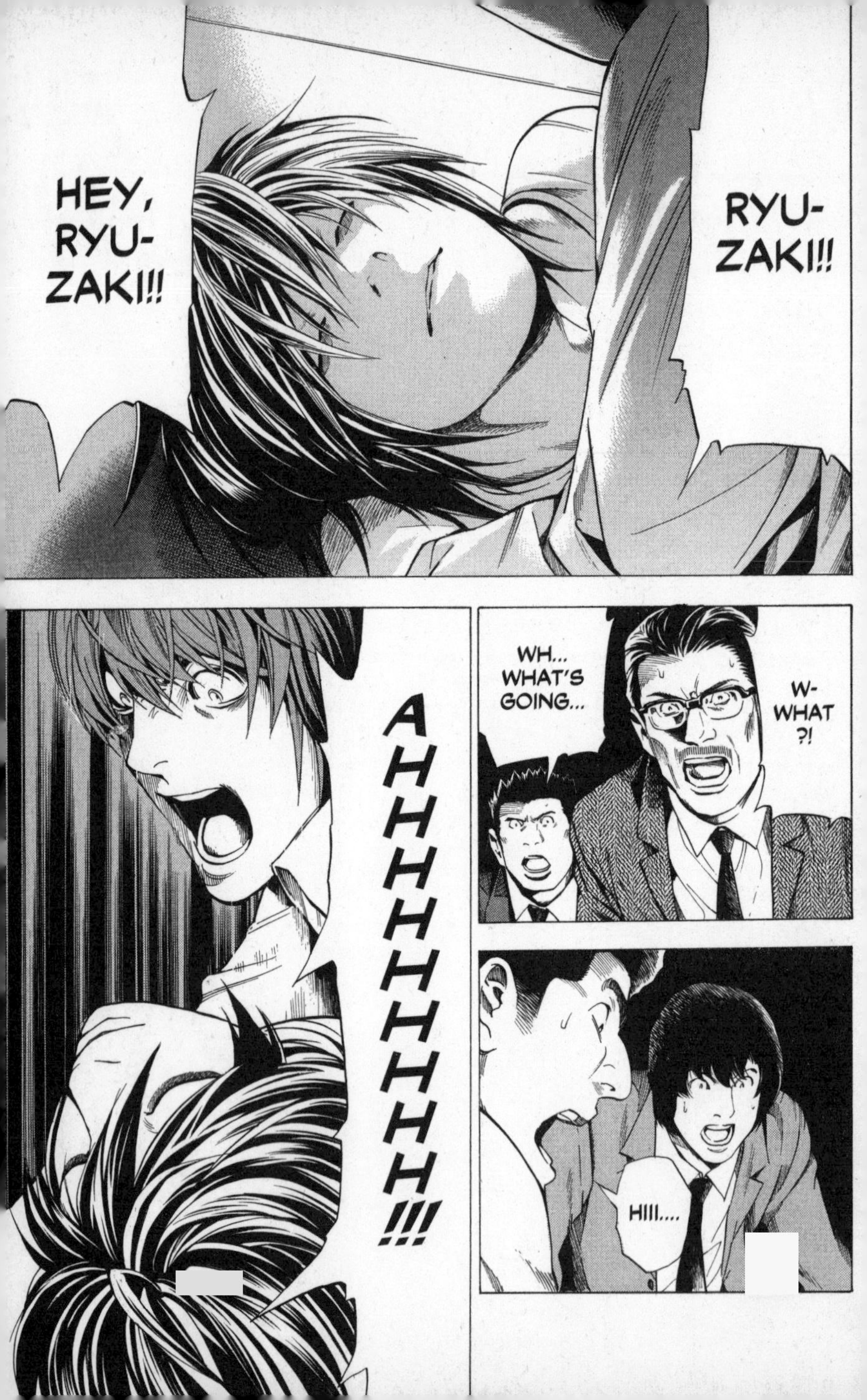
RYU-ZAKI!!!
HEY, RYU-ZAKI!!
W-WHAT ?!
WH... WHAT'S GOING...
HIII....
AHHHHHHHHH!!!

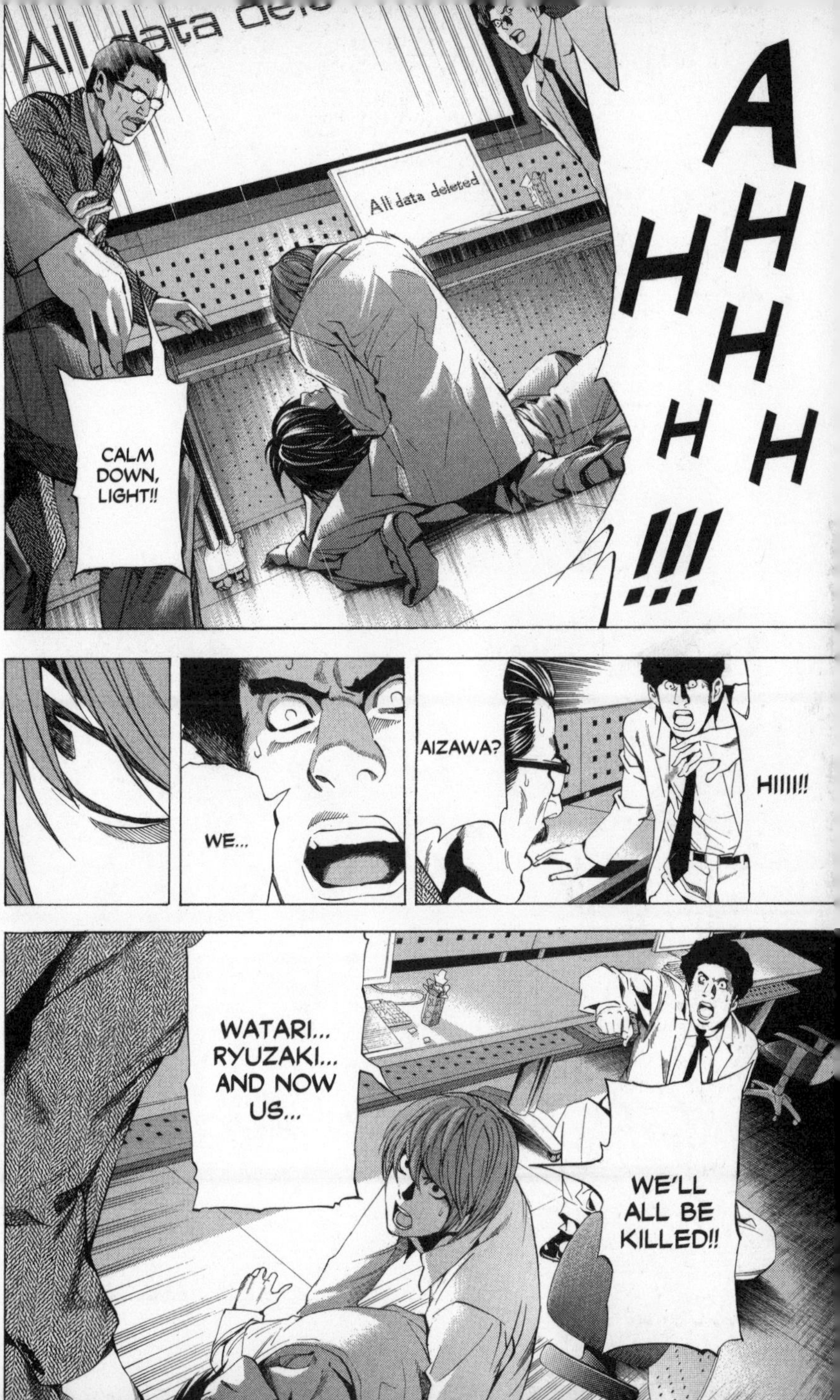
AHHHHH!!!
All data dele
All data deleted
CALM DOWN, LIGHT!!
HIIII!!
AIZAWA?
WE...
WATARI... RYUZAKI... AND NOW US...
WE'LL ALL BE KILLED!!

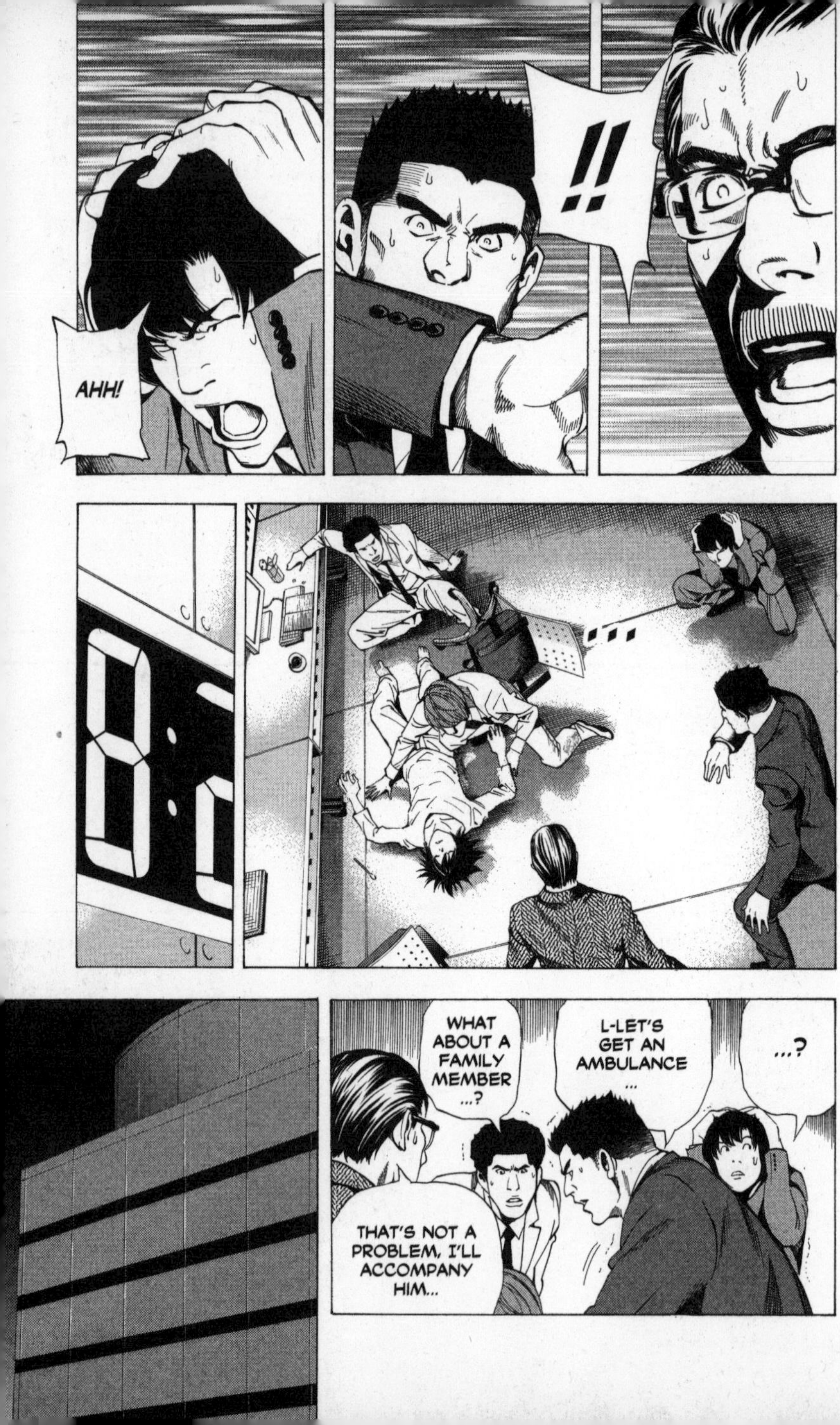
!!
AHH!
...
...?
L-LET'S GET AN AMBULANCE ...
WHAT ABOUT A FAMILY MEMBER ...?
THAT'S NOT A PROBLEM, I'LL ACCOMPANY HIM...

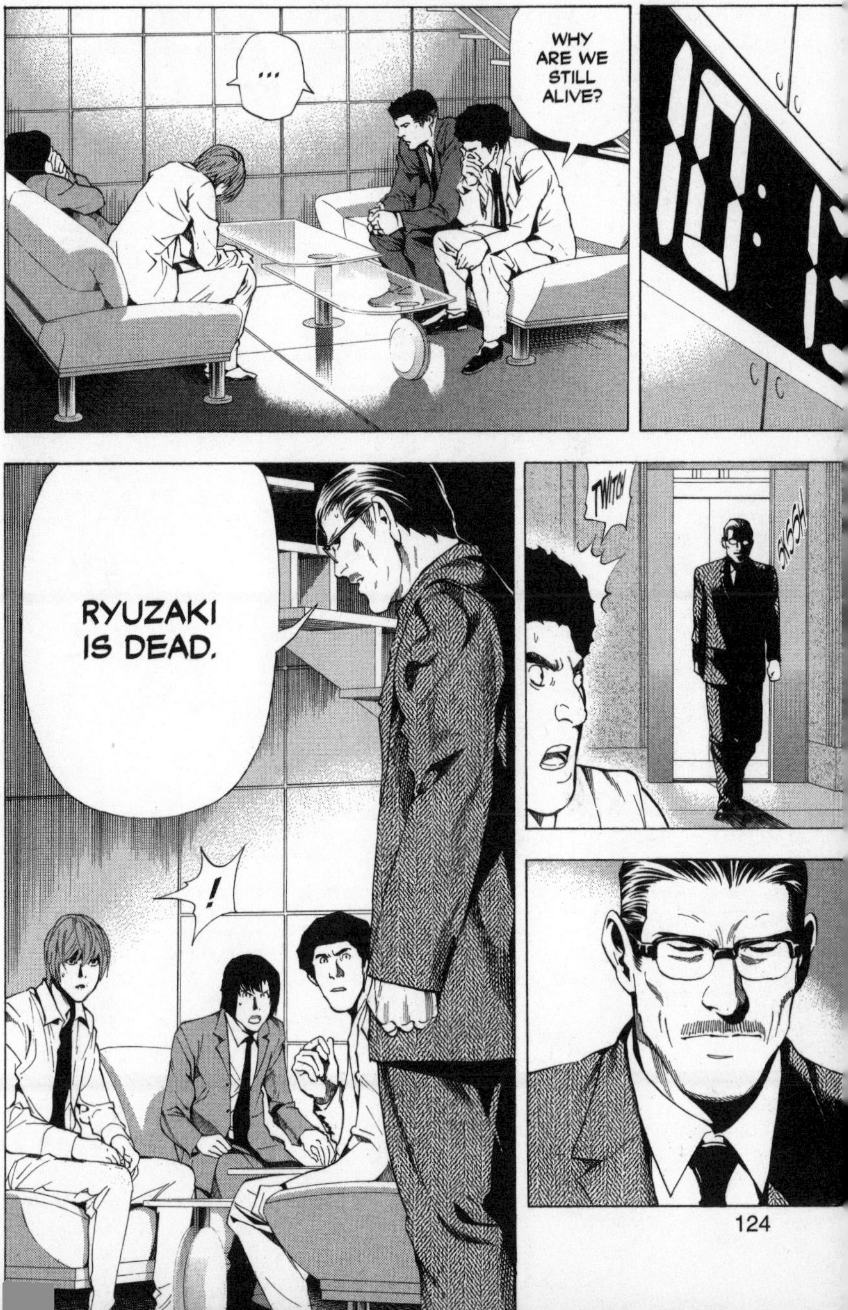
WHY ARE WE STILL ALIVE?
...
SWSSH
TWITCH
RYUZAKI IS DEAD.
!

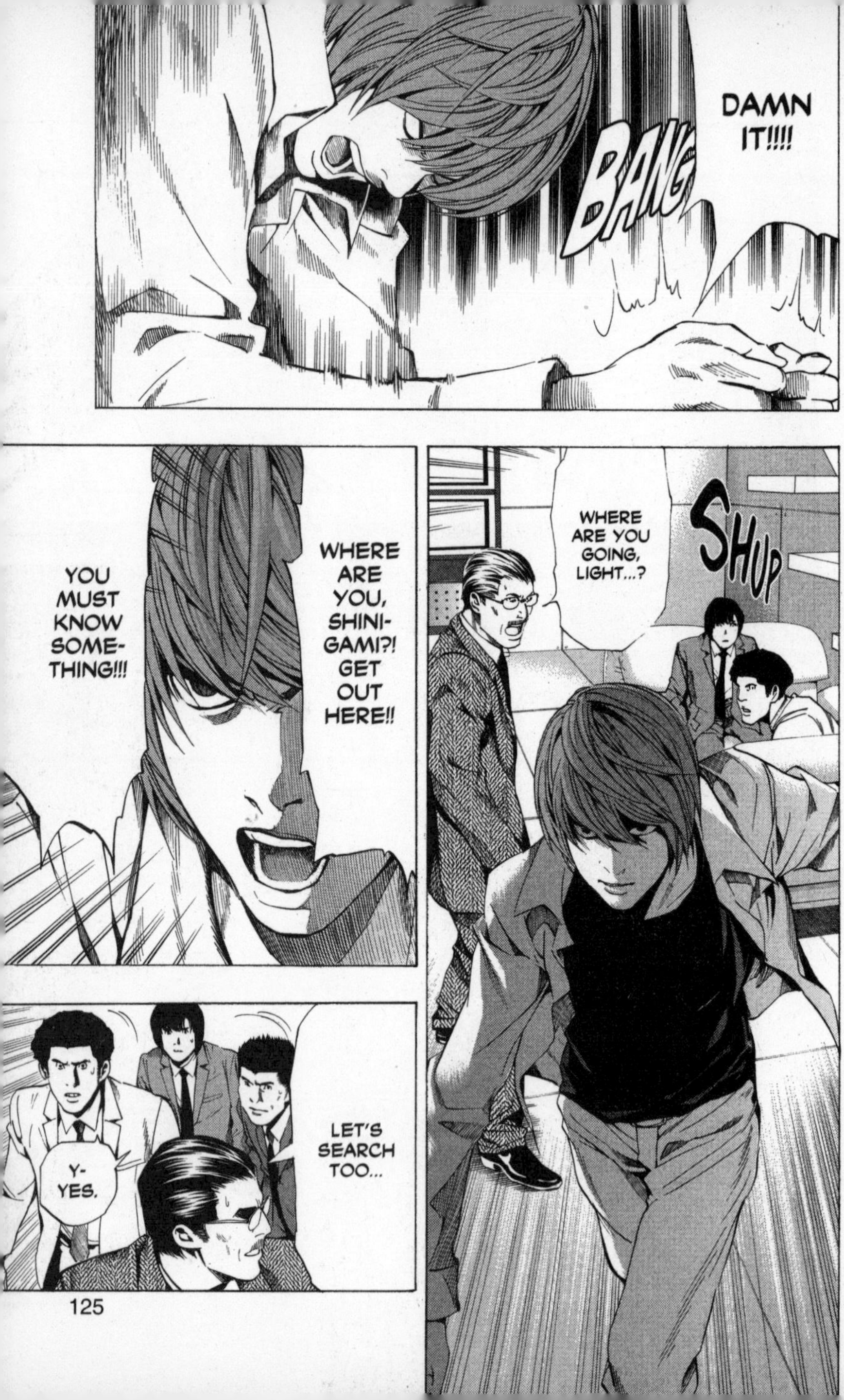
DAMN IT!!!!
BANG
SHUP
WHERE ARE YOU GOING, LIGHT...?
WHERE ARE YOU, SHINI-GAMI?! GET OUT HERE!!
YOU MUST KNOW SOME-THING!!!
LET'S SEARCH TOO...
Y-YES.

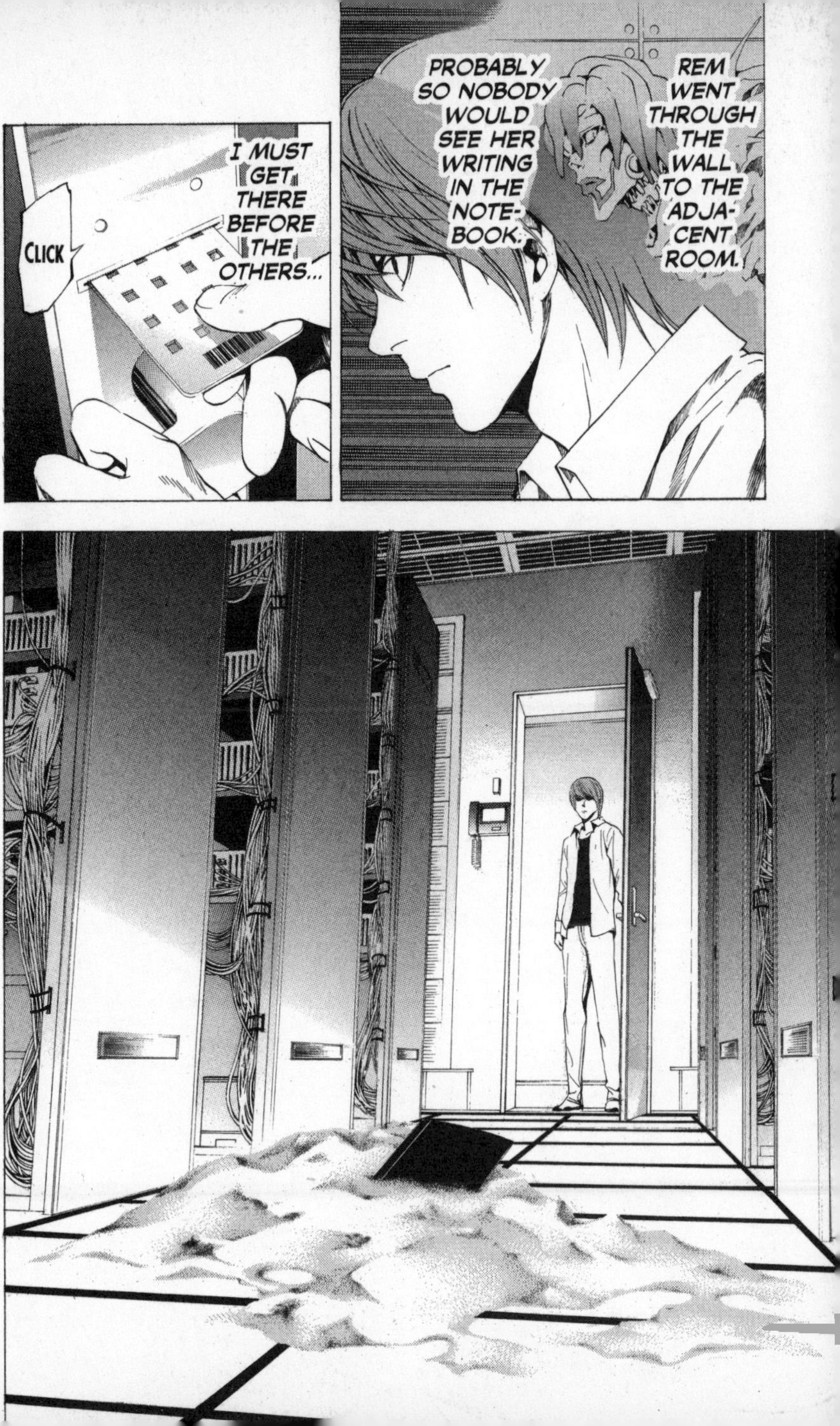
REM WENT THROUGH THE WALL TO THE ADJACENT ROOM.
PROBABLY SO NOBODY WOULD SEE HER WRITING IN THE NOTEBOOK.
CLICK
I MUST GET THERE BEFORE THE OTHERS...

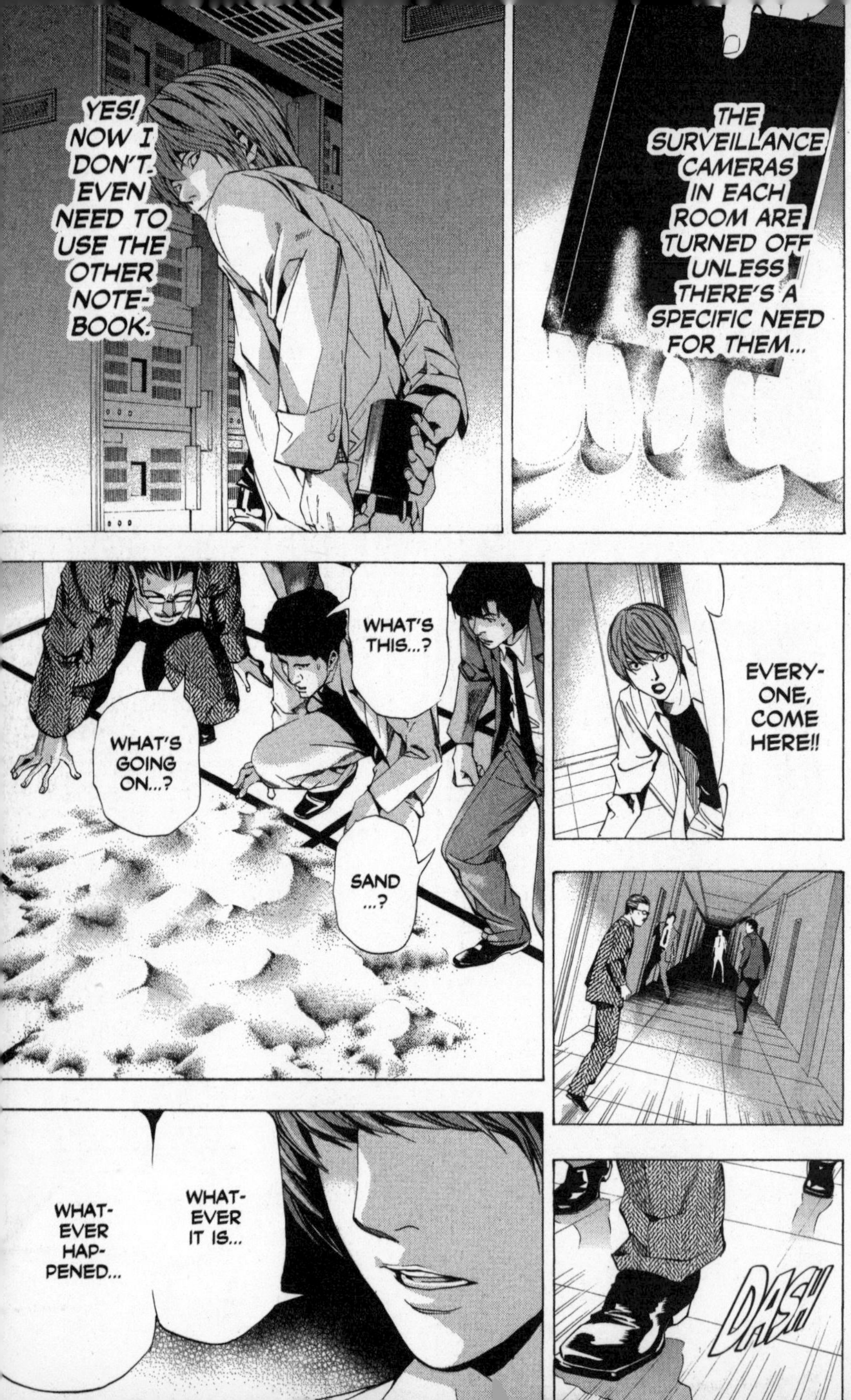
THE SURVEILLANCE CAMERAS IN EACH ROOM ARE TURNED OFF UNLESS THERE'S A SPECIFIC NEED FOR THEM...
YES! NOW I DON'T EVEN NEED TO USE THE OTHER NOTE-BOOK.
EVERY-ONE, COME HERE!!
DASH
WHAT'S THIS...?
WHAT'S GOING ON...?
SAND ...?
WHAT-EVER IT IS...
WHAT-EVER HAP-PENED...

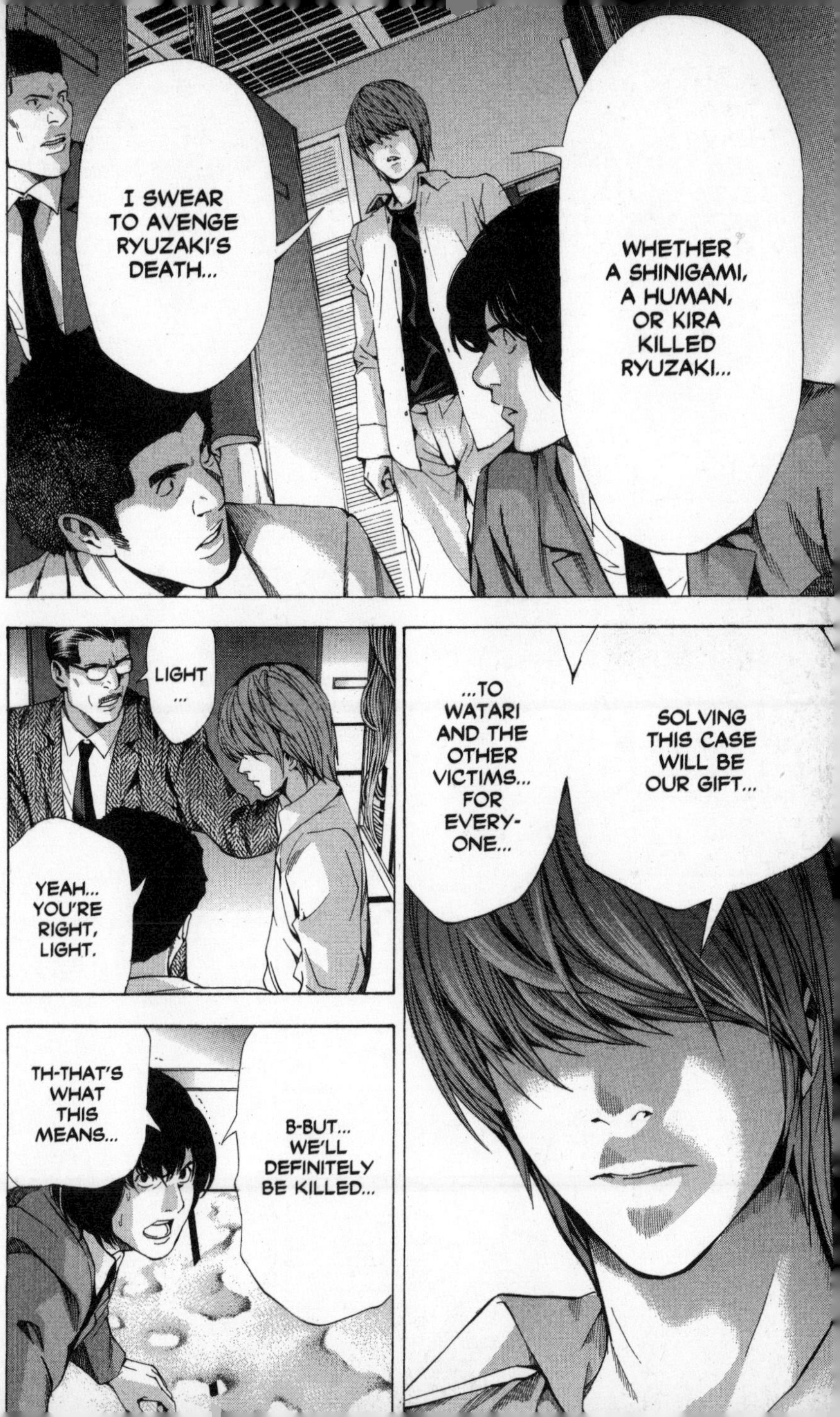
WHETHER A SHINIGAMI, A HUMAN, OR KIRA KILLED RYUZAKI...
I SWEAR TO AVENGE RYUZAKI'S DEATH...
SOLVING THIS CASE WILL BE OUR GIFT...
...TO WATARI AND THE OTHER VICTIMS... FOR EVERY-ONE...
LIGHT ...
YEAH... YOU'RE RIGHT, LIGHT.
B-BUT... WE'LL DEFINITELY BE KILLED...
TH-THAT'S WHAT THIS MEANS...

READ THIS WAY

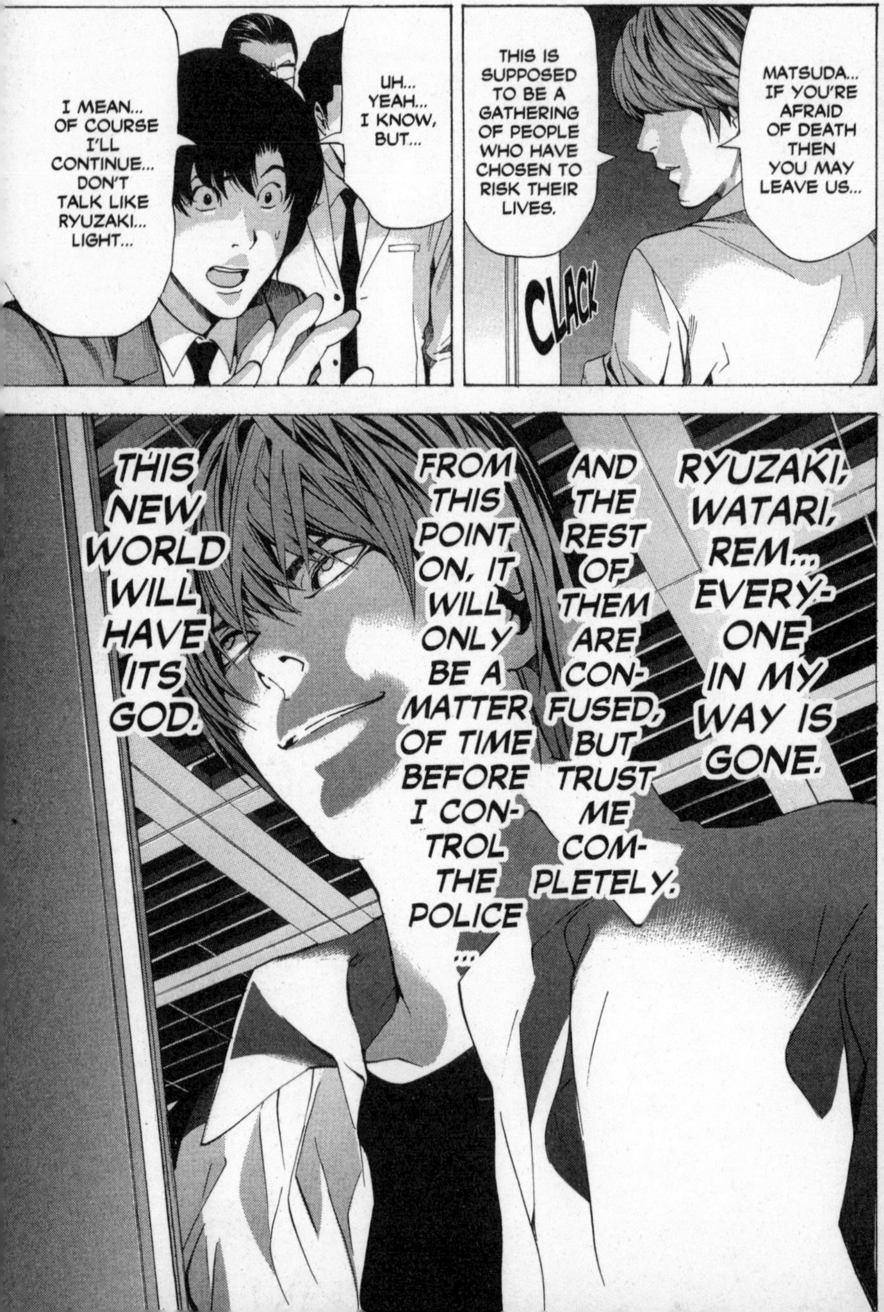
MATSUDA... IF YOU'RE AFRAID OF DEATH THEN YOU MAY LEAVE US...
THIS IS SUPPOSED TO BE A GATHERING OF PEOPLE WHO HAVE CHOSEN TO RISK THEIR LIVES.
CLACK
UH... YEAH... I KNOW, BUT...
I MEAN... OF COURSE I'LL CONTINUE... DON'T TALK LIKE RYUZAKI... LIGHT...
RYUZAKI, WATARI, REM... EVERY-ONE IN MY WAY IS GONE.
AND THE REST OF THEM ARE CON-FUSED, BUT TRUST ME COM-PLETELY.
FROM THIS POINT ON, IT WILL ONLY BE A MATTER OF TIME BEFORE I CON-TROL THE POLICE ...
THIS NEW WORLD WILL HAVE ITS GOD.

DEATH NOTE
How to use it
XL

○ Whenever a god of death who had been in the human world dies and the DEATH NOTE is left behind and is picked up by a human, that person becomes the owner.

人間界にいた死神が死に、人間界に残されたデスノートは、人間が拾えばその人間のものとなる。

○ However, in this case, only the human that can recognize the god of death and its voice is able to see and touch the DEATH NOTE.

しかしこの場合、その死神の姿や声を認知できていた人間でなければ、ノートを見る事も触る事もできない。

○ It is very unlikely, but if by any chance a god of death picks up the DEATH NOTE, that god of death becomes the owner.

可能性として極めて低いが、死神が拾えばその死神の物となる。

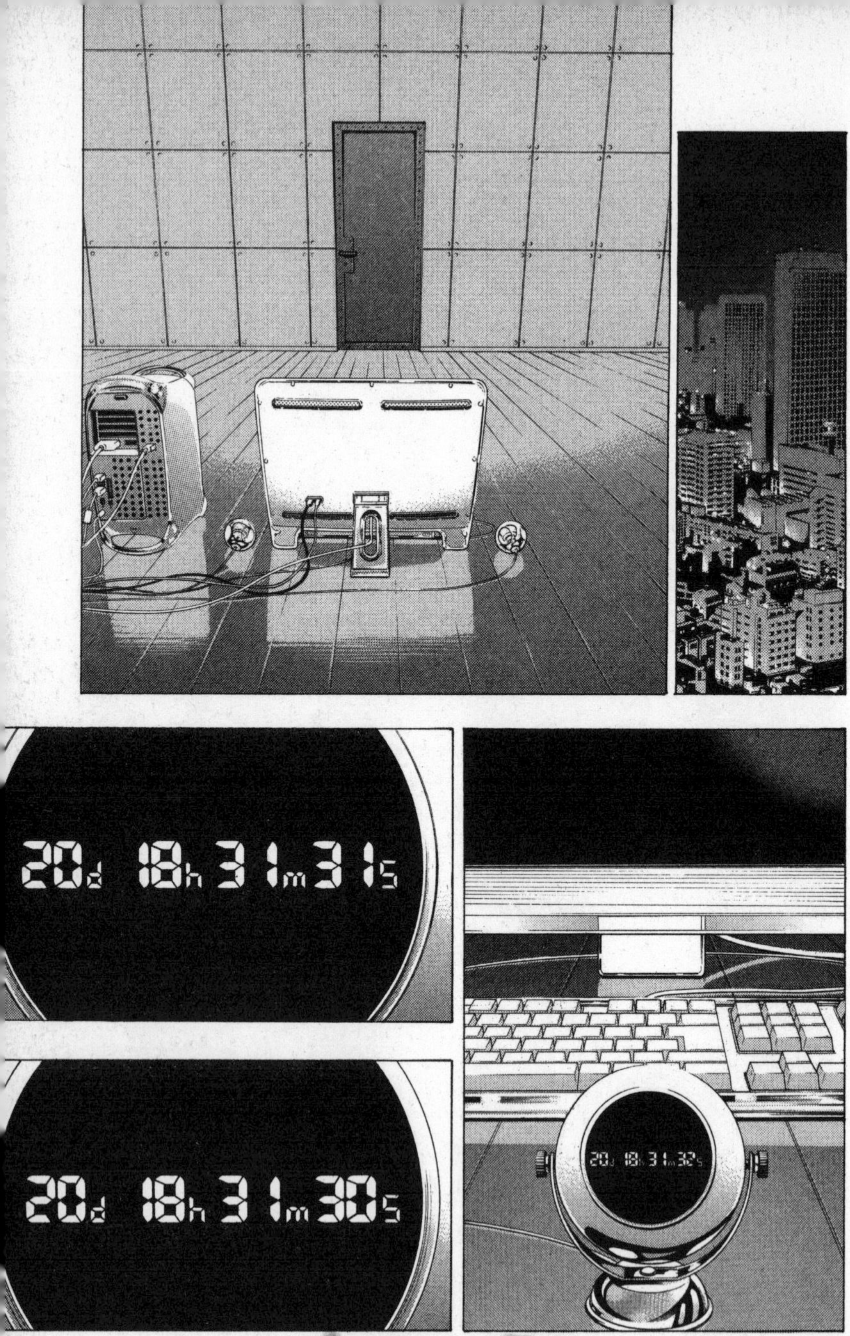
20d 18h 31m 32s
20d 18h 31m 31s
20d 18h 31m 30s

chapter 59 Zero

chapter 59 Zero

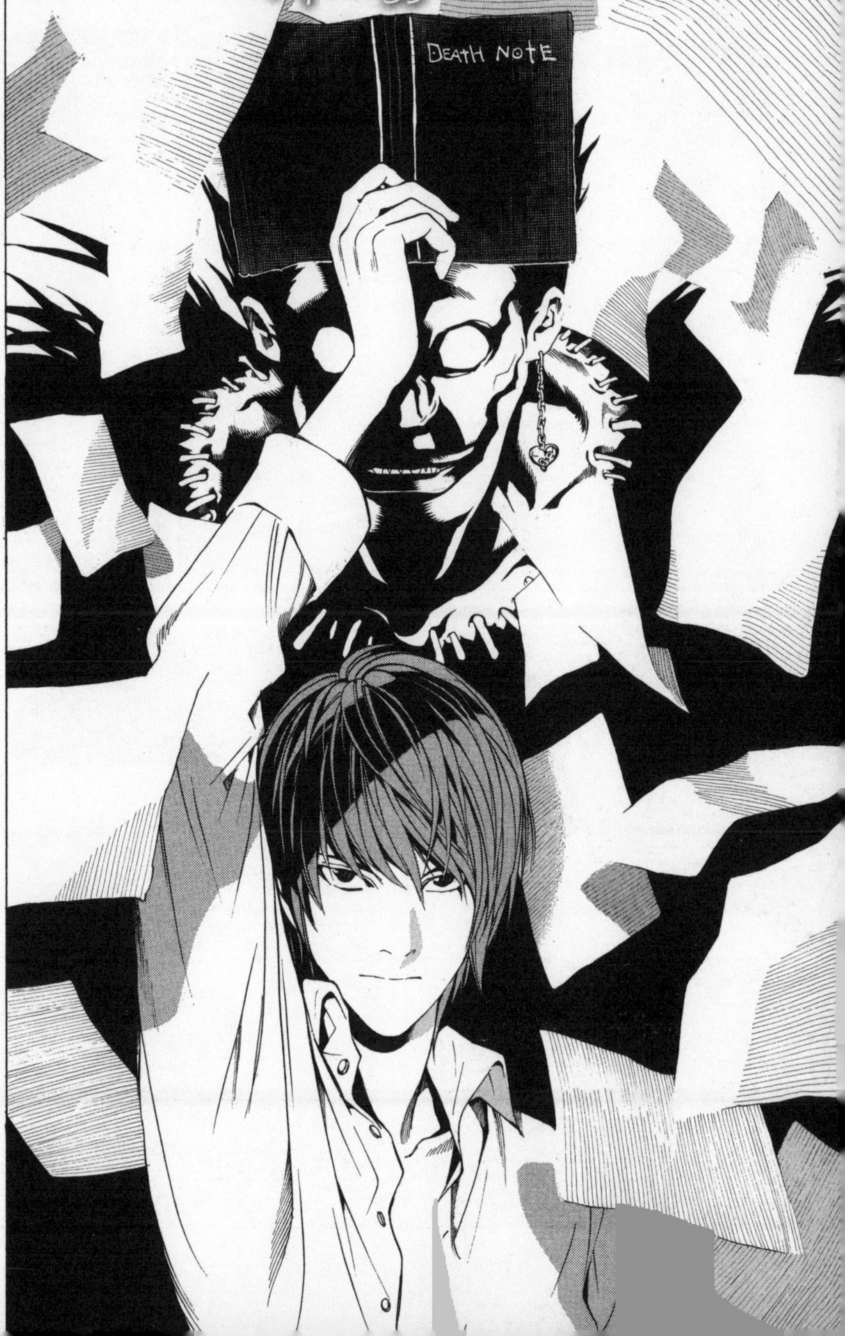
DEATH NOTE

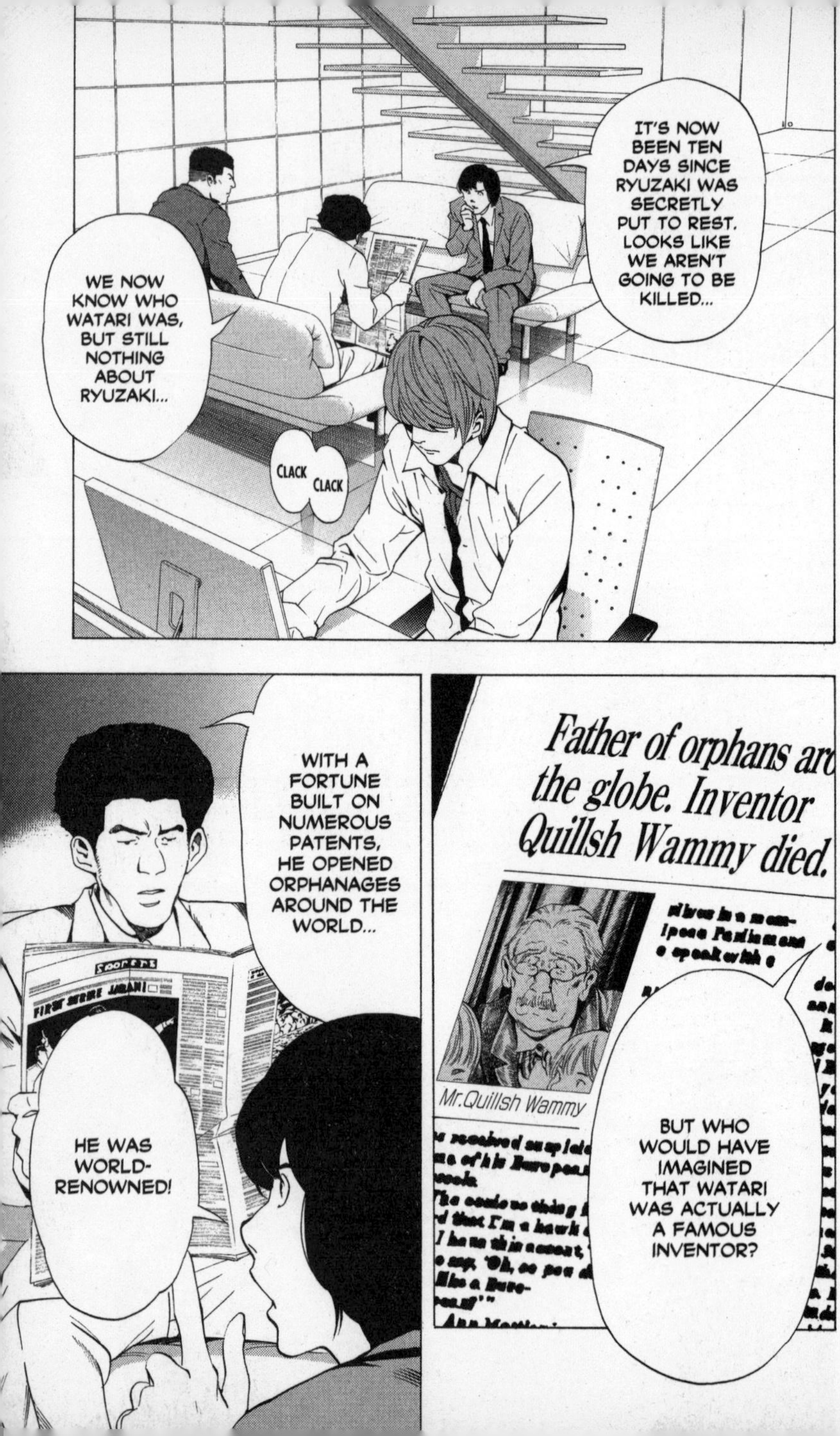

IT'S NOW BEEN TEN DAYS SINCE RYUZAKI WAS SECRETLY PUT TO REST. LOOKS LIKE WE AREN'T GOING TO BE KILLED...
WE NOW KNOW WHO WATARI WAS, BUT STILL NOTHING ABOUT RYUZAKI...
CLACK CLACK
Father of orphans ar
the globe. Inventor
Quillsh Wammy died.
Mr.Quillsh Wammy
BUT WHO WOULD HAVE IMAGINED THAT WATARI WAS ACTUALLY A FAMOUS INVENTOR?
WITH A FORTUNE BUILT ON NUMEROUS PATENTS, HE OPENED ORPHANAGES AROUND THE WORLD...
HE WAS WORLD-RENOWNED!

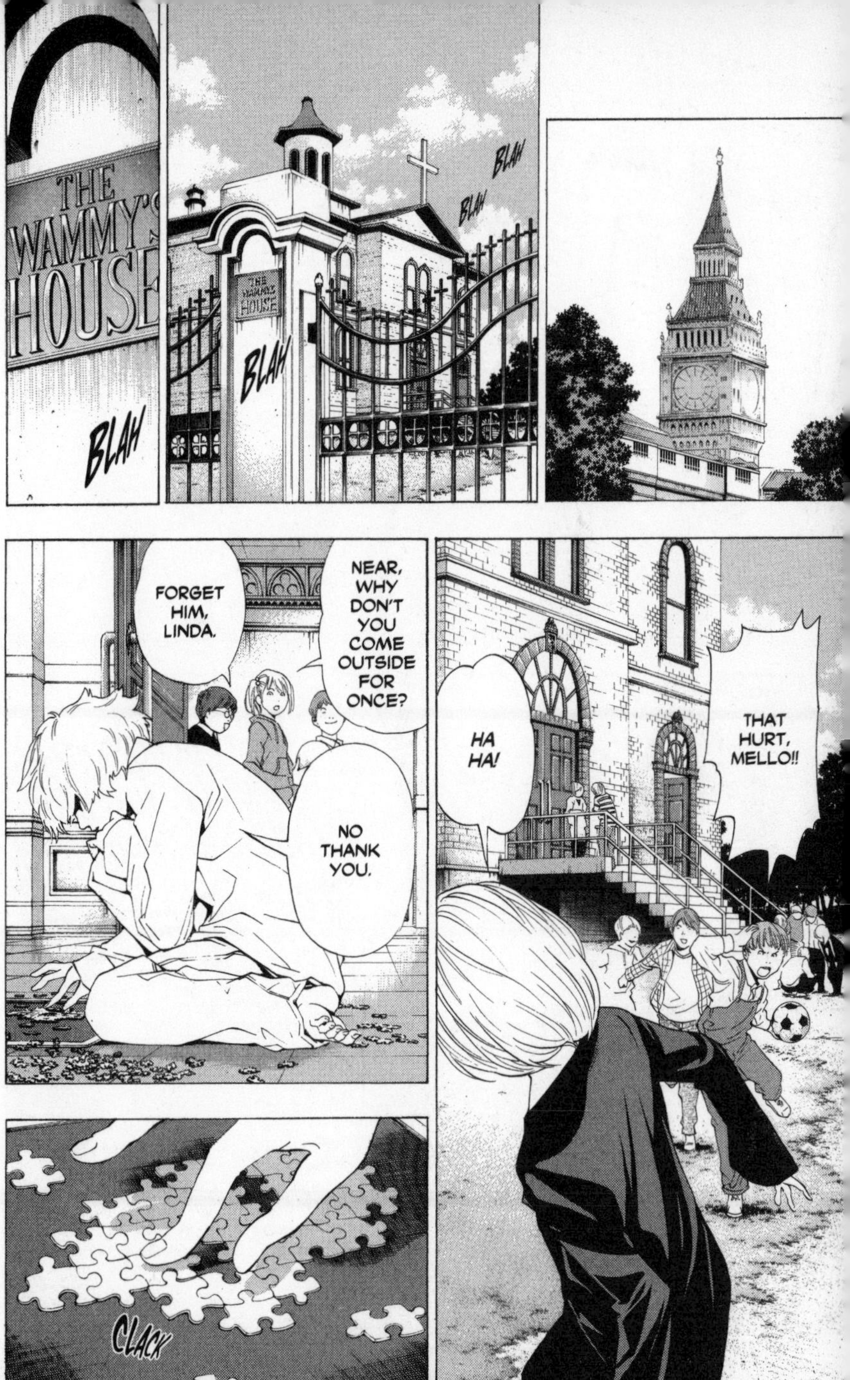
BLAH
BLAH
THE WAMMY'S HOUSE
BLAH
THE WAMMY'S HOUSE
BLAH
THAT HURT, MELLO!!
HA HA!
NEAR, WHY DON'T YOU COME OUTSIDE FOR ONCE?
FORGET HIM, LINDA.
NO THANK YOU.
CLACK

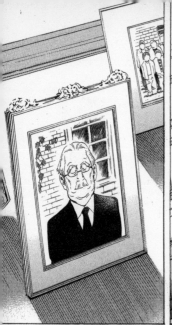

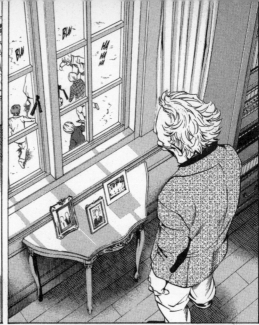

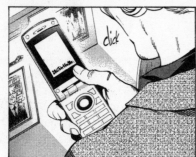

click

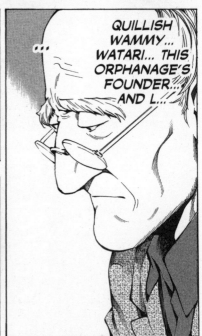

... QUILLISH WAMMY... WATARI... THIS ORPHANAGE'S FOUNDER... AND L...!

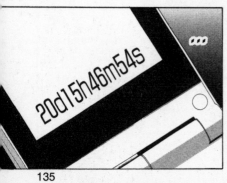

20d15h46m54s

...

135

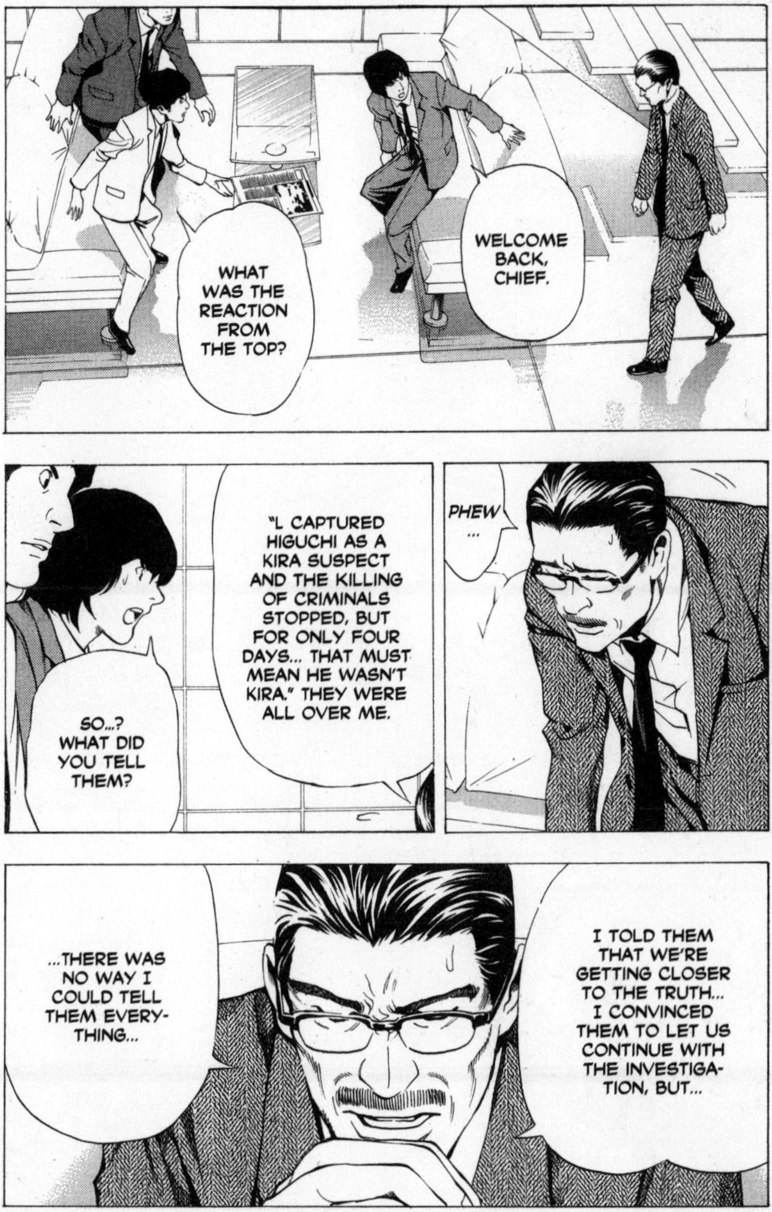
WELCOME BACK, CHIEF.
WHAT WAS THE REACTION FROM THE TOP?
PHEW ...
"L CAPTURED HIGUCHI AS A KIRA SUSPECT AND THE KILLING OF CRIMINALS STOPPED, BUT FOR ONLY FOUR DAYS... THAT MUST MEAN HE WASN'T KIRA." THEY WERE ALL OVER ME.
SO...? WHAT DID YOU TELL THEM?
I TOLD THEM THAT WE'RE GETTING CLOSER TO THE TRUTH... I CONVINCED THEM TO LET US CONTINUE WITH THE INVESTIGA-TION, BUT...
...THERE WAS NO WAY I COULD TELL THEM EVERY-THING...

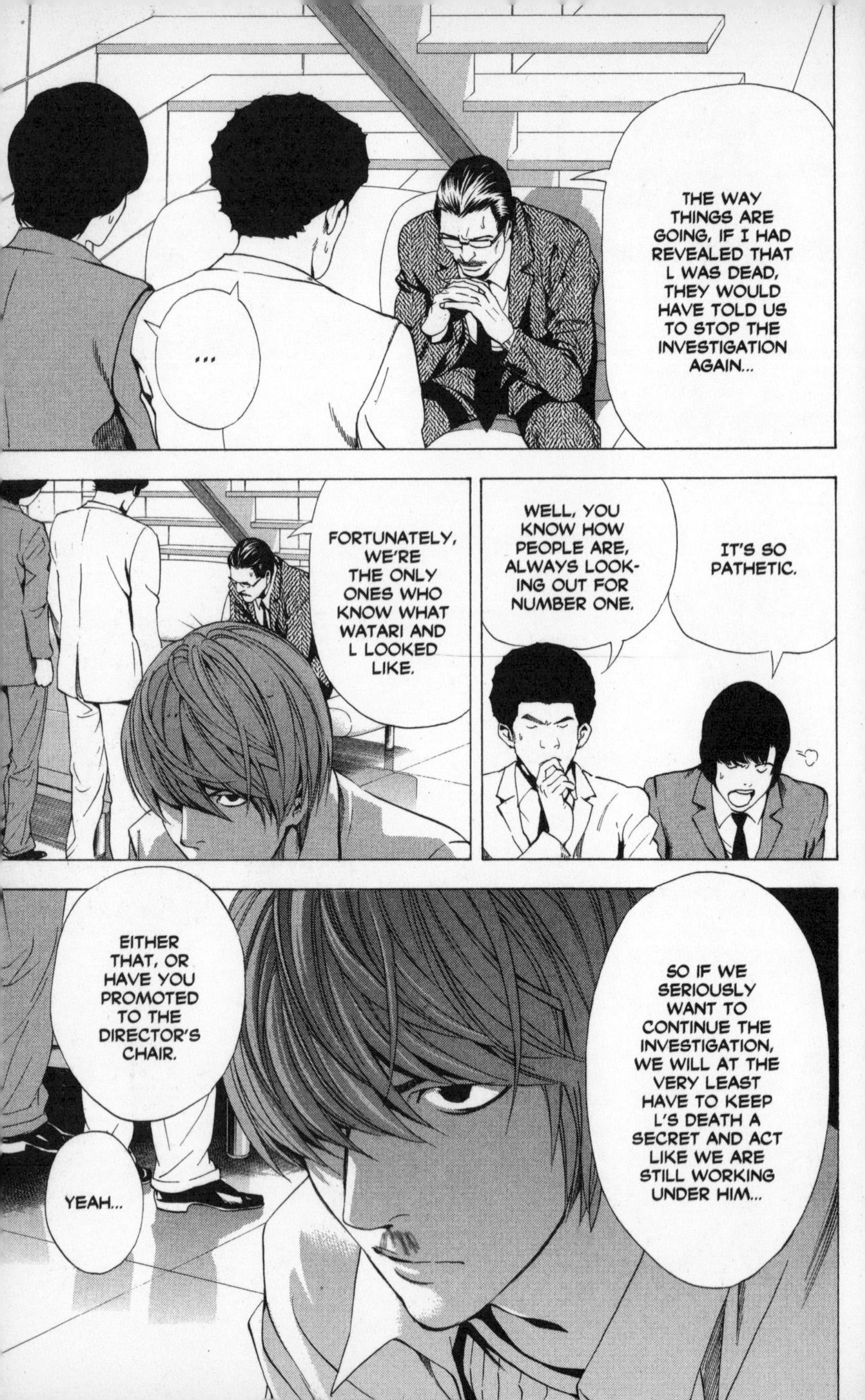
THE WAY THINGS ARE GOING, IF I HAD REVEALED THAT L WAS DEAD, THEY WOULD HAVE TOLD US TO STOP THE INVESTIGATION AGAIN...
...
IT'S SO PATHETIC.
WELL, YOU KNOW HOW PEOPLE ARE, ALWAYS LOOK-ING OUT FOR NUMBER ONE.
FORTUNATELY, WE'RE THE ONLY ONES WHO KNOW WHAT WATARI AND L LOOKED LIKE.
SO IF WE SERIOUSLY WANT TO CONTINUE THE INVESTIGATION, WE WILL AT THE VERY LEAST HAVE TO KEEP L'S DEATH A SECRET AND ACT LIKE WE ARE STILL WORKING UNDER HIM...
EITHER THAT, OR HAVE YOU PROMOTED TO THE DIRECTOR'S CHAIR.
YEAH...

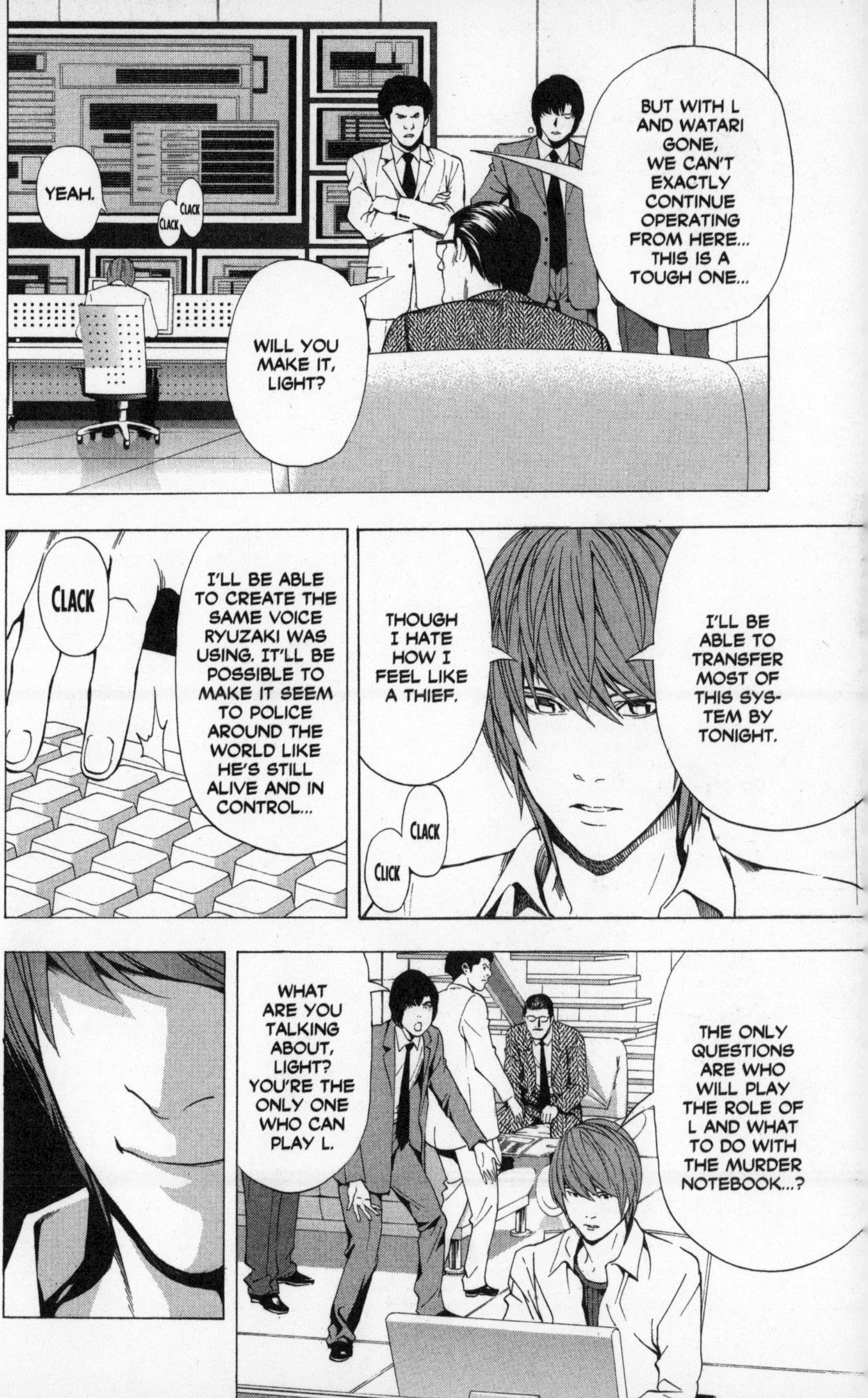
BUT WITH L AND WATARI GONE, WE CAN'T EXACTLY CONTINUE OPERATING FROM HERE... THIS IS A TOUGH ONE...
WILL YOU MAKE IT, LIGHT?
YEAH.
CLACK
CLACK
I'LL BE ABLE TO TRANSFER MOST OF THIS SYS-TEM BY TONIGHT.
THOUGH I HATE HOW I FEEL LIKE A THIEF.
CLACK
CLICK
CLACK
I'LL BE ABLE TO CREATE THE SAME VOICE RYUZAKI WAS USING. IT'LL BE POSSIBLE TO MAKE IT SEEM TO POLICE AROUND THE WORLD LIKE HE'S STILL ALIVE AND IN CONTROL...
THE ONLY QUESTIONS ARE WHO WILL PLAY THE ROLE OF L AND WHAT TO DO WITH THE MURDER NOTEBOOK...?
WHAT ARE YOU TALKING ABOUT, LIGHT? YOU'RE THE ONLY ONE WHO CAN PLAY L.

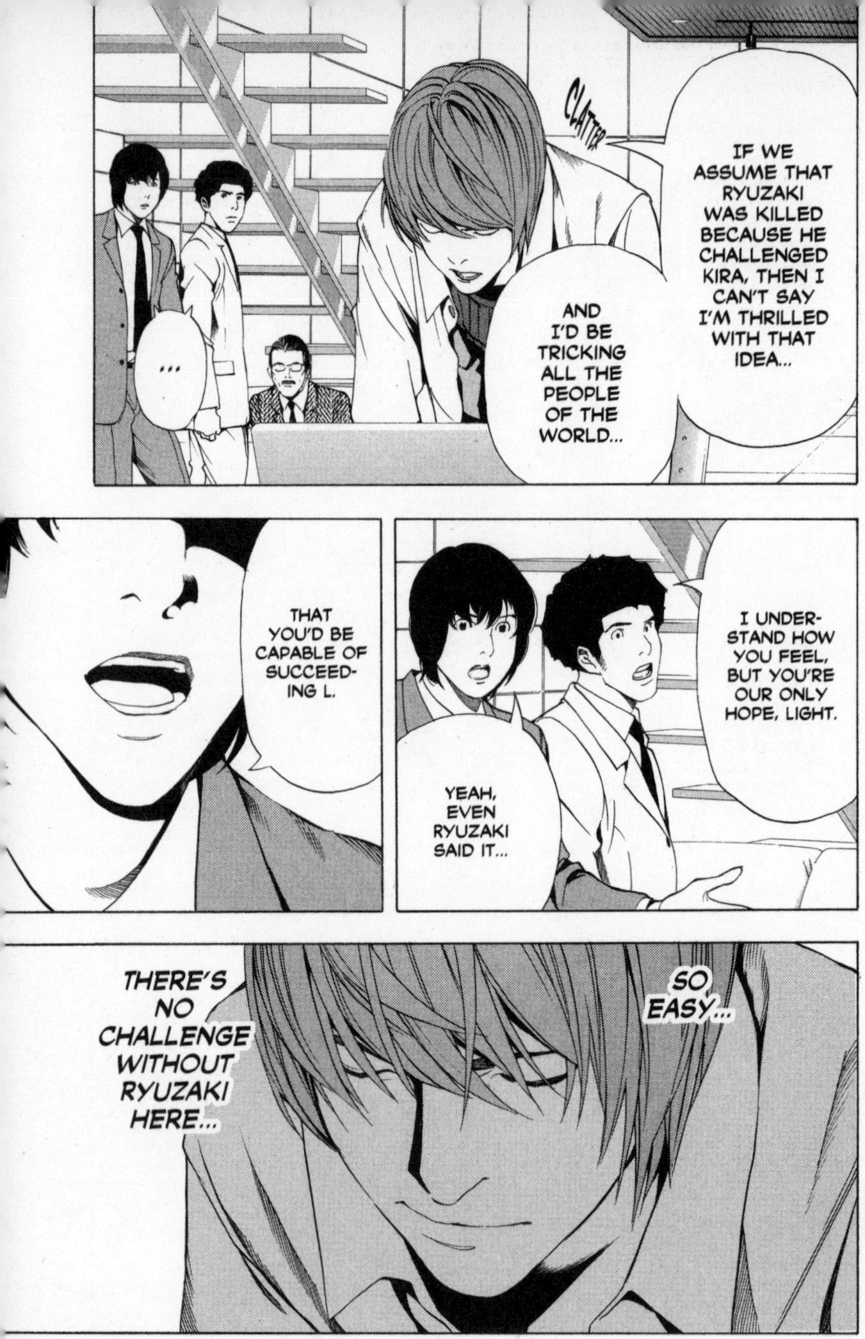
CLATTER
IF WE ASSUME THAT RYUZAKI WAS KILLED BECAUSE HE CHALLENGED KIRA, THEN I CAN'T SAY I'M THRILLED WITH THAT IDEA...
AND I'D BE TRICKING ALL THE PEOPLE OF THE WORLD...
...
I UNDER-STAND HOW YOU FEEL, BUT YOU'RE OUR ONLY HOPE, LIGHT.
YEAH, EVEN RYUZAKI SAID IT...
THAT YOU'D BE CAPABLE OF SUCCEED-ING L.
SO EASY...
THERE'S NO CHALLENGE WITHOUT RYUZAKI HERE...

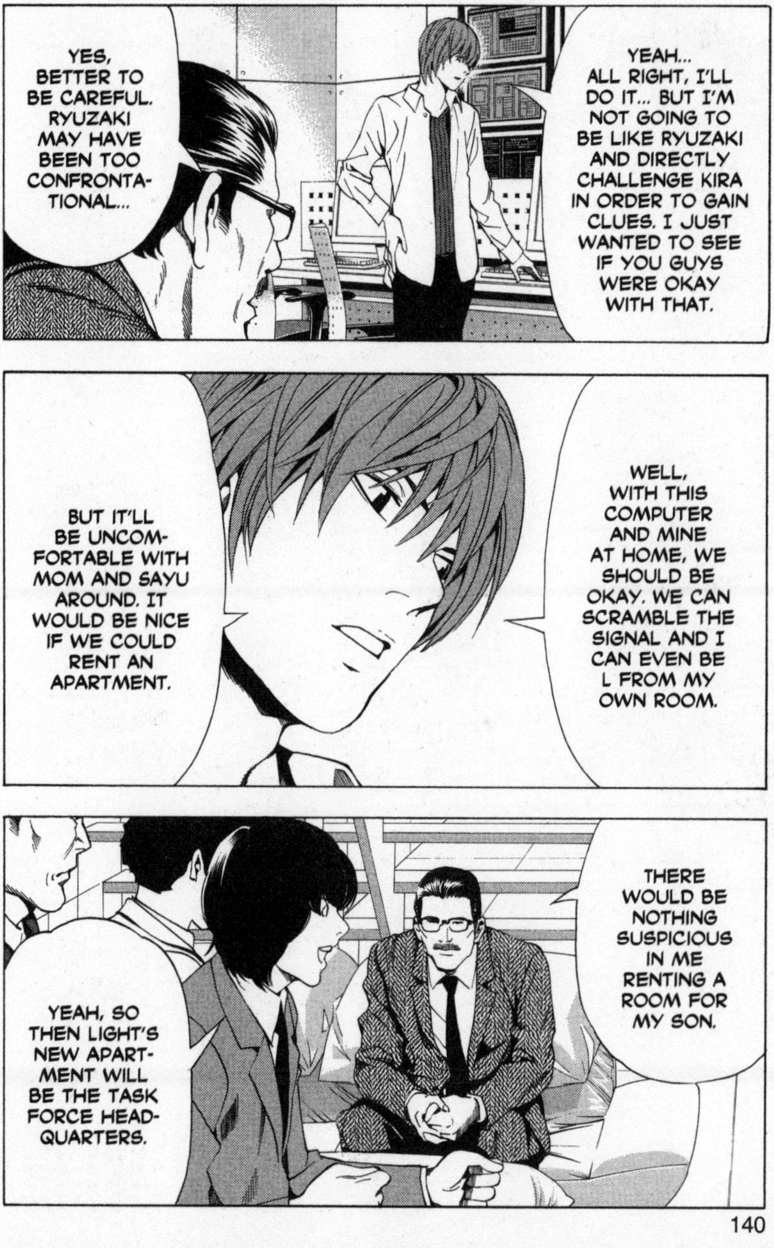
YEAH... ALL RIGHT, I'LL DO IT... BUT I'M NOT GOING TO BE LIKE RYUZAKI AND DIRECTLY CHALLENGE KIRA IN ORDER TO GAIN CLUES. I JUST WANTED TO SEE IF YOU GUYS WERE OKAY WITH THAT.
YES, BETTER TO BE CAREFUL. RYUZAKI MAY HAVE BEEN TOO CONFRONTA-TIONAL...
WELL, WITH THIS COMPUTER AND MINE AT HOME, WE SHOULD BE OKAY. WE CAN SCRAMBLE THE SIGNAL AND I CAN EVEN BE L FROM MY OWN ROOM.
BUT IT'LL BE UNCOM-FORTABLE WITH MOM AND SAYU AROUND. IT WOULD BE NICE IF WE COULD RENT AN APARTMENT.
THERE WOULD BE NOTHING SUSPICIOUS IN ME RENTING A ROOM FOR MY SON.
YEAH, SO THEN LIGHT'S NEW APART-MENT WILL BE THE TASK FORCE HEAD-QUARTERS.

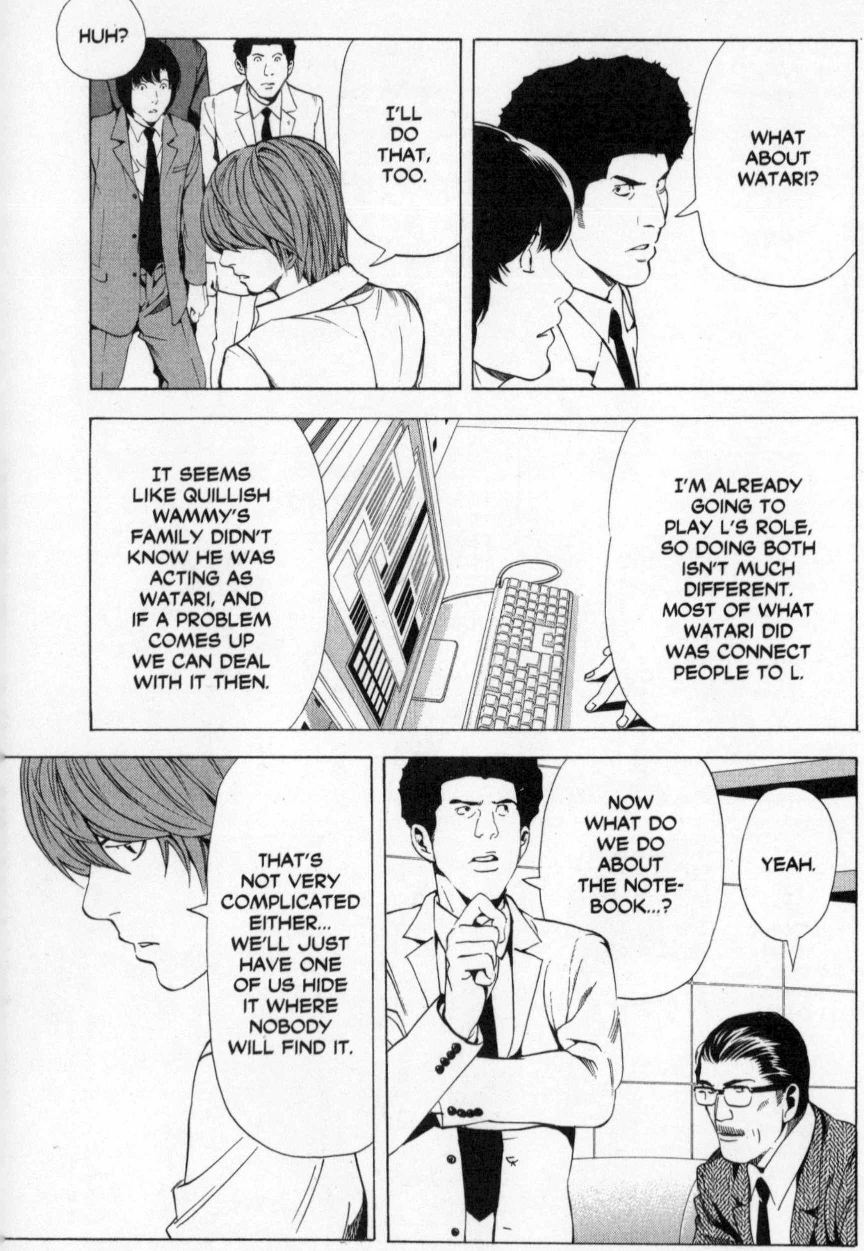
WHAT ABOUT WATARI?
I'LL DO THAT, TOO.
HUH?
I'M ALREADY GOING TO PLAY L'S ROLE, SO DOING BOTH ISN'T MUCH DIFFERENT. MOST OF WHAT WATARI DID WAS CONNECT PEOPLE TO L.
IT SEEMS LIKE QUILLISH WAMMY'S FAMILY DIDN'T KNOW HE WAS ACTING AS WATARI, AND IF A PROBLEM COMES UP WE CAN DEAL WITH IT THEN.
YEAH.
NOW WHAT DO WE DO ABOUT THE NOTE-BOOK...?
THAT'S NOT VERY COMPLICATED EITHER... WE'LL JUST HAVE ONE OF US HIDE IT WHERE NOBODY WILL FIND IT.

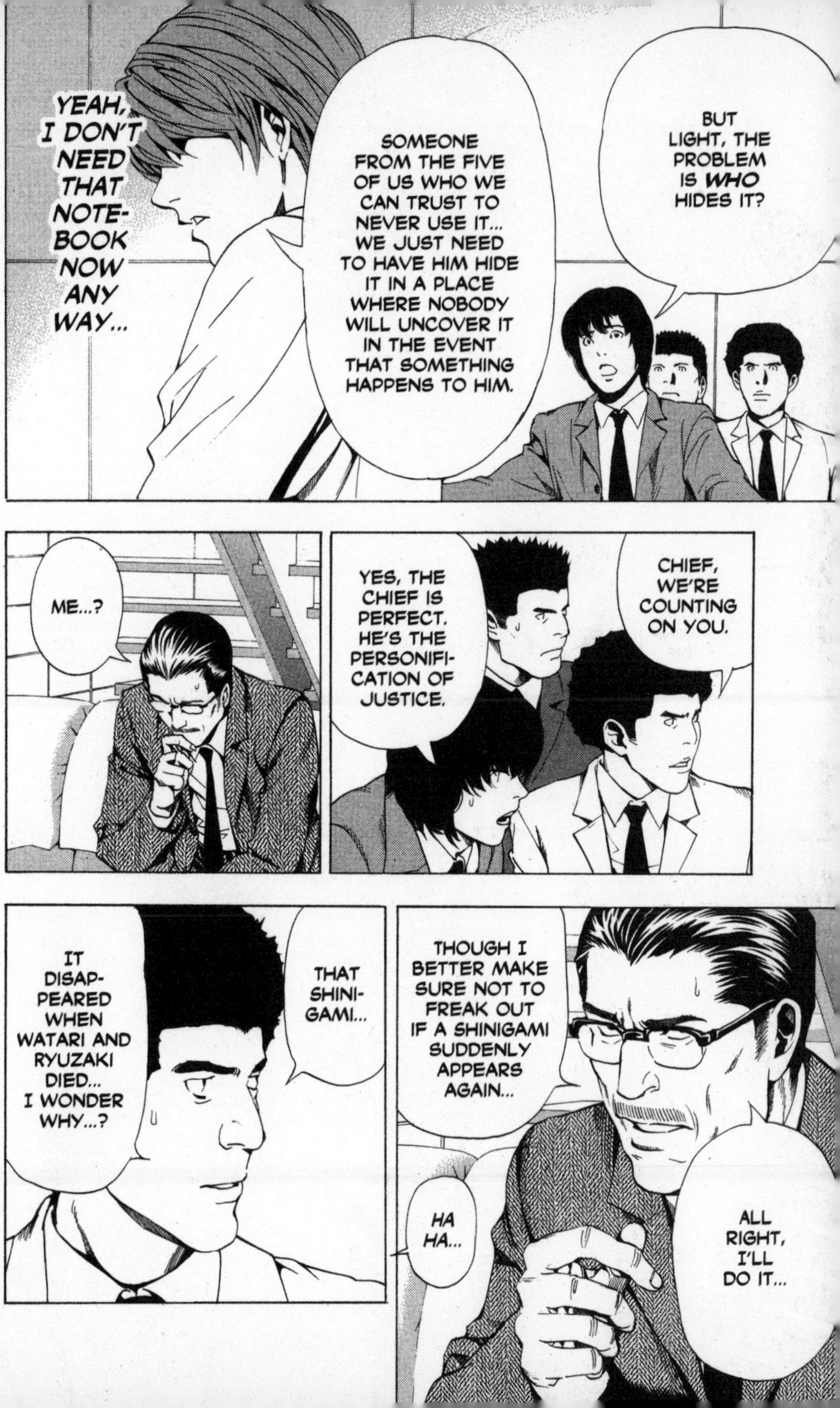
BUT LIGHT, THE PROBLEM IS *WHO* HIDES IT?
SOMEONE FROM THE FIVE OF US WHO WE CAN TRUST TO NEVER USE IT... WE JUST NEED TO HAVE HIM HIDE IT IN A PLACE WHERE NOBODY WILL UNCOVER IT IN THE EVENT THAT SOMETHING HAPPENS TO HIM.
YEAH, I DON'T NEED THAT NOTE-BOOK NOW ANY WAY...
CHIEF, WE'RE COUNTING ON YOU.
YES, THE CHIEF IS PERFECT. HE'S THE PERSONIFI-CATION OF JUSTICE.
ME...?
ALL RIGHT, I'LL DO IT...
THOUGH I BETTER MAKE SURE NOT TO FREAK OUT IF A SHINIGAMI SUDDENLY APPEARS AGAIN...
HA HA...
THAT SHINI-GAMI...
IT DISAP-PEARED WHEN WATARI AND RYUZAKI DIED... I WONDER WHY...?

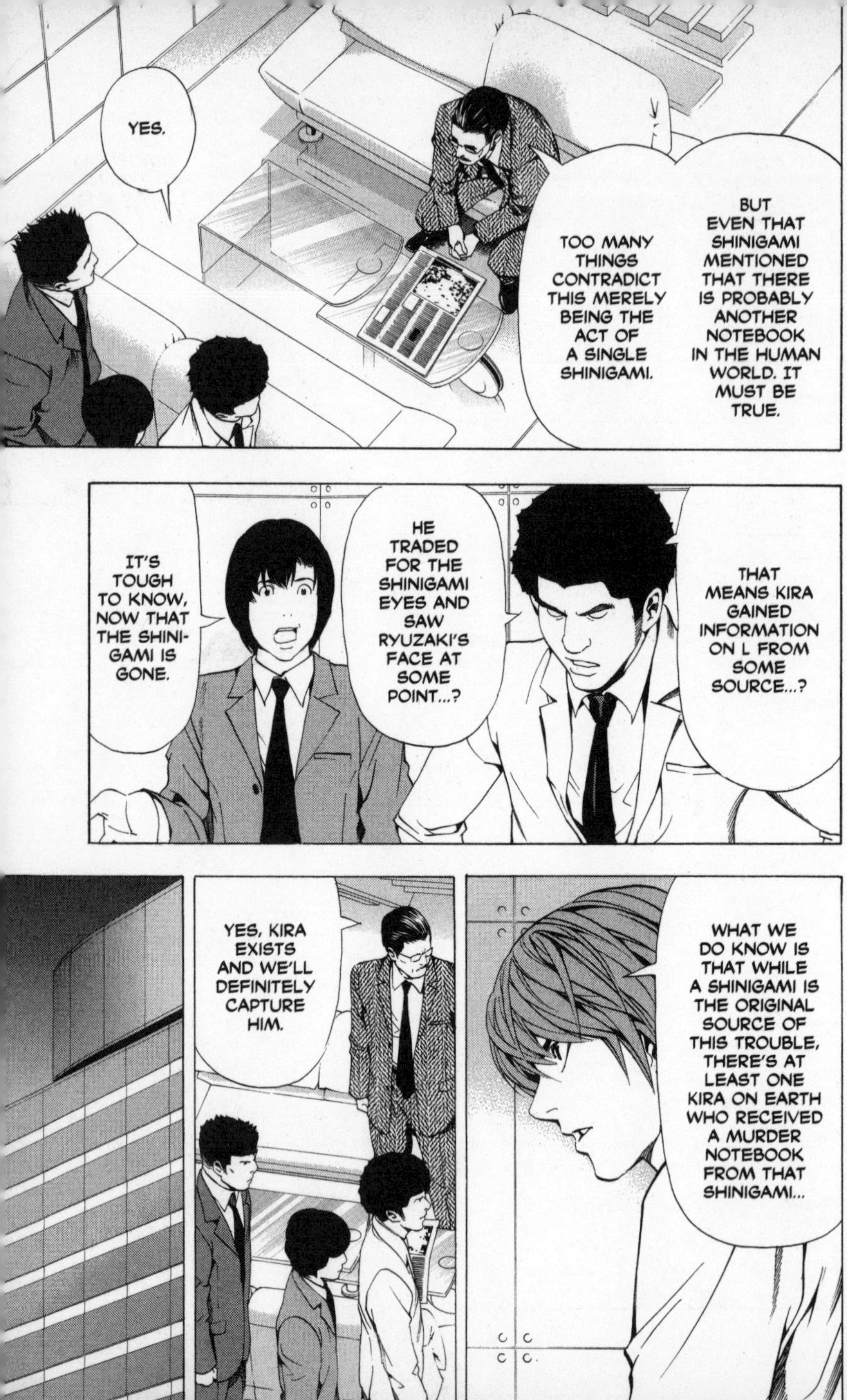
BUT EVEN THAT SHINIGAMI MENTIONED THAT THERE IS PROBABLY ANOTHER NOTEBOOK IN THE HUMAN WORLD. IT MUST BE TRUE.
TOO MANY THINGS CONTRADICT THIS MERELY BEING THE ACT OF A SINGLE SHINIGAMI.
YES.
THAT MEANS KIRA GAINED INFORMATION ON L FROM SOME SOURCE...?
HE TRADED FOR THE SHINIGAMI EYES AND SAW RYUZAKI'S FACE AT SOME POINT...?
IT'S TOUGH TO KNOW, NOW THAT THE SHINIGAMI IS GONE.
WHAT WE DO KNOW IS THAT WHILE A SHINIGAMI IS THE ORIGINAL SOURCE OF THIS TROUBLE, THERE'S AT LEAST ONE KIRA ON EARTH WHO RECEIVED A MURDER NOTEBOOK FROM THAT SHINIGAMI...
YES, KIRA EXISTS AND WE'LL DEFINITELY CAPTURE HIM.

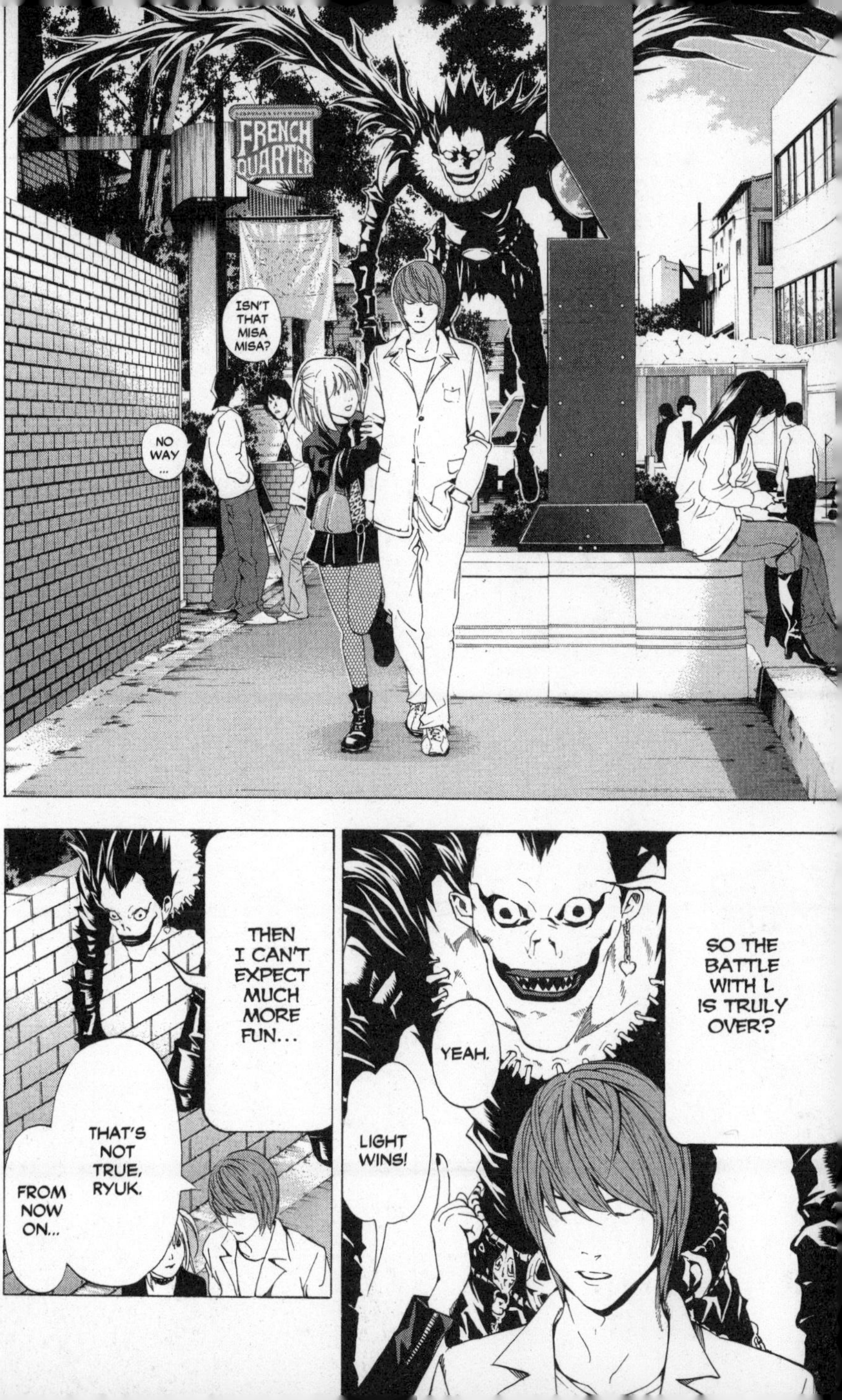
ISN'T THAT MISA MISA?
NO WAY...
SO THE BATTLE WITH L IS TRULY OVER?
YEAH.
LIGHT WINS!
THEN I CAN'T EXPECT MUCH MORE FUN...
THAT'S NOT TRUE, RYUK.
FROM NOW ON...

READ THIS WAY

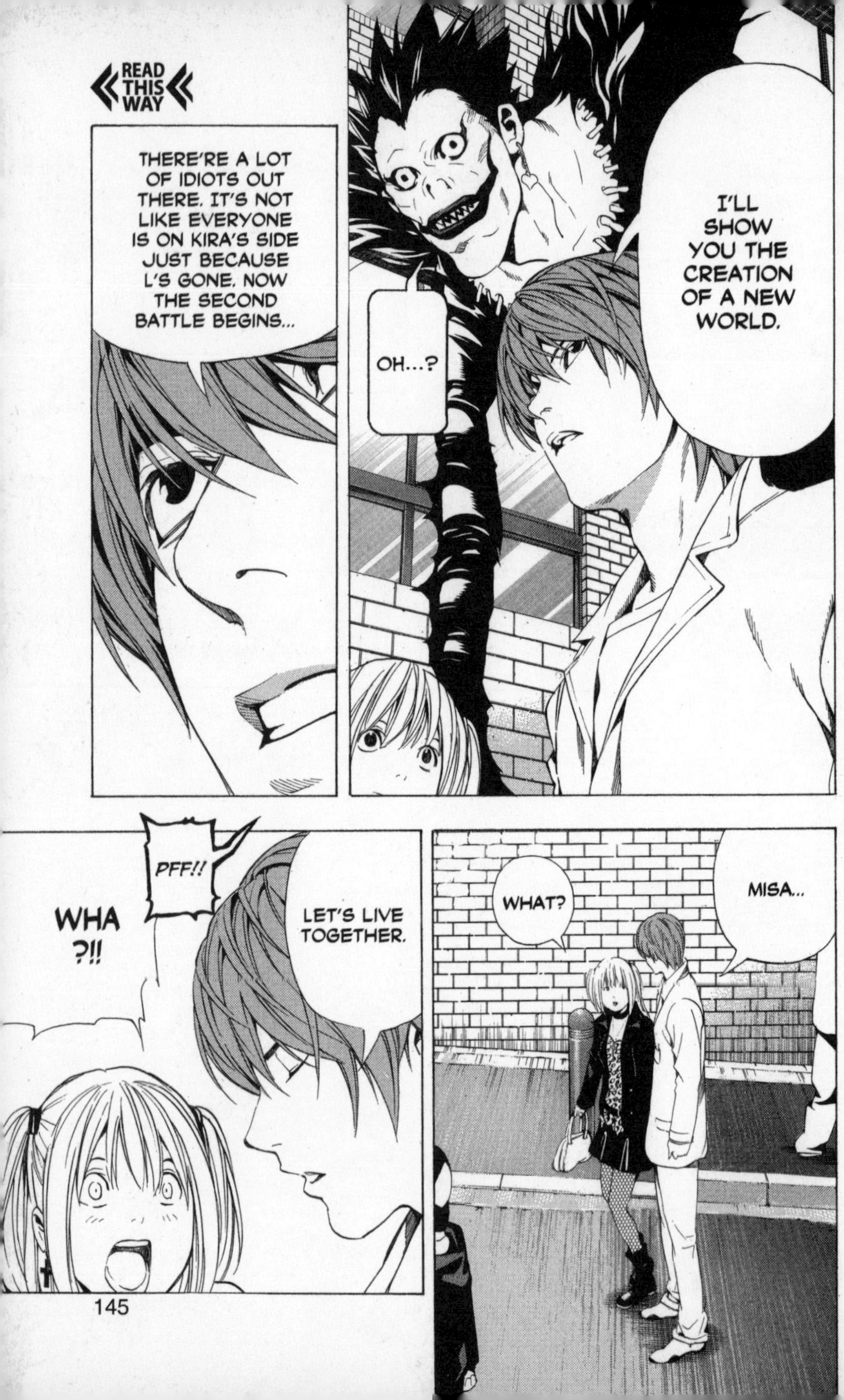

I'LL SHOW YOU THE CREATION OF A NEW WORLD.
OH...?
THERE'RE A LOT OF IDIOTS OUT THERE. IT'S NOT LIKE EVERYONE IS ON KIRA'S SIDE JUST BECAUSE L'S GONE. NOW THE SECOND BATTLE BEGINS...
MISA...
WHAT?
LET'S LIVE TOGETHER.
PFF!!
WHA ?!!

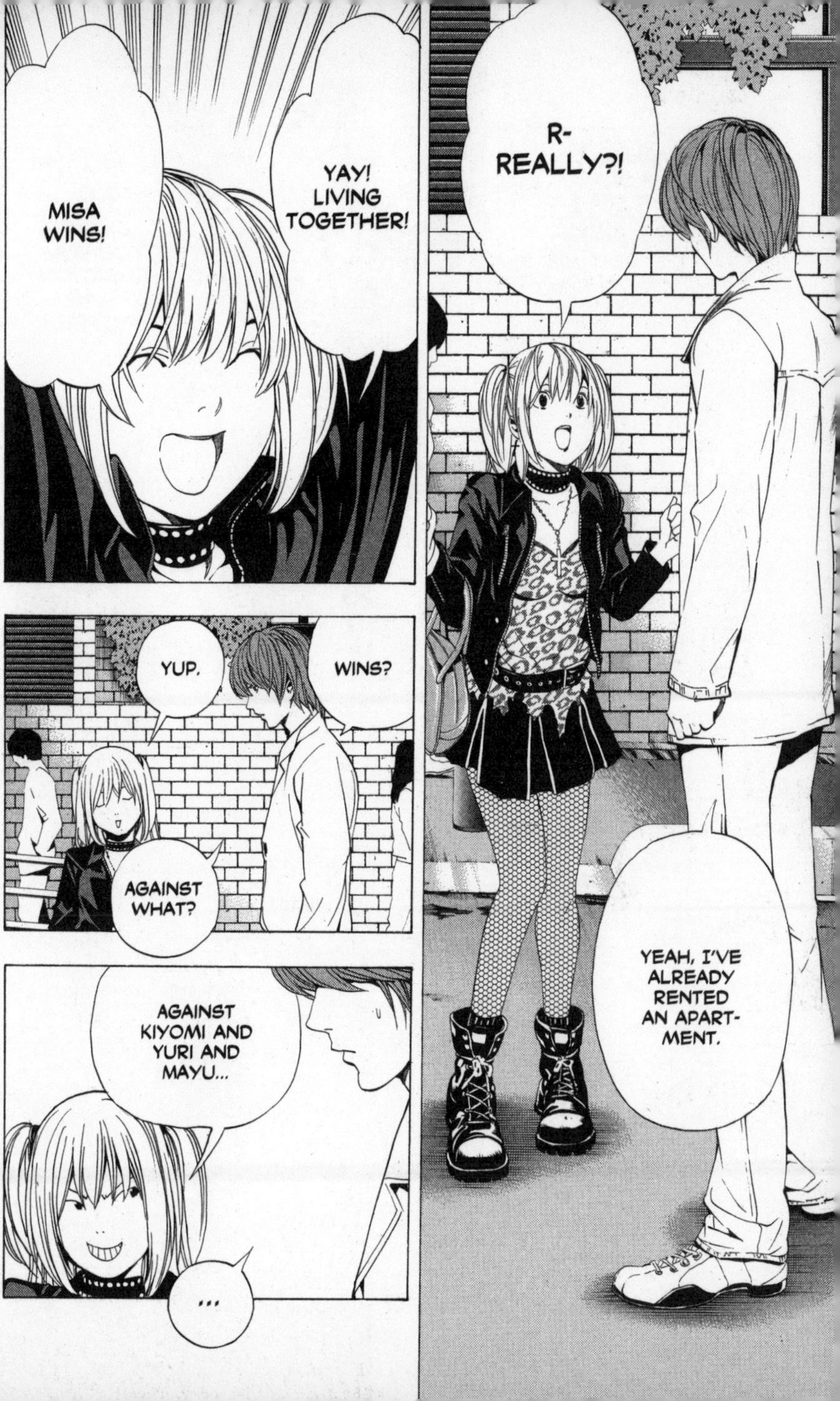
R-
REALLY?!
YEAH, I'VE ALREADY RENTED AN APARTMENT.
YAY! LIVING TOGETHER!
MISA WINS!
WINS?
YUP.
AGAINST WHAT?
AGAINST KIYOMI AND YURI AND MAYU...
...

READ THIS WAY

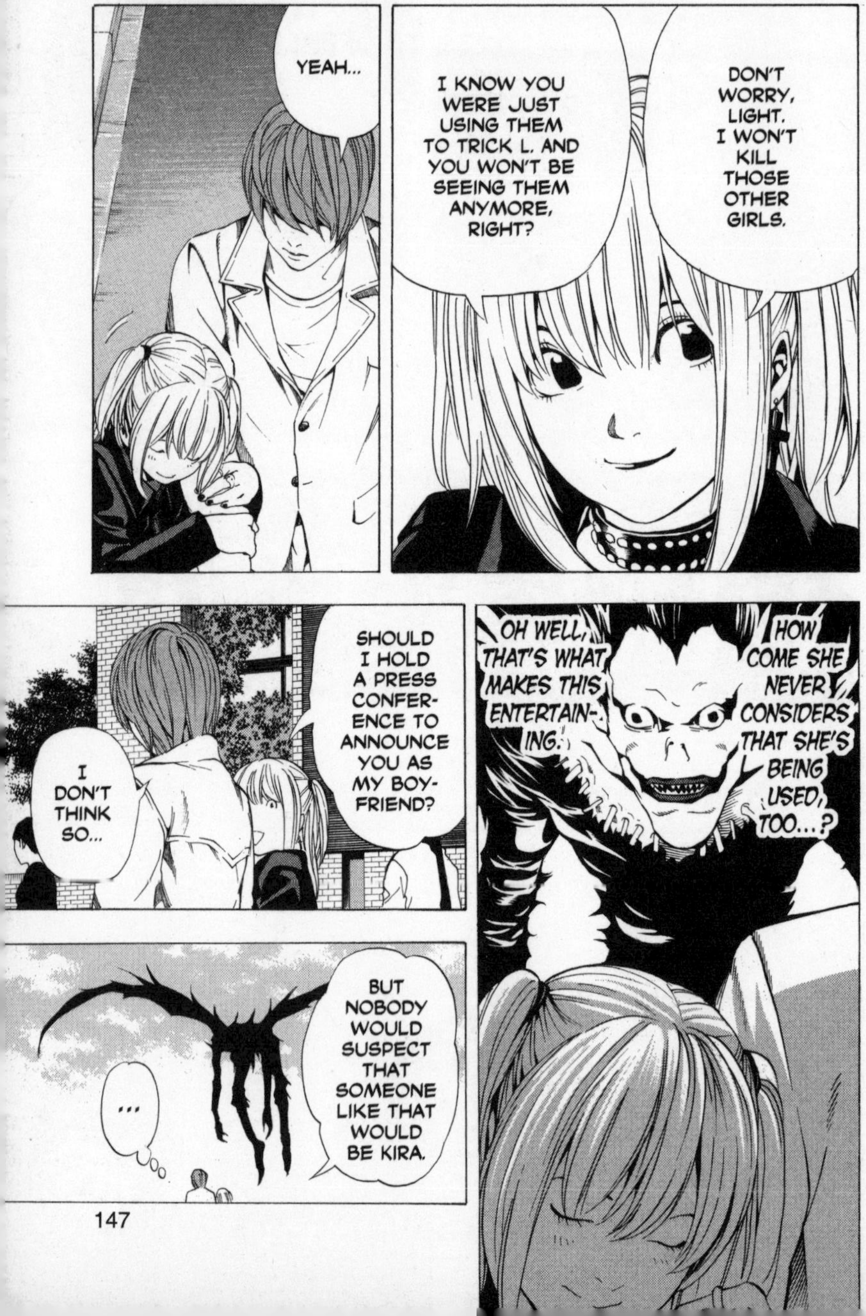
DON'T WORRY, LIGHT. I WON'T KILL THOSE OTHER GIRLS.
I KNOW YOU WERE JUST USING THEM TO TRICK L. AND YOU WON'T BE SEEING THEM ANYMORE, RIGHT?
YEAH...
HOW COME SHE NEVER CONSIDERS THAT SHE'S BEING USED, TOO...?
OH WELL, THAT'S WHAT MAKES THIS ENTERTAIN-ING.
SHOULD I HOLD A PRESS CONFER-ENCE TO ANNOUNCE YOU AS MY BOY-FRIEND?
I DON'T THINK SO...
BUT NOBODY WOULD SUSPECT THAT SOMEONE LIKE THAT WOULD BE KIRA.
...

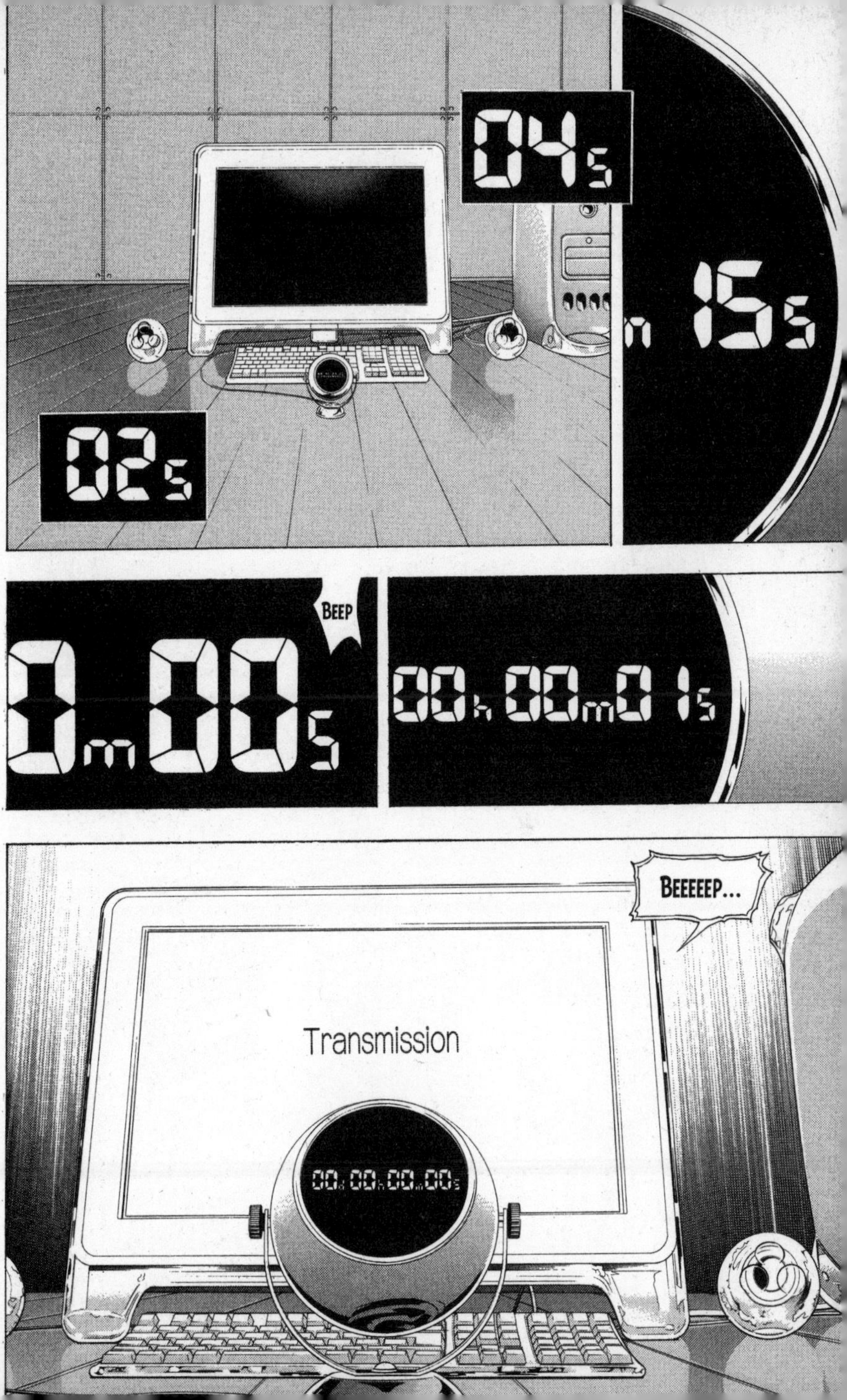
m 15s
04s
02s
00h 00m 01s
BEEP
0m 00s
BEEEEEP...
Transmission
00d 00h 00m 00s

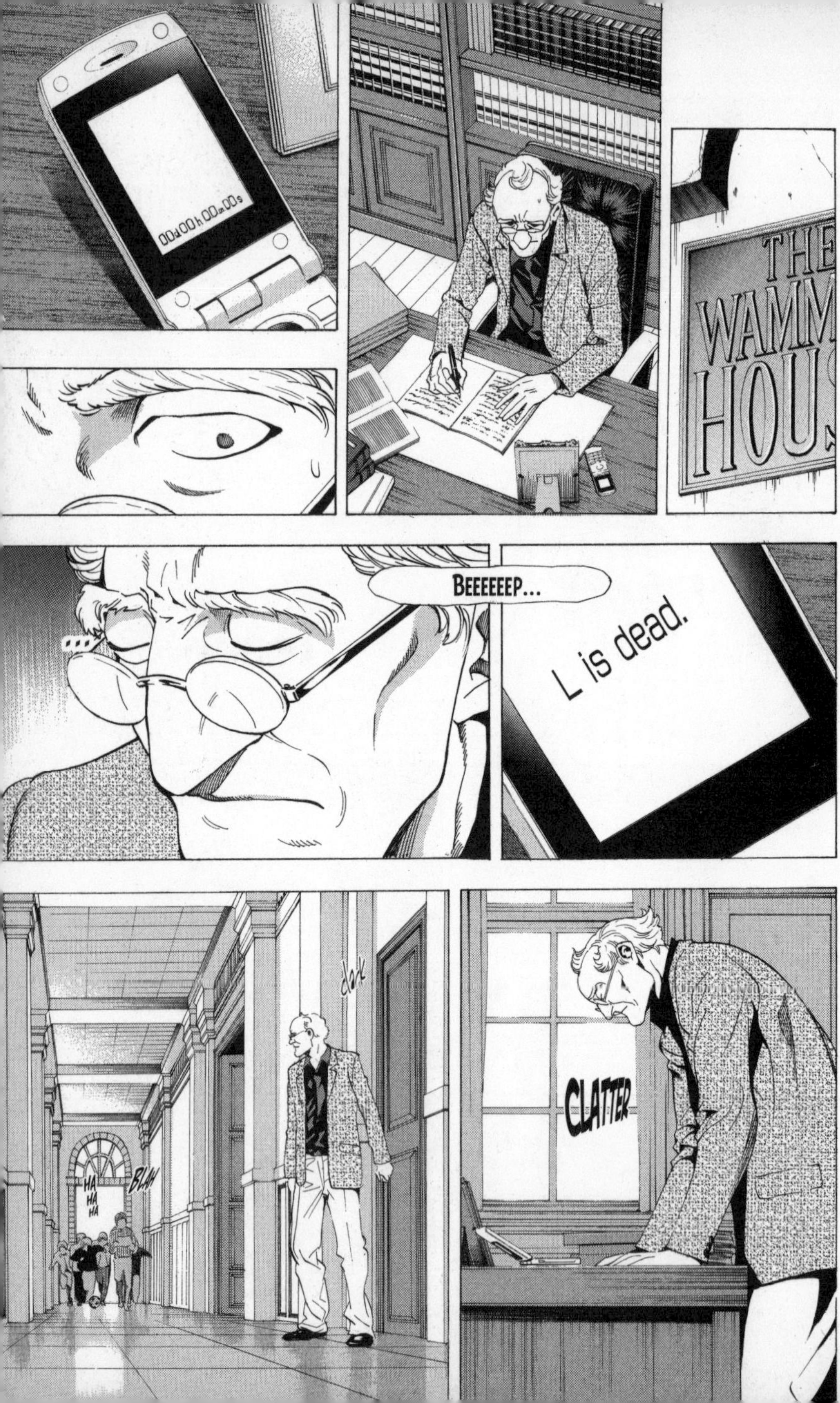
THE
WAMM
HOUS
00d00h00m00s
L is dead.
BEEEEEEP...
...
CLATTER
clack
HA
HA
HA
BLAH

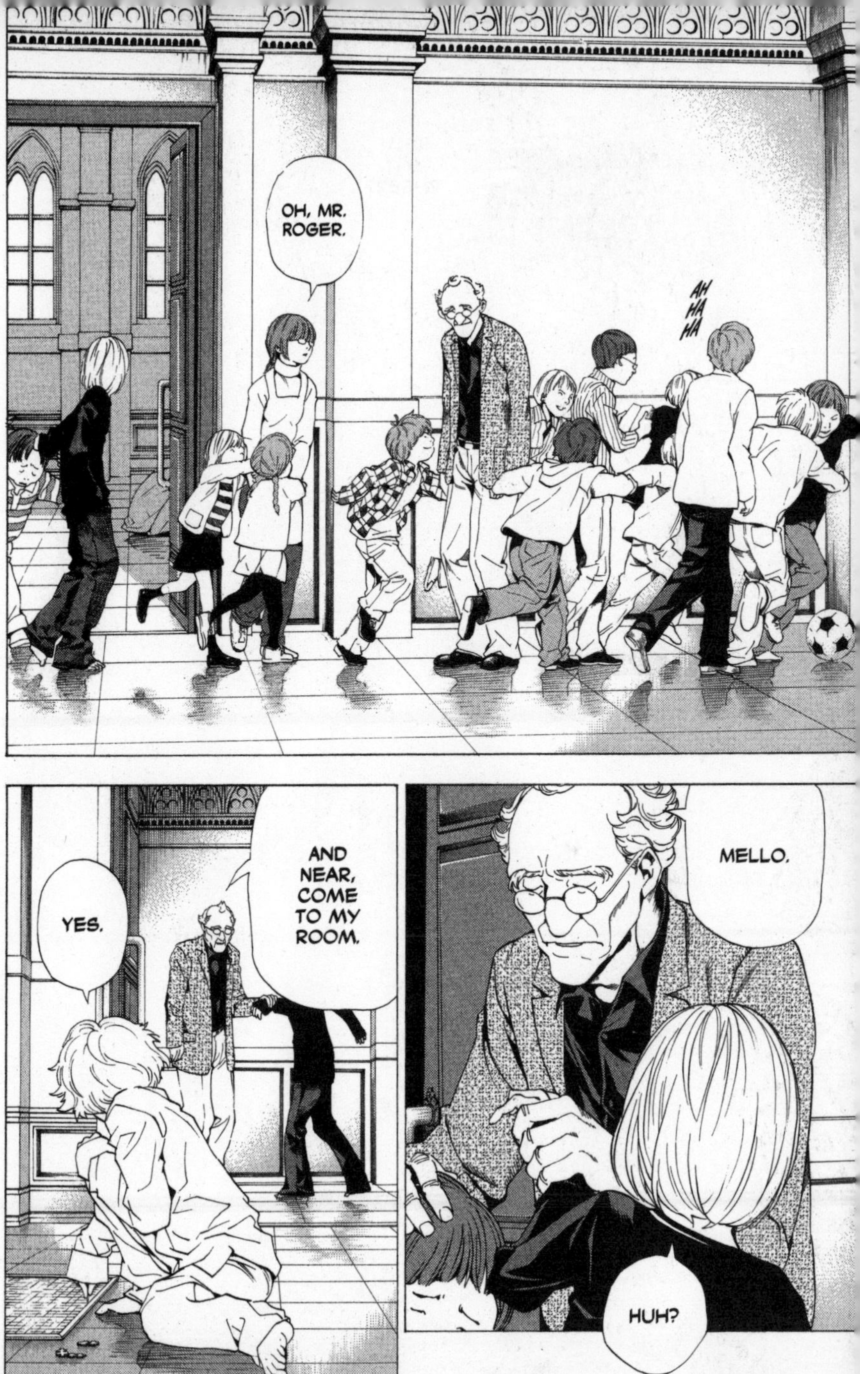
AH HA HA
OH, MR. ROGER.
MELLO.
HUH?
AND NEAR, COME TO MY ROOM.
YES.

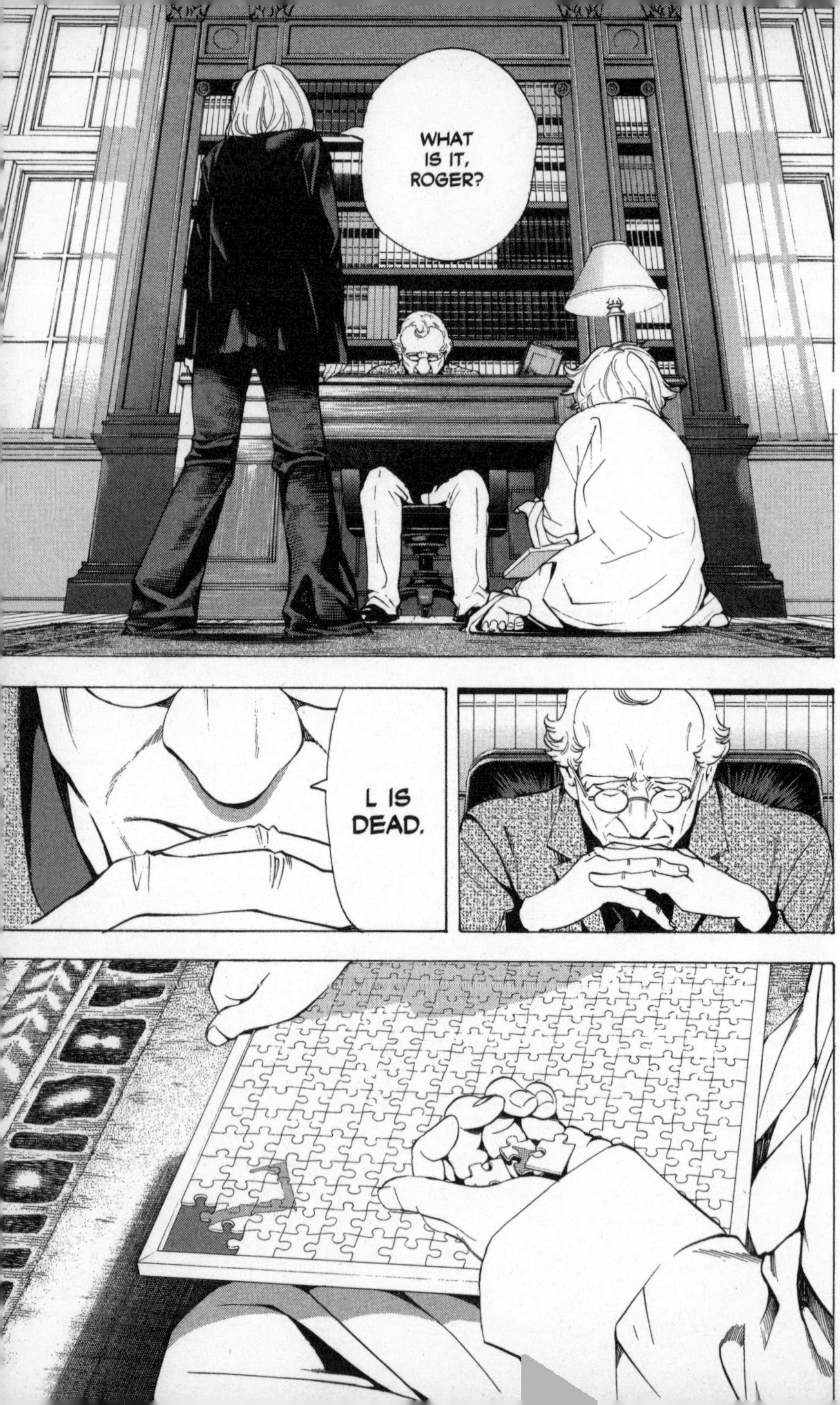
WHAT IS IT, ROGER?
L IS DEAD.

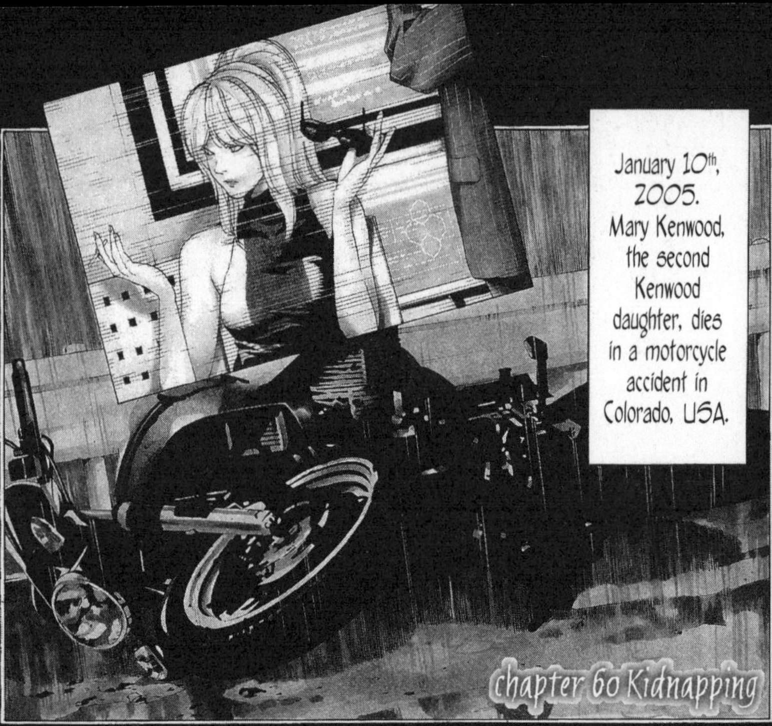
January 10th, 2005. Mary Kenwood, the second Kenwood daughter, dies in a motorcycle accident in Colorado, USA.
chapter 60 Kidnapping

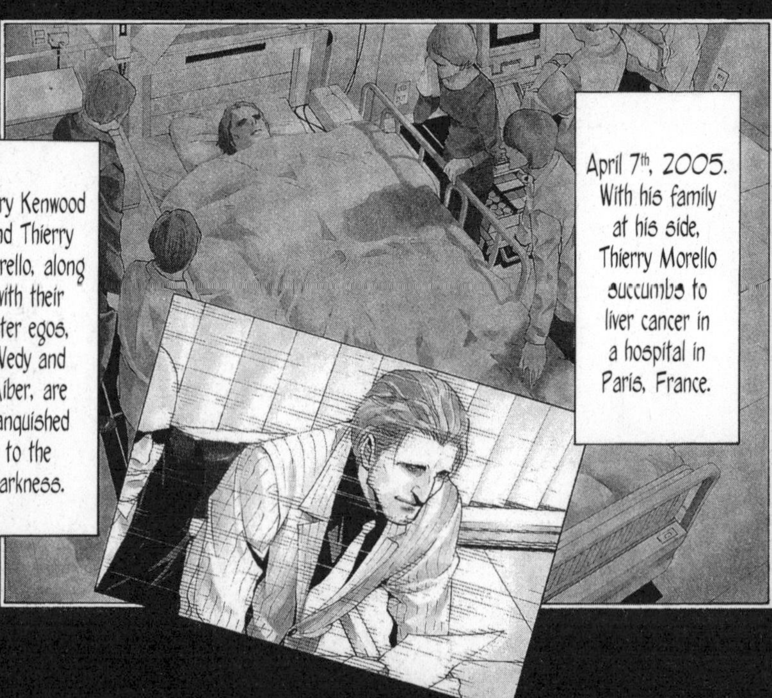
April 7th, 2005. With his family at his side, Thierry Morello succumbs to liver cancer in a hospital in Paris, France.
Mary Kenwood and Thierry Morello, along with their alter egos, Wedy and Aiber, are vanquished to the darkness.

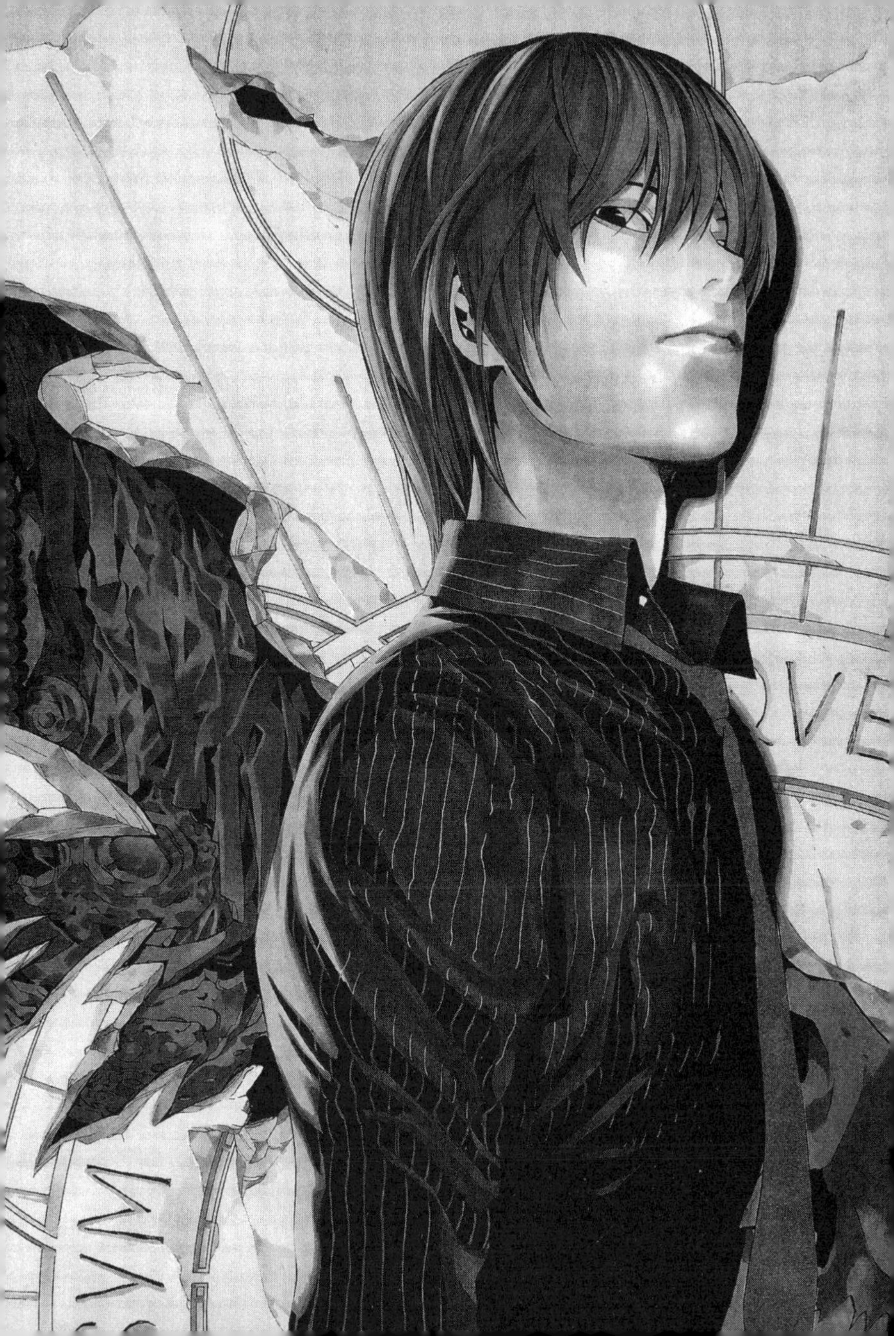

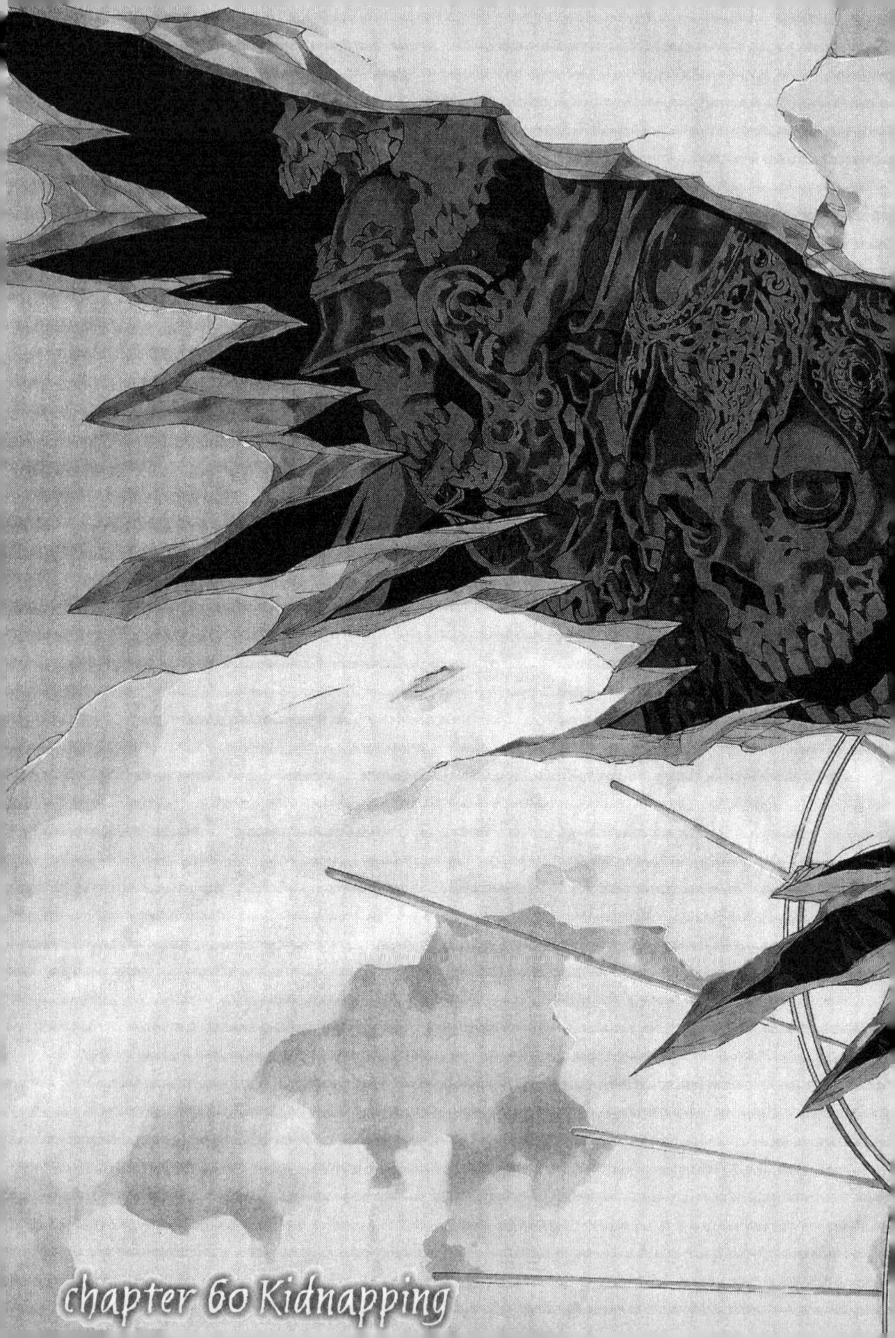

chapter 60 Kidnapping

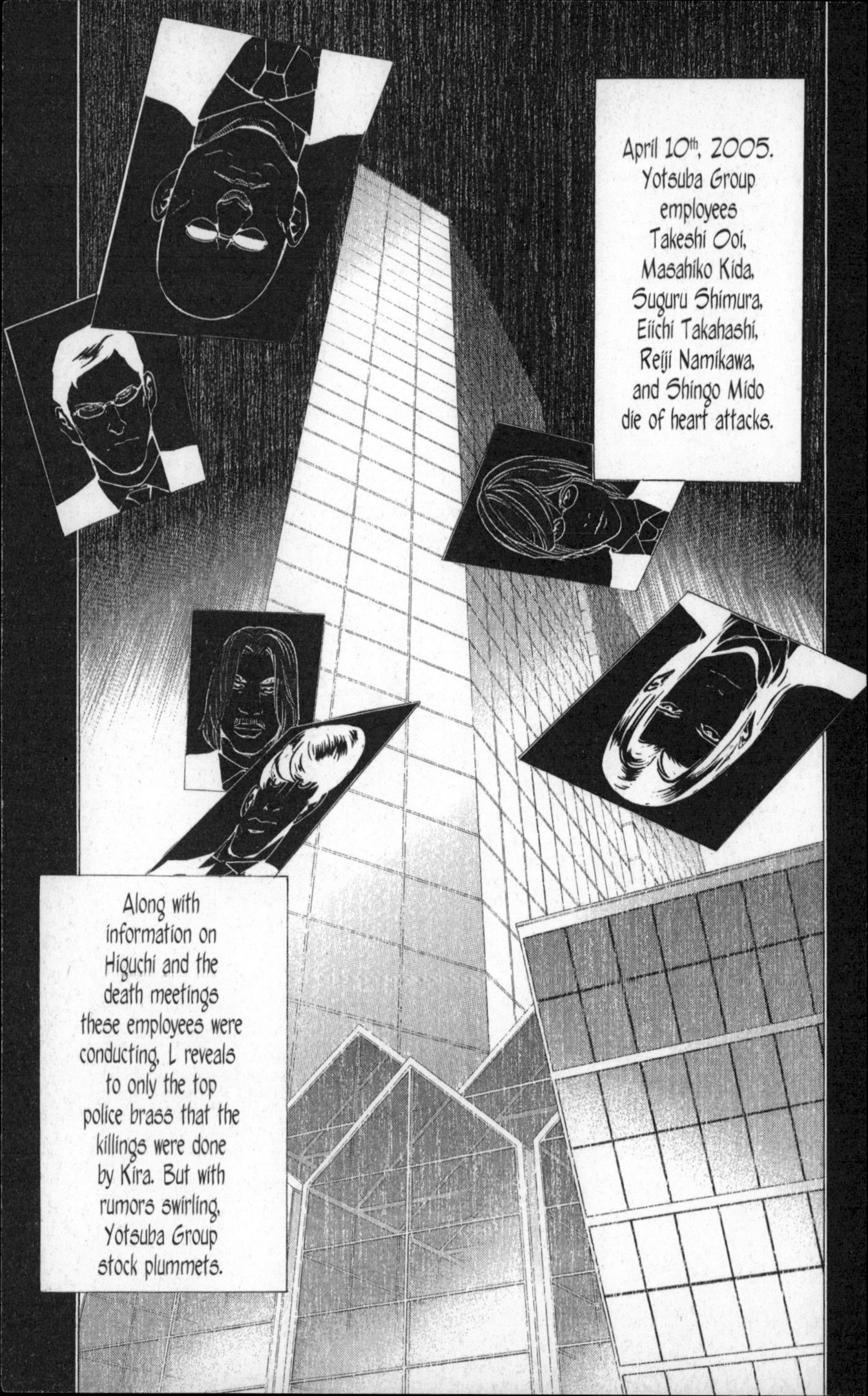
April 10th, 2005. Yotsuba Group employees Takeshi Ooi, Masahiko Kida, Suguru Shimura, Eiichi Takahashi, Reiji Namikawa, and Shingo Mido die of heart attacks.
Along with information on Higuchi and the death meetings these employees were conducting, L reveals to only the top police brass that the killings were done by Kira. But with rumors swirling, Yotsuba Group stock plummets.

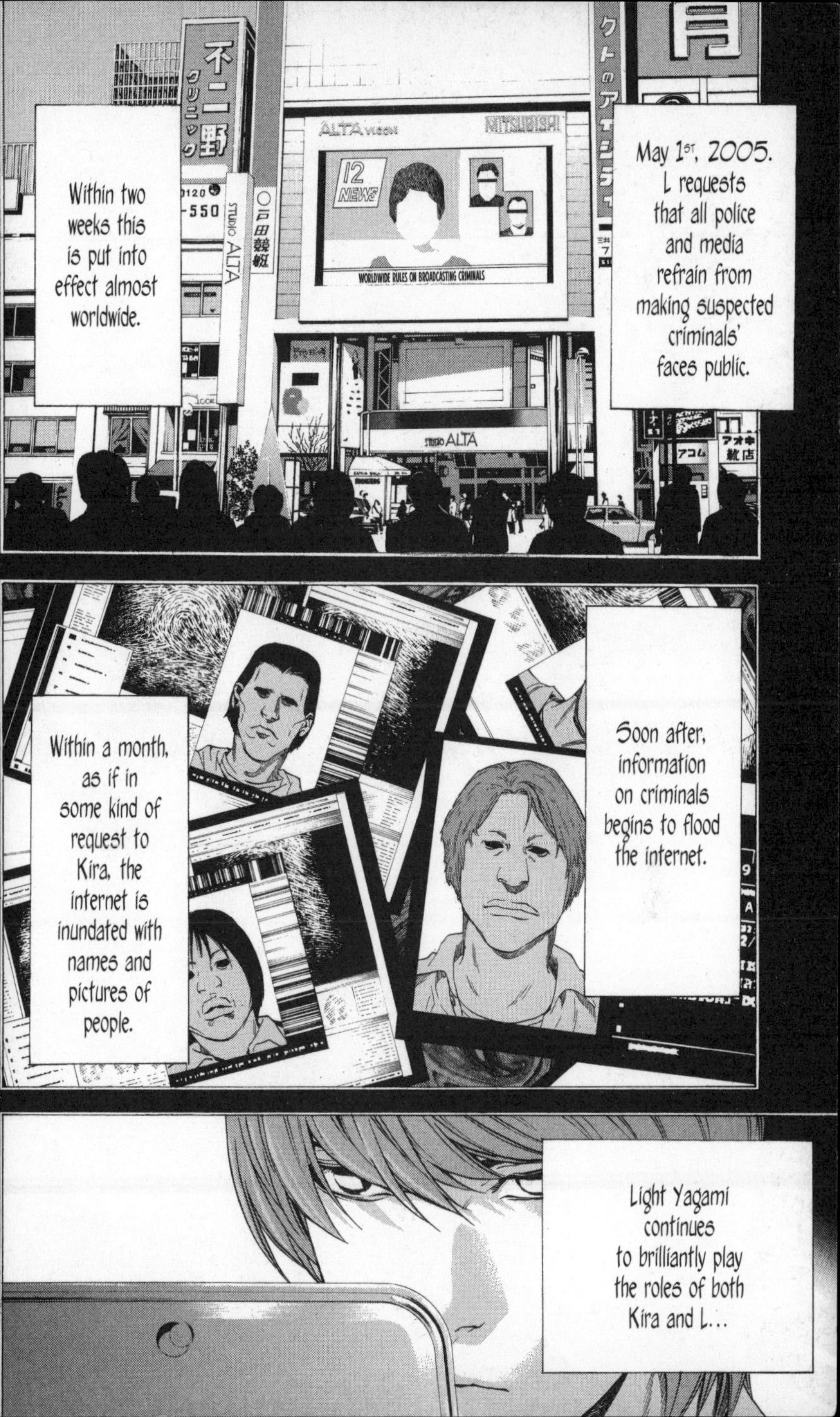
May 1st, 2005. L requests that all police and media refrain from making suspected criminals' faces public.
MITSUBISHI
ALTA VISION
12 NEWS
WORLDWIDE RULES ON BROADCASTING CRIMINALS
STUDIO ALTA
Within two weeks this is put into effect almost worldwide.
Soon after, information on criminals begins to flood the internet.
Within a month, as if in some kind of request to Kira, the internet is inundated with names and pictures of people.
Light Yagami continues to brilliantly play the roles of both Kira and L...

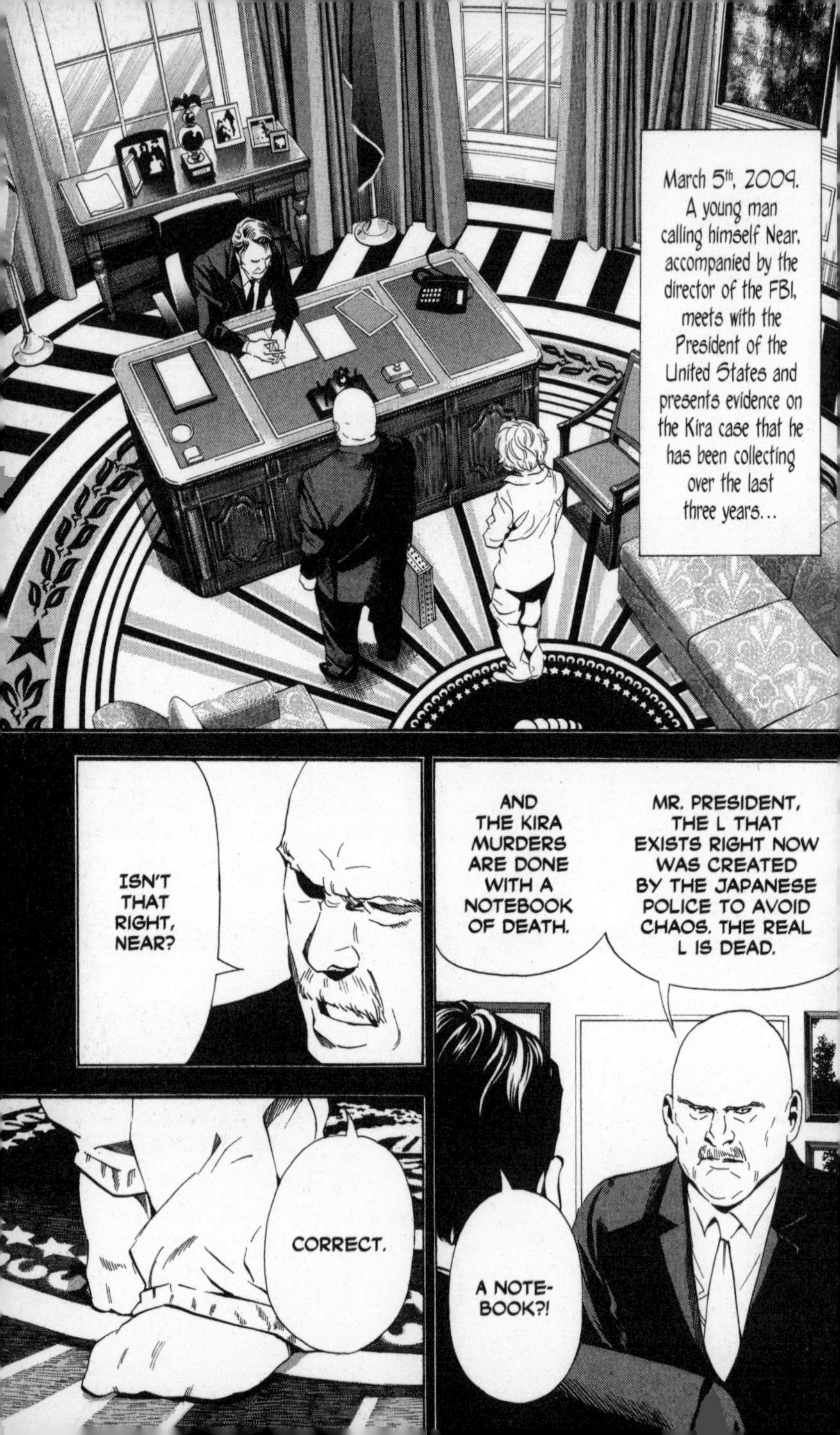
March 5th, 2009. A young man calling himself Near, accompanied by the director of the FBI, meets with the President of the United States and presents evidence on the Kira case that he has been collecting over the last three years...
MR. PRESIDENT, THE L THAT EXISTS RIGHT NOW WAS CREATED BY THE JAPANESE POLICE TO AVOID CHAOS. THE REAL L IS DEAD.
AND THE KIRA MURDERS ARE DONE WITH A NOTEBOOK OF DEATH.
A NOTE-BOOK?!
ISN'T THAT RIGHT, NEAR?
CORRECT.

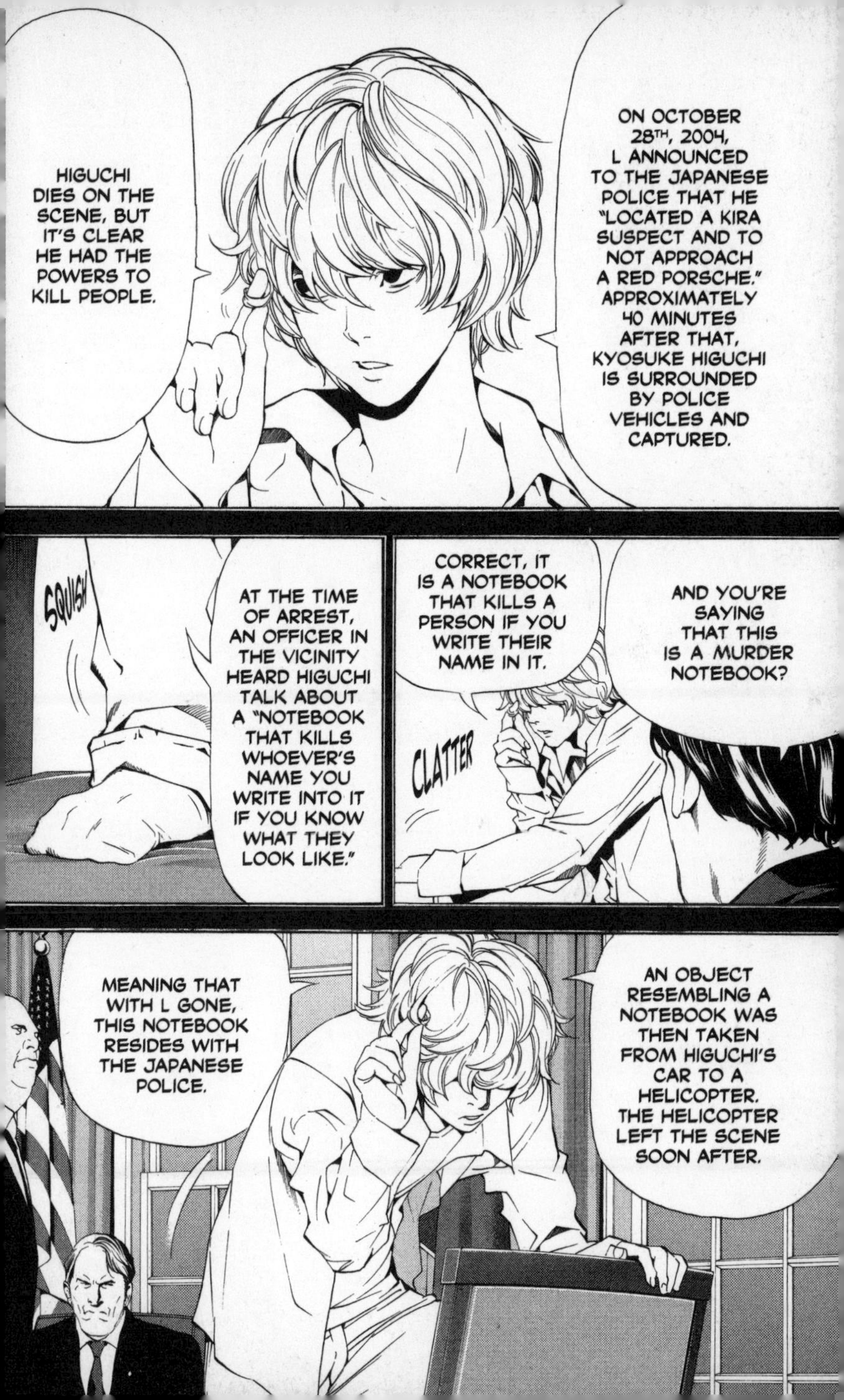
ON OCTOBER 28TH, 2004, L ANNOUNCED TO THE JAPANESE POLICE THAT HE "LOCATED A KIRA SUSPECT AND TO NOT APPROACH A RED PORSCHE." APPROXIMATELY 40 MINUTES AFTER THAT, KYOSUKE HIGUCHI IS SURROUNDED BY POLICE VEHICLES AND CAPTURED.
HIGUCHI DIES ON THE SCENE, BUT IT'S CLEAR HE HAD THE POWERS TO KILL PEOPLE.
AND YOU'RE SAYING THAT THIS IS A MURDER NOTEBOOK?
CORRECT, IT IS A NOTEBOOK THAT KILLS A PERSON IF YOU WRITE THEIR NAME IN IT.
CLATTER
AT THE TIME OF ARREST, AN OFFICER IN THE VICINITY HEARD HIGUCHI TALK ABOUT A "NOTEBOOK THAT KILLS WHOEVER'S NAME YOU WRITE INTO IT IF YOU KNOW WHAT THEY LOOK LIKE."
SQUISH
AN OBJECT RESEMBLING A NOTEBOOK WAS THEN TAKEN FROM HIGUCHI'S CAR TO A HELICOPTER. THE HELICOPTER LEFT THE SCENE SOON AFTER.
MEANING THAT WITH L GONE, THIS NOTEBOOK RESIDES WITH THE JAPANESE POLICE.

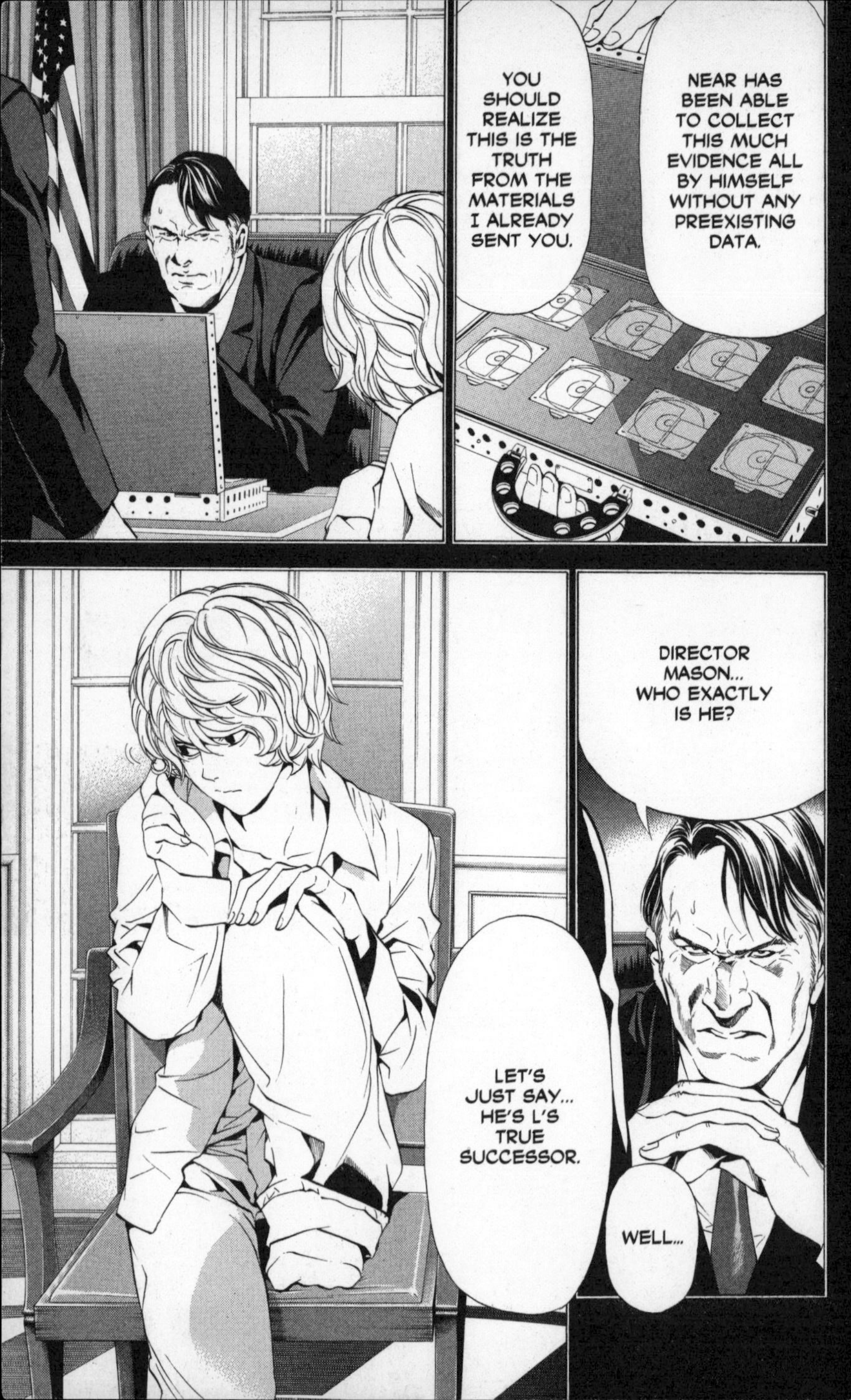
NEAR HAS BEEN ABLE TO COLLECT THIS MUCH EVIDENCE ALL BY HIMSELF WITHOUT ANY PREEXISTING DATA.
YOU SHOULD REALIZE THIS IS THE TRUTH FROM THE MATERIALS I ALREADY SENT YOU.
DIRECTOR MASON... WHO EXACTLY IS HE?
WELL...
LET'S JUST SAY... HE'S L'S TRUE SUCCESSOR.

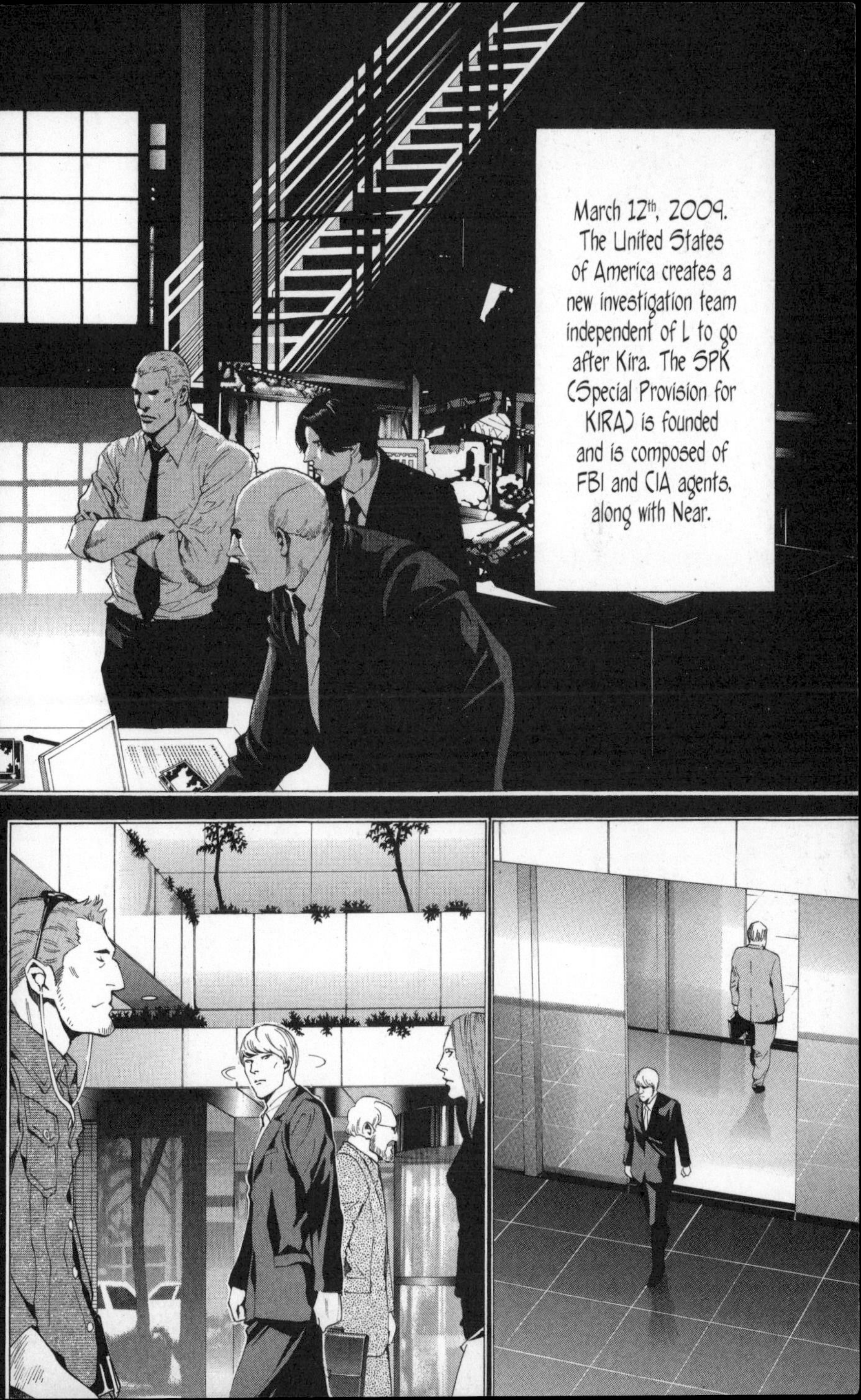
March 12th, 2009. The United States of America creates a new investigation team independent of L to go after Kira. The SPK (Special Provision for KIRA) is founded and is composed of FBI and CIA agents, along with Near.

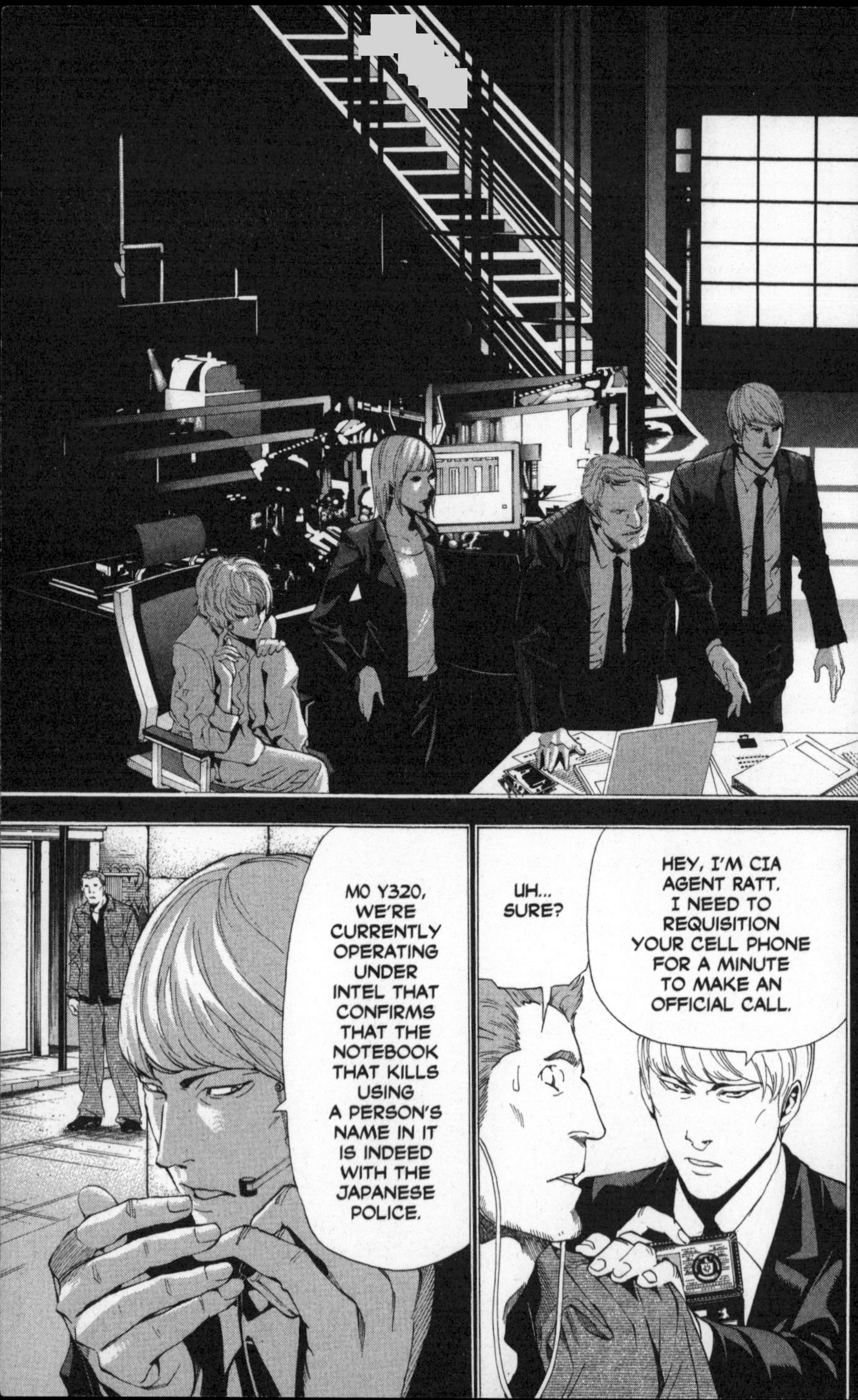
HEY, I'M CIA AGENT RATT. I NEED TO REQUISITION YOUR CELL PHONE FOR A MINUTE TO MAKE AN OFFICIAL CALL.
UH... SURE?
MO Y320, WE'RE CURRENTLY OPERATING UNDER INTEL THAT CONFIRMS THAT THE NOTEBOOK THAT KILLS USING A PERSON'S NAME IN IT IS INDEED WITH THE JAPANESE POLICE.

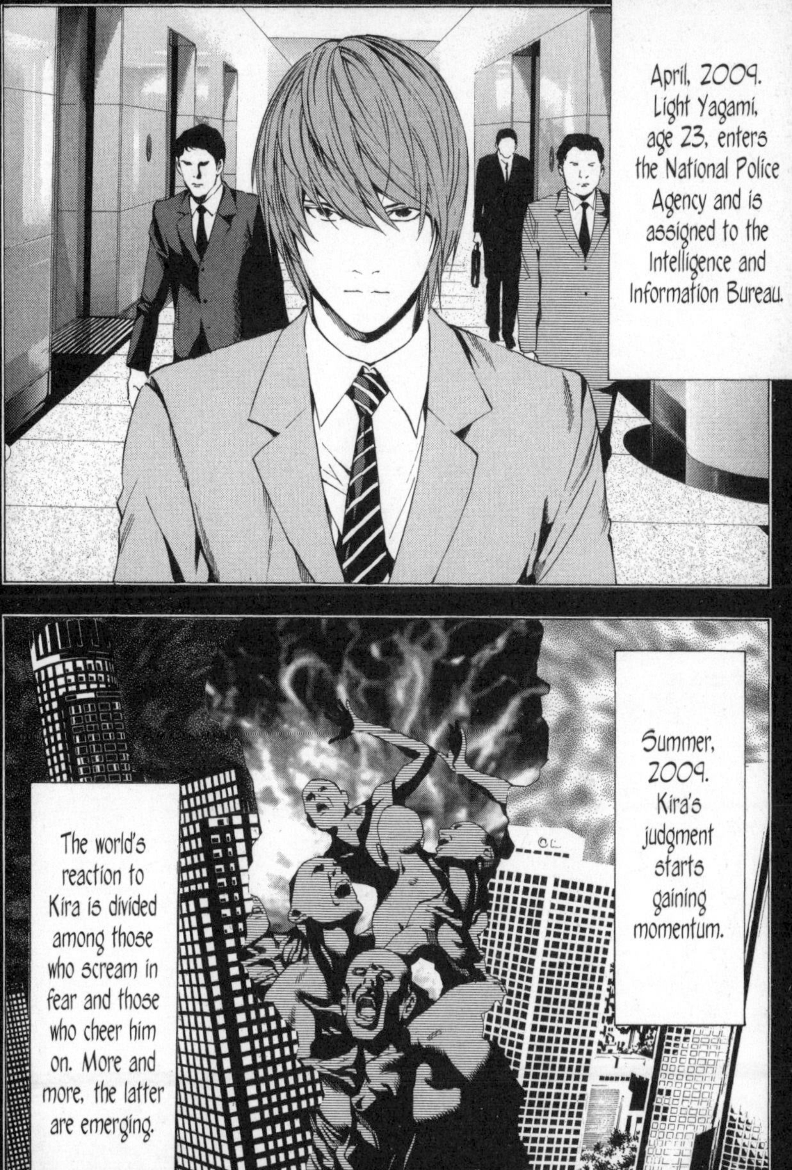
April, 2009. Light Yagami, age 23, enters the National Police Agency and is assigned to the Intelligence and Information Bureau.
Summer, 2009. Kira's judgment starts gaining momentum.
The world's reaction to Kira is divided among those who scream in fear and those who cheer him on. More and more, the latter are emerging.

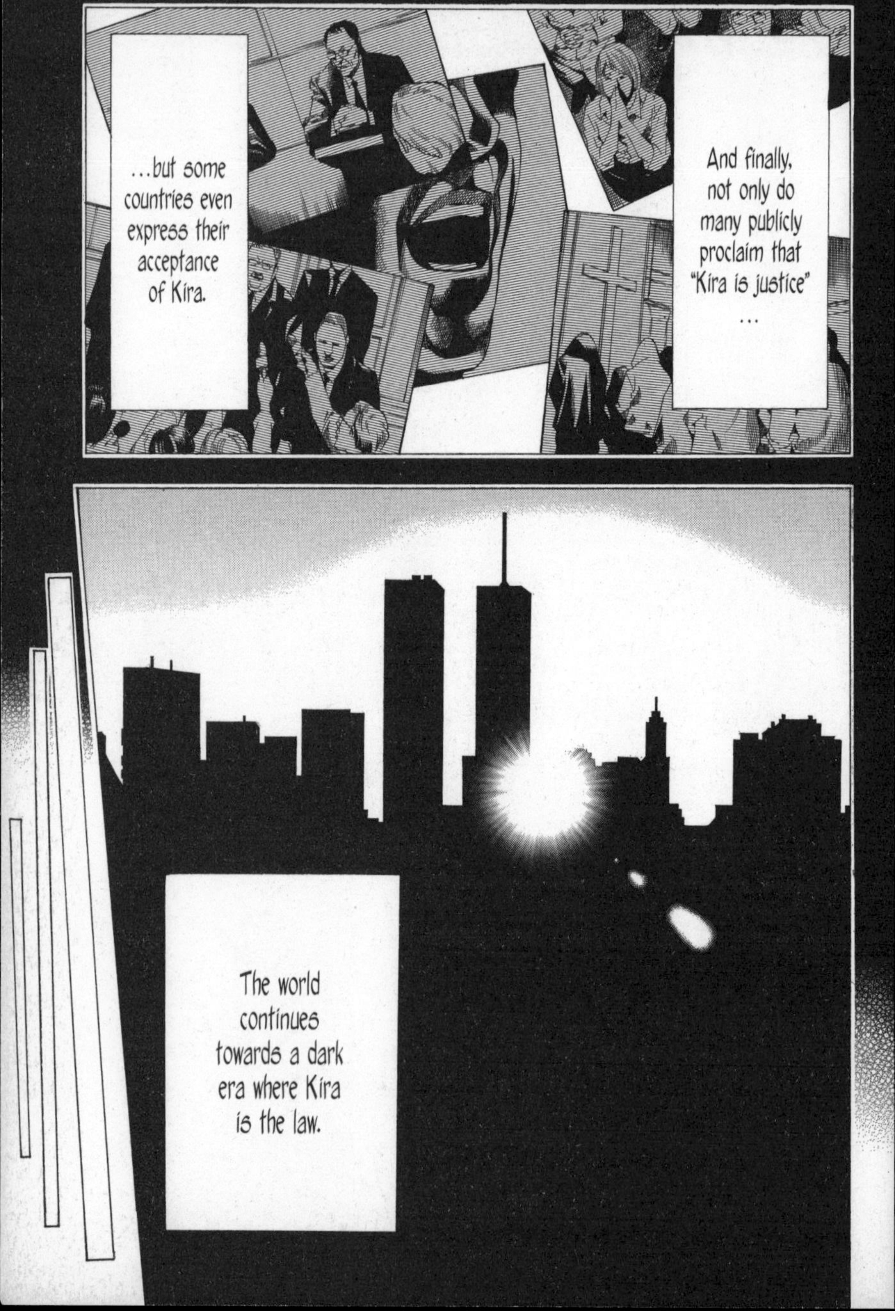
And finally, not only do many publicly proclaim that "Kira is justice" ...
...but some countries even express their acceptance of Kira.
The world continues towards a dark era where Kira is the law.

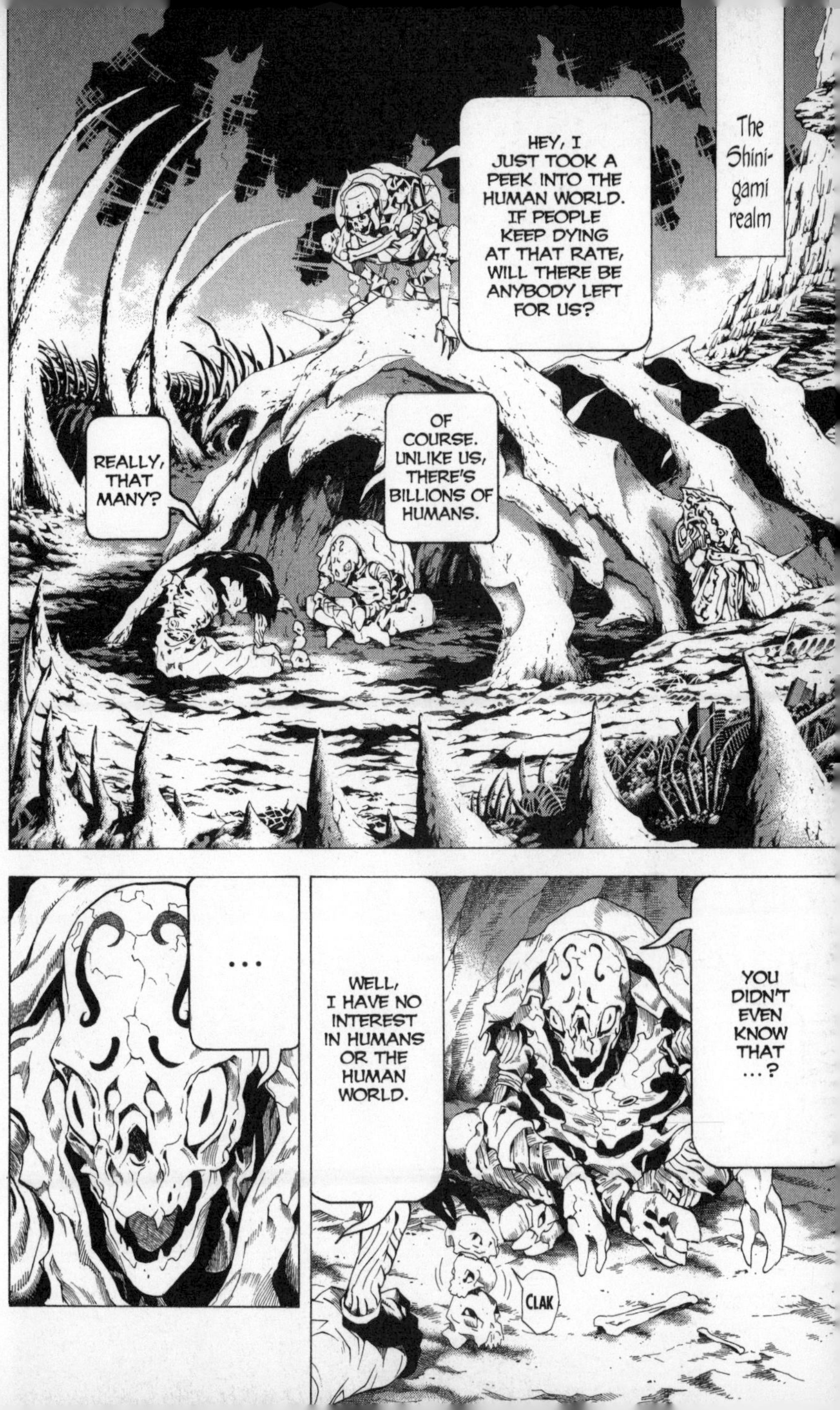
The Shinigami realm
HEY, I JUST TOOK A PEEK INTO THE HUMAN WORLD. IF PEOPLE KEEP DYING AT THAT RATE, WILL THERE BE ANYBODY LEFT FOR US?
OF COURSE. UNLIKE US, THERE'S BILLIONS OF HUMANS.
REALLY, THAT MANY?
YOU DIDN'T EVEN KNOW THAT ...?
WELL, I HAVE NO INTEREST IN HUMANS OR THE HUMAN WORLD.
CLAK
. . .

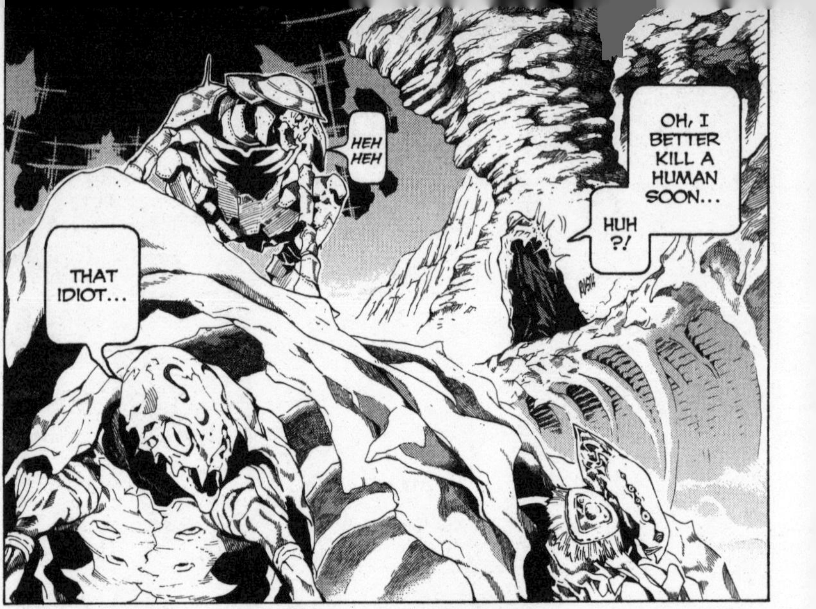
OH, I BETTER KILL A HUMAN SOON...
HUH ?!
HEH HEH
THAT IDIOT...

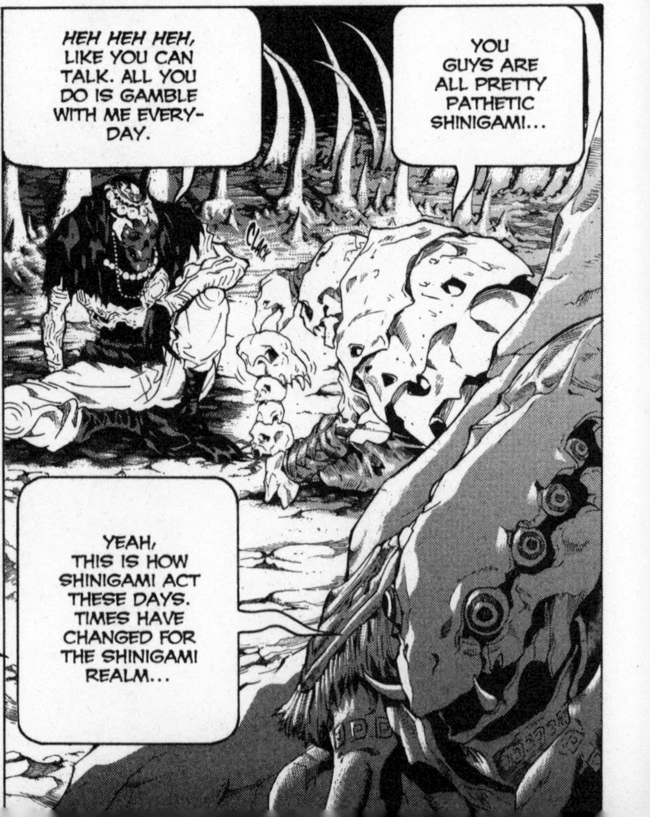
YOU GUYS ARE ALL PRETTY PATHETIC SHINIGAMI...
HEH HEH HEH, LIKE YOU CAN TALK. ALL YOU DO IS GAMBLE WITH ME EVERY-DAY.
CLACK
YEAH, THIS IS HOW SHINIGAMI ACT THESE DAYS. TIMES HAVE CHANGED FOR THE SHINIGAMI REALM...

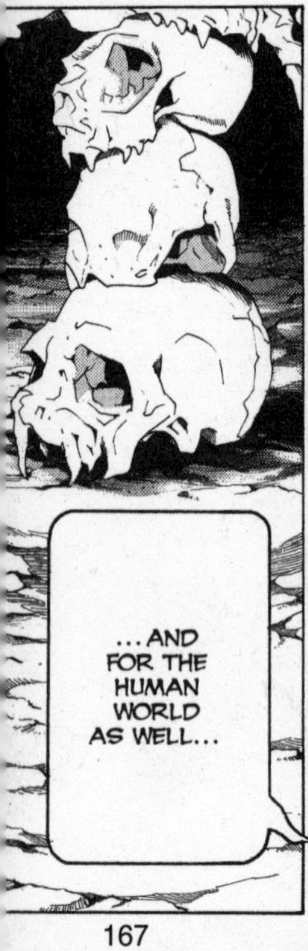
...AND FOR THE HUMAN WORLD AS WELL...

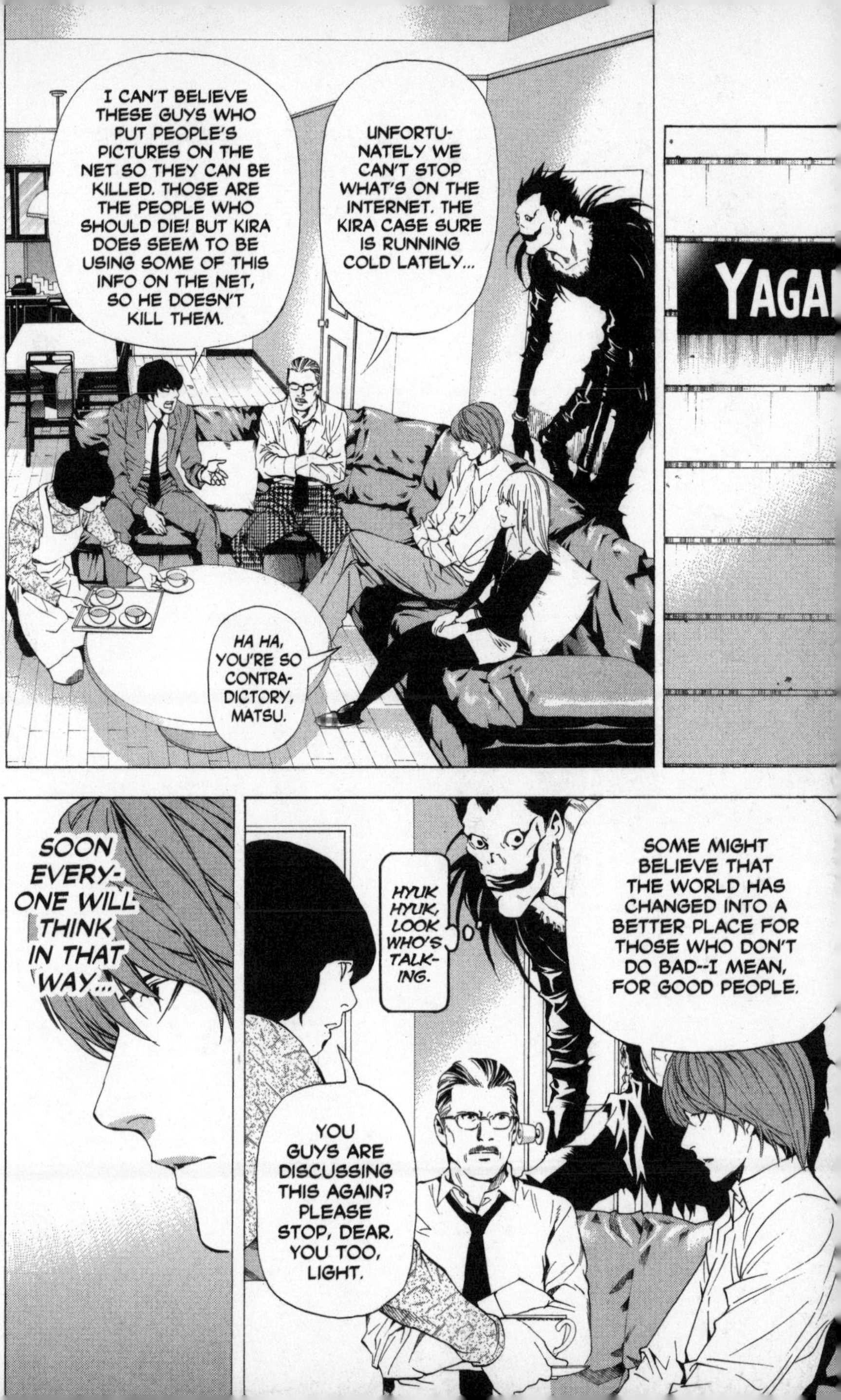
YAGA
UNFORTU-NATELY WE CAN'T STOP WHAT'S ON THE INTERNET. THE KIRA CASE SURE IS RUNNING COLD LATELY...
I CAN'T BELIEVE THESE GUYS WHO PUT PEOPLE'S PICTURES ON THE NET SO THEY CAN BE KILLED. THOSE ARE THE PEOPLE WHO SHOULD DIE! BUT KIRA DOES SEEM TO BE USING SOME OF THIS INFO ON THE NET, SO HE DOESN'T KILL THEM.
HA HA, YOU'RE SO CONTRA-DICTORY, MATSU.
SOME MIGHT BELIEVE THAT THE WORLD HAS CHANGED INTO A BETTER PLACE FOR THOSE WHO DON'T DO BAD--I MEAN, FOR GOOD PEOPLE.
HYUK HYUK, LOOK WHO'S TALK-ING.
YOU GUYS ARE DISCUSSING THIS AGAIN? PLEASE STOP, DEAR. YOU TOO, LIGHT.
SOON EVERY-ONE WILL THINK IN THAT WAY...

READ THIS WAY

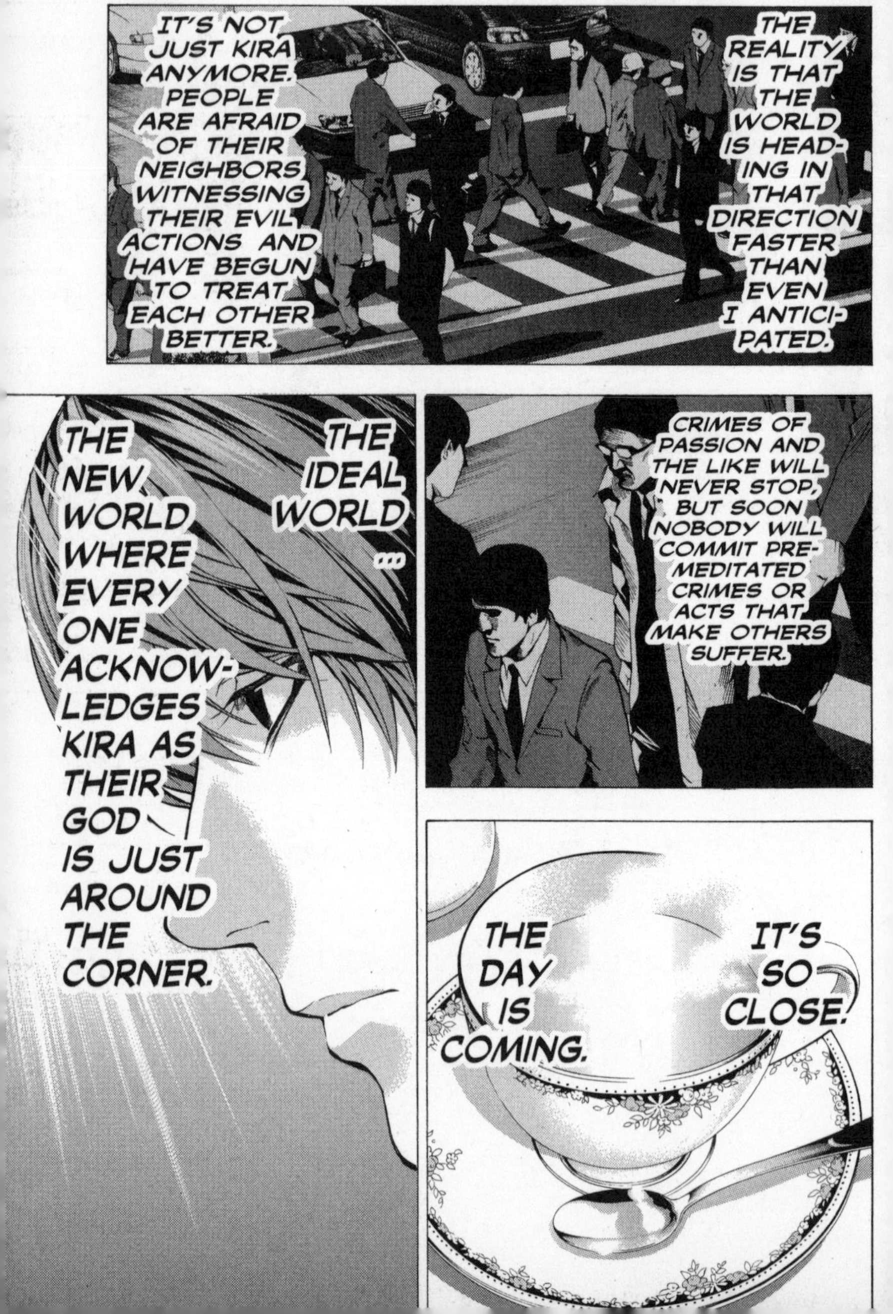
THE REALITY IS THAT THE WORLD IS HEADING IN THAT DIRECTION FASTER THAN EVEN I ANTICIPATED.
IT'S NOT JUST KIRA ANYMORE. PEOPLE ARE AFRAID OF THEIR NEIGHBORS WITNESSING THEIR EVIL ACTIONS AND HAVE BEGUN TO TREAT EACH OTHER BETTER.
CRIMES OF PASSION AND THE LIKE WILL NEVER STOP, BUT SOON NOBODY WILL COMMIT PREMEDITATED CRIMES OR ACTS THAT MAKE OTHERS SUFFER.
IT'S SO CLOSE.
THE DAY IS COMING.
THE IDEAL WORLD...
THE NEW WORLD WHERE EVERYONE ACKNOWLEDGES KIRA AS THEIR GOD IS JUST AROUND THE CORNER.

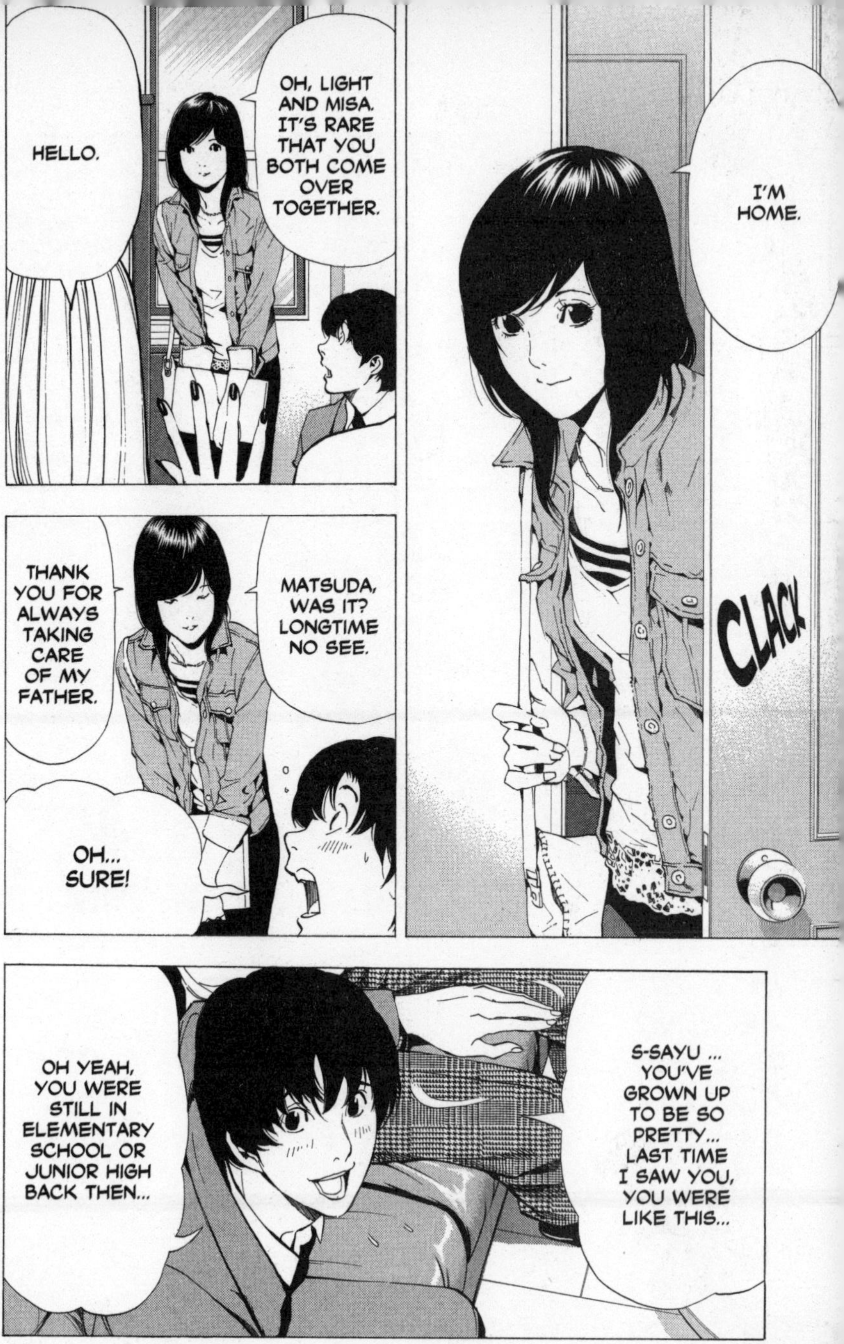
I'M HOME.
CLACK
OH, LIGHT AND MISA. IT'S RARE THAT YOU BOTH COME OVER TOGETHER.
HELLO.
MATSUDA, WAS IT? LONGTIME NO SEE.
THANK YOU FOR ALWAYS TAKING CARE OF MY FATHER.
OH... SURE!
S-SAYU ... YOU'VE GROWN UP TO BE SO PRETTY... LAST TIME I SAW YOU, YOU WERE LIKE THIS...
OH YEAH, YOU WERE STILL IN ELEMENTARY SCHOOL OR JUNIOR HIGH BACK THEN...

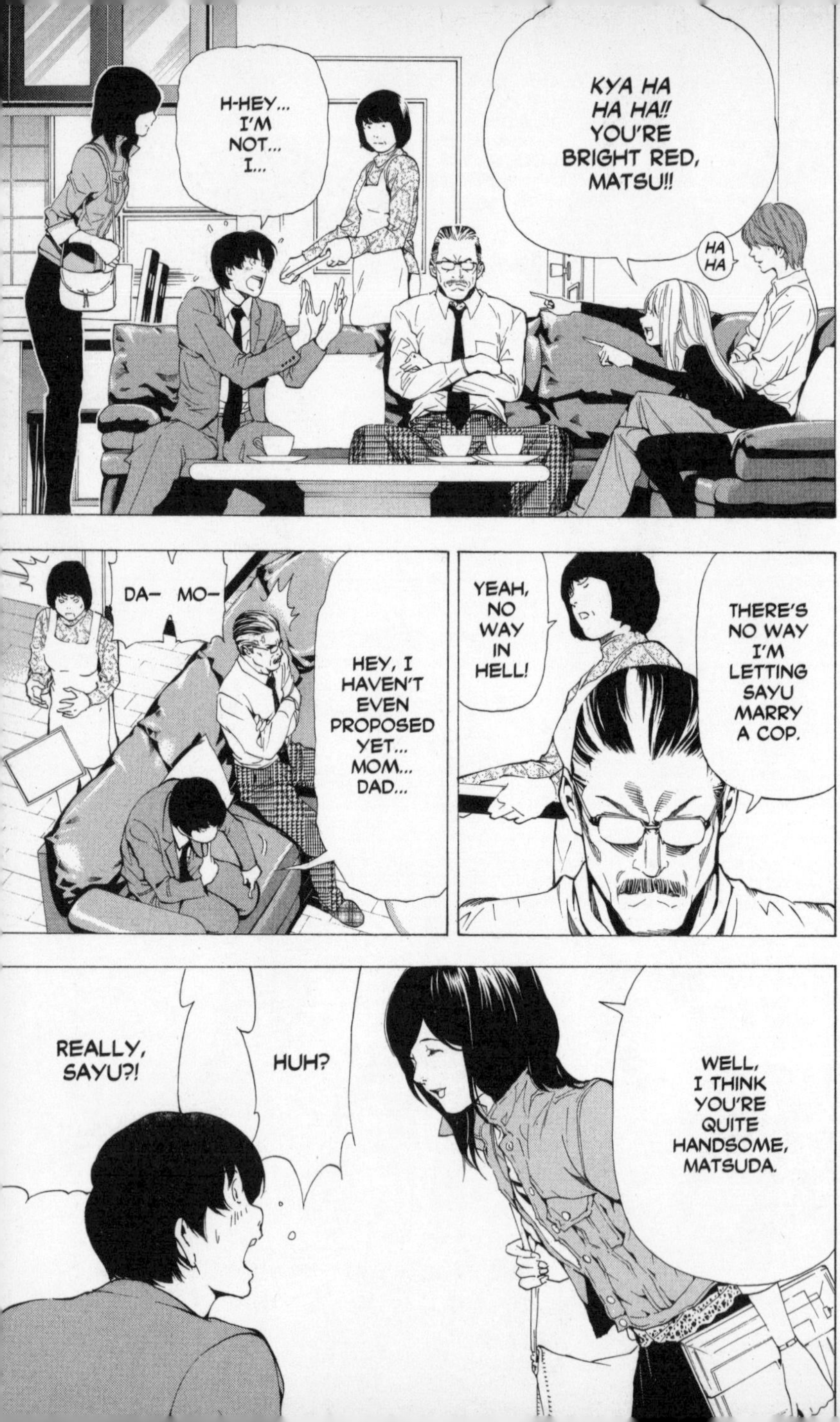
KYA HA HA HA!! YOU'RE BRIGHT RED, MATSU!!
HA HA
H-HEY... I'M NOT... I...
THERE'S NO WAY I'M LETTING SAYU MARRY A COP.
YEAH, NO WAY IN HELL!
HEY, I HAVEN'T EVEN PROPOSED YET... MOM... DAD...
DA— MO—
WELL, I THINK YOU'RE QUITE HANDSOME, MATSUDA.
HUH?
REALLY, SAYU?!

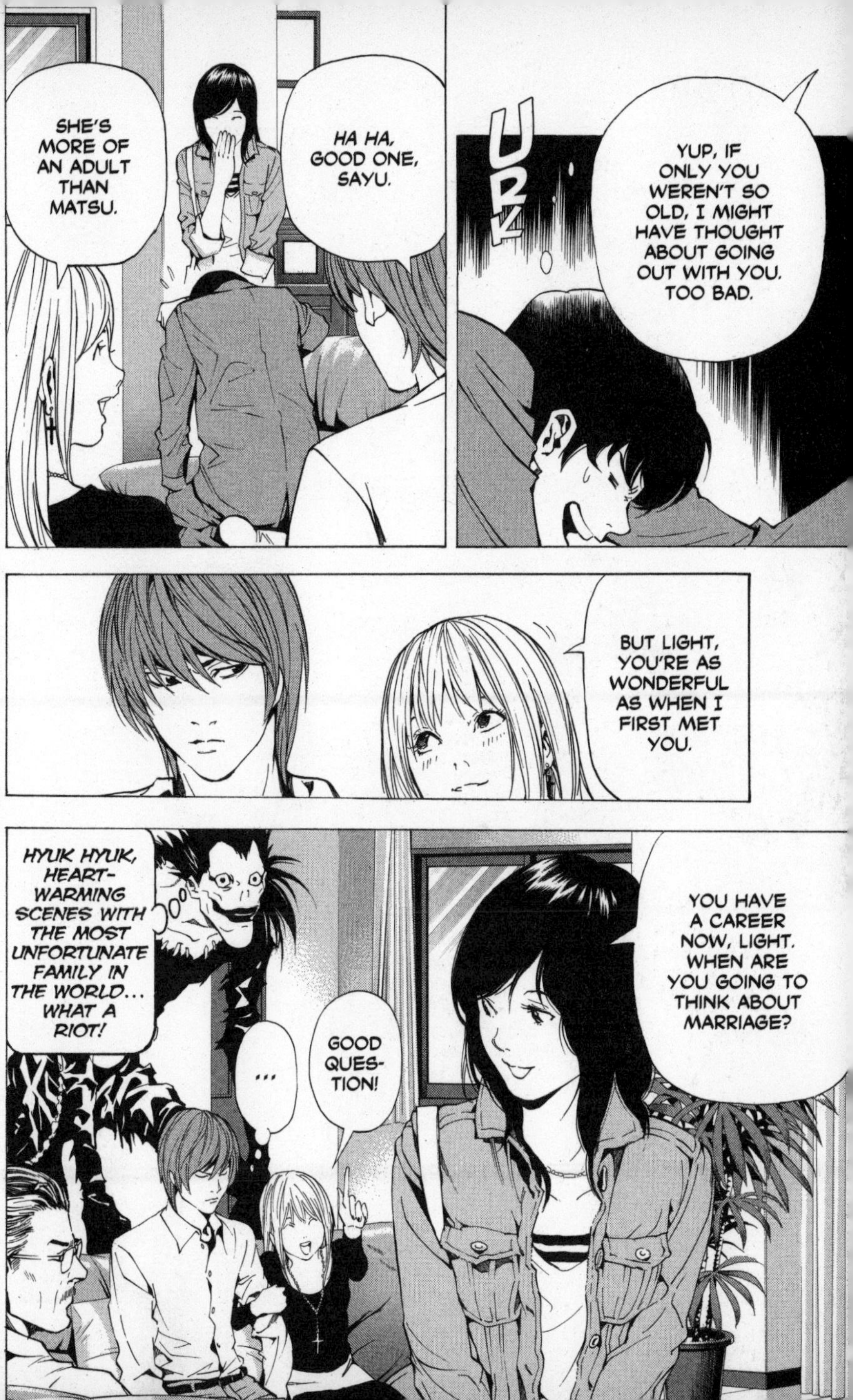
URK
YUP, IF ONLY YOU WEREN'T SO OLD, I MIGHT HAVE THOUGHT ABOUT GOING OUT WITH YOU. TOO BAD.
HA HA, GOOD ONE, SAYU.
SHE'S MORE OF AN ADULT THAN MATSU.
BUT LIGHT, YOU'RE AS WONDERFUL AS WHEN I FIRST MET YOU.
YOU HAVE A CAREER NOW, LIGHT. WHEN ARE YOU GOING TO THINK ABOUT MARRIAGE?
GOOD QUES-TION!
...
HYUK HYUK, HEART-WARMING SCENES WITH THE MOST UNFORTUNATE FAMILY IN THE WORLD... WHAT A RIOT!

READ THIS WAY

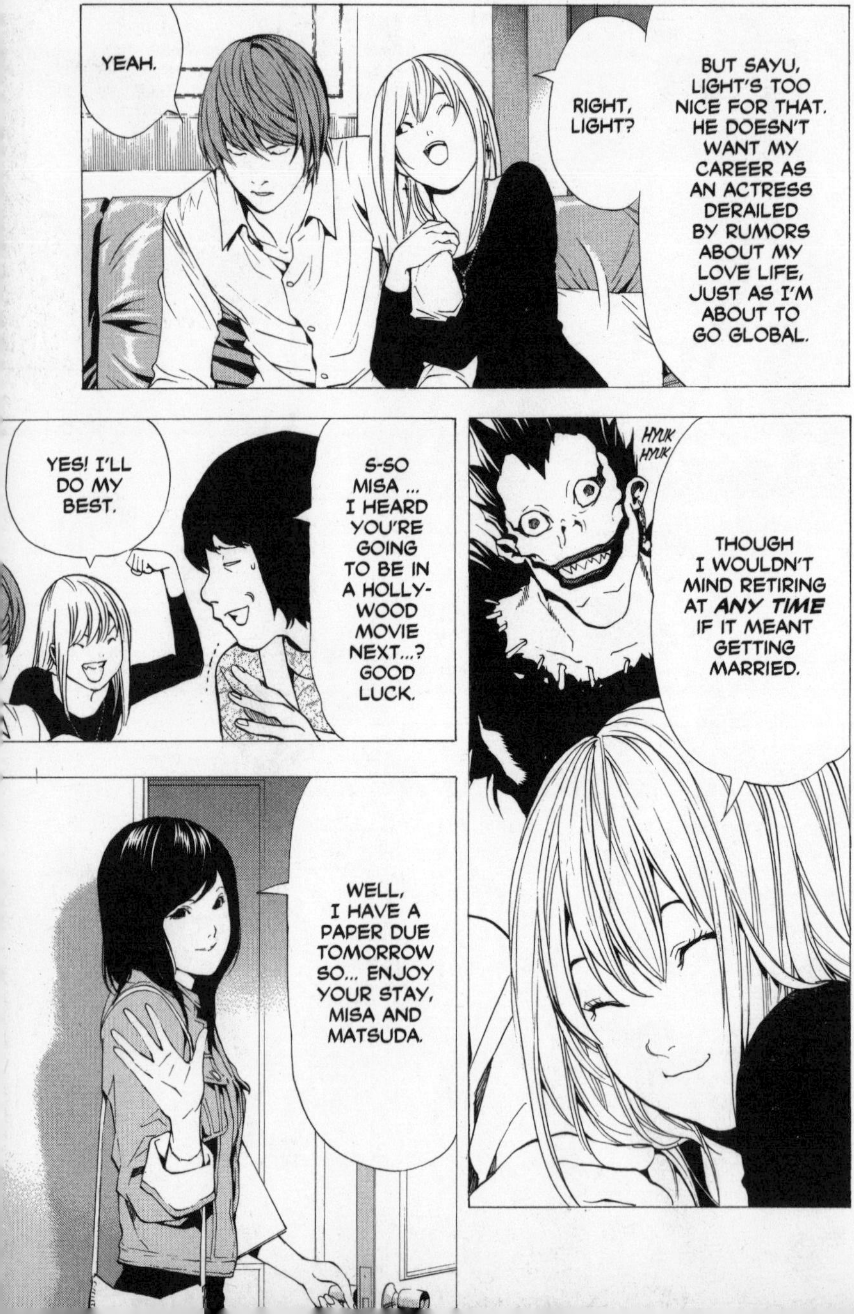
BUT SAYU, LIGHT'S TOO NICE FOR THAT. HE DOESN'T WANT MY CAREER AS AN ACTRESS DERAILED BY RUMORS ABOUT MY LOVE LIFE, JUST AS I'M ABOUT TO GO GLOBAL.
RIGHT, LIGHT?
YEAH.
THOUGH I WOULDN'T MIND RETIRING AT *ANY TIME* IF IT MEANT GETTING MARRIED.
HYUK HYUK
S-SO MISA ... I HEARD YOU'RE GOING TO BE IN A HOLLY-WOOD MOVIE NEXT...? GOOD LUCK.
YES! I'LL DO MY BEST.
WELL, I HAVE A PAPER DUE TOMORROW SO... ENJOY YOUR STAY, MISA AND MATSUDA.

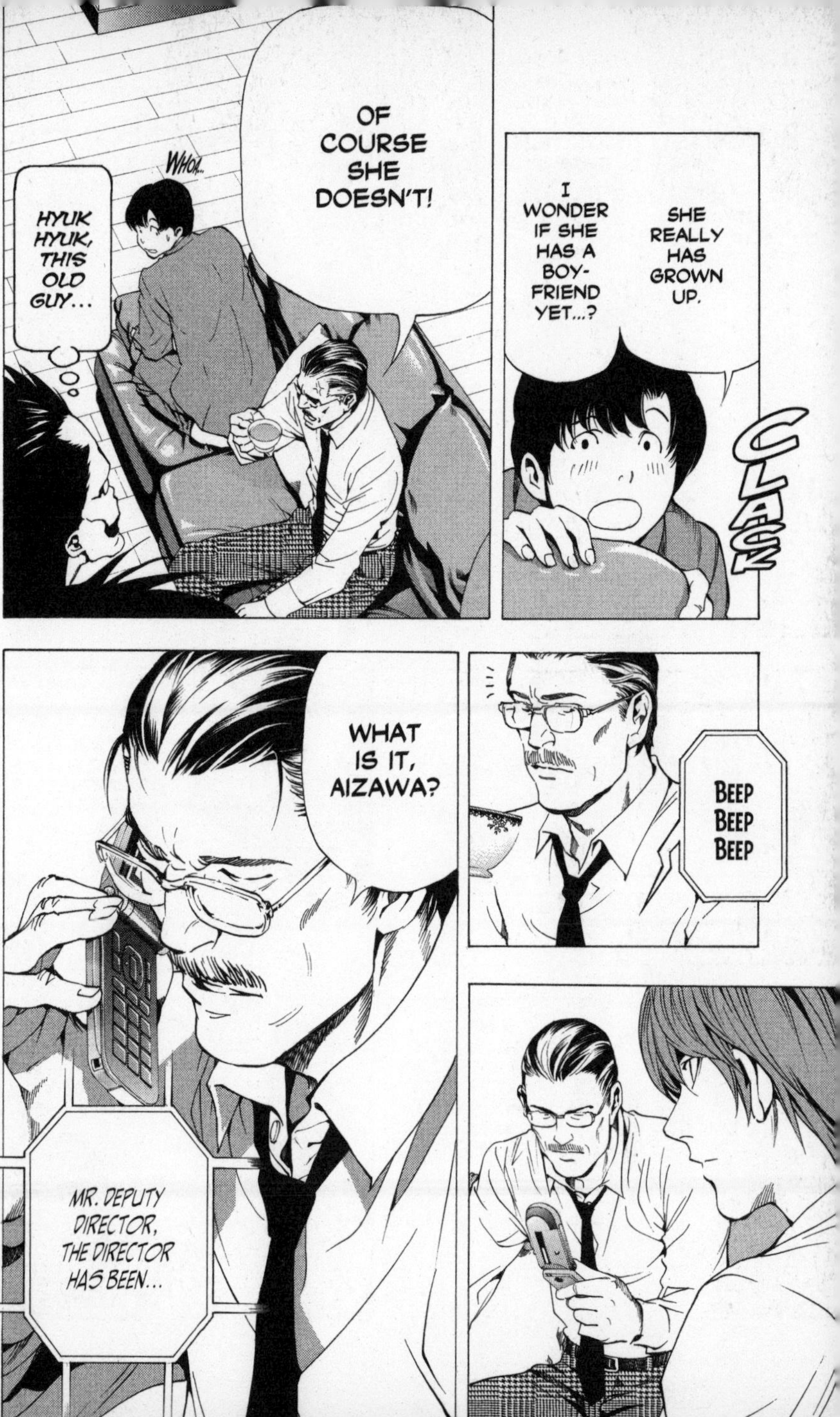
SHE REALLY HAS GROWN UP.
I WONDER IF SHE HAS A BOY-FRIEND YET...?
CLACK
OF COURSE SHE DOESN'T!
WHOA...
HYUK HYUK, THIS OLD GUY...
BEEP BEEP BEEP
WHAT IS IT, AIZAWA?
MR. DEPUTY DIRECTOR, THE DIRECTOR HAS BEEN...

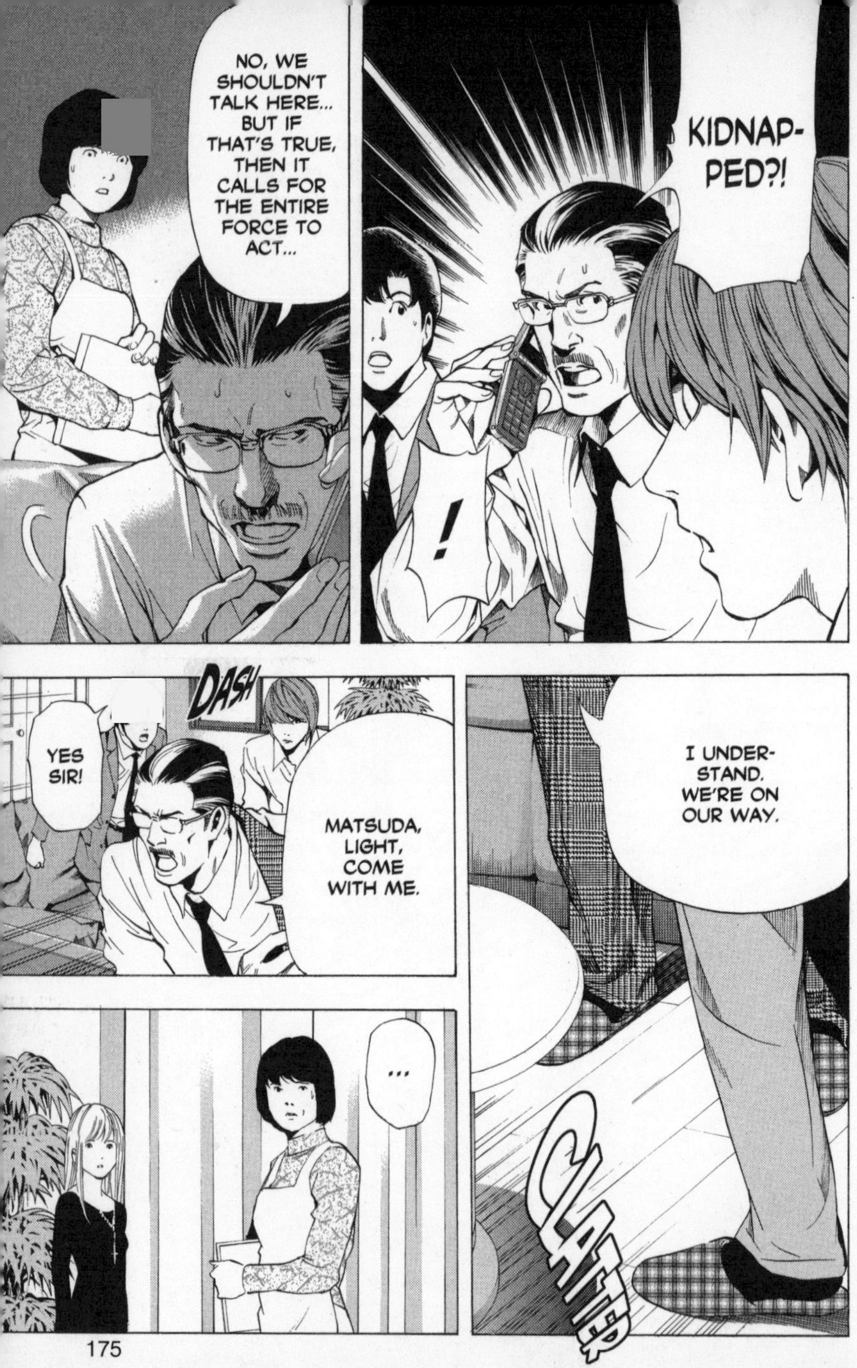
KIDNAP-PED?!
!
NO, WE SHOULDN'T TALK HERE... BUT IF THAT'S TRUE, THEN IT CALLS FOR THE ENTIRE FORCE TO ACT...
I UNDER-STAND. WE'RE ON OUR WAY.
CLATTER
MATSUDA, LIGHT, COME WITH ME.
DASH
YES SIR!
...

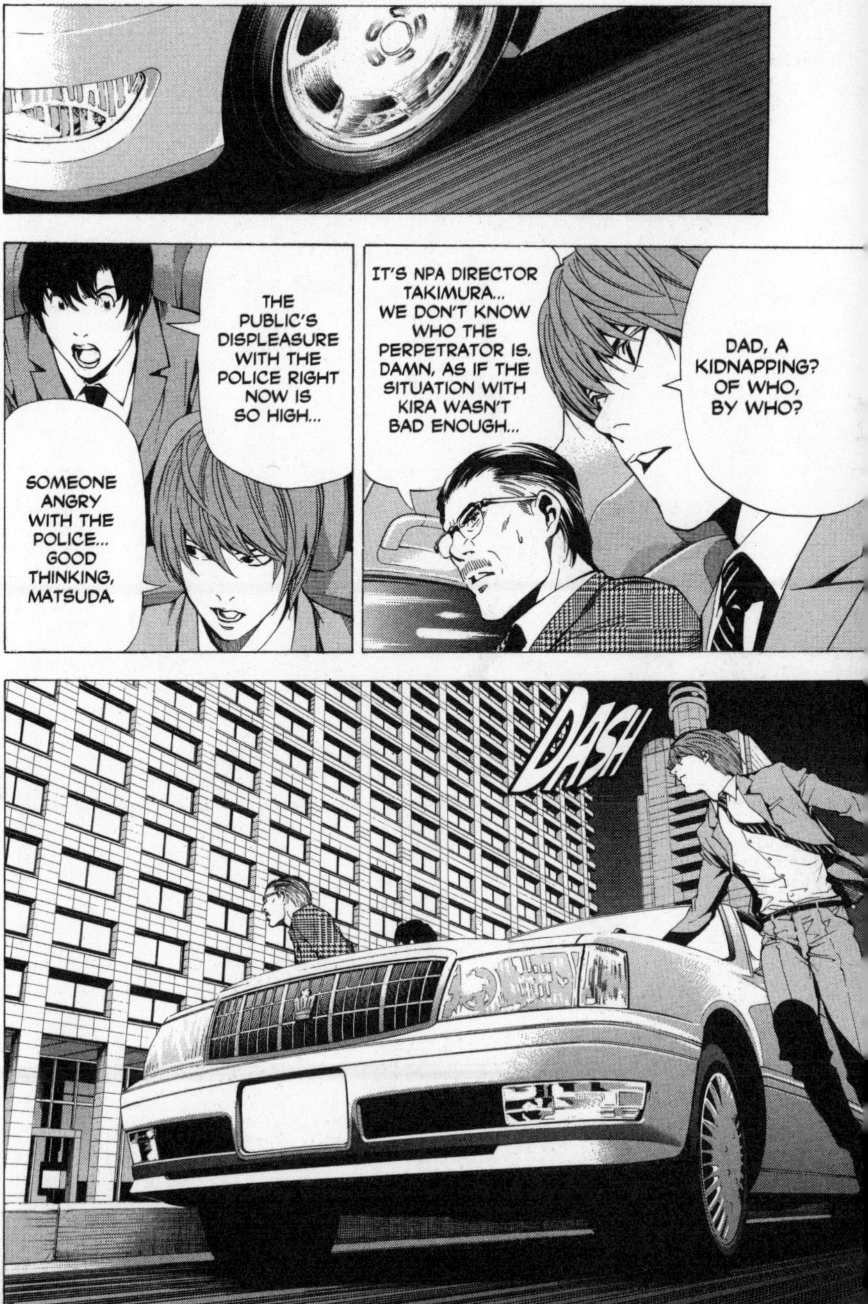
DAD, A KIDNAPPING? OF WHO, BY WHO?
IT'S NPA DIRECTOR TAKIMURA... WE DON'T KNOW WHO THE PERPETRATOR IS. DAMN, AS IF THE SITUATION WITH KIRA WASN'T BAD ENOUGH...
THE PUBLIC'S DISPLEASURE WITH THE POLICE RIGHT NOW IS SO HIGH...
SOMEONE ANGRY WITH THE POLICE... GOOD THINKING, MATSUDA.
DASH

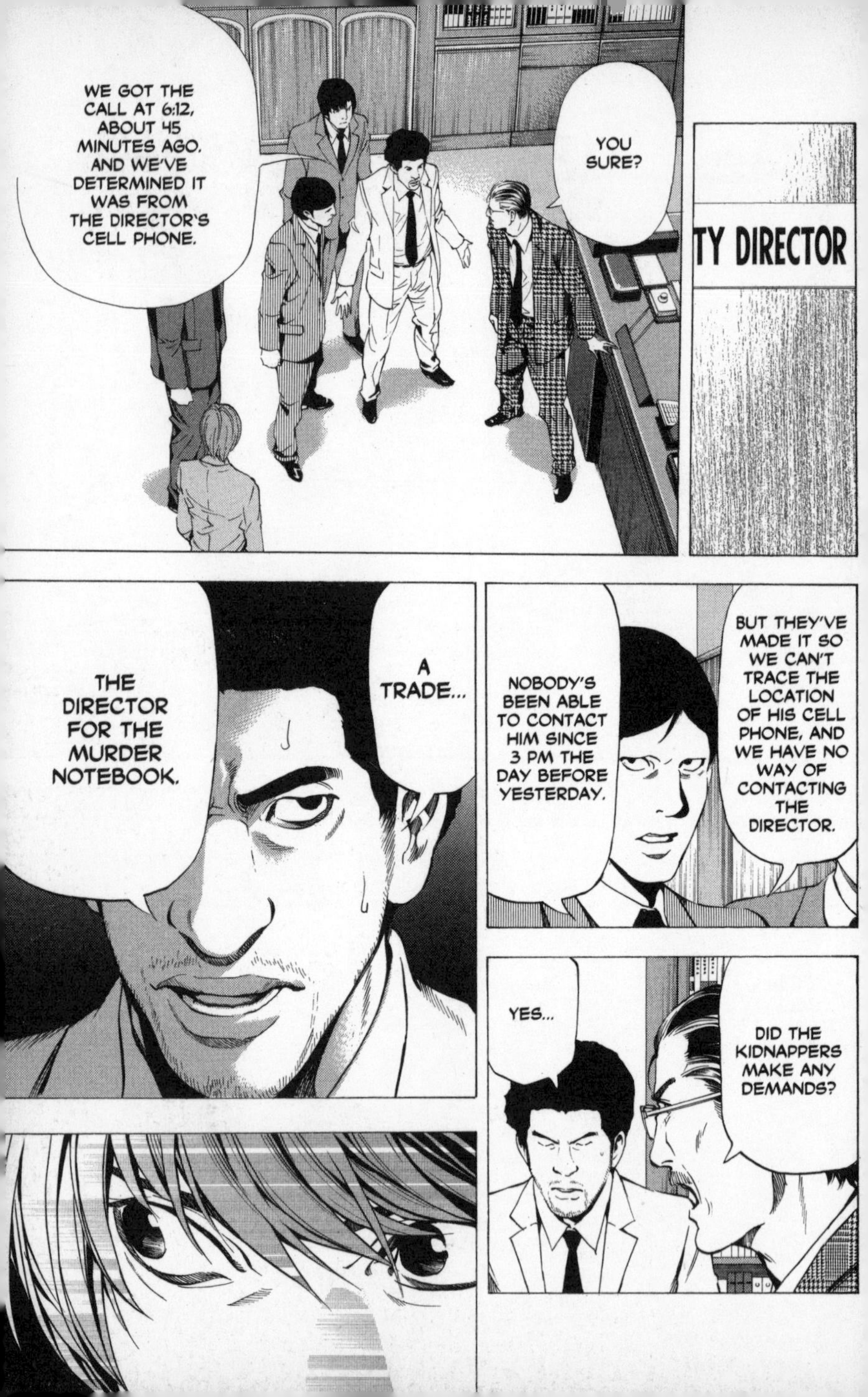
TY DIRECTOR
YOU SURE?
WE GOT THE CALL AT 6:12, ABOUT 45 MINUTES AGO. AND WE'VE DETERMINED IT WAS FROM THE DIRECTOR'S CELL PHONE.
BUT THEY'VE MADE IT SO WE CAN'T TRACE THE LOCATION OF HIS CELL PHONE, AND WE HAVE NO WAY OF CONTACTING THE DIRECTOR.
NOBODY'S BEEN ABLE TO CONTACT HIM SINCE 3 PM THE DAY BEFORE YESTERDAY.
DID THE KIDNAPPERS MAKE ANY DEMANDS?
YES...
A TRADE...
THE DIRECTOR FOR THE MURDER NOTEBOOK.

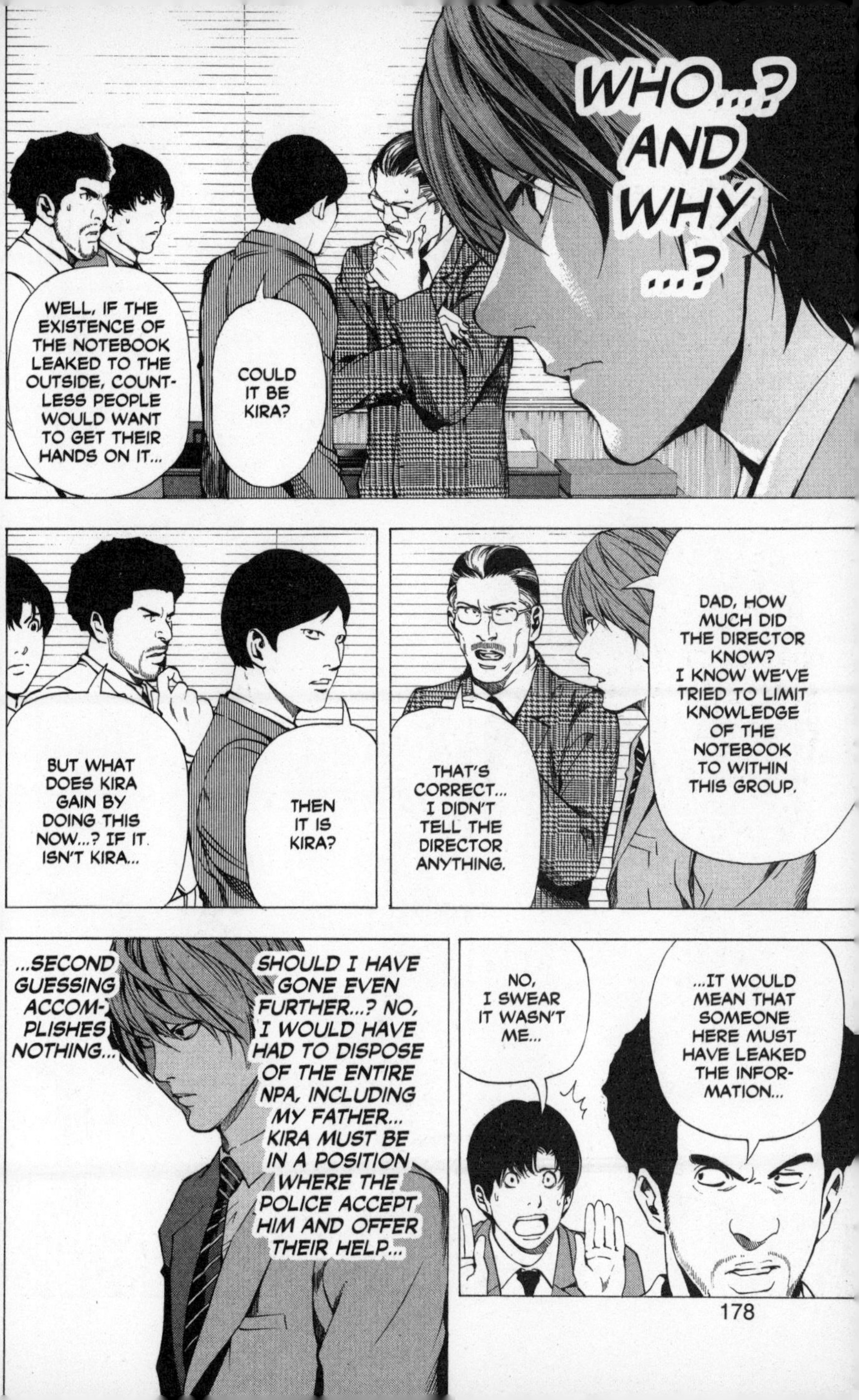
WHO...? AND WHY...?
COULD IT BE KIRA?
WELL, IF THE EXISTENCE OF THE NOTEBOOK LEAKED TO THE OUTSIDE, COUNT-LESS PEOPLE WOULD WANT TO GET THEIR HANDS ON IT...
DAD, HOW MUCH DID THE DIRECTOR KNOW? I KNOW WE'VE TRIED TO LIMIT KNOWLEDGE OF THE NOTEBOOK TO WITHIN THIS GROUP.
THAT'S CORRECT... I DIDN'T TELL THE DIRECTOR ANYTHING.
THEN IT IS KIRA?
BUT WHAT DOES KIRA GAIN BY DOING THIS NOW...? IF IT ISN'T KIRA...
...IT WOULD MEAN THAT SOMEONE HERE MUST HAVE LEAKED THE INFOR-MATION...
NO, I SWEAR IT WASN'T ME...
SHOULD I HAVE GONE EVEN FURTHER...? NO, I WOULD HAVE HAD TO DISPOSE OF THE ENTIRE NPA, INCLUDING MY FATHER... KIRA MUST BE IN A POSITION WHERE THE POLICE ACCEPT HIM AND OFFER THEIR HELP...
...SECOND GUESSING ACCOM-PLISHES NOTHING...

READ THIS WAY

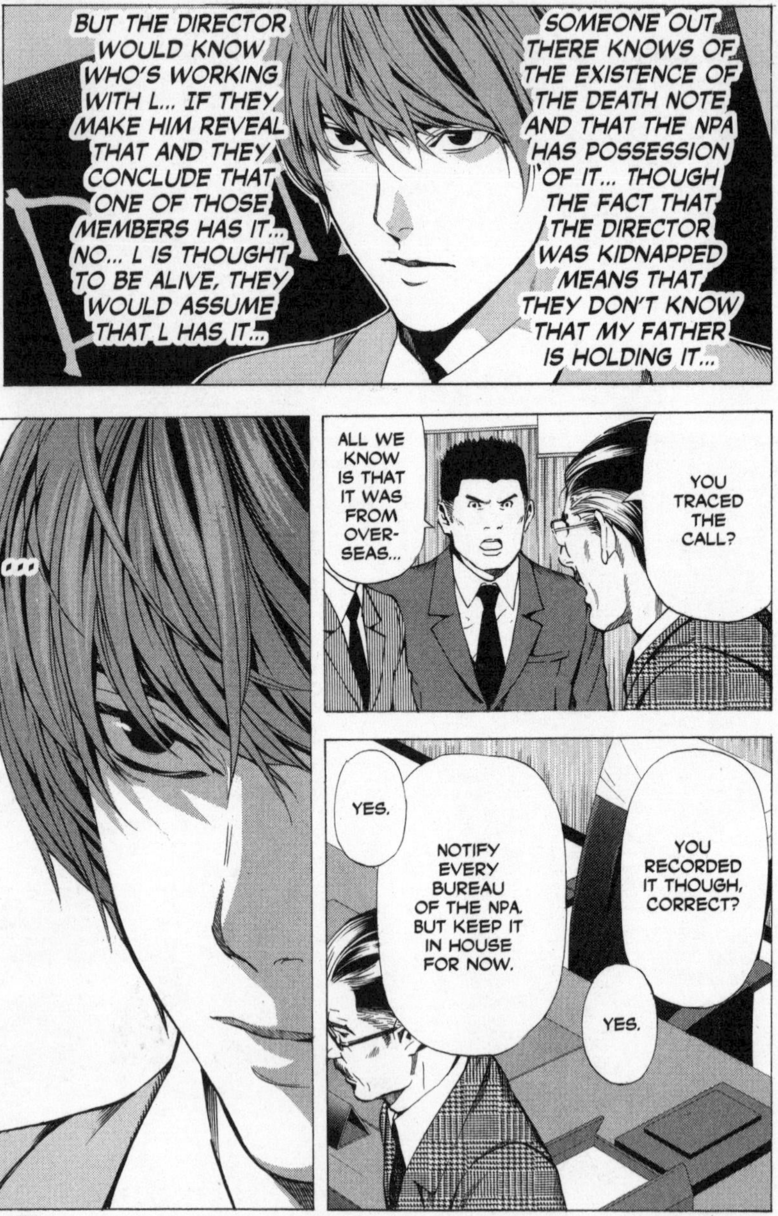

SOMEONE OUT THERE KNOWS OF THE EXISTENCE OF THE DEATH NOTE AND THAT THE NPA HAS POSSESSION OF IT... THOUGH THE FACT THAT THE DIRECTOR WAS KIDNAPPED MEANS THAT THEY DON'T KNOW THAT MY FATHER IS HOLDING IT...
BUT THE DIRECTOR WOULD KNOW WHO'S WORKING WITH L... IF THEY MAKE HIM REVEAL THAT AND THEY CONCLUDE THAT ONE OF THOSE MEMBERS HAS IT... NO... L IS THOUGHT TO BE ALIVE, THEY WOULD ASSUME THAT L HAS IT...
YOU TRACED THE CALL?
ALL WE KNOW IS THAT IT WAS FROM OVERSEAS...
YOU RECORDED IT THOUGH, CORRECT?
YES.
NOTIFY EVERY BUREAU OF THE NPA. BUT KEEP IT IN HOUSE FOR NOW.
YES.
...

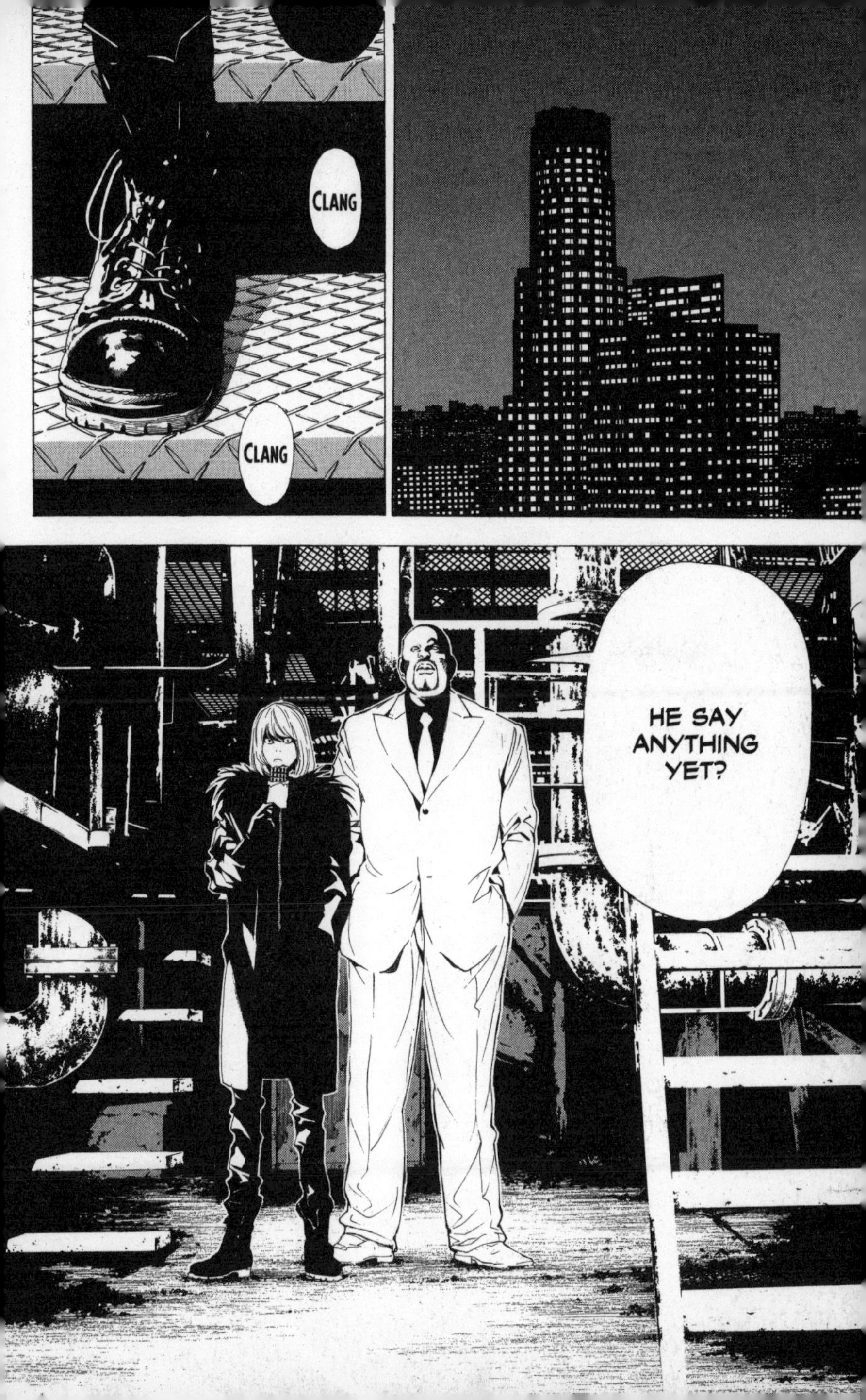
CLANG
CLANG
HE SAY ANYTHING YET?

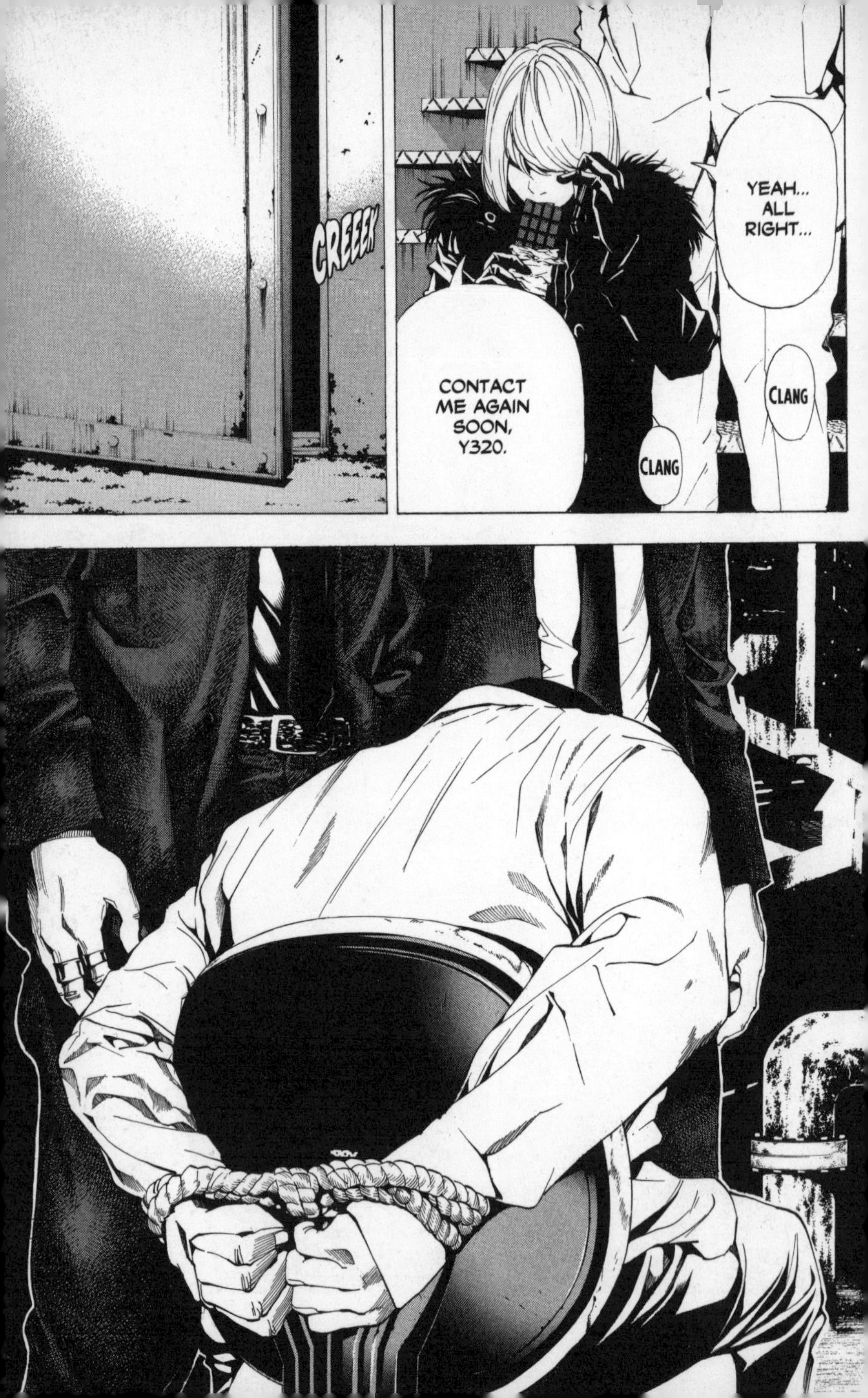
YEAH... ALL RIGHT...
CLANG
CONTACT ME AGAIN SOON, Y320.
CLANG
CREEEK

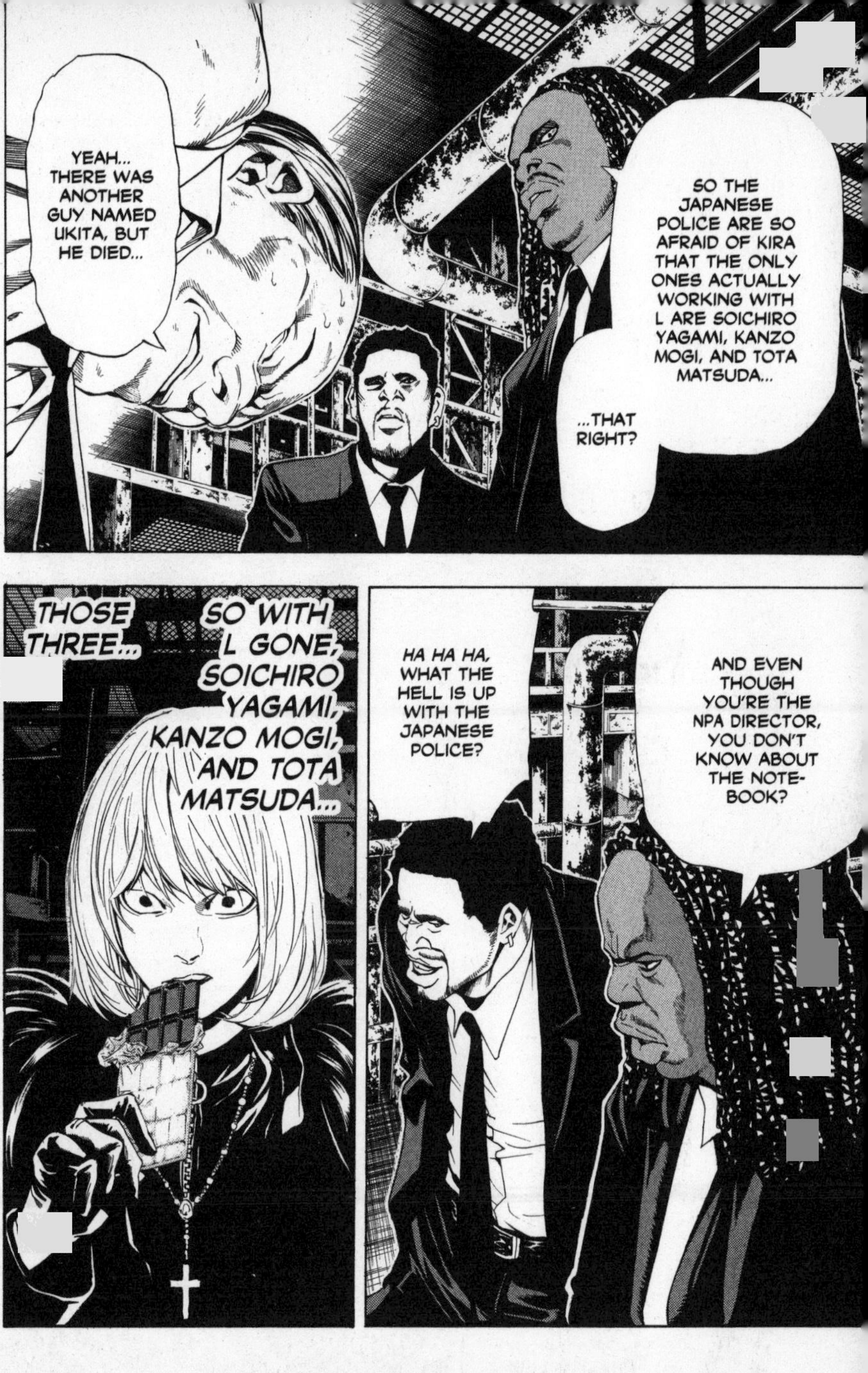
SO THE JAPANESE POLICE ARE SO AFRAID OF KIRA THAT THE ONLY ONES ACTUALLY WORKING WITH L ARE SOICHIRO YAGAMI, KANZO MOGI, AND TOTA MATSUDA...
...THAT RIGHT?
YEAH... THERE WAS ANOTHER GUY NAMED UKITA, BUT HE DIED...
AND EVEN THOUGH YOU'RE THE NPA DIRECTOR, YOU DON'T KNOW ABOUT THE NOTE-BOOK?
HA HA HA, WHAT THE HELL IS UP WITH THE JAPANESE POLICE?
SO WITH L GONE, SOICHIRO YAGAMI, KANZO MOGI, AND TOTA MATSUDA...
THOSE THREE...

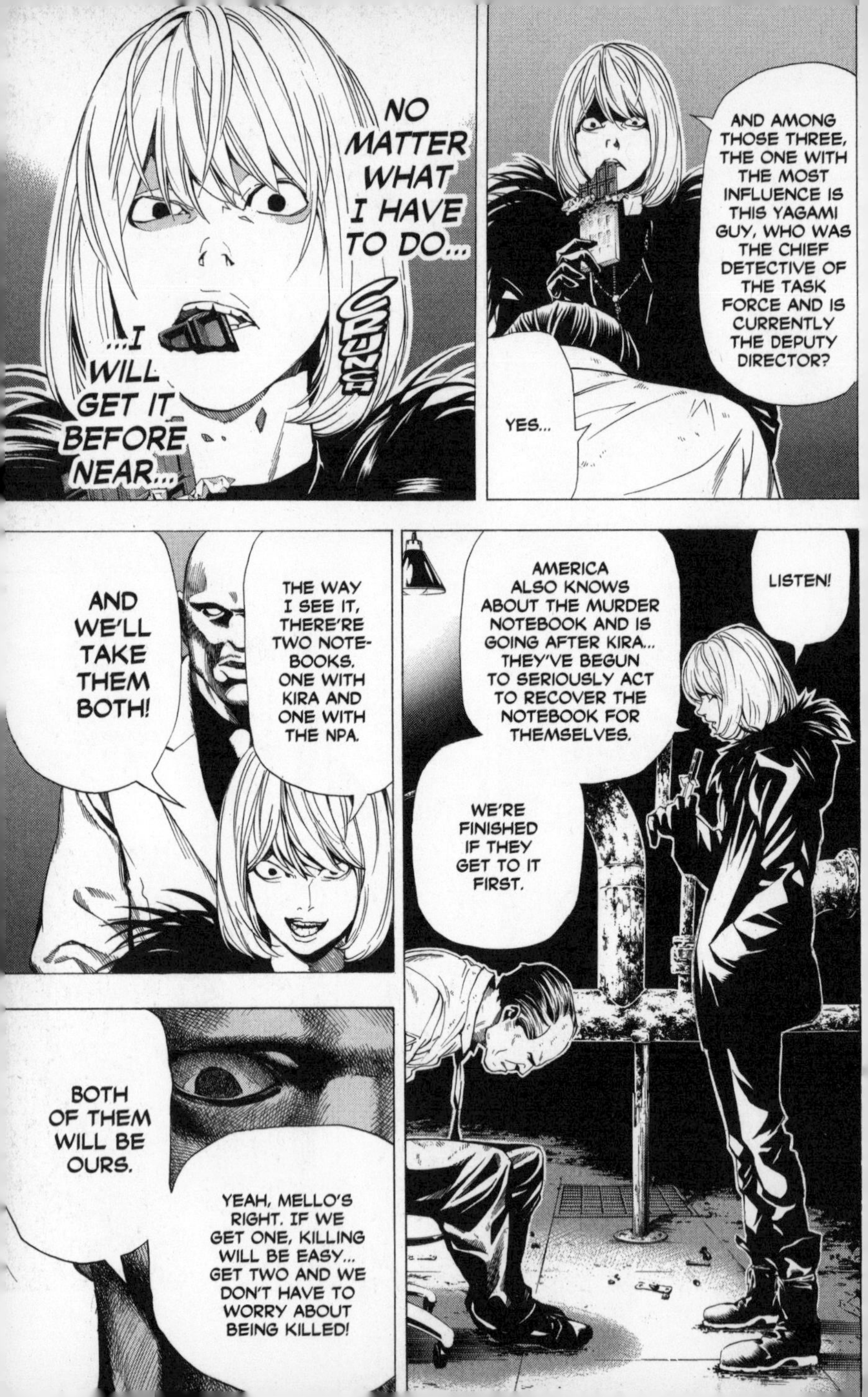
AND AMONG THOSE THREE, THE ONE WITH THE MOST INFLUENCE IS THIS YAGAMI GUY, WHO WAS THE CHIEF DETECTIVE OF THE TASK FORCE AND IS CURRENTLY THE DEPUTY DIRECTOR?
YES...
NO MATTER WHAT I HAVE TO DO...
CRUNCH
...I WILL GET IT BEFORE NEAR...
LISTEN!
AMERICA ALSO KNOWS ABOUT THE MURDER NOTEBOOK AND IS GOING AFTER KIRA... THEY'VE BEGUN TO SERIOUSLY ACT TO RECOVER THE NOTEBOOK FOR THEMSELVES.
WE'RE FINISHED IF THEY GET TO IT FIRST.
THE WAY I SEE IT, THERE'RE TWO NOTE-BOOKS. ONE WITH KIRA AND ONE WITH THE NPA.
AND WE'LL TAKE THEM BOTH!
BOTH OF THEM WILL BE OURS.
YEAH, MELLO'S RIGHT. IF WE GET ONE, KILLING WILL BE EASY... GET TWO AND WE DON'T HAVE TO WORRY ABOUT BEING KILLED!

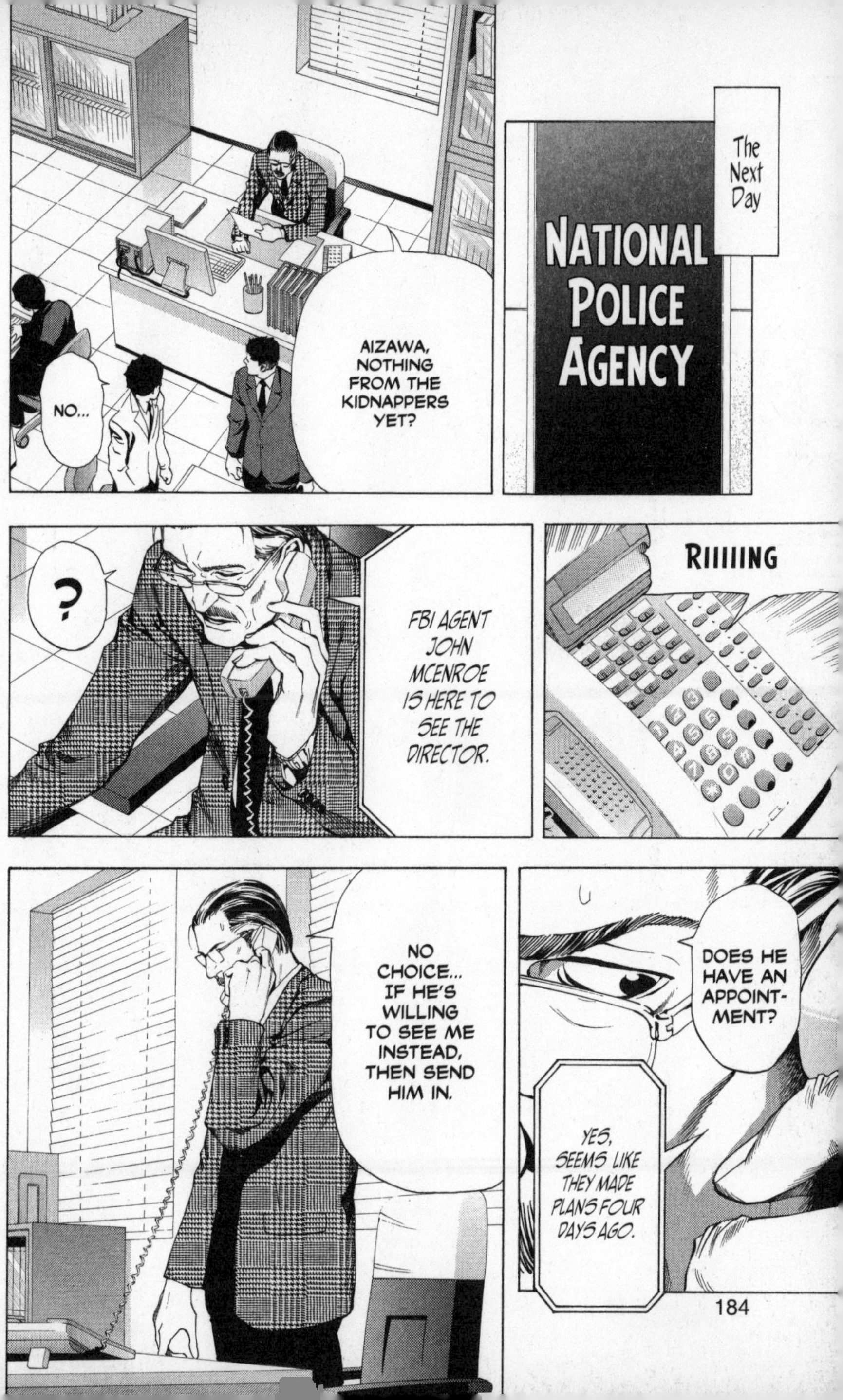
The Next Day
NATIONAL POLICE AGENCY
AIZAWA, NOTHING FROM THE KIDNAPPERS YET?
NO...
RIIIIIING
FBI AGENT JOHN MCENROE IS HERE TO SEE THE DIRECTOR.
?
DOES HE HAVE AN APPOINT-MENT?
YES, SEEMS LIKE THEY MADE PLANS FOUR DAYS AGO.
NO CHOICE... IF HE'S WILLING TO SEE ME INSTEAD, THEN SEND HIM IN.

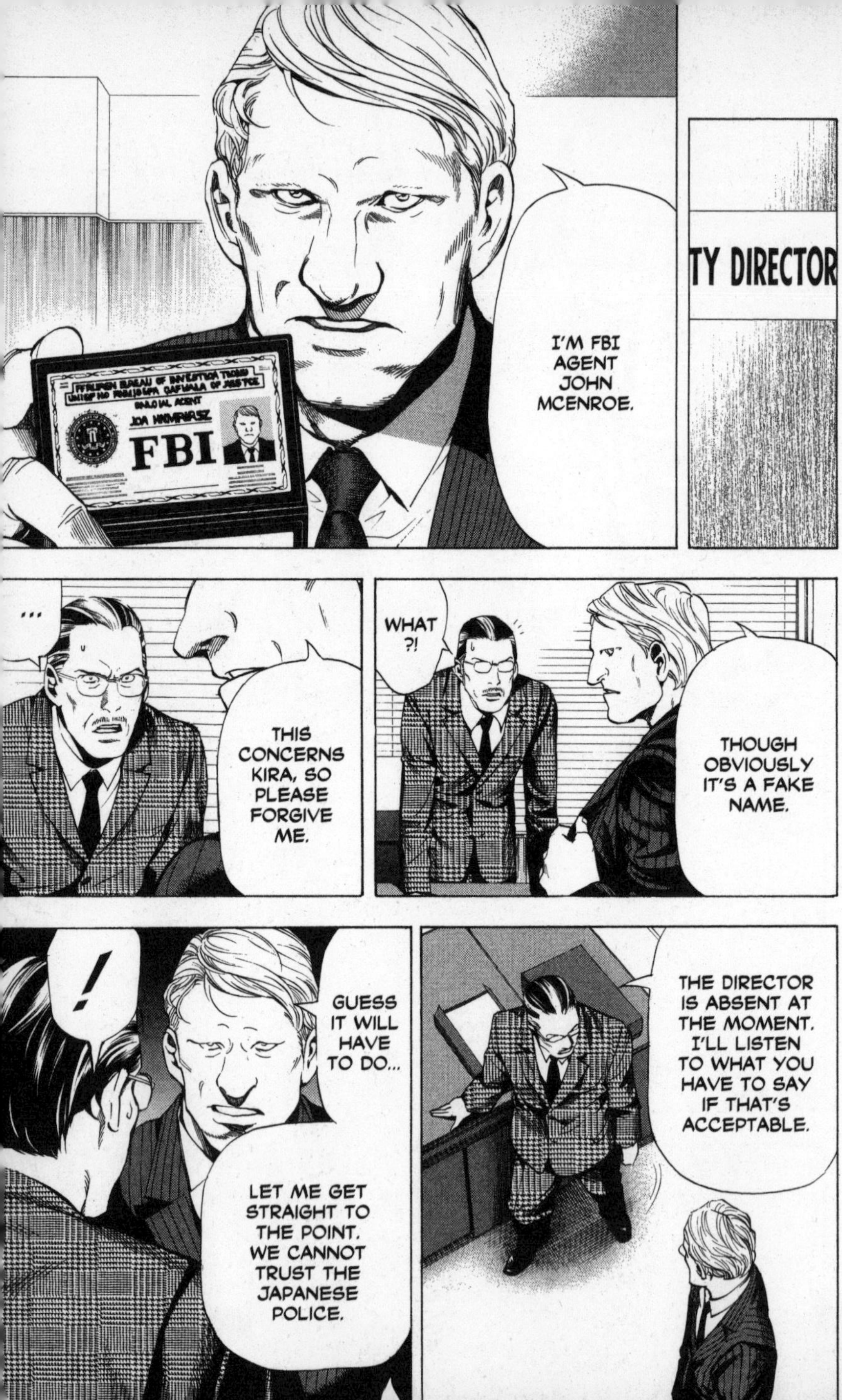
TY DIRECTOR
I'M FBI AGENT JOHN MCENROE.
FBI
THOUGH OBVIOUSLY IT'S A FAKE NAME.
WHAT ?!
THIS CONCERNS KIRA, SO PLEASE FORGIVE ME.
...
THE DIRECTOR IS ABSENT AT THE MOMENT. I'LL LISTEN TO WHAT YOU HAVE TO SAY IF THAT'S ACCEPTABLE.
GUESS IT WILL HAVE TO DO...
!
LET ME GET STRAIGHT TO THE POINT. WE CANNOT TRUST THE JAPANESE POLICE.

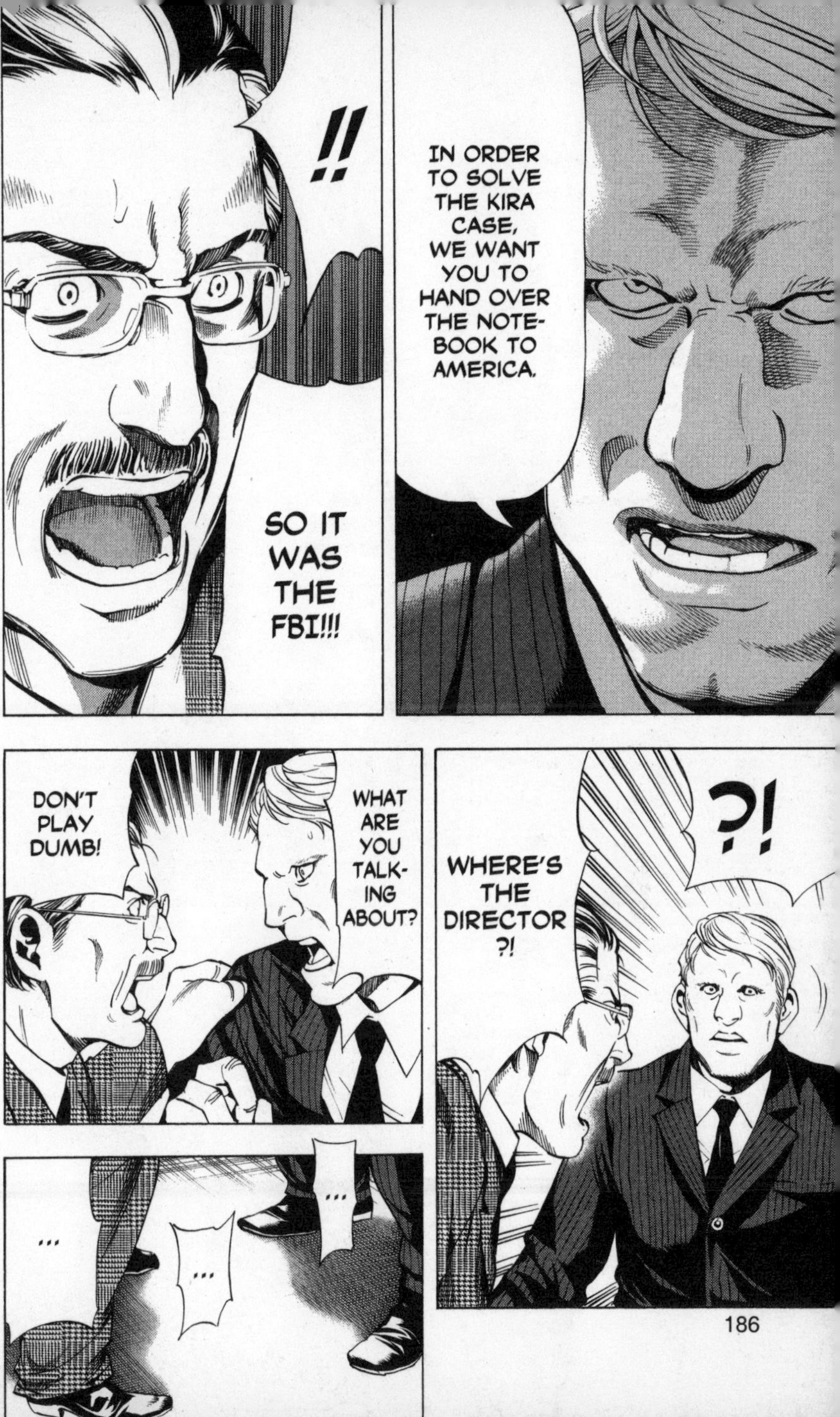
IN ORDER TO SOLVE THE KIRA CASE, WE WANT YOU TO HAND OVER THE NOTEBOOK TO AMERICA.
!!
SO IT WAS THE FBI!!!
?!
WHERE'S THE DIRECTOR?!
WHAT ARE YOU TALKING ABOUT?
DON'T PLAY DUMB!
...
...
...

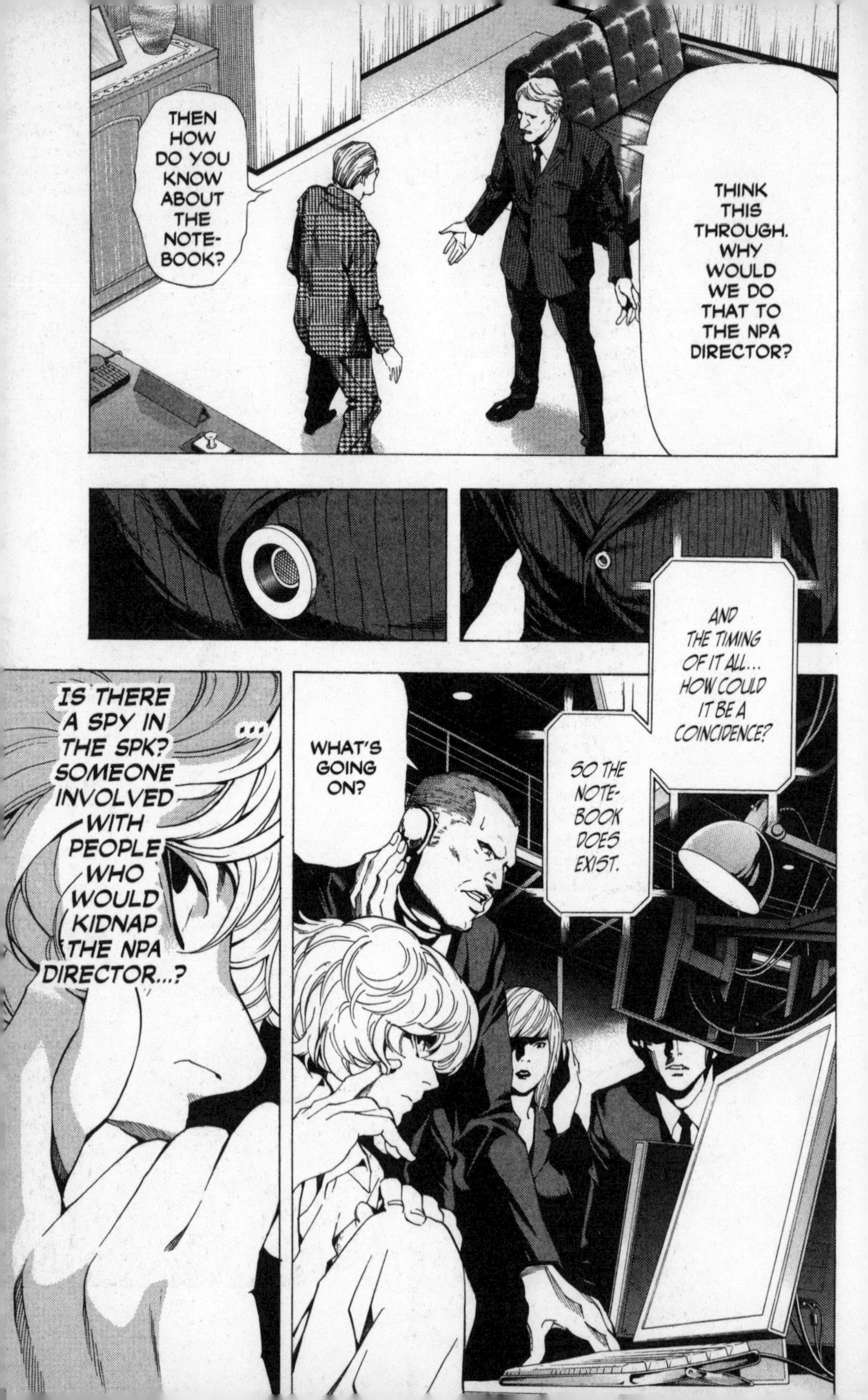
THINK THIS THROUGH. WHY WOULD WE DO THAT TO THE NPA DIRECTOR?
THEN HOW DO YOU KNOW ABOUT THE NOTE-BOOK?
AND THE TIMING OF IT ALL... HOW COULD IT BE A COINCIDENCE?
SO THE NOTE-BOOK DOES EXIST.
WHAT'S GOING ON?
...
IS THERE A SPY IN THE SPK? SOMEONE INVOLVED WITH PEOPLE WHO WOULD KIDNAP THE NPA DIRECTOR...?

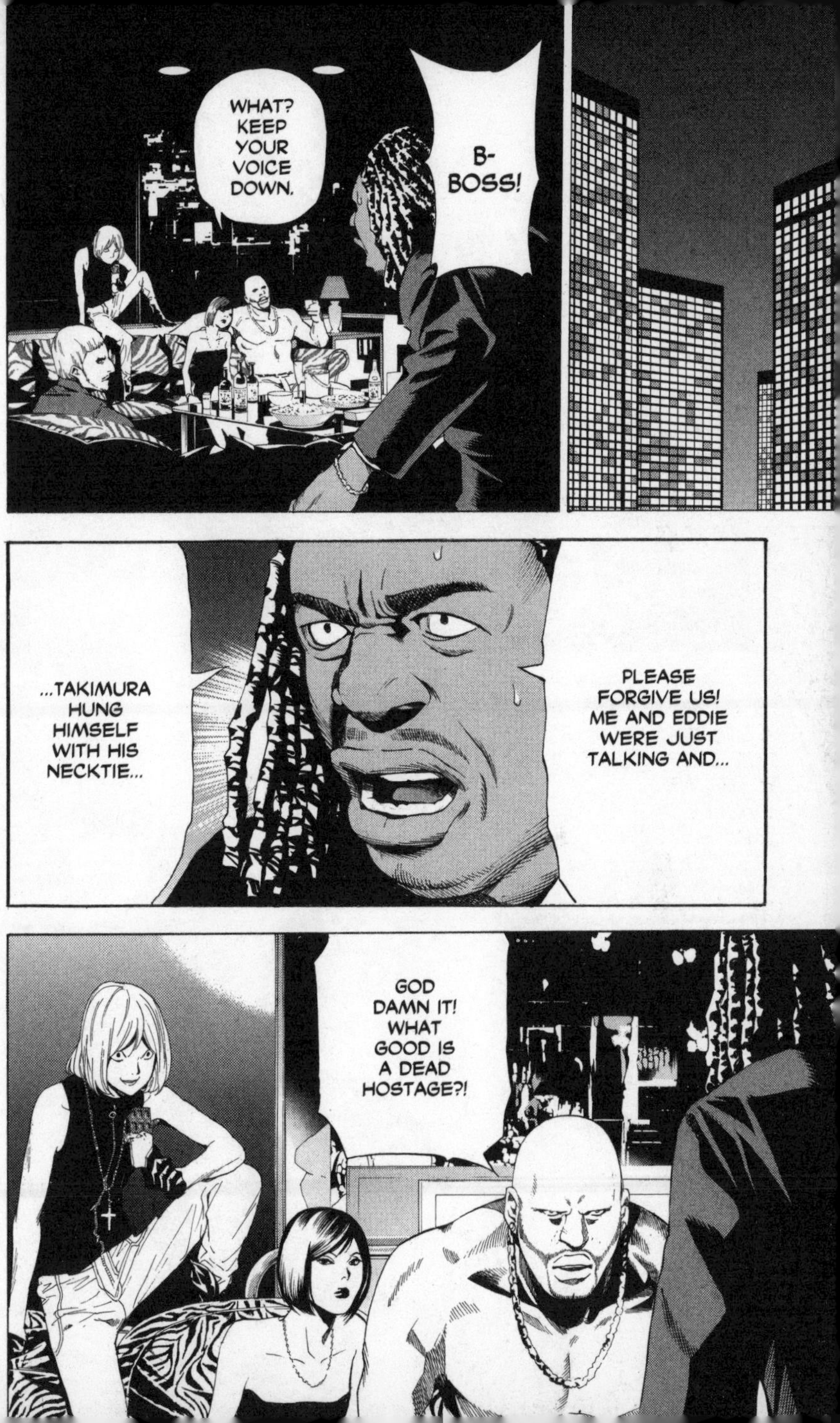
B-BOSS!
WHAT? KEEP YOUR VOICE DOWN.
PLEASE FORGIVE US! ME AND EDDIE WERE JUST TALKING AND...
...TAKIMURA HUNG HIMSELF WITH HIS NECKTIE...
GOD DAMN IT! WHAT GOOD IS A DEAD HOSTAGE?!

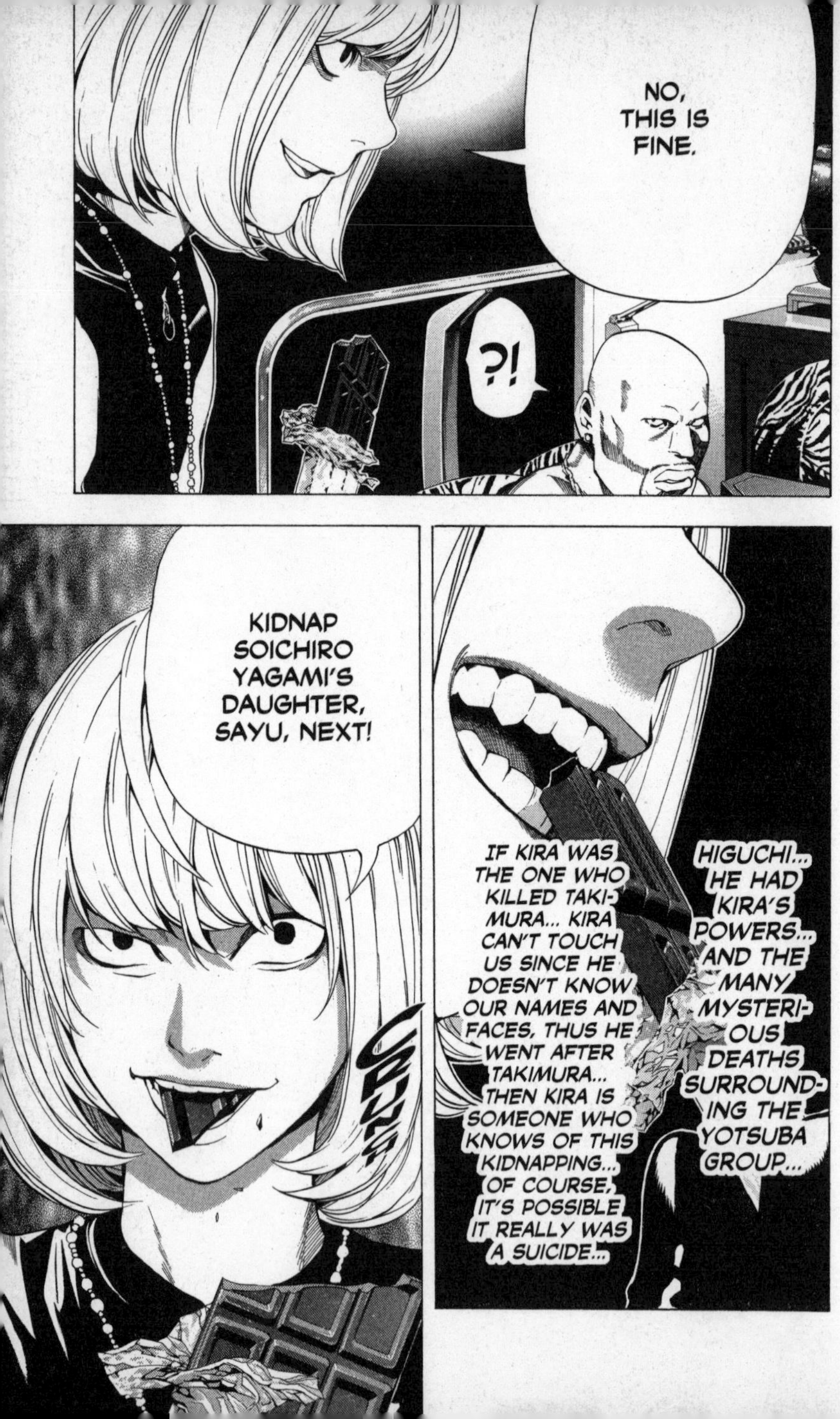
NO, THIS IS FINE.
?!
HIGUCHI... HE HAD KIRA'S POWERS... AND THE MANY MYSTERIOUS DEATHS SURROUNDING THE YOTSUBA GROUP...
IF KIRA WAS THE ONE WHO KILLED TAKIMURA... KIRA CAN'T TOUCH US SINCE HE DOESN'T KNOW OUR NAMES AND FACES, THUS HE WENT AFTER TAKIMURA... THEN KIRA IS SOMEONE WHO KNOWS OF THIS KIDNAPPING... OF COURSE, IT'S POSSIBLE IT REALLY WAS A SUICIDE...
KIDNAP SOICHIRO YAGAMI'S DAUGHTER, SAYU, NEXT!

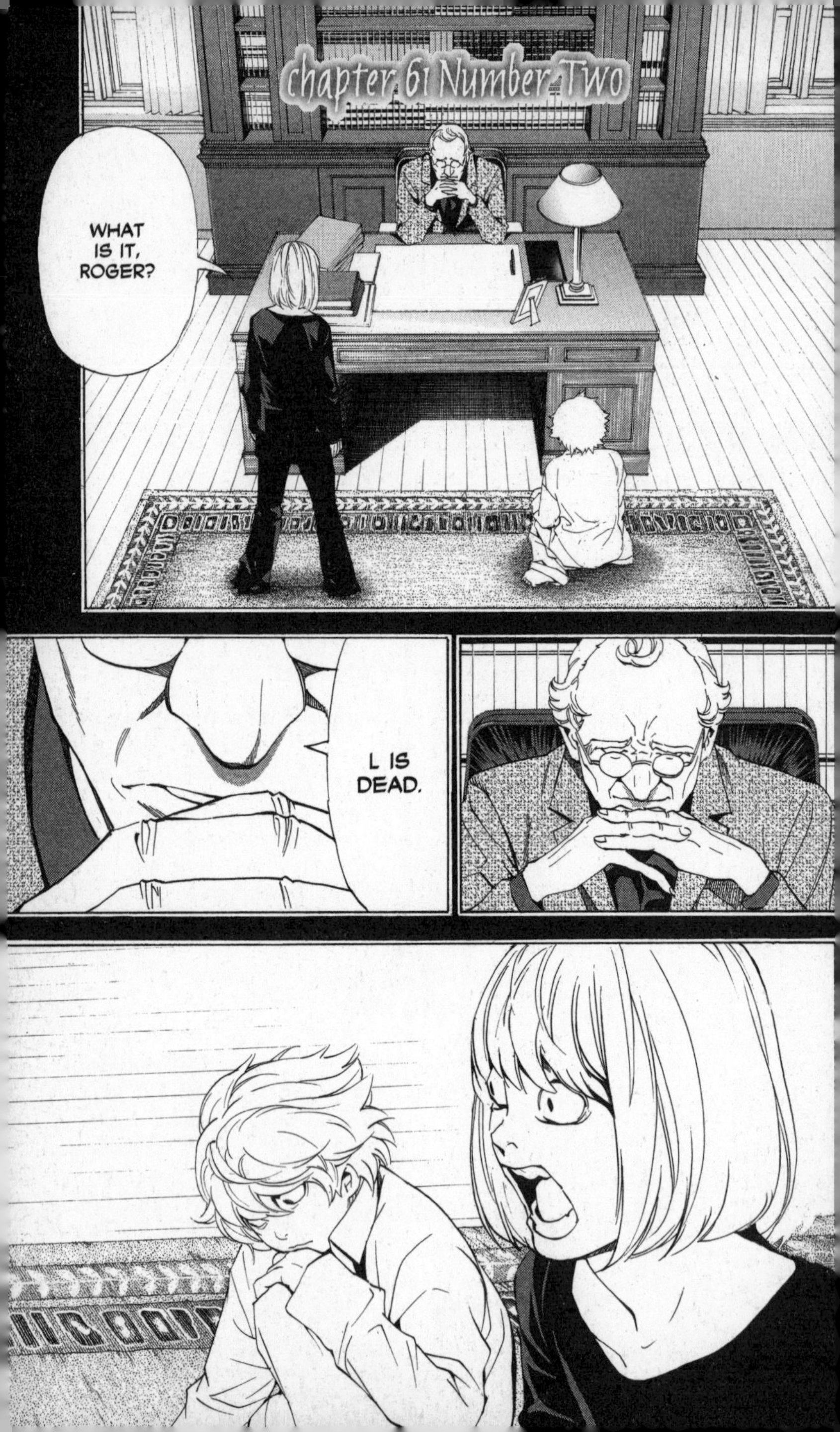
chapter 61 Number Two
WHAT IS IT, ROGER?
L IS DEAD.

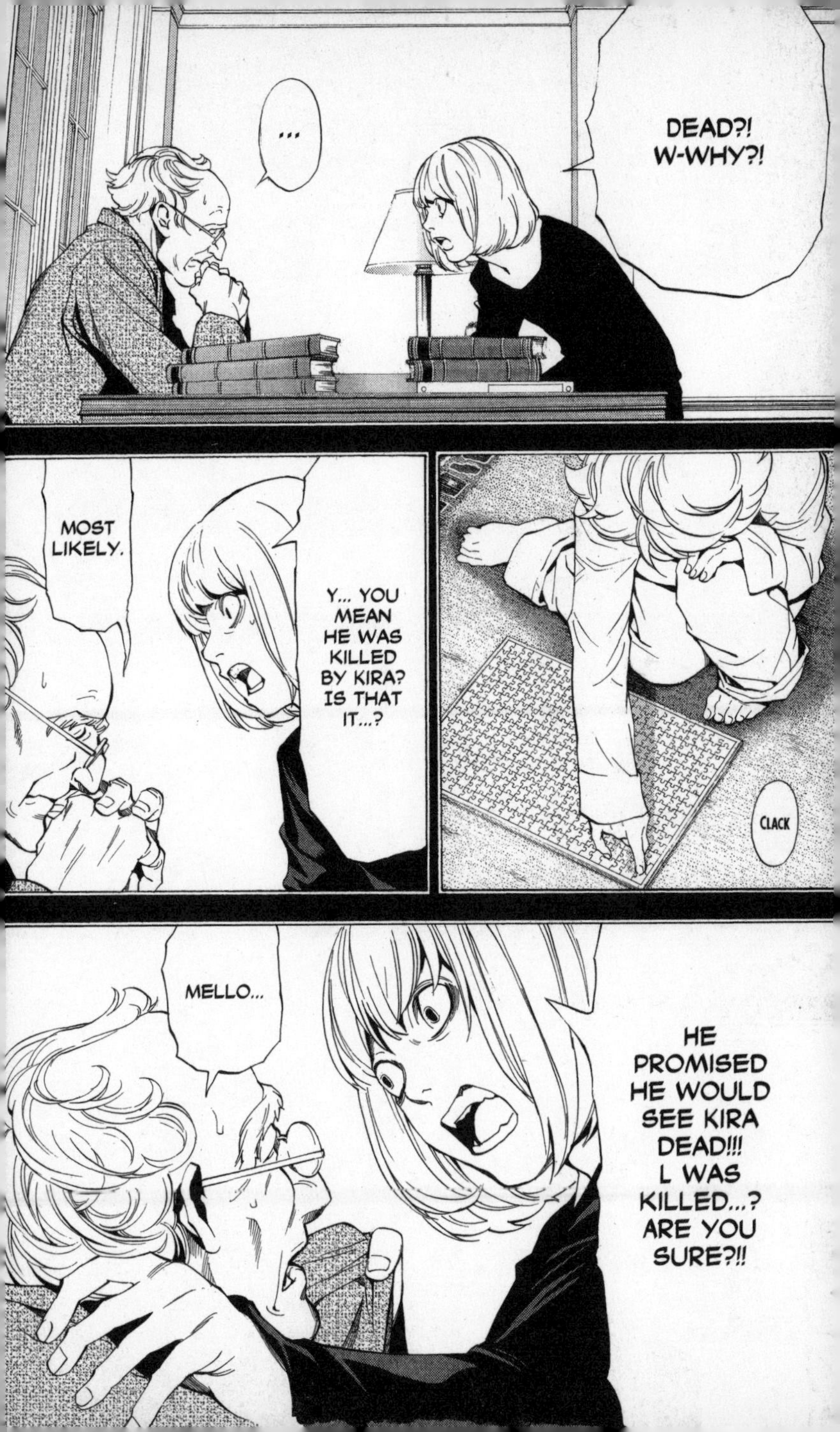
DEAD?! W-WHY?!
...
CLACK
Y... YOU MEAN HE WAS KILLED BY KIRA? IS THAT IT...?
MOST LIKELY.
HE PROMISED HE WOULD SEE KIRA DEAD!!! L WAS KILLED...? ARE YOU SURE?!!
MELLO...

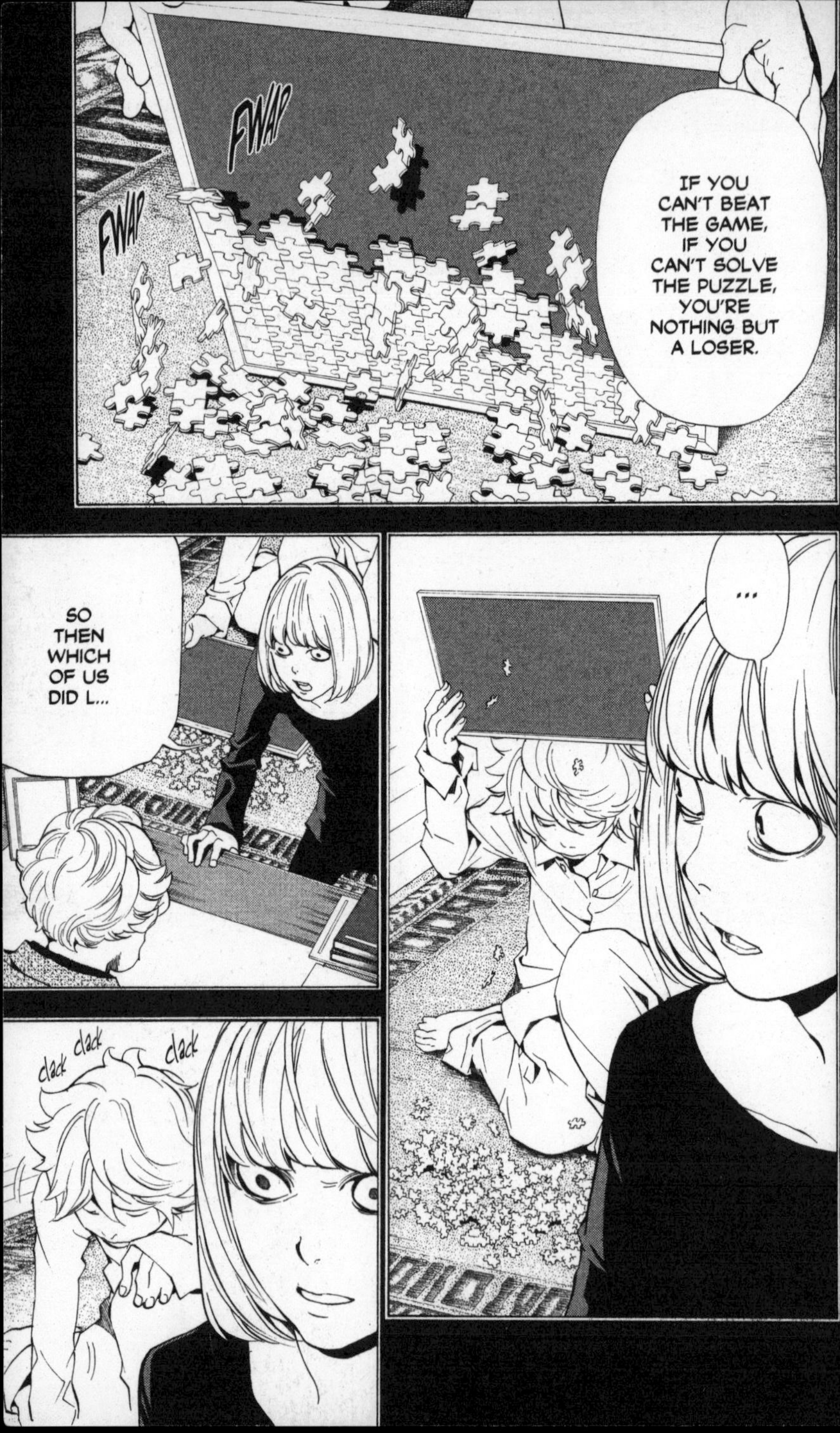
FWAP
FWAP
IF YOU CAN'T BEAT THE GAME, IF YOU CAN'T SOLVE THE PUZZLE, YOU'RE NOTHING BUT A LOSER.
...
SO THEN WHICH OF US DID L...
clack
clack
clack

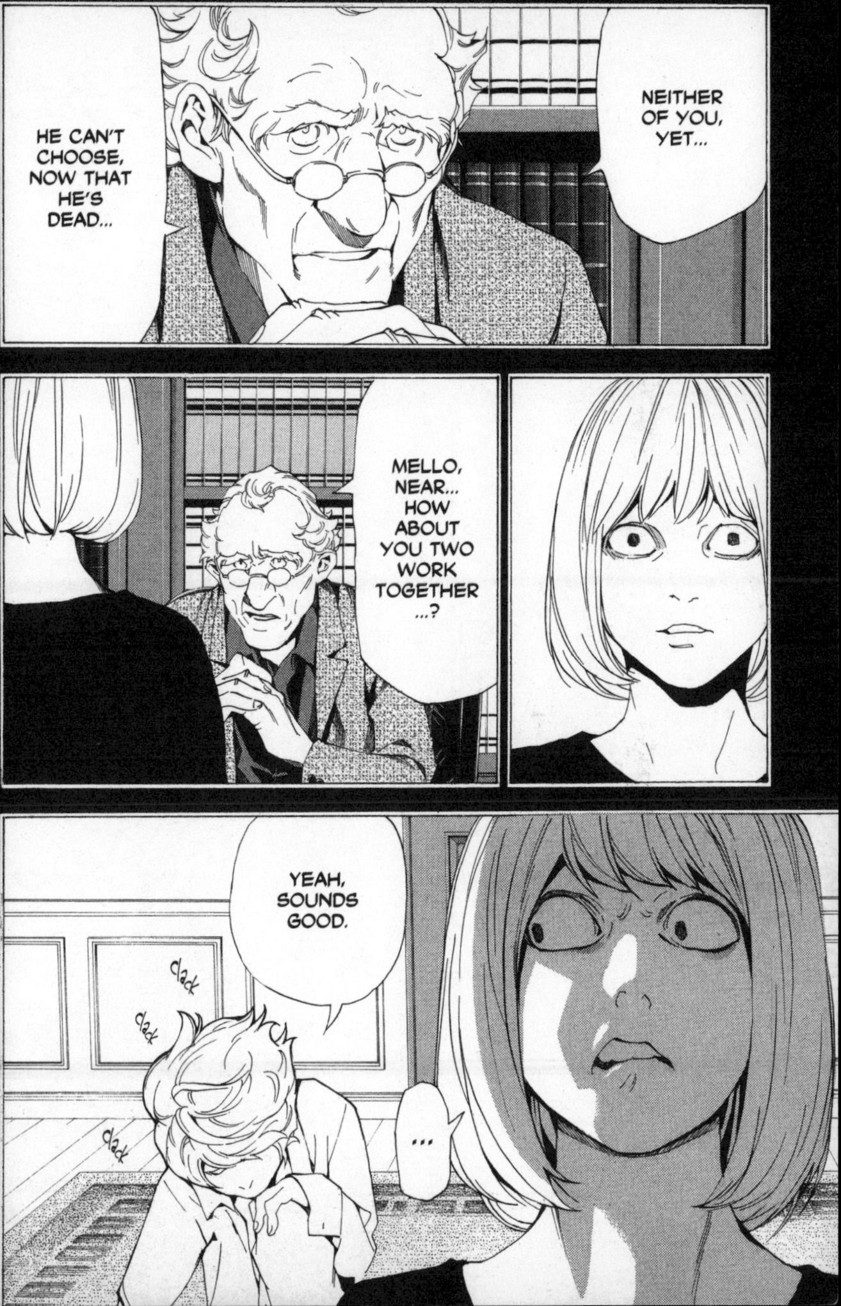
NEITHER OF YOU, YET...
HE CAN'T CHOOSE, NOW THAT HE'S DEAD...
MELLO, NEAR... HOW ABOUT YOU TWO WORK TOGETHER ...?
YEAH, SOUNDS GOOD.
clack
clack
...
clack

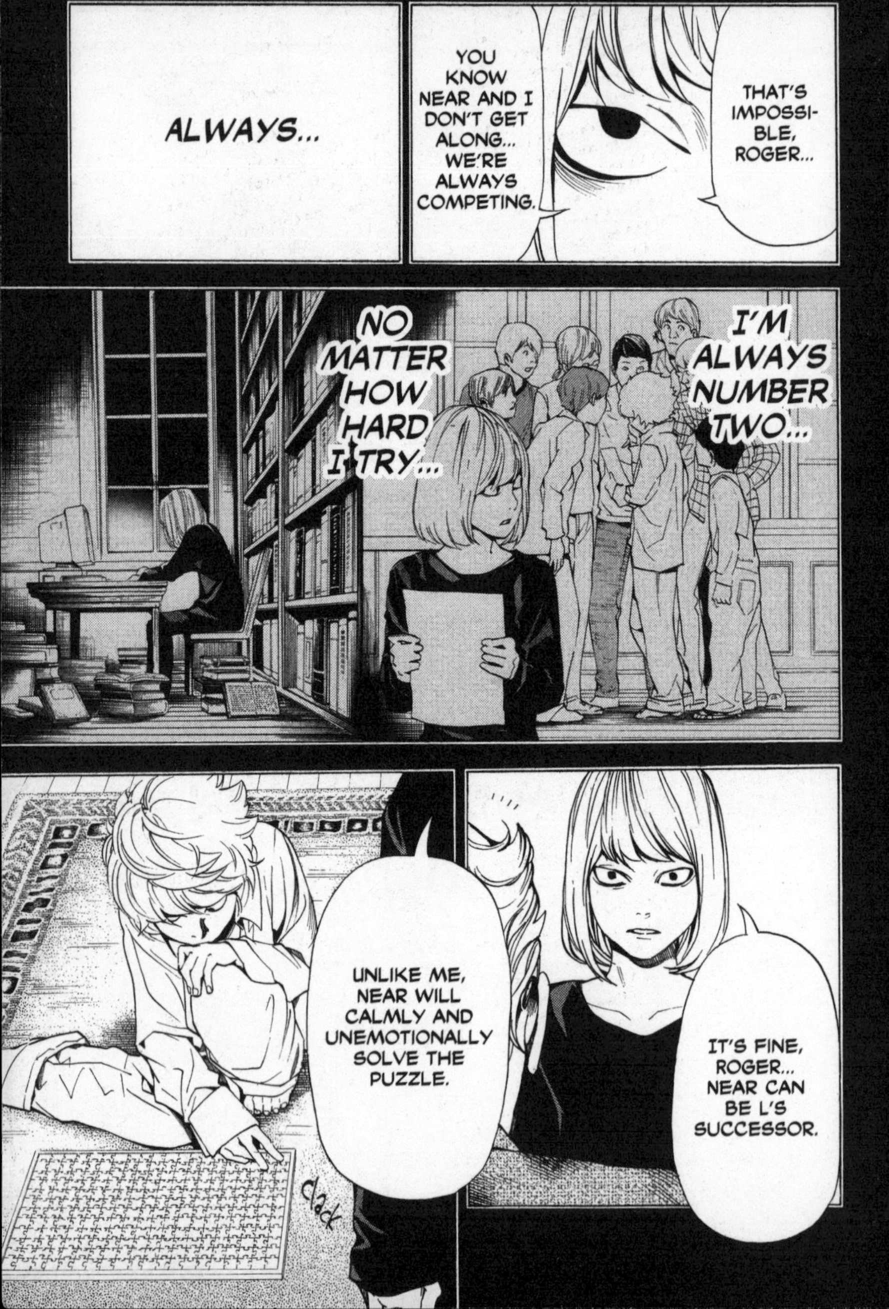

THAT'S IMPOSSIBLE, ROGER...
YOU KNOW NEAR AND I DON'T GET ALONG... WE'RE ALWAYS COMPETING.
ALWAYS...
I'M ALWAYS NUMBER TWO...
NO MATTER HOW HARD I TRY...
IT'S FINE, ROGER... NEAR CAN BE L'S SUCCESSOR.
UNLIKE ME, NEAR WILL CALMLY AND UNEMOTIONALLY SOLVE THE PUZZLE.
clack

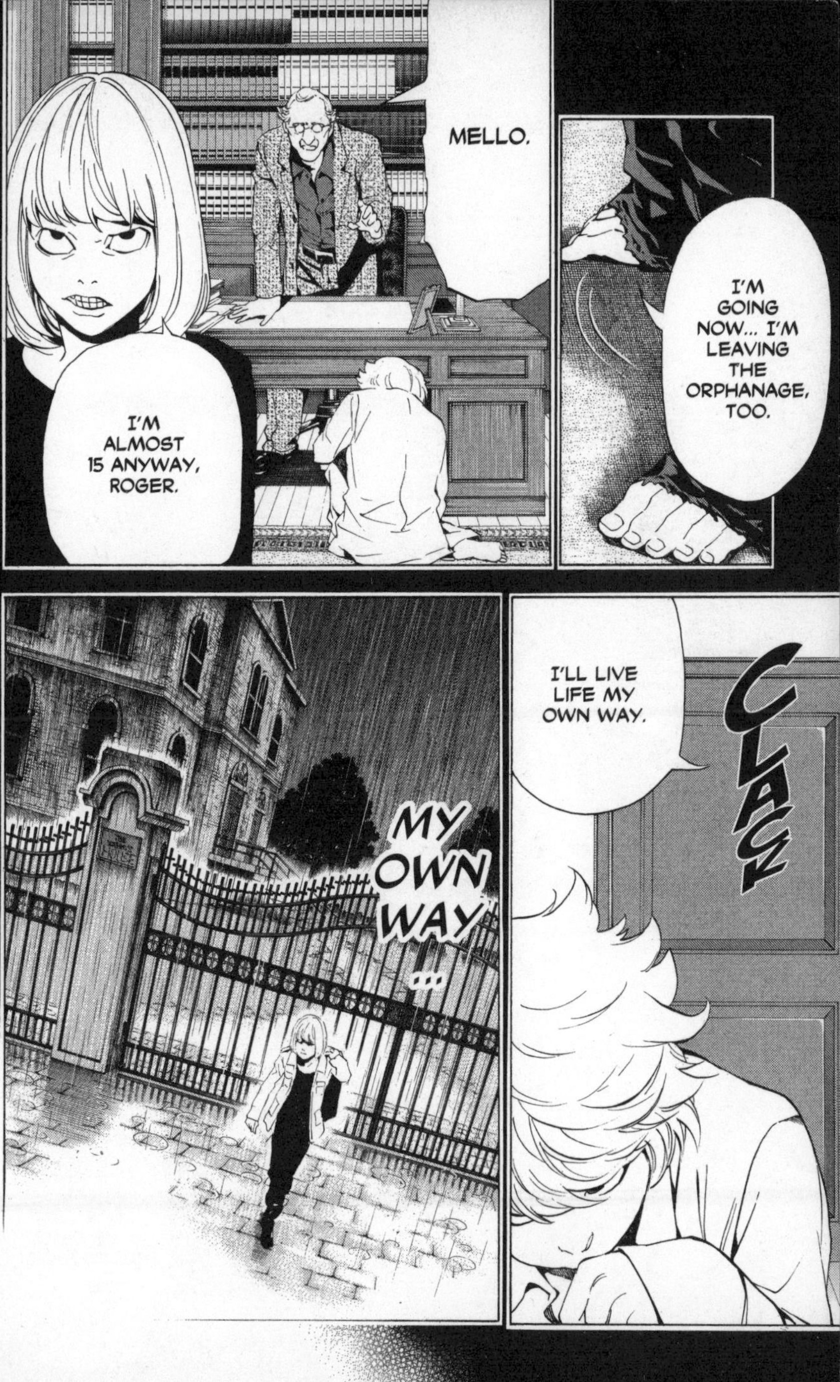
I'M GOING NOW... I'M LEAVING THE ORPHANAGE, TOO.
MELLO.
I'M ALMOST 15 ANYWAY, ROGER.
I'LL LIVE LIFE MY OWN WAY.
CLACK
MY OWN WAY...

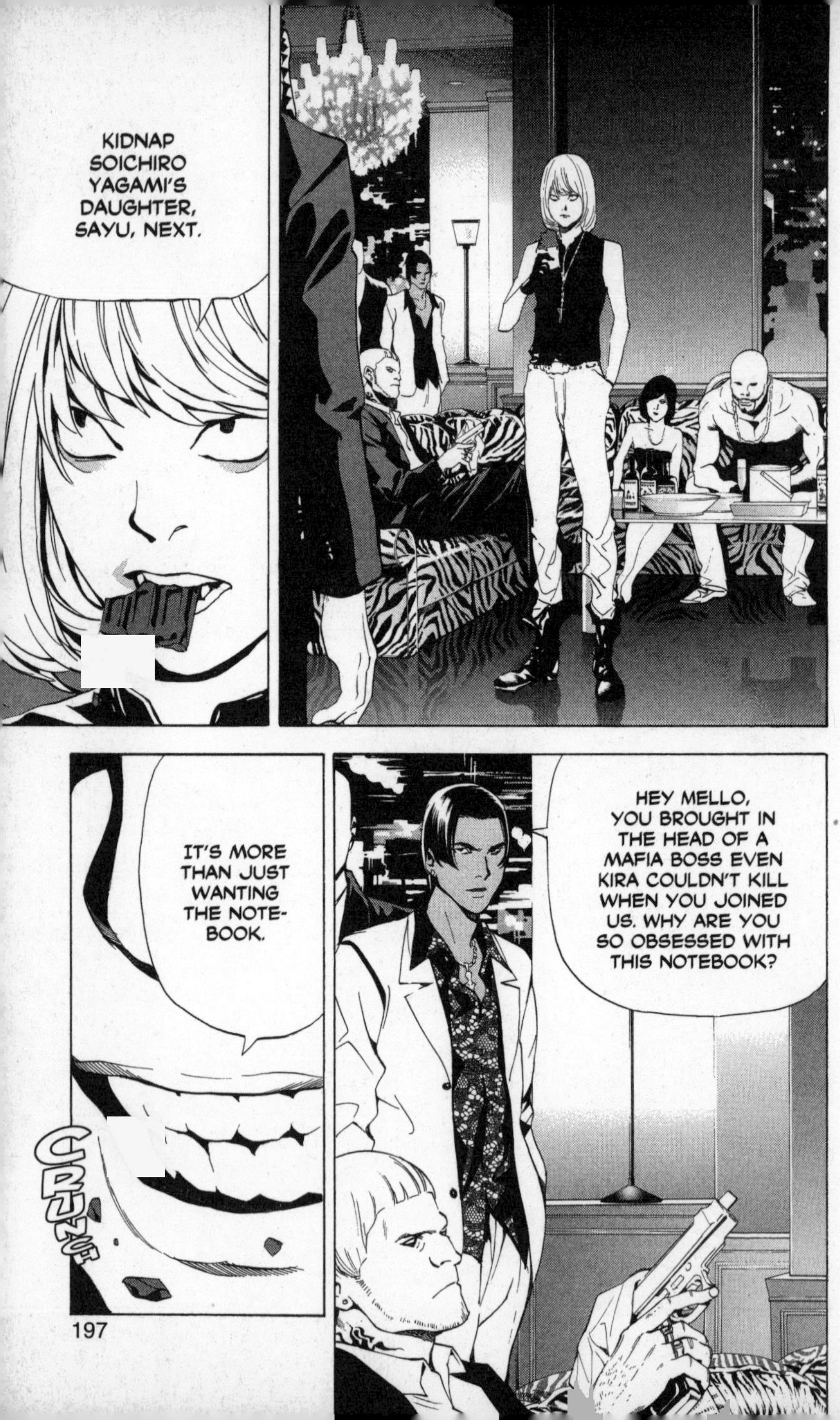
KIDNAP SOICHIRO YAGAMI'S DAUGHTER, SAYU, NEXT.
HEY MELLO, YOU BROUGHT IN THE HEAD OF A MAFIA BOSS EVEN KIRA COULDN'T KILL WHEN YOU JOINED US. WHY ARE YOU SO OBSESSED WITH THIS NOTEBOOK?
IT'S MORE THAN JUST WANTING THE NOTE-BOOK.
CRUNCH

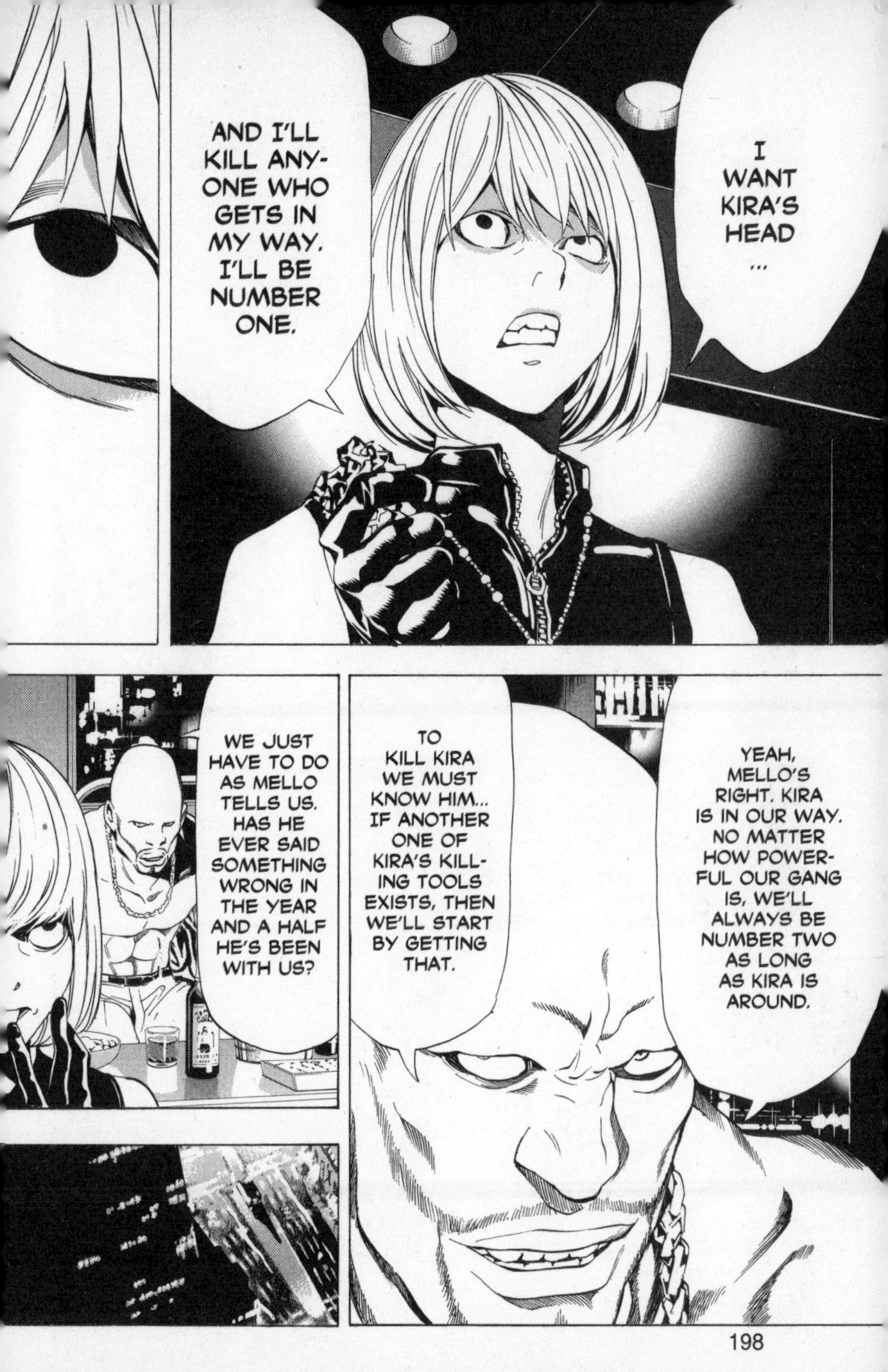
I WANT KIRA'S HEAD ...
AND I'LL KILL ANY-ONE WHO GETS IN MY WAY. I'LL BE NUMBER ONE.
YEAH, MELLO'S RIGHT. KIRA IS IN OUR WAY. NO MATTER HOW POWER-FUL OUR GANG IS, WE'LL ALWAYS BE NUMBER TWO AS LONG AS KIRA IS AROUND.
TO KILL KIRA WE MUST KNOW HIM... IF ANOTHER ONE OF KIRA'S KILL-ING TOOLS EXISTS, THEN WE'LL START BY GETTING THAT.
WE JUST HAVE TO DO AS MELLO TELLS US. HAS HE EVER SAID SOMETHING WRONG IN THE YEAR AND A HALF HE'S BEEN WITH US?

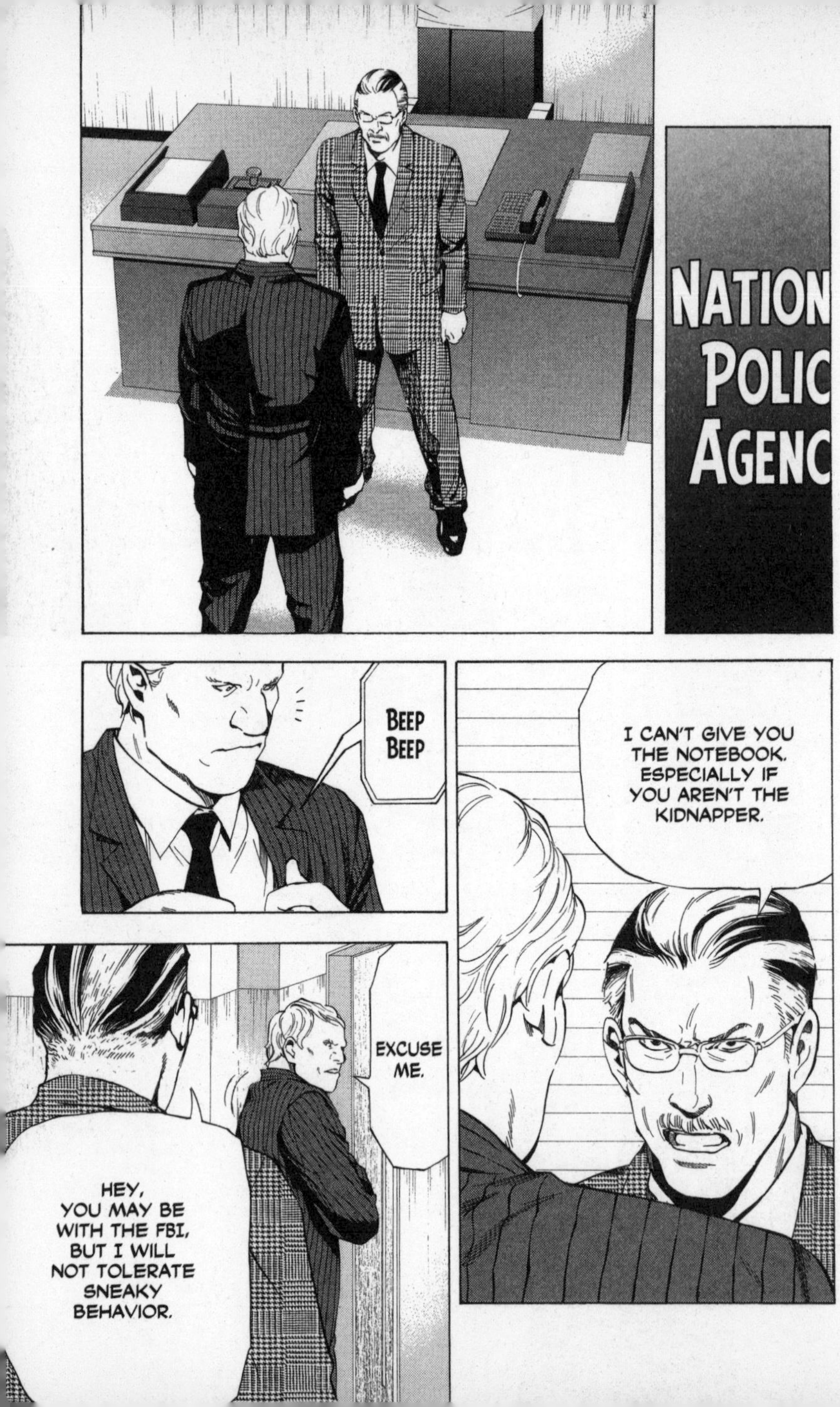
NATION POLIC AGENC
I CAN'T GIVE YOU THE NOTEBOOK. ESPECIALLY IF YOU AREN'T THE KIDNAPPER.
BEEP BEEP
EXCUSE ME.
HEY, YOU MAY BE WITH THE FBI, BUT I WILL NOT TOLERATE SNEAKY BEHAVIOR.

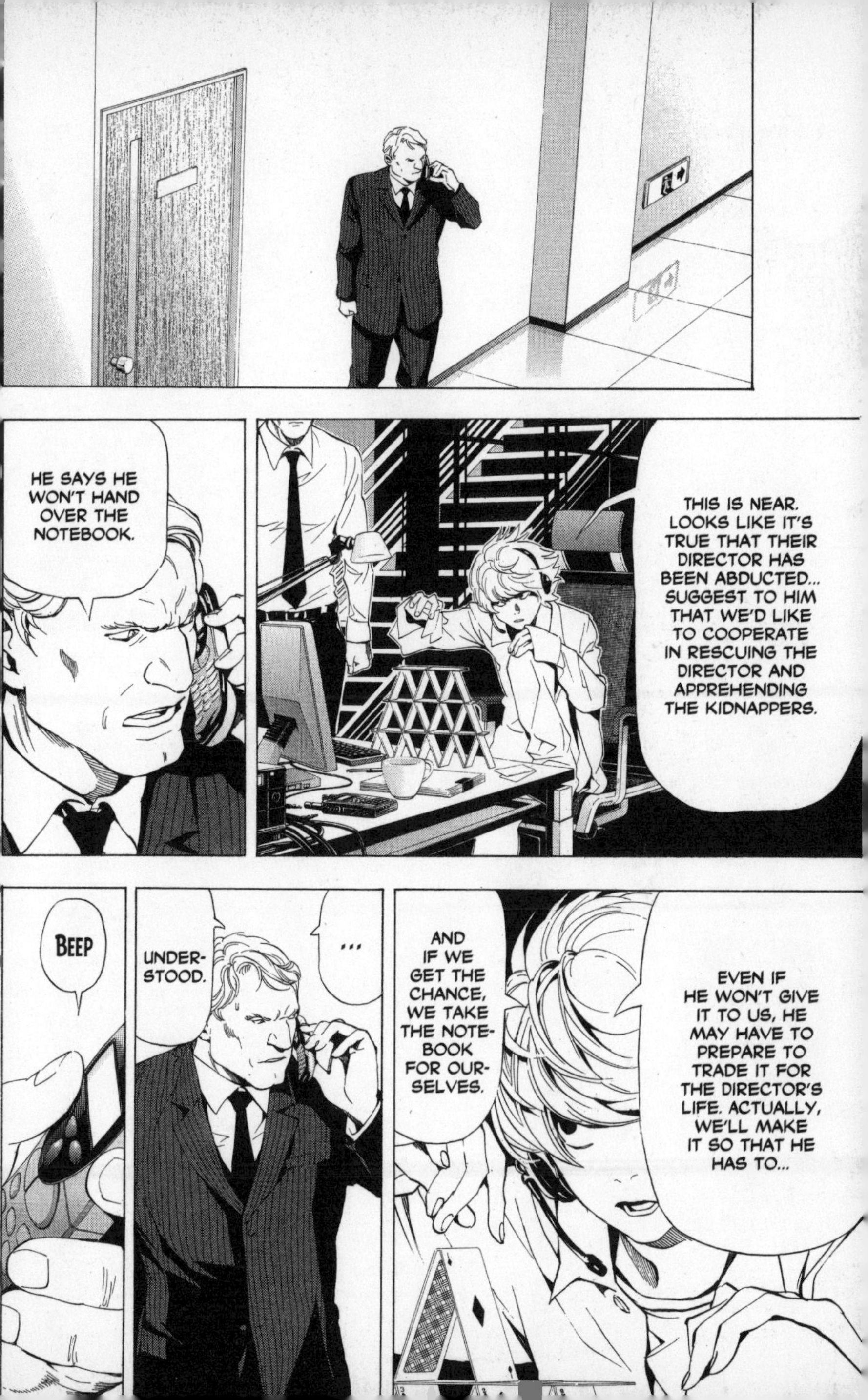
THIS IS NEAR. LOOKS LIKE IT'S TRUE THAT THEIR DIRECTOR HAS BEEN ABDUCTED... SUGGEST TO HIM THAT WE'D LIKE TO COOPERATE IN RESCUING THE DIRECTOR AND APPREHENDING THE KIDNAPPERS.
HE SAYS HE WON'T HAND OVER THE NOTEBOOK.
EVEN IF HE WON'T GIVE IT TO US, HE MAY HAVE TO PREPARE TO TRADE IT FOR THE DIRECTOR'S LIFE. ACTUALLY, WE'LL MAKE IT SO THAT HE HAS TO...
AND IF WE GET THE CHANCE, WE TAKE THE NOTE-BOOK FOR OUR-SELVES.
...
UNDER-STOOD.
BEEP

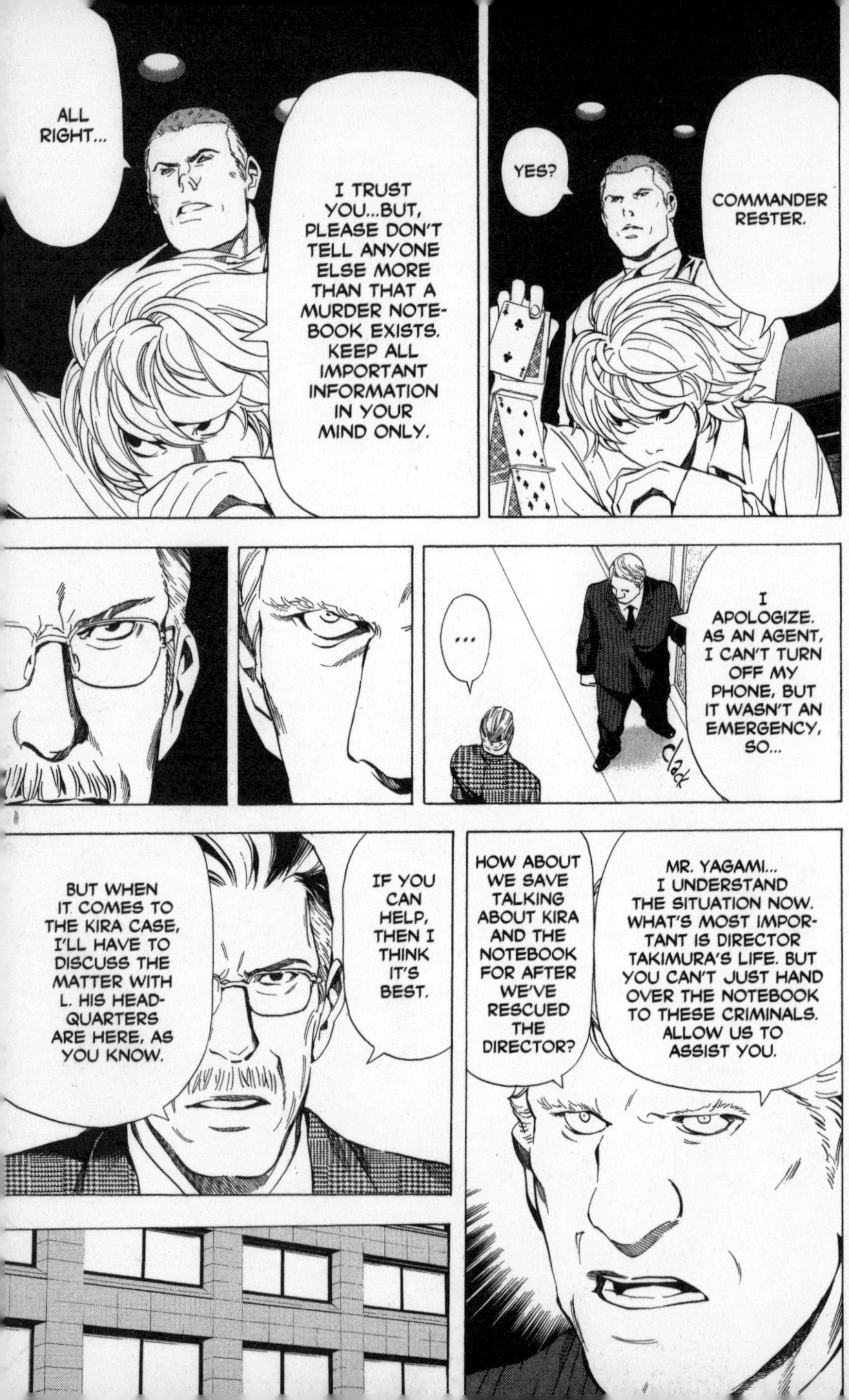
COMMANDER RESTER.
YES?
I TRUST YOU...BUT, PLEASE DON'T TELL ANYONE ELSE MORE THAN THAT A MURDER NOTE-BOOK EXISTS. KEEP ALL IMPORTANT INFORMATION IN YOUR MIND ONLY.
ALL RIGHT...
I APOLOGIZE. AS AN AGENT, I CAN'T TURN OFF MY PHONE, BUT IT WASN'T AN EMERGENCY, SO...
clack
...
MR. YAGAMI... I UNDERSTAND THE SITUATION NOW. WHAT'S MOST IMPOR-TANT IS DIRECTOR TAKIMURA'S LIFE. BUT YOU CAN'T JUST HAND OVER THE NOTEBOOK TO THESE CRIMINALS. ALLOW US TO ASSIST YOU.
HOW ABOUT WE SAVE TALKING ABOUT KIRA AND THE NOTEBOOK FOR AFTER WE'VE RESCUED THE DIRECTOR?
IF YOU CAN HELP, THEN I THINK IT'S BEST.
BUT WHEN IT COMES TO THE KIRA CASE, I'LL HAVE TO DISCUSS THE MATTER WITH L. HIS HEAD-QUARTERS ARE HERE, AS YOU KNOW.

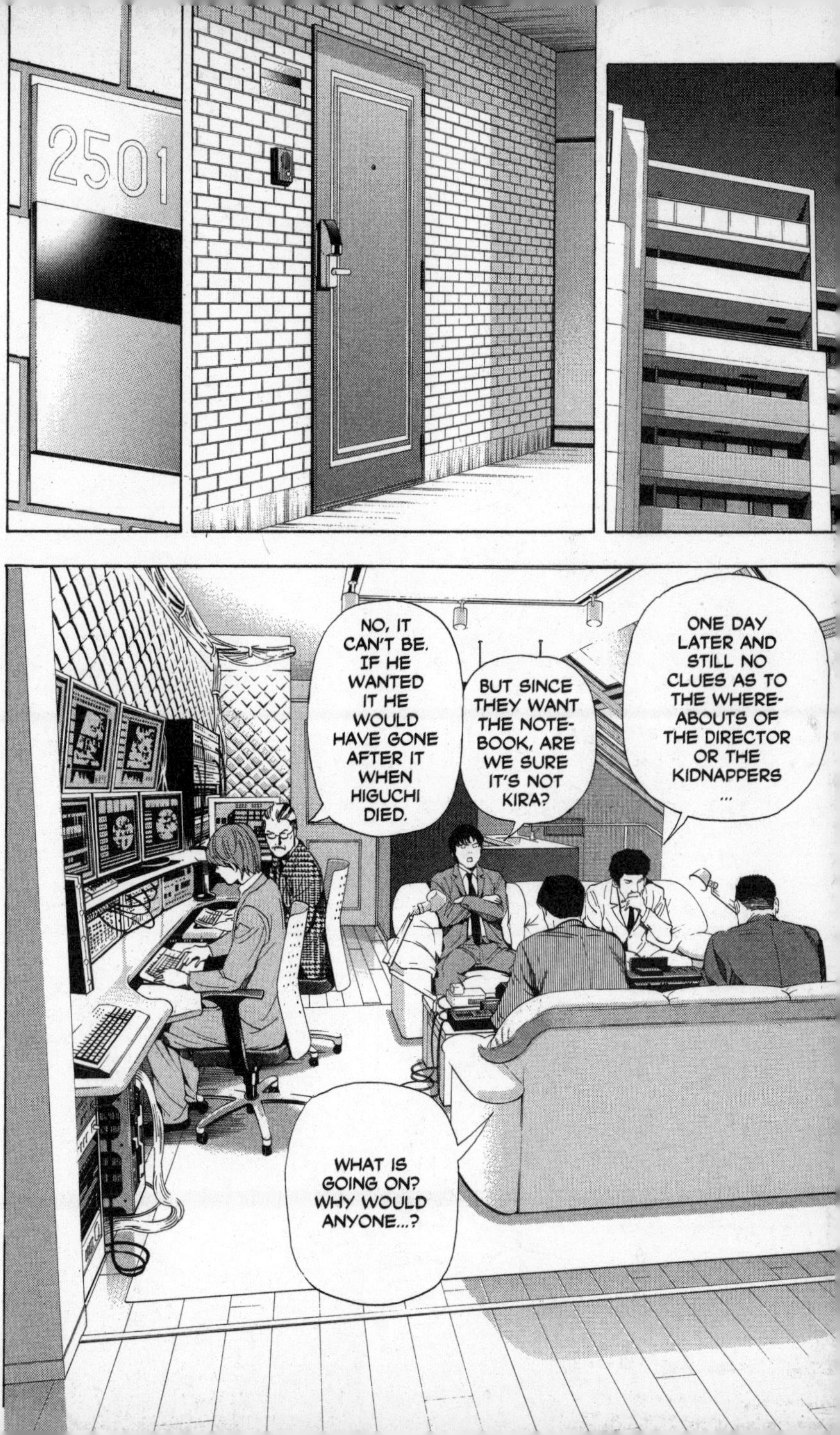
ONE DAY LATER AND STILL NO CLUES AS TO THE WHEREABOUTS OF THE DIRECTOR OR THE KIDNAPPERS ...
BUT SINCE THEY WANT THE NOTEBOOK, ARE WE SURE IT'S NOT KIRA?
NO, IT CAN'T BE. IF HE WANTED IT HE WOULD HAVE GONE AFTER IT WHEN HIGUCHI DIED.
WHAT IS GOING ON? WHY WOULD ANYONE...?

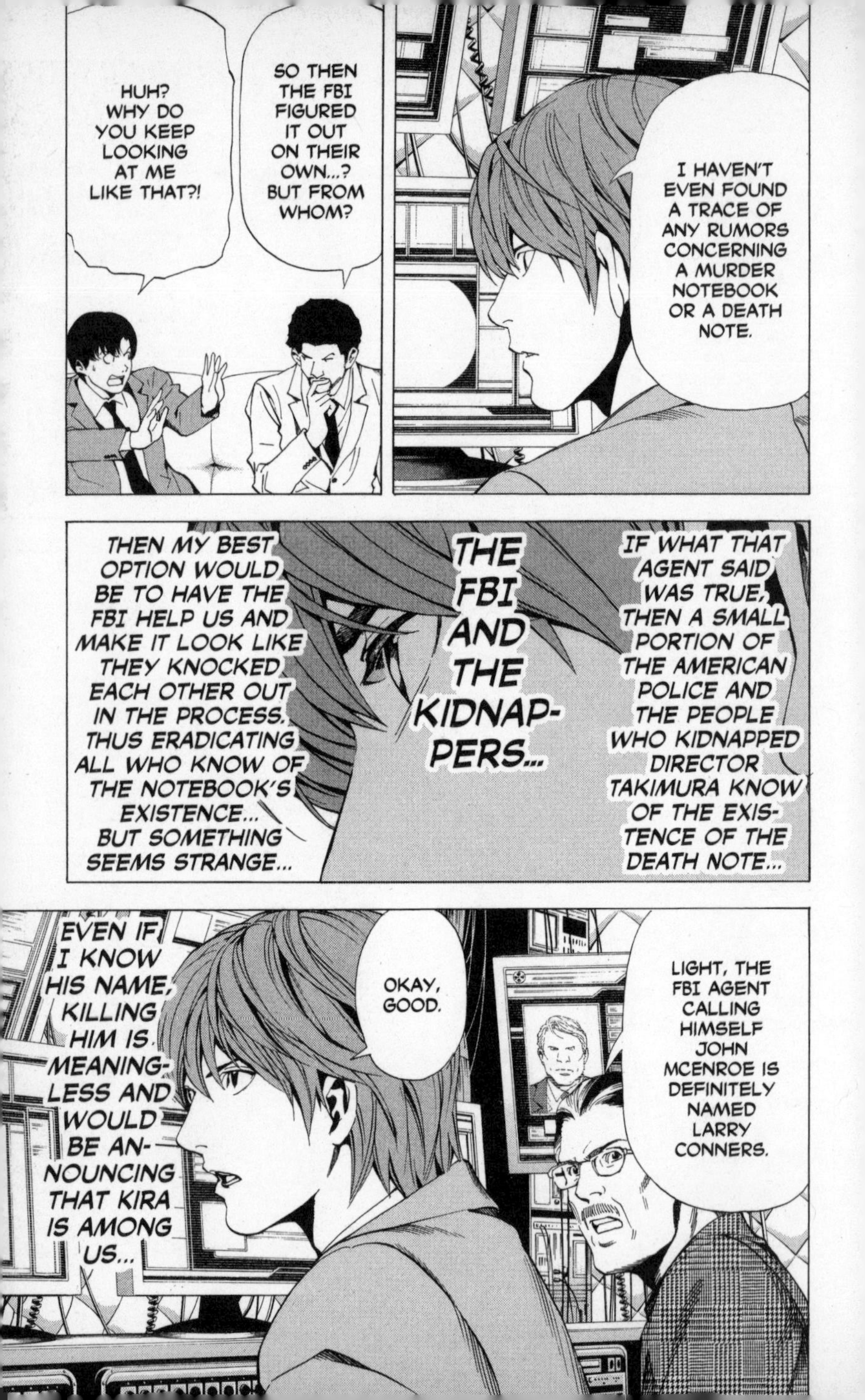
I HAVEN'T EVEN FOUND A TRACE OF ANY RUMORS CONCERNING A MURDER NOTEBOOK OR A DEATH NOTE.
SO THEN THE FBI FIGURED IT OUT ON THEIR OWN...? BUT FROM WHOM?
HUH? WHY DO YOU KEEP LOOKING AT ME LIKE THAT?!
IF WHAT THAT AGENT SAID WAS TRUE, THEN A SMALL PORTION OF THE AMERICAN POLICE AND THE PEOPLE WHO KIDNAPPED DIRECTOR TAKIMURA KNOW OF THE EXIS-TENCE OF THE DEATH NOTE...
THE FBI AND THE KIDNAP-PERS...
THEN MY BEST OPTION WOULD BE TO HAVE THE FBI HELP US AND MAKE IT LOOK LIKE THEY KNOCKED EACH OTHER OUT IN THE PROCESS. THUS ERADICATING ALL WHO KNOW OF THE NOTEBOOK'S EXISTENCE... BUT SOMETHING SEEMS STRANGE...
LIGHT, THE FBI AGENT CALLING HIMSELF JOHN MCENROE IS DEFINITELY NAMED LARRY CONNERS.
OKAY, GOOD.
EVEN IF I KNOW HIS NAME, KILLING HIM IS MEANING-LESS AND WOULD BE AN-NOUNCING THAT KIRA IS AMONG US...

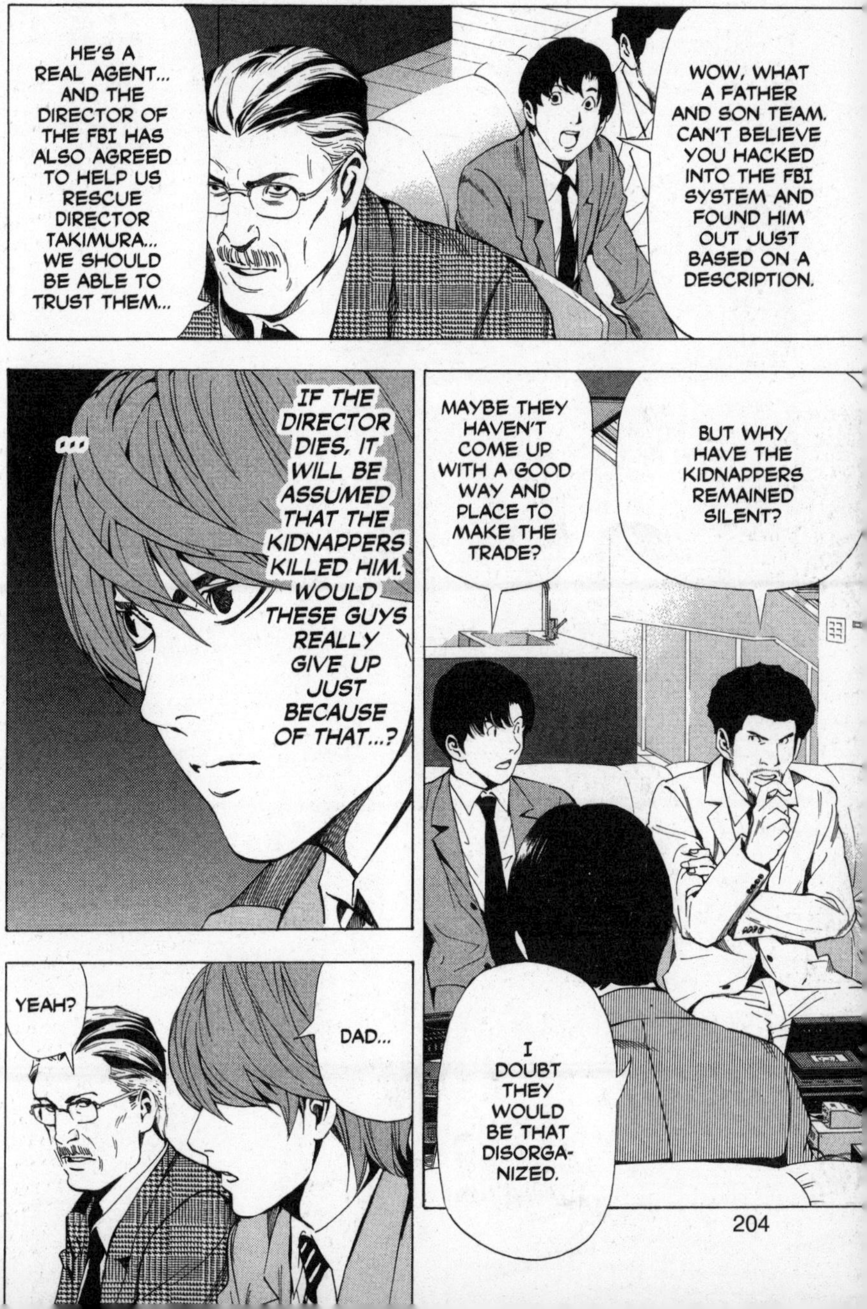
WOW, WHAT A FATHER AND SON TEAM. CAN'T BELIEVE YOU HACKED INTO THE FBI SYSTEM AND FOUND HIM OUT JUST BASED ON A DESCRIPTION.
HE'S A REAL AGENT... AND THE DIRECTOR OF THE FBI HAS ALSO AGREED TO HELP US RESCUE DIRECTOR TAKIMURA... WE SHOULD BE ABLE TO TRUST THEM...
BUT WHY HAVE THE KIDNAPPERS REMAINED SILENT?
MAYBE THEY HAVEN'T COME UP WITH A GOOD WAY AND PLACE TO MAKE THE TRADE?
I DOUBT THEY WOULD BE THAT DISORGA-NIZED.
IF THE DIRECTOR DIES, IT WILL BE ASSUMED THAT THE KIDNAPPERS KILLED HIM. WOULD THESE GUYS REALLY GIVE UP JUST BECAUSE OF THAT...?
...
DAD...
YEAH?

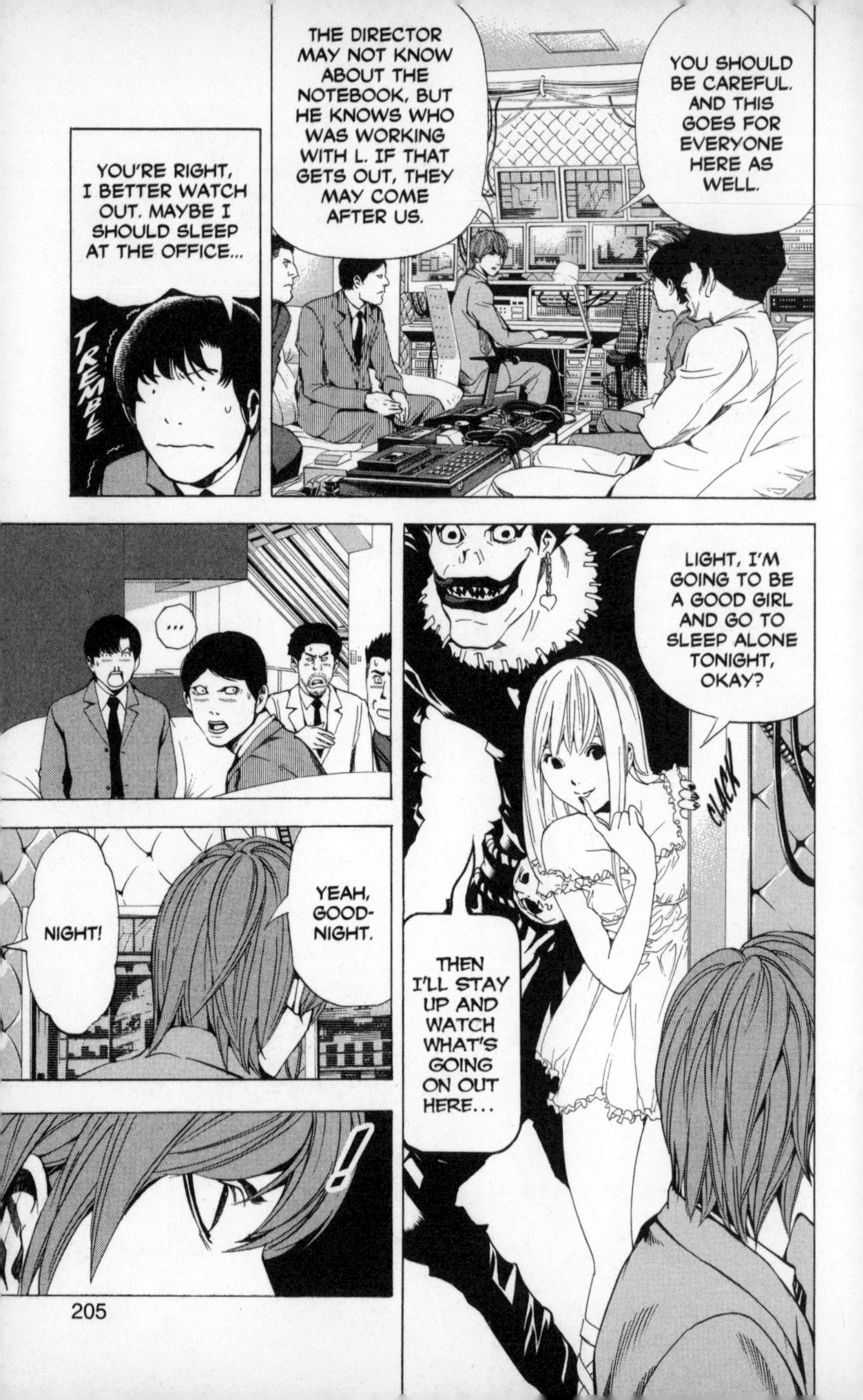
YOU SHOULD BE CAREFUL. AND THIS GOES FOR EVERYONE HERE AS WELL.
THE DIRECTOR MAY NOT KNOW ABOUT THE NOTEBOOK, BUT HE KNOWS WHO WAS WORKING WITH L. IF THAT GETS OUT, THEY MAY COME AFTER US.
YOU'RE RIGHT, I BETTER WATCH OUT. MAYBE I SHOULD SLEEP AT THE OFFICE...
TREMBLE
LIGHT, I'M GOING TO BE A GOOD GIRL AND GO TO SLEEP ALONE TONIGHT, OKAY?
CLACK
THEN I'LL STAY UP AND WATCH WHAT'S GOING ON OUT HERE...
...
YEAH, GOOD-NIGHT.
NIGHT!
!

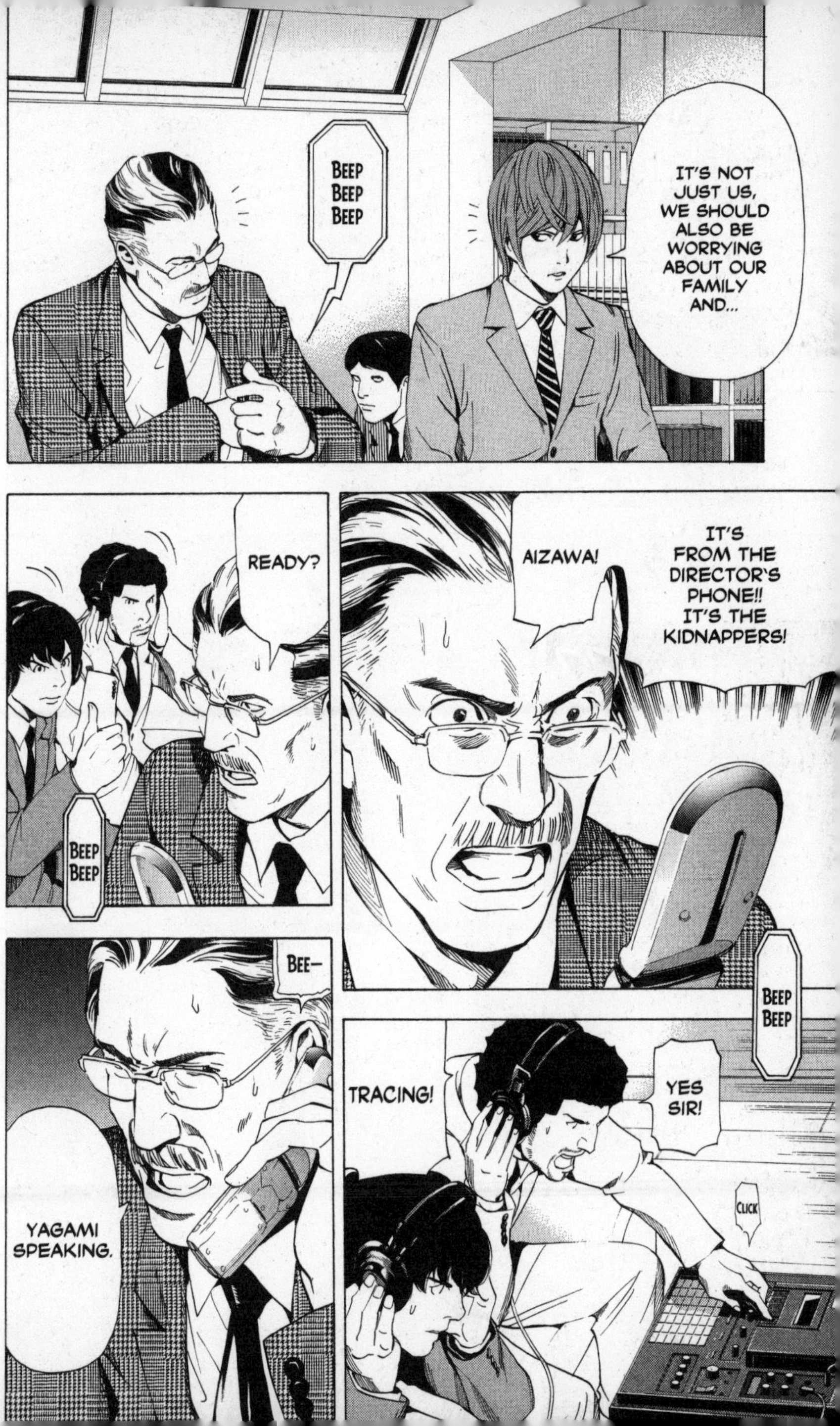
IT'S NOT JUST US, WE SHOULD ALSO BE WORRYING ABOUT OUR FAMILY AND...
BEEP BEEP BEEP
IT'S FROM THE DIRECTOR'S PHONE!! IT'S THE KIDNAPPERS!
AIZAWA!
READY?
BEEP BEEP
BEEP BEEP
YES SIR!
TRACING!
CLICK
BEE-
YAGAMI SPEAKING.

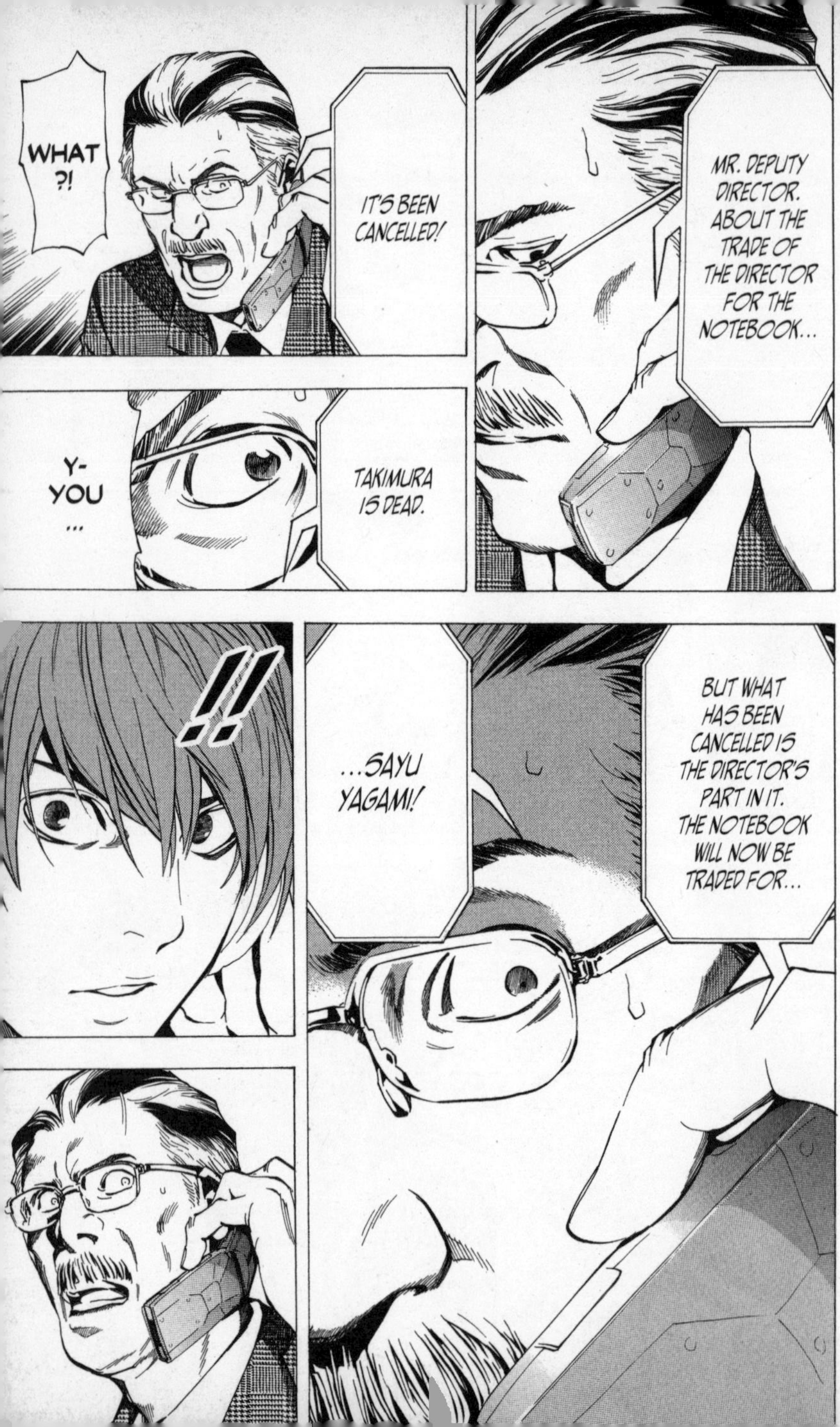
MR. DEPUTY DIRECTOR. ABOUT THE TRADE OF THE DIRECTOR FOR THE NOTEBOOK...
IT'S BEEN CANCELLED!
WHAT?!
TAKIMURA IS DEAD.
Y-YOU...
BUT WHAT HAS BEEN CANCELLED IS THE DIRECTOR'S PART IN IT. THE NOTEBOOK WILL NOW BE TRADED FOR...
...SAYU YAGAMI!
!!

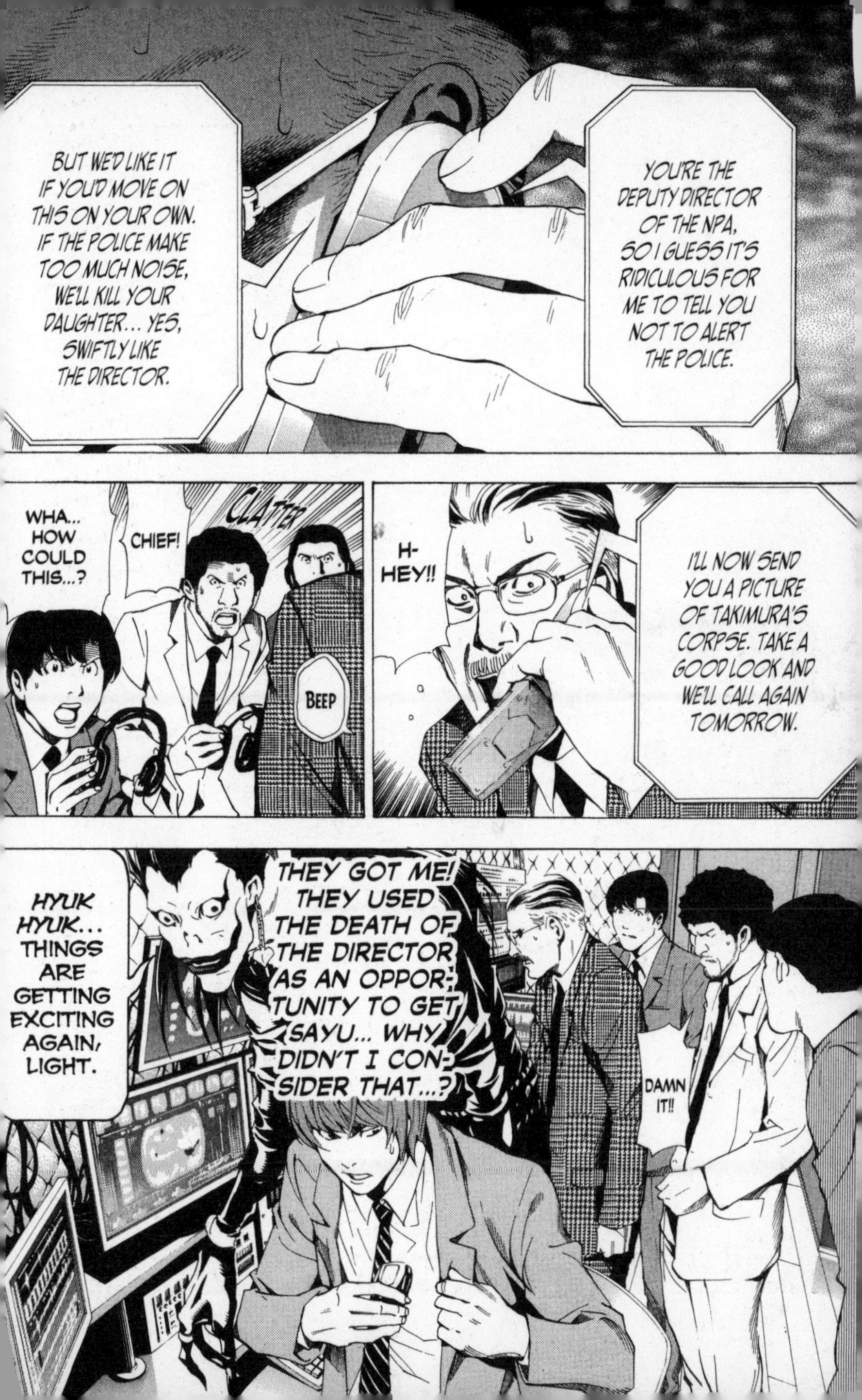

YOU'RE THE DEPUTY DIRECTOR OF THE NPA, SO I GUESS IT'S RIDICULOUS FOR ME TO TELL YOU NOT TO ALERT THE POLICE.
BUT WE'D LIKE IT IF YOU'D MOVE ON THIS ON YOUR OWN. IF THE POLICE MAKE TOO MUCH NOISE, WE'LL KILL YOUR DAUGHTER... YES, SWIFTLY LIKE THE DIRECTOR.
I'LL NOW SEND YOU A PICTURE OF TAKIMURA'S CORPSE. TAKE A GOOD LOOK AND WE'LL CALL AGAIN TOMORROW.
H- HEY!!
CLATTER
CHIEF!
WHA... HOW COULD THIS...?
BEEP
DAMN IT!!
THEY GOT ME! THEY USED THE DEATH OF THE DIRECTOR AS AN OPPOR-TUNITY TO GET SAYU... WHY DIDN'T I CON-SIDER THAT...?
HYUK HYUK... THINGS ARE GETTING EXCITING AGAIN, LIGHT.

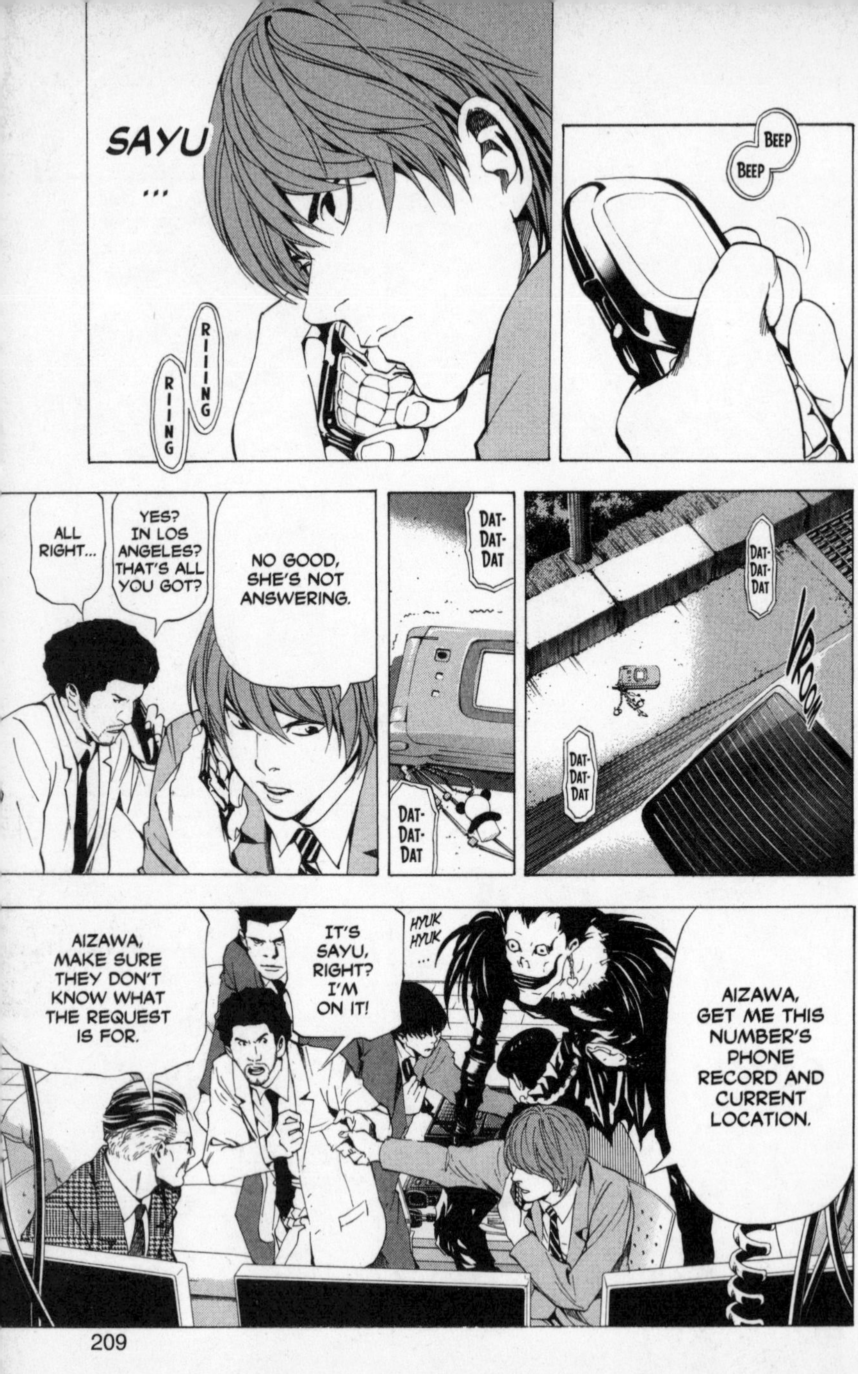
BEEP
BEEP
SAYU
...
RIIING
RIIING
DAT-DAT-DAT
VROOM
DAT-DAT-DAT
DAT-DAT-DAT
DAT-DAT-DAT
NO GOOD, SHE'S NOT ANSWERING.
YES? IN LOS ANGELES? THAT'S ALL YOU GOT?
ALL RIGHT...
AIZAWA, GET ME THIS NUMBER'S PHONE RECORD AND CURRENT LOCATION.
HYUK HYUK ...
IT'S SAYU, RIGHT? I'M ON IT!
AIZAWA, MAKE SURE THEY DON'T KNOW WHAT THE REQUEST IS FOR.

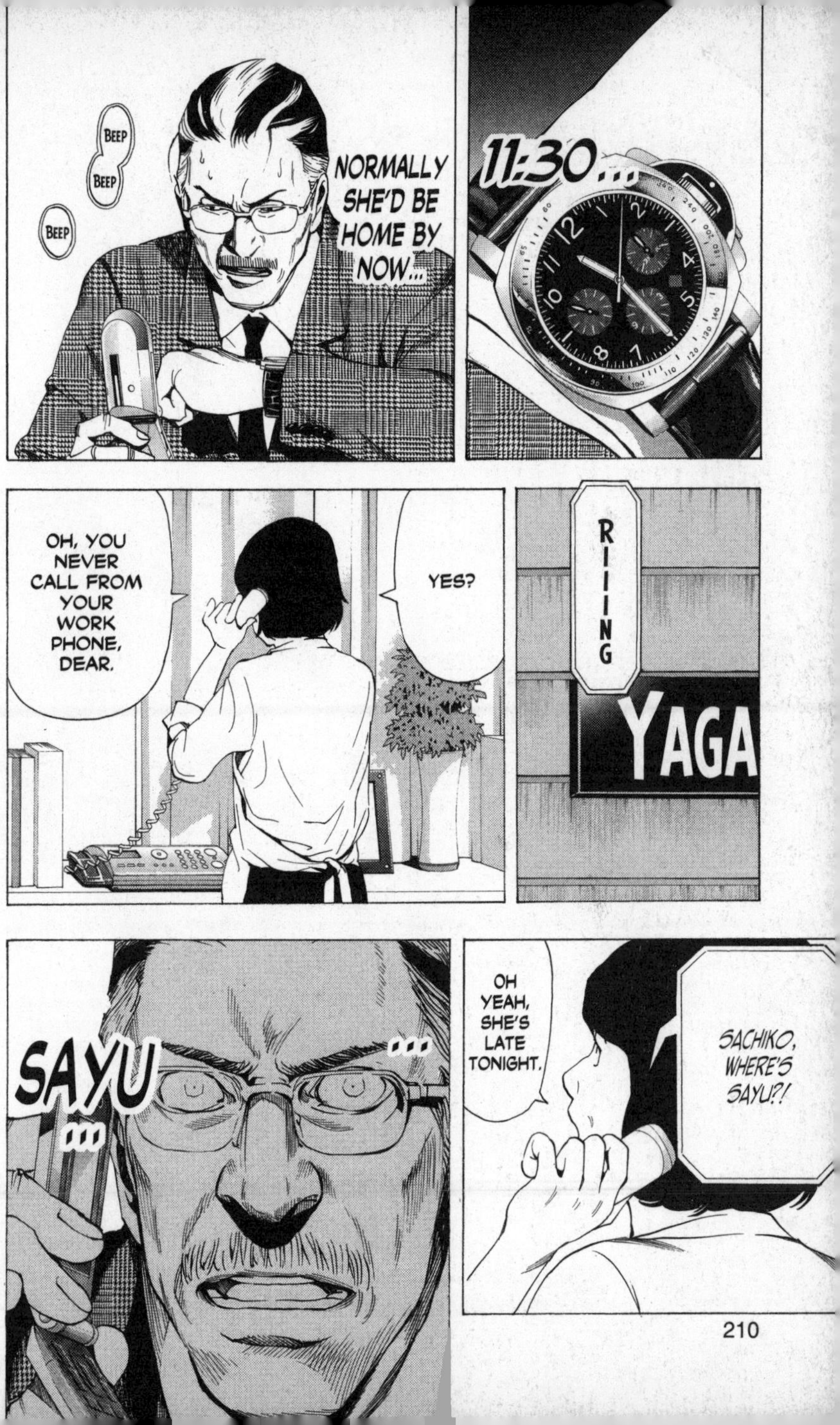
11:30...
BEEP
BEEP
BEEP
NORMALLY SHE'D BE HOME BY NOW...
RIIING
YAGA
YES?
OH, YOU NEVER CALL FROM YOUR WORK PHONE, DEAR.
SACHIKO, WHERE'S SAYU?!
OH YEAH, SHE'S LATE TONIGHT.
SAYU...
...

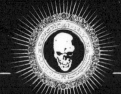

DEATH NOTE
How to use it
XLI

○ It is useless trying to erase names written in the DEATH NOTE with erasers or white-out.

デスノートに書いた名前・文字等を
消しゴム・インク消し・修正液等で消しても何の意味もなさない。

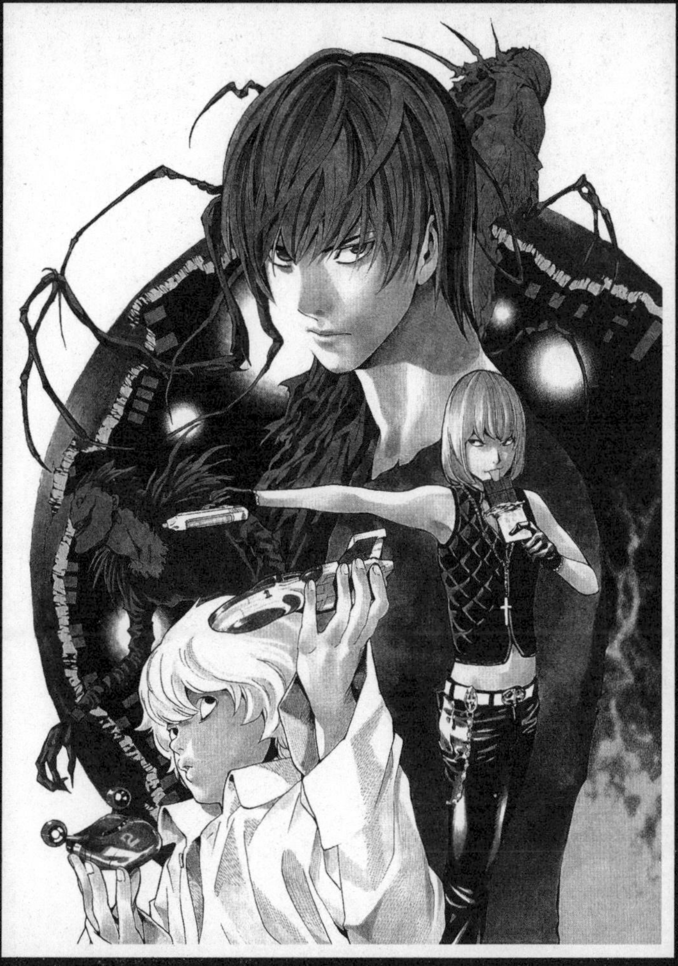

In the Next Volume

With L no longer a problem, Light is closer than ever to creating his ideal world. But after years of uncontested victory as Kira *and* the new L, Light finally has some opposition. Can Light handle an attack from two sides, or will he have to choose between his life as Kira and the lives of his family?!

Available Now

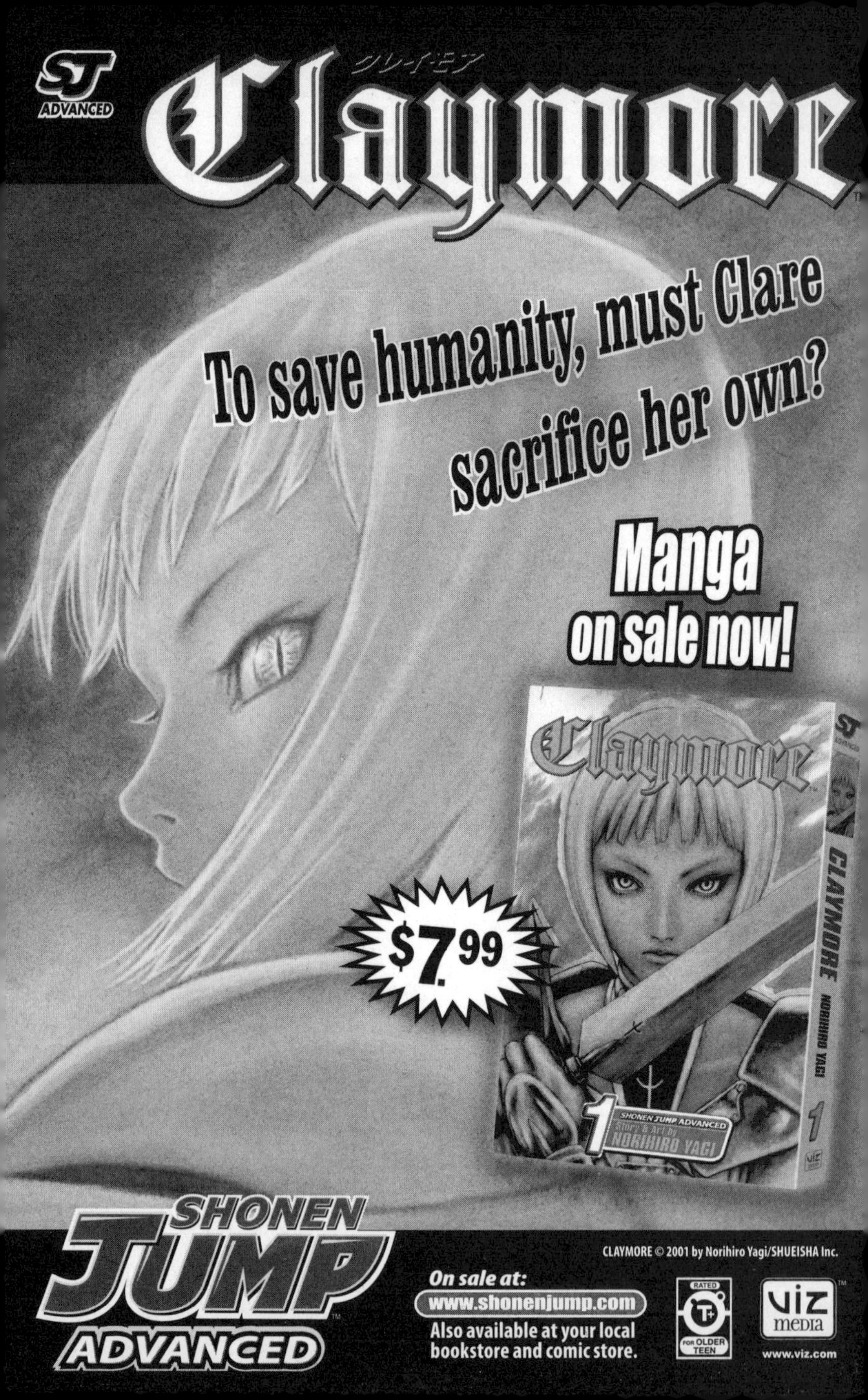
SJ ADVANCED
クレイモア
Claymore
To save humanity, must Clare sacrifice her own?
Manga on sale now!
$7.99
Claymore
CLAYMORE
NORIHIRO YAGI
1
SHONEN JUMP ADVANCED
Story & Art by NORIHIRO YAGI
SHONEN JUMP ADVANCED
CLAYMORE © 2001 by Norihiro Yagi/SHUEISHA Inc.
On sale at:
www.shonenjump.com
Also available at your local bookstore and comic store.
RATED T+ FOR OLDER TEEN
VIZ media
www.viz.com

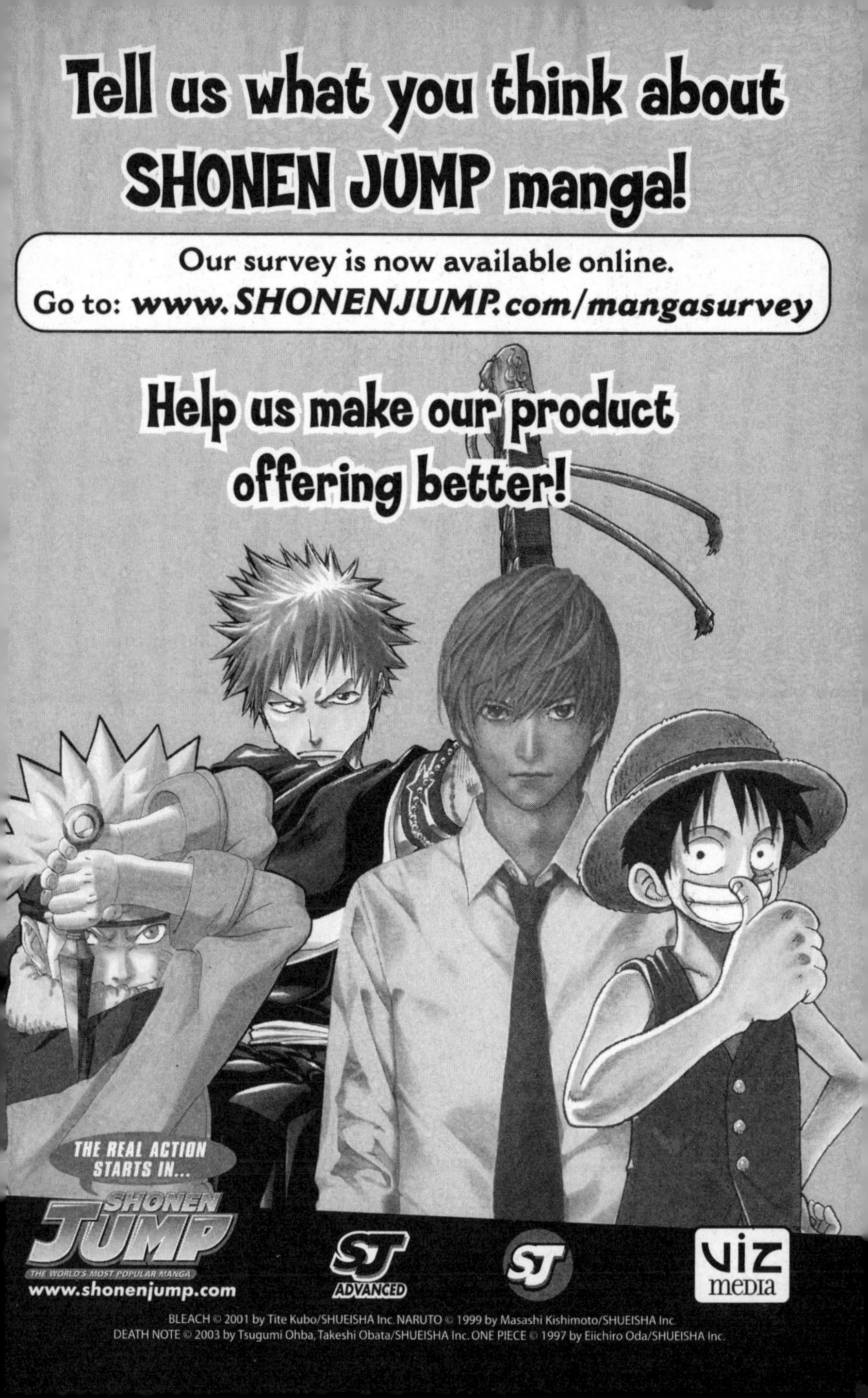
Tell us what you think about SHONEN JUMP manga!
Our survey is now available online.
Go to: www.SHONENJUMP.com/mangasurvey
Help us make our product offering better!
THE REAL ACTION STARTS IN...
SHONEN JUMP
THE WORLD'S MOST POPULAR MANGA
www.shonenjump.com
SJ ADVANCED
SJ
VIZ media
BLEACH © 2001 by Tite Kubo/SHUEISHA Inc. NARUTO © 1999 by Masashi Kishimoto/SHUEISHA Inc.
DEATH NOTE © 2003 by Tsugumi Ohba, Takeshi Obata/SHUEISHA Inc. ONE PIECE © 1997 by Eiichiro Oda/SHUEISHA Inc.

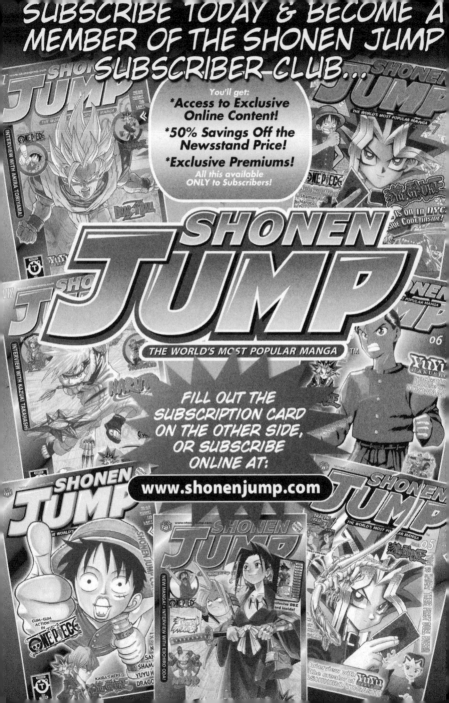

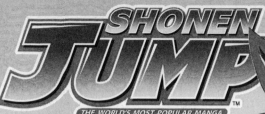
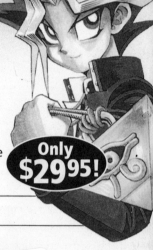